# The Audit Committee Handbook

**Fifth Edition**

# THE AUDIT COMMITTEE HANDBOOK

## Fifth Edition

**LOUIS BRAIOTTA, JR.**
**R. TRENT GAZZAWAY**
**ROBERT H. COLSON**
**SRIDHAR RAMAMOORTI**

WILEY

John Wiley & Sons, Inc.

Published by John Wiley & Sons, Inc., Hoboken, New Jersey.
Published simultaneously in Canada.

For general information on our other products and services or for technical support, please contact our Customer Care Department within the United States at (800) 762-2974, outside the United States at (317) 572-3993 or fax (317) 572-4002.

Wiley also publishes its books in a variety of electronic formats. Some content that appears in print may not be available in electronic books. For more information about Wiley products, visit our Web site at www.wiley.com.

*Library of Congress Cataloging-in-Publication Data*

Braiotta, Louis,
    The audit committee handbook / Louis Braiotta, Trent Gazzaway. — 5th ed.
        p. cm.
    Includes index.
    ISBN 978-0-470-56048-8 (cloth)    1. Audit committees.    I. Gazzaway,
Trent.    II. Title.
    HF5667.15.B7 2010
    658.15—dc22

                                                                    2009046293


Printed in the United States of America

10 9 8 7 6 5 4 3 2 1

*Dedicated to the men and women who, through their audit committee service, selflessly devote their time and energy to the preservation of the public trust and the advancement of the organizations they serve.*

# Contents

# Preface

What differentiates world-class audit committee members from caretakers? The answer is dedication and preparation. That fact has been true for as long as audit committees have existed, but the degree of separation between the two camps has never been greater. Business moves faster and financial reporting is more complicated than at any point in history—and the future promises more of the same. How are audit committee members to be adequately prepared to fulfill their obligations to stakeholders?

An audit committee's primary job is to oversee the financial reporting processes of the organization it serves (public or private, for-profit or not-for-profit). The audit committee also frequently assumes some level of oversight responsibility for enterprise risk management and treasury functions, but its raison d'être is centered on the organization's need for independent checks and balances over financial reporting.

Audit Analytics reports that financial statement restatements for U.S. public companies totaled 616 in 2000. The number rose to a staggering 1,800 in 2006, before falling to a total of 869 in 2008.[1] Even with the recent decline, 2008 still saw approximately 6 percent of public companies restating their financial statements (sometimes more than once). If an average company experienced a 6 percent failure rate in the quality of its primary product, we would be concerned for that company's future. We should be equally concerned about the quality of financial reporting. That quality affects the trust investors and creditors place in the financial statements and the price they are willing to pay for a share of stock. Thus, the quality of financial reporting has a direct impact on the cost of capital.

The good news is that the tide is turning. Management, internal audit, external audit, and audit committees have made great strides in recent years in improving the quality of financial reporting. The Sarbanes-Oxley Act of 2002, for all of its initial pain, has helped to refocus attention on financial reporting and to provide audit committees with some of the resources they need to perform their oversight duties. Greater efficiencies need to be built into the oversight process—especially the internal control evaluation process—but the tools needed to do so are now available. The Securities and Exchange Commission (SEC) and the Committee of

---

[1] Audit Analytics, *2008 Financial Restatements, An Eight Year Comparison* (February 2009).

Sponsoring Organizations (COSO) have provided guidance for companies that is designed to help them more efficiently and effectively evaluate internal control effectiveness. In addition, the Public Company Accounting Oversight Board (PCAOB) has revised its related U.S. auditing standards, and both the PCAOB and the Center for Audit Quality (CAQ) have developed guidance to help auditors of smaller public companies better audit internal control over financial reporting.

All of this brings us back to the book you hold in your hands right now. Audit committee members need a comprehensive yet practical guide to help them execute their duties. *The Audit Committee Handbook*, now in its fifth edition, is that guide. In these pages you will find everything from the history of how we got here to practical recommendations regarding things to look for as you work to oversee internal and external auditors.

One of our primary goals in editing this edition is to leave you with a flavor for the dynamics of the role of the audit committee, yet provide you with practical recommendations and tools you can use in the boardroom. Along those lines, Chapters 1 through 5—which focus on the history and current state of the audit committee role—are designed to provide the context for today's audit committee member role. Chapters 6 through 10 have been completely re-written with a how-to focus on areas critical to effective audit committees—the audit planning process and the oversight of internal and external audit. Chapters 11 through 14 complete the work with a focus on fraud and audit-related communications.

Effective audit committees are critical to the quality of financial reporting and the proper conduct of business. The best audit committee members see their role as one of great responsibility as well as of great honor. We hope *The Audit Committee Handbook, Fifth Edition* contributes in a meaningful way to the effective execution of those important duties.

R. TRENT GAZZAWAY
National Managing Partner of Audit Services
Grant Thornton LLP
December 2009

# Part One

# Getting Acquainted with Your Responsibilities

# Chapter 1

# Corporate Accountability

## Focus on the Audit Committee

Audit committee responsibilities have increased significantly in recent years because of the uncertainties arising from (1) a changing statutory, regulatory, legal, and risk environment for corporations, directors and officers; and (2) the accounting and auditing substance of audit committees' jobs. Certain questions are sure to concern audit committee members and those considering audit committee membership. How can I tell if the company has complied with the spirit and letter of new regulations? Am I going to be second-guessed by someone outside the company for my best efforts? Will that second-guess expose me to legal liability or personal embarrassment? How can I satisfy all these new responsibilities in a few meetings a year? How can the company best comply with myriad regulations while managing costs and maintaining a business focus rather than one of compliance? The purpose of this handbook is to help form responses to such questions.

Sections 205 and 301 of the Sarbanes-Oxley Act of 2002 establish three fundamental roles for audit committees. First, they have oversight responsibility for the accounting and financial reporting processes of the company and for its financial statement audits. Second, they are responsible for appointing, compensating, and overseeing the external auditor. Third, they must establish procedures for "receipt, retention, and treatment of complaints" about accounting, internal control, or auditing matters and for "the confidential, anonymous submission by employees" regarding questionable accounting or auditing issues. In the aftermath of the various regulatory activities that were initiated by Sarbanes-Oxley, audit committees also have responsibility, as part of exchange listing requirements, for ensuring that the company has appropriate systems in place for the effective monitoring and management of risk. Unlike the first three responsibilities, this last one is not necessarily one that must be fulfilled by the audit committee itself. Rather, the intent of the stock exchange listing rules is for the audit committee to ensure that the board has adequately addressed this important issue.

In essence, the audit committee's role is to stand objectively between management, the external auditors, and capital providers—creditors, investors, owners, or donors—to ensure that they receive complete, timely, and accurate financial information that has been subjected to the appropriate, but not excessive, level of scrutiny, both internally and by an external auditor. Audit committees accomplish this goal by focusing on five key areas:

1. Appropriate accounting skills in management
2. Internal control oversight
3. External auditor oversight
4. Adequate resources for the committee's functions
5. Understanding the economics behind every transaction

## APPROPRIATE ACCOUNTING SKILLS

The need has never been greater for organizations to hire or engage individuals who have accounting skills that are commensurate with the complexity and scope of their business. Most companies continuously accelerate their business transactions to increase their number and to extend them to new markets, whether domestically or abroad, but increasingly in foreign countries. The flow of business information coming from these innovations continues to grow in quantity and speed. Similarly, the complexity and extent of accounting and financial reporting expands to accommodate increasingly creative business transactions. Because every organization that depends on external capital must exercise diligence in accounting for and reporting its financial information, the right personnel with the right skills and the right authority must be in the right positions.

Management is responsible for making sure the company has the right people with the proper accounting and financial reporting skills, and the commitment to apply them with integrity. The audit committee's job is to make certain that management is doing its job. Audit committees can begin to assess management's job by understanding the accounting complexities and challenges that arise because of their company's industry, geography, or business practices. The next step is to gain assurance about the quality and adequacy of the related knowledge and skills. For example, revenue recognition in the software industry is highly complex. A reasonable question for an audit committee in this industry is whether the company has people with the knowledge, skills, experience, training, and authority to account properly for software revenue.

Internal audit can help audit committees by continuously providing an objective assessment of the state of the necessary accounting skills. External auditors' assessments also may be helpful to an audit committee in fulfilling its oversight responsibilities. Audit committees may find value in listing complex and high-risk financial reporting areas such as revenue recognition, cost capitalization, structured transactions like derivatives and other financial instruments measured at fair value, and accounts based on significant judgments like reserves and asset retirement obligations. Geographic issues may involve the use of international financial reporting standards (IFRS), transfer pricing, and other tax-related issues. Whatever the issues may be, once they are identified it becomes much easier to assess whether the organization has the appropriate expertise to manage them appropriately.

## INTERNAL CONTROL OVERSIGHT

Just as an organization cannot produce reliable services or products without good controls over service delivery or manufacturing processes, it cannot produce consistently reliable financial statements without good internal control over financial reporting.

Management should have a basis for knowing whether its financial reporting processes are working properly. Having a general conviction without persuasive evidence is inadequate. "We have good people and have not had a problem in the past" is a phrase repeated by managements and audit committees in almost all accounting restatements, whether the restatements result from errors or fraud.

Well-run organizations establish controls to manage and mitigate risks. They also establish proper oversight and monitoring functions, because systems deteriorate over time. Internal control monitoring, and ways of determining its effectiveness, should be part of the DNA of the organization. While not every risk and control requires equal monitoring, management should do all of the following:

1. Know the financial reporting risks and have methods for prioritizing them and identifying changes over time
2. Know what controls are in place to manage and mitigate those risks that are critical to the organization's objectives
3. Implement monitoring procedures that provide persuasive and timely assessments of the effectiveness of those controls

The audit committee's job is to make sure that management performs these three tasks routinely and effectively. Asking the right questions of management and probing their answers for reasonableness is an effective approach to ensuring proper internal control. Here are some questions to consider:

- How does management identify and prioritize financial reporting risks?
- How often is this analysis updated for changes?
- Do the procedures and outcomes reasonably match the organization's structure and operations?
- Does management involve the appropriate people?
- What controls are focused on the most critical aspects of the financial reporting process?
- How does management determine whether controls are working?
- Does management listen to critical viewpoints?

These are good questions for all organizations' audit committees—public or private, for-profit or not-for-profit.

Monitoring is such an important part of internal control that the Committee of Sponsoring Organizations (COSO)—a body recognized internationally for its internal control framework—has devoted itself to monitoring an entire series of guidance, applications, and examples.[1] COSO's monitoring guidance draws on two fundamental principles of the COSO Integrated Framework for Internal Control:

1. Ongoing and/or separate evaluations enable management to determine whether the other components of internal control continue to function over time.
2. Internal control deficiencies are identified and communicated in a timely manner to those parties responsible for taking corrective action, and to management and the board as appropriate.

The monitoring guidance develops three broad elements for achieving these principles:

1. Establishing a foundation for monitoring, which includes:
   - A proper tone at the top
   - An effective organizational structure that assigns monitoring roles to people with appropriate capabilities, objectivity, and authority
   - A starting point or "baseline" of known effective internal control from which ongoing monitoring and separate evaluations can be implemented
2. Designing and executing monitoring procedures that:
   - Are focused on persuasive information
   - Are about the operation of key controls
   - Address meaningful risks to organizational objectives
3. Assessing and reporting results, which includes:
   - Evaluating the severity of any identified deficiencies
   - Reporting the monitoring results to the appropriate personnel and the board for timely action and follow-up if needed

See Chapter 8 for further discussion of internal control monitoring and COSO's related guidance.

## AUDITOR OVERSIGHT

Two aspects of the audit committee's responsibility for oversight of the external auditor are paramount. First, the audit committee should determine whether the auditors have the capability and commitment to address properly the areas of greatest financial reporting risk. Once the audit committee has established its assessment of financial reporting risk, it needs to make certain that its auditors

---

[1] See COSO's Guidance on Monitoring Internal Control Systems (2009). Available at www.coso.org/guidance.htm.

have the characteristics that match up well. These characteristics usually come down to whether the auditor has the following capabilities:

- Sufficient technical knowledge of accounting and the company's industry to be able to handle the transactions inherent in the company's business
- The capacity to handle the company's accounting issues on a timely basis
- A service delivery model that matches well with the company's needs
- The geographical presence to handle the company's operations

Audit committees can get a good idea of different auditors' capabilities through interviews and interactions with auditors during the proposal process.

The second aspect is somewhat more intangible, relating to whether the audit committee can count on the auditors to have the integrity and fortitude to be frank and honest about their assessments of organizational processes, skills, and attitudes related to financial reporting. Such strength of character is especially important if management executives have aggressive personalities or management styles. The audit committee should be confident about the auditors' commitment to tell them the truth, the whole truth, and nothing but the truth. This confidence should extend beyond the individuals on the audit engagement to the reputation and support systems internal to the audit firm. One way to obtain specific impressions about the auditors' capabilities and commitment to integrity is to ask them challenging, open-ended questions about the organization, its policies, the management team, internal control, accounting knowledge and skills, and then gauge the frankness of their responses. Such discussions are most effective when conducted privately with the auditors, but every audit committee should know whether their auditors are willing to tell management the hard truth just as they will tell the audit committee.

Reviewing audit plans, monitoring cost effectiveness, and evaluating the auditors' reports are other important aspects of auditor oversight, but all such activities fall appropriately into place only if the auditors have the right people on the engagement team, the right internal support system for those people, and the integrity to stand up for what is right.

## AUDIT COMMITTEE RESOURCES

To meet its oversight responsibilities, the audit committee needs adequate resources, which typically come from the knowledge, skills, and time of individual audit committee members, internal audit personnel, external auditors, and other experts engaged independently of management.

Audit committees also depend on the active support and engagement of management in fulfilling their duties. It's not enough to have high-quality people on audit committees devoting time and energy to understanding the organization's operations and financial reporting risk. Audit committees need the raw materials for their work, which consist of financial and other information provided far enough in advance of meetings for members' appropriate review and development of questions or concerns.

Audit committee members may also need to observe certain operations or accounting systems, especially those related to areas of high financial reporting risk. To that end, an appropriately staffed, supervised, and autonomous internal audit function can be of great assistance to audit committees by becoming their eyes, ears, arms, and legs. As organizations grow in size or complexity, the relationship between the audit committee and the internal audit group becomes increasingly important.

Audit committees also can follow up on areas of concern raised by the external auditors. The external auditors' independence requirements prohibit them from becoming a part of the organization's internal control, but their observations can be the springboard for further work by internal audit, management, the audit committee or board, or other experts. Because external auditors operate on a sampling basis, they cannot test every transaction (doing so would not be practical). Accordingly, while professional standards require auditors to report problems that they find, audit committees should be aware that the auditor may not identify every problem.

Audit committees also can hire subject matter experts or other counselors where specialized skills may be required, such as in accounting for acquisitions, asset impairments, fair value measurements, intangibles, derivatives, and complex financial instruments.

## TRANSACTIONAL ECONOMICS

The proper accounting for a transaction depends heavily on understanding the transaction's economic consequences to the organization. From both a financial reporting and an economic perspective, high-risk transactions include complex derivatives, sale-leaseback agreements of assets unrelated to the organization's core activities, and contracts or agreements in locations where the organization normally does not do business. Management is responsible for understanding and communicating the business purpose and economic outcomes of every significant transaction. The audit committee must be confident that management and those responsible for recording transactions understand the underlying economics. Management's responses to probing questions about the business purpose, expected cash flows, and anticipated risks associated with transactions can help an audit committee gauge whether management is fulfilling its responsibilities in this area.

## THE NATURE AND IMPORTANCE OF CORPORATE ACCOUNTABILITY

### The Meaning of Corporate Accountability

The concept of corporate accountability may be stated in this way:

> The board of directors is charged with safeguarding and advancing the interest of the stockholders, acting as their representatives in establishing corporate policies, and

reviewing management's execution of those policies. Accordingly, the directors have a fiduciary responsibility to the stockholders. They have an obligation to inform themselves about the company's affairs and to act diligently and capably in fulfilling their responsibilities.[2]

The Business Roundtable has described corporate accountability as follows:

The board of directors is ultimately accountable to the shareholders for the long-term successful economic performance of the corporation consistent with its underlying public purpose. Directors are held accountable for their performance in a variety of ways.

First, there is the powerful accountability imposed by markets. The impact of consumer dissatisfaction with products and services is quick and visible. Financial markets also quickly reflect their evaluation of the quality of accountability through the price of equity and debt.

Accountability is also imposed through the numerous statutes and regulations enacted by governmental bodies to limit and control corporate action. Directors are held accountable to regulatory mechanisms.

There is also a body of law—part statutory, part court-made—which defines the duties of directors and the principles and boundaries within which they must keep their decisions. If they overstep, their decisions are subject to reversal by the courts. Directors can also be held personally liable, without limitation, to the extent of their personal assets if they violate their duty of loyalty to the corporation.

A final form of board accountability comes through the election of directors by the shareholders at the corporation's annual meeting. Annual meetings may also include shareholder resolutions which are a form of governance by referendum.

Each of these forms of accountability is dynamic, not static. The developing specifics of each form of accountability must be judged as to its overall potential to contribute to the successful long-term performance of the corporation. Each specific new item of accountability carries with it the potential for harm as well as good.[3]

More recently, the Business Roundtable has restated its guiding principles of corporate governance:

First, the paramount duty of the board of directors of a public corporation is to select a chief executive officer and to oversee the CEO and other senior management in the competent and ethical operation of the corporation on a day-to-day basis.

Second, it is the responsibility of management to operate the corporation in an effective and ethical manner in order to produce value for stockholders. Senior management is expected to know how the corporation earns its income and what risks the corporation is undertaking in the course of carrying out its business.

---

[2] American Institute of Certified Public Accountants, *Audit Committees, Answers to Typical Questions about Their Organization and Operations* (New York: AICPA, 1978), 7.

[3] Business Roundtable, *Corporate Governance and American Competitiveness* (New York: Business Roundtable, 1990), 15–16.

Management should never put personal interests ahead of or in conflict with the interests of the corporation.

Third, it is the responsibility of management, under the oversight of the board and its audit committee, to produce financial statements that fairly present the financial condition and results of operations of the corporation, and to make the timely disclosures investors need to permit them to assess the financial and business soundness and risks of the corporation.

Fourth, it is the responsibility of the board and its audit committee to engage an independent accounting firm to audit the financial statements prepared by management and to issue an opinion on those statements based on Generally Accepted Accounting Principles. The board, its audit committee, and management must be vigilant to ensure that no actions are taken by the corporation or its employees that compromise the independence of the outside auditor.

Fifth, it is the responsibility of the independent accounting firm to ensure that it is in fact independent, is without conflicts of interest, employs highly competent staff, and carries out its work in accordance with Generally Accepted Auditing Standards. It is also the responsibility of the independent accounting firm to inform the board, through the audit committee, of any concerns the auditor may have about the appropriateness or quality of significant accounting treatments, business transactions that affect the fair presentation of the corporation's financial condition and results of operations, and weaknesses in internal control systems. The auditor should do so in a forthright manner and on a timely basis, whether or not management has also communicated with the board or the audit committee on these matters.

Sixth, the corporation has a responsibility to deal with its employees in a fair and equitable manner.

These responsibilities, and others, are critical to the functioning of the modern public corporation and the integrity of the public markets. No law or regulation alone can be a substitute for the voluntary adherence to these principles by corporate directors and management and by the accounting firms retained to serve American corporations.

The Business Roundtable continues to believe that the most effective way to enhance corporate governance is through conscientious and forward-looking action by a business community that focuses on generating long-term stockholder value with the highest degree of integrity.

The principles discussed here are intended to assist corporate management and boards of directors in their individual efforts to implement best practices of corporate governance, and also to serve as guideposts for the public dialogue on evolving governance standards.[4]

In addition to their fiduciary duties of care and loyalty, directors are expected to attend board meetings and their appropriate standing committee meetings. Directors must keep informed on the affairs of the corporation and use reasonable care and diligence in the performance of their duties. It is imperative that the

---

[4] Business Roundtable, *Principles of Corporate Governance* (Washington, DC: Business Roundtable, May 2002), iv–vi.

directors keep abreast of the corporate developments since they are directly responsible for participating in the decisions that affect the management of the corporation. Directors may be held liable for losses sustained by the corporation as a result of their neglect.

Practically speaking, the concept of corporate accountability extends not only to the stockholders but also to the other constituencies of the board of directors, such as credit grantors and governmental agencies. The extension of corporate accountability to the other constituencies is discussed by the American Assembly. The discussion leaders focused their attention on questions central to running the corporation vis-à-vis its many constituencies. With respect to a framework for corporate accountability, the participants generally agreed that:

> Boards of directors have a primary role in interpreting society's expectations and standards for management.
>
> The five key board functions are:
>
> (a) Appraisal of management performance and provision for management and board succession;
>
> (b) Determination of significant policies and actions with respect to present and future profitability and strategic direction of the enterprise;
>
> (c) Determination of policies and actions with a potential for significant financial, economic, and social impact;
>
> (d) Establishment of policies and procedures designed to obtain compliance with the law; and
>
> (e) Responsibility for monitoring the totality of corporate performance.
>
> Boards should continue to be the central focus in improving the way corporations are governed.[5]

The subject of corporate accountability is a dynamic concept in the governance of the corporation. It is dynamic because the directors must not only assess the changing needs of their constituencies but also render a stewardship accountability based on legal pressures from their constituencies.

In a 2009 report, "Rebuilding Corporate Leadership: How Directors Can Link Long-Term Performance with Public Goals," the Committee for Economic Development links shareholders' prosperity to the health of society. In its view (page 2), "Directors have a legal obligation and duty to address the long-term performance of the corporation. Directors' fiduciary duties include broader societal concerns that affirmatively affect the corporation's performance and long-term sustainability."

## The Need for Corporate Accountability

In an effort to address the credibility gap or expectation gap that arose from the corporate accounting scandals involving Enron, WorldCom, Tyco, and others, the

---

[5] American Assembly, *Corporate Governance in America,* Pamphlet 54 (New York: Columbia University, April 1978), 6.

U.S. Congress passed the Sarbanes-Oxley Act of 2002 (Sarbanes-Oxley) on July 25 of that year, and President George W. Bush signed the bill into law on July 30, 2002.[6] Sarbanes-Oxley incorporated many standards of corporate accountability into a federal statute that has changed securities laws and self-regulatory organizations' listing standards. This legislation provides a framework that can be used to measure the performance of audit committee members, independent auditors, chief executive officers, and chief financial officers.[7] As a consequence of the expansion of federal statutes into an area traditionally left more to state common law, directors of publicly held corporations likely will face more sources of lawsuits as well as an increased risk of liability. Although some qualified persons may be reluctant to accept a position on a board of directors because of a perception of heightened risk, others will appreciate that due diligence, care, and loyalty will go a long way in mitigating any possible risks.

## DEVELOPMENTS IN CORPORATE ACCOUNTABILITY

During the late 1990s, unprecedented public attention was focused on the role and responsibility of audit committees in promoting corporate accountability and investor confidence in the integrity of the audit and financial reporting. Although audit committees had been recognized and accepted for more than 20 years, unexpected failures of major corporations and disclosures of questionable financial reporting practices dashed investors' confidence in the capital marketplace. Notwithstanding, the common question asked by investors was "Where were the auditors?" Another question was "Where was the audit committee?" As a result, a number of public and private sector initiatives were undertaken in the late 1990s and in the post-Enron, post-WorldCom period in response to high-profile accounting scandals and the demise of a large accounting firm.

This timeline shown in Exhibit 1.1 provides a chronology of the important developments or studies related to audit committees (The timeline presents major developments; the reader may wish to visit the Web sites noted parenthetically for further reading.)

### Public and Private Sector Initiatives

*Securities and Exchange Commission*   In September 1998 SEC Chairman Arthur Levitt, in a keynote speech entitled "The Numbers Game," expressed his concerns about "hocus pocus accounting." In addition to his remarks regarding the decline in the quality of financial reporting (e.g., earnings management strategies to meet analyst and market quarterly expectations via creative acquisition accounting, premature revenue recognition, restructuring charges, "cookie

---

[6] Sarbanes-Oxley Act of 2002, H.R. Rep. No. 107-610, July 25, 2002, and Title 1 of Public Law No. 107-204, July 30, 2002.

[7] The initial implementation of some aspects of Sarbanes-Oxley—in particular Section 404—was fraught with difficulty and high costs. Chapter 8 addresses some of the causes of and solutions to those problems.

---

**EXHIBIT 1.1**   Important Audit Committee Developments Timeline

---

1998   SEC chairman Arthur Levitt's speech, "The Numbers Game" (remarks at New York University's Center for Law and Business and the SEC's Nine-Point Action Plan).

1999   Blue Ribbon Committee on Improving the Effectiveness of Corporate Audit Committees,

      *Report and Recommendations of the Blue Ribbon Committee on Improving the Effectiveness of Corporate Audit Committees.*

      Securities and Exchange Commission, *Final Rules, Audit Committee Disclosure*, and approval of the New York Stock Exchange, NASDAQ, and American Stock Exchange.

      American Institute of Certified Public Accountants' Auditing Standards Board, *Statement on Auditing Standards No. 90, "Audit Committee Communication."* Available at www.aicpa.org.

      National Association of Corporate Directors (NACD), *Report of the NACD Blue Ribbon Commission on Audit Committees.* Available at www.nacdonline.org.

      Committee of Sponsoring Organizations of the Treadway Commission, *Fraudulent Financial Reporting: 1987–1997 An Analysis of U.S. Public Companies.* Available at www.coso.org.

      Independence Standards Board

      *No. 1 "Independence Discussion with Audit Committees."* Available at ISB-Independence Discussion with Audit Committees.

2000   Public Oversight Board, Panel on Audit Effectiveness (O'Malley Panel), *The Panel on Audit Effectiveness, Report and Recommendations.*

2001   Chairman Arthur Levitt's Letter to Audit Committees, Public Oversight Board, Final Annual Report (May 1, 2002, the POB terminated its existence; visit the POB Web site, www.publicoversightboard.org.

2002   The Business Roundtable, *Principles of Corporate Governance.*

      NYSE Corporate Accountability and Listing Standards Committee, *Report on Proposed Changes to the Corporate Governance Listing Standards.*

      NASDAQ Listing and Hearing Review Council, *Letter of recommendations proposing corporate governance reforms.* Available at www.nasdaq.com/newsroom.

      Sarbanes-Oxley Act of 2002. Available at www.sec.gov.

      Public Company Accounting Oversight Board. Available at www.pcaobus.org.

2003   Implementation of the sections of the Sarbanes-Oxley Act of 2002 through amendments to Sec. 10A of the Securities Exchange of 1934.

2004   PCAOB Standard No. 2, *Integrated Audits of Financial Statements and Internal Control over Financial Reporting.* Available at www.pcaobus.org.

2006   COSO, *Internal Control over Financial Reporting — Guidance for Smaller Public Companies.* Available at www.coso.org/guidance.htm.

      The Committee for Economic Development, *Private Enterprise, Public Trust: The State of Corporate America After Sarbanes-Oxley.* Available at www.ced.org.

*(continued)*

---

**EXHIBIT 1.1**   *(Continued)*

---

2007    PCAOB Standard No. 5 replaces Standard No. 2 on *Integrated Audits of Financial Statements and Internal Control over Financial Reporting*. Available at www.pcaobus.org.

The Committee for Economic Development, *Built to Last: Focusing Corporations on Long-Term Performance*. Available at www.ced.org.

2008    SEC, *Report of the Advisory Committee on Improvements to Financial Reporting*. Available at www.sec.gov.

U.S. Treasury, *Report of the Advisory Committee on the Auditing Profession*. Available at www.treas.gov.

2009    PCAOB Staff View, *An Audit of Internal Control over Financial Reporting That Is Integrated with An Audit of Financial Statements: Guidance for Auditors of Smaller Public Companies*. Available at www.pcaobus.org.

Center for Audit Quality, *Lessons Learned—Performing an Audit of Internal Control in an Integrated Audit*. Available at www.thecaq.org/resources/library.htm.

COSO, *Internal Control—Integrated Framework: Guidance on Monitoring Internal Control Systems*. Available at www.coso.org/guidance.htm.

The Committee for Economic Development, *Rebuilding Corporate Leadership: How Directors Can Link Long-Term Performance with Public Goals*. Available at www.ced.org.

---

jar reserves," and materiality judgments) as well as the related decline in market capitalization, Levitt stated that with respect to audit committees:

> [Q]ualified, committed, independent and tough minded audit committees represent the most reliable guardians of the public interest. Sadly, stories abound of audit committees whose members lack expertise in the basic principles of financial reporting as well as the mandate to ask probing questions.[8]

Recognizing the problem with respect to the decline in the integrity and credibility of financial reporting, Levitt set forth the SEC's nine-point action plan (see Exhibit 1.2), which included, in point eight, an action item to strengthen the audit committee process. Subsequently the SEC, the New York Stock Exchange (NYSE), and the National Association of Securities Dealers[9] agreed that both self-regulatory organizations would sponsor a Blue Ribbon Committee (BRC) called Improving the Effectiveness of Corporate Audit Committees. In September 1998, the BRC was formed. It issued its final report and recommendations in February 1999. The BRC's primary goal was to produce a report "geared toward effecting pragmatic, progressive changes in the functions and expectations placed

---

[8] See remarks by Chairman Arthur Levitt, Securities and Exchange Commission, "The Numbers Game," NYU Center for Law and Business, New York, September 28, 1998. Available at www.sec .gov/news/speech/speecharchive/1998/spch220.txt.
[9] Now the Financial Industry Regulatory Authority (FINRA).

---

**EXHIBIT 1.2**   Summary of the Securities and Exchange's Nine-Point Action Plan

---

First, I have instructed the SEC staff to require well-detailed disclosures about the impact of changes in accounting assumptions. This should include a supplement to the financial statement showing beginning and ending balances as well as activity in between, including any adjustments. This will, I believe, enable the market to better understand the nature and effects of the restructuring liabilities and other loss accruals.

Second, we are challenging the profession, through the AICPA, to clarify the ground rules for auditing of purchased R&D. We also are requesting that they augment existing guidance on restructurings, large acquisition write-offs, and revenue recognition practices. It's time for the accounting profession to better qualify for auditors what's acceptable and what's not.

Third, I reject the notion that the concept of materiality can be used to excuse deliberate misstatements of performance. I know of one Fortune 500 company who had recorded a significant accounting error, and whose auditors told them so. But they still used a materiality ceiling of six percent earnings to justify the error. I have asked the SEC staff to focus on this problem and publish guidance that emphasizes the need to consider qualitative, not just quantitative factors of earnings. Materiality is not a bright line cutoff of three or five percent. It requires consideration of all relevant factors that could impact an investor's decision.

Fourth, SEC staff will immediately consider interpretive accounting guidance on the do's and don'ts of revenue recognition. The staff will also determine whether recently published standards for the software industry can be applied to other service companies.

Fifth, I am asking private sector standard setters to take action where current standards and guidance are inadequate. I encourage a prompt resolution of the FASB's projects, currently underway, that should bring greater clarity to the definition of a liability.

Sixth, the SEC's review and enforcement teams will reinforce these regulatory initiatives. We will formally target reviews of public companies that announce restructuring liability reserves, major write-offs or other practices that appear to manage earnings. Likewise, our enforcement team will continue to root out and aggressively act on abuses of the financial reporting process.

**Improved Outside Auditing in the Financial Reporting Process**
Seventh, I don't think it should surprise anyone here that recent headlines of accounting failures have led some people to question the thoroughness of audits. I need not remind auditors they are the public's watchdog in the financial reporting process. We rely on auditors to put something like the good housekeeping seal of approval on the information investors receive. The integrity of that information must take priority over a desire for cost efficiencies or competitive advantage in the audit process. High quality auditing requires well-trained, well-focused and well-supervised auditors.

As I look at some of the failures today, I can't help but wonder if the staff in the trenches of the profession have the training and supervision they need to ensure that audits are being done right. We cannot permit thorough audits to be sacrificed for re-engineered approaches that are efficient, but less effective. I have just proposed that the Public Oversight Board form a group of all the major constituencies to review the way audits are performed and assess the impact of recent trends on the public interest.

**Strengthening the Audit Committee Process**
And, finally, qualified, committed, independent and tough-minded audit committees represent the most reliable guardians of the public interest. Sadly, stories abound of

*(continued)*

---

**EXHIBIT 1.2**   *(Continued)*

---

audit committees whose members lack expertise in the basic principles of financial reporting as well as the mandate to ask probing questions. In fact, I've heard of one audit committee that convenes only twice a year before the regular board meeting for 15 minutes and whose duties are limited to a perfunctory presentation.

Compare that situation with the audit committee which meets twelve times a year before each board meeting; where every member has a financial background; where there are no personal ties to the chairman or the company; where they have their own advisers; where they ask tough questions of management and outside auditors; and where, ultimately, the investor interest is being served.

The SEC stands ready to take appropriate action if that interest is not protected. But, a private sector response that empowers audit committees and obviates the need for public sector dictates seems the wisest choice. I am pleased to announce that the financial community has agreed to accept this challenge.

As part eight of this comprehensive effort to address earnings management, the New York Stock Exchange and the National Association of Securities Dealers have agreed to sponsor a "blue-ribbon" panel to be headed by John Whitehead, former Deputy Secretary of State and retired senior partner of Goldman, Sachs, and Ira Millstein, a lawyer and noted corporate governance expert. Within the next 90 days, this distinguished group will develop a series of far-ranging recommendations intended to empower audit committees and function as the ultimate guardian of investor interests and corporate accountability. They are going to examine how we can get the right people to do the right things and ask the right questions.

**Need for a Cultural Change**
Finally, I'm challenging corporate management and Wall Street to re-examine our current environment. I believe we need to embrace nothing less than a cultural change. For corporate managers, remember, the integrity of the numbers in the financial reporting system is directly related to the long-term interests of a corporation. While the temptations are great, and the pressures strong, illusions in numbers are only that—ephemeral, and ultimately self-destructive.

To Wall Street, I say, look beyond the latest quarter. Punish those who rely on deception, rather than the practice of openness and transparency.

---

*Source:* See remarks by Chairman Arthur Levitt, Securities and Exchange Commission, "The Numbers Game," New York: NYU Center for Law and Business, September 28, 1998, www.sec .gov/news/speech/speecharchive/1998/spch220.txt.

---

on corporate boards, audit committees, senior and financial management, the internal audit, and the outside auditors regarding financial reporting and the oversight process."[10] Furthermore, the BRC noted that its final recommendations were based on two essentials: "First, an audit committee, with actual practice and overall performance that reflects the professionalism embodied by the full board of which it is a part, and second, a legal, regulatory, and self-regulating framework that emphasizes disclosure and transparency and accountability."[11] (See Exhibit 1.3 for a summary of the BRC's recommendations.)

---

[10] The report is available at www.nyse.com and www.finra.org.
[11] Ibid., 8.

**EXHIBIT 1.3**   Summary of Recommendations of the Blue Ribbon Committee on Improving the Effectiveness of Corporate Audit Committees

The first two recommendations are aimed at strengthening the independence of the audit committee:

### Recommendation 1

The Committee recommends that both the New York Stock Exchange (NYSE) and the Financial Industry Regulatory Authority (FINRA)* adopt the following definitions of independence for purposes of service on the audit committee for listed companies with a market capitalization above $200 million (or a more appropriate measure for identifying smaller-sized companies as determined jointly by the NYSE and FINRA).

Members of the audit committee shall be considered independent if they have no relationship to the corporation that may interfere with the exercise of their independence from management and the corporation. Examples of such relationships include.

- a director being employed by the corporation or any of its affiliates for the current year or any of the past five years;
- a director accepting any compensation from the corporation or any of its affiliates other than compensation for board service or benefits under a tax-qualified retirement plan;
- a director being a member of the immediate family of an individual who is, or has been in any of the past five years, employed by the corporation or any of its affiliates as an executive officer;
- a director being a partner in, or a controlling shareholder or an executive officer of, any for-profit business organizations to which the corporation made, or from which the corporation received, payments that are or have been significant** to the corporation or business organization in any of the past five years;
- a director being employed as an executive of another company where any of the corporation's executives serve on that company's compensation committee.

A director who has one or more of these relationships may be appointed to the audit committee, if the board, under exceptional and limited circumstances, determines that membership on the committee by the individual is required by the best interests of the corporation and its shareholders, and the board discloses, in the next annual proxy statement subsequent to such determination, the nature of the relationship and the reasons for that determination.

### Recommendation 2

The Committee recommends that in addition to adopting and complying with the definition of independence set forth above for purposes of service on the audit committee, the NYSE and FINRA require that listed companies with a market capitalization above $200 million (or a more appropriate measure for identifying smaller-sized companies as determined jointly by the NYSE and FINRA) have an audit committee comprised solely of independent directors.

---

*Formerly the National Association of Securities Dealers (NASD).
**The committee views the term "significant" in the spirit of Section 1.34(a)(4) of the American Law Institute Principles of Corporate Governance and the accompanying commentary to that section.

*(continued)*

**EXHIBIT 1.3**   *(Continued)*

The Committee recommends that the NYSE and FINRA maintain their respective current audit committee independence requirements as well as their respective definitions of independence for listed companies with a market capitalization of $200 million or below (or a more appropriate measure for identifying smaller-sized companies as determined jointly by the NYSE and FINRA).

**Our second set of recommendations is aimed at making the audit committee more effective:**

### Recommendation 3

The Committee recommends that the NYSE and FINRA require listed companies with a market capitalization above $200 million (or a more appropriate measure for identifying smaller-sized companies as determined jointly by the NYSE and FINRA) to have an audit committee comprised of a minimum of three directors, each of whom is financially literate (as described in the section of this report entitled "Financial Literacy") or becomes financially literate within a reasonable period of time after his or her appointment to the audit committee, and further that at least one member of the audit committee have accounting or related financial management expertise.

The Committee recommends that the NYSE and FINRA maintain their respective current audit committee size and membership requirements for companies with a market capitalization of $200 million or below (or a more appropriate measure for identifying smaller-sized companies as determined jointly by the NYSE and FINRA).

### Recommendation 4

The Committee recommends that the NYSE and FINRA require the audit committee of each listed company to (i) adopt a formal written charter that is approved by the full board of directors and that specifies the scope of the committee's responsibilities, and how it carries out those responsibilities, including structure, processes, and membership requirements, and (ii) review and reassess the adequacy of the audit committee charter on an annual basis.

### Recommendation 5

The Committee recommends that the Securities and Exchange Commission (SEC) promulgate rules that require the audit committee for each reporting company to disclose in the company's proxy statement for its annual meeting of shareholders whether the audit committee has adopted a formal written charter, and, if so, whether the audit committee satisfied its responsibilities during the prior year in compliance with its charter, which charter shall be disclosed at least triennially in the annual report to shareholders or proxy statement and in the next annual report to shareholders or proxy statement after any significant amendment to that charter.

The Committee further recommends that the SEC adopt a "safe harbor" applicable to all disclosure referenced in the Recommendation 5.

**Our final group of recommendations addresses mechanisms for accountability among the audit committee, the outside auditors, and management:**

### Recommendation 6

The Committee recommends that the listing rules for both the NYSE and FINRA require that the audit committee charter for every listed company specify that the outside auditor is ultimately accountable to the board of directors and the audit committee, as representatives of shareholders, and that these shareholder representatives have the ultimate authority and responsibility to select, evaluate, and, where appropriate, replace the outside auditor (or to nominate the outside auditor to be proposed for shareholder approval in any proxy statement).

### Recommendation 7

The Committee recommends that the listing rules for both the NYSE and FINRA require that the audit committee charter for every listed company specify that the audit committee is responsible for ensuring its receipt from the outside auditors of a formal written statement delineating all relationships between the auditor and the company, consistent with Independence Standards Board Standard 1, and that the audit committee is also responsible for actively engaging in a dialogue with the auditor with respect to any disclosed relationships or services that may impact the objectivity and independence of the auditor and for taking, or recommending that the full board take, appropriate action to ensure the independence of the outside auditor.

### Recommendation 8

The Committee recommends that Generally Accepted Auditing Standards (GAAS) require that a company's outside auditor discuss with the audit committee the auditor's judgments about the quality, not just the acceptability, of the company's accounting principles as applied in its financial reporting; the discussion should include such issues as the clarity of the company's financial disclosures and degree of aggressiveness or conservatism of the company's accounting principles and underlying estimates and other significant decisions made by management in preparing the financial disclosure and reviewed by the outside auditors. This requirement should be written in a way to encourage open, frank discussion and to avoid boilerplate.

### Recommendation 9

The Committee recommends that the SEC require all reporting companies to include a letter from the audit committee in the company's annual report to shareholders and Form 10-K Annual Report disclosing whether or not, with respect to the prior fiscal year: (i) management has reviewed the audited financial statements with the audit committee, including a discussion of the quality of the accounting principles as applied and significant judgments affecting the company's financial statements; (ii) the outside auditors have discussed with the audit committee the outside auditors' judgments of the quality of those principles as applied and judgments referenced in (i) above under the circumstances; (iii) the members of the audit committee have discussed among themselves, without management or the outside auditors present, the information disclosed to the audit committee described in (i) and (ii) above; and (iv) the audit committee, in reliance on the review and discussions conducted with management and the outside auditors pursuant to (i) and (ii) above, believes that the company's financial statements are fairly presented in conformity with Generally Accepted Accounting Principles (GAAP) in all material aspects.

The Committee further recommends that the SEC adopt a "safe harbor" applicable to any disclosure referenced in this Recommendation 9.

### Recommendation 10

The Committee recommends that the SEC require that a reporting company's outside auditor conduct a SAS 71 Interim Financial Review prior to the company's filing of its Form 10-Q.

*(continued)*

**EXHIBIT 1.3**   (*Continued*)

The Committee further recommends that SAS 71 be amended to require that a reporting company's outside auditor discuss with the audit committee, or at least its chairman, and a representative of financial management, in person, or by telephone conference call, the matters described in AU Section 380, Communications With the Audit Committee, prior to the filing of the Form 10-Q (and preferably prior to any public announcement of financial results), including significant adjustments, management judgments and accounting estimates, significant new accounting policies, and disagreements with management.

*Source:* Blue Ribbon Committee on Improving the Effectiveness of Corporate Audit Committees, *Report and Recommendations of the Blue Ribbon Committee on Improving the Effectiveness of Corporate Audit Committees* (New York: The Blue Ribbon Committee on Improving the Effectiveness of Corporate Audit Committees, 1999), pp. 10–16.

Between February and December 1999, boards of directors and audit committee members studied the BRC's recommendations and reevaluated the responsibilities of their audit committees.[12] Additionally, the SEC and self-regulatory organizations (SROs) issued proposed rules and changes to the SROs' listing standards. Finally, in December 1999, the SEC, the SROs, and the AICPA's Auditing Standards Board adopted new rules, listing standards, and auditing standards for improving the effectiveness of audit committees. Exhibit 1.4 contains a flow chart that delineates the items to meet the new SEC disclosure rules, the SROs' listing standards, and professional auditing standards.

In January 1999, the Public Oversight Board agreed to sponsor the Panel on Audit Effectiveness. The major objective of the panel was to review and evaluate ways to improve independent audits in the financial reporting process and to assess the impact of recent trends on the public interest. In August 2000, the panel issued its report and recommendations. With respect to audit committees, the panel made these recommendations:

**2.88** The Panel recommends that audit committees increase the time and attention they devote to discussions of internal control with management and both the internal and external auditors. Specifically, audit committees should:

- Obtain a written report from management on the effectiveness of internal control over financial reporting (ordinarily using the criteria in the 1992 report of the Committee of Sponsoring Organizations of the Treadway Commission [COSO]). Annual reporting by management on internal control to the audit committee is necessary for the effective discharge of the audit committee's responsibilities and will serve as a catalyst for its more substantive involvement in the area of internal control and a more meaningful dialogue with the internal and external auditors about controls. It also should provide a basis for discussions about the degree of

---

[12] See, for example, *Report of the NACD Blue Ribbon Commission on Audit Committees* (Washington, DC: NACD, 1999); see also Financial Executives Institute and Arthur Andersen, *The Audit Symposium: A Balanced Responsibility* (Morristown, NJ: Financial Executives Institute); *Fraudulent Financial Reporting: 1987–1997, An Analysis of U.S. Public Companies* (New York: COSO of the Treadway Commission, 1999).

**EXHIBIT 1.4** The New Requirements and Disclosure Rules for Audit Committees: A Flow Chart

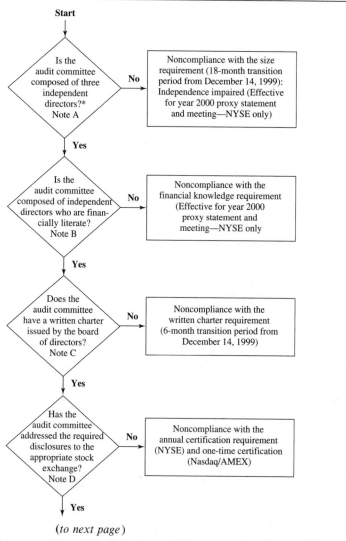

*(to next page)*

*Notes:* A. If the board of directors determines in its business judgment that the relationship (e.g., certain business relationships and/or one non-independent member relationship) does not interfere with the director's exercise of independent judgment, then independence is not impaired.

B. The board of directors determines in its business judgment whether each member of the audit committee is financially literate. Based on the board's business judgment, at least one member must have accounting or related financial management expertise.

C. Each listed company must have an audit committee charter that guides its activities.

D. Each listed company (NYSE) is required to furnish a written certification letter, submitted annually, affirming the aforementioned points in A, B, and C. NASDAQ/AMEX listed companies require a one-time certification with respect to A, B, and C above.

E. After December 15, 2000, the SEC requires proxy statement disclosure of a report from the audit committee indicating whether the committee: (1) reviewed and discussed financial statements with management and the

*(continued)*

*(from previous page)*

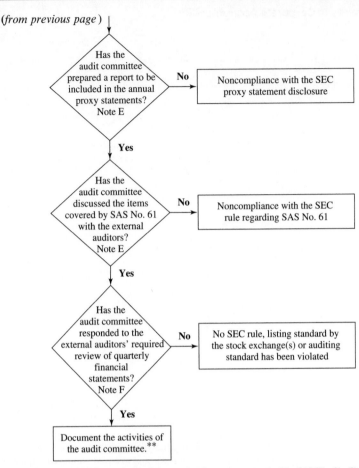

Has the audit committee prepared a report to be included in the annual proxy statements? Note E

**No** → Noncompliance with the SEC proxy statement disclosure

**Yes**

Has the audit committee discussed the items covered by SAS No. 61 with the external auditors? Note E

**No** → Noncompliance with the SEC rule regarding SAS No. 61

**Yes**

Has the audit committee responded to the external auditors' required review of quarterly financial statements? Note F

**No** → No SEC rule, listing standard by the stock exchange(s) or auditing standard has been violated

**Yes**

Document the activities of the audit committee.**

external auditors; (2) discussed with the external auditors matters required by SAS No. 61; (3) received a written letter from the external auditors required by ISBS No. 1 and discussed independence issues; and (4) based on the aforementioned review and discussions, recommended to the board that the audited financial statements be included in the company's annual SEC 10-K report. Additionally, after December 15, 2000, the SEC requires proxy statement disclosures of whether the audit committee is governed by a written charter, and if it is, each registrant must attach a copy to the proxy statement once every three years. Finally, each SEC registrant is required to disclose in its proxy statements whether audit committee members are independent and provide information about members that are not. (See Note A above).

F. Starting with the fiscal quarter ending on or after March 15, 2000, SEC rules mandate that the external auditors review the quarterly financial statements prior to the filing of Form 10-Q or 10-QSB. In its 1987 report, the National Commission on Fraudulent Financial Reporting (NCFFR) recommended that "the audit committee oversight responsibilities undertaken on behalf of the board of directors extend to the quarterly reporting process. The audit committee should review the controls that management has established to protect the integrity of the quarterly reporting process. This review should be ongoing" (p. 48). In February 1999, the Blue Ribbon Committee reaffirmed the NCFFR's position (p. 16).

*The SEC approved amendments to the NYSE, FINRA, and AMEX listing standards that require all audit committee members to be independent; however, one non-independent member can serve on the committee. See Order Approving Proposed Rule Change SEC Release No. NYSE 34-42233, SEC Release No. NASD 34-42231, and SEC Release No. AMEX 34-42232.

**It may be advisable to have in-house general counsel review the above documentation as well as a review by outside legal counsel.

*Source:* This flow chart, prepared by Louis Braiotta, Jr., is included and adopted from an article by Robert W. Rouse and Mark R. Borrelli, "Audit Committees in an Era of Increased Scrutiny," *CPA Journal* 70, no. 6 (June 2000): 30–31. Copyright © 2000 by the New York State Society of Certified Public Accountants, 530 Fifth Avenue, New York, NY 10036-5101. All rights reserved.

the external auditor's involvement with internal control during the financial statement audit.

• Establish specific expectations with management and the internal and external auditors about the qualitative information needs of the committee related to internal control. Particular emphasis should be given to understanding management's and the auditors' views on (1) the control environment and (2) the controls (or lack thereof) over financial reporting, with particular attention to controls in higher-risk areas of the company's information systems. In addition, these discussions should include the effects of technology on current and future information systems [pp. 32–33].

**2.164** The Panel recommends that audit committees evaluate the nature of entities' reserves and review activity in them with both management and the auditors [p. 55].

**2.219** The Panel recommends that audit committees:

• Specify in their charters and reflect in their actions, as recommended by the Blue Ribbon Committee, "that the outside auditor is ultimately accountable to the board of directors and the audit committee, as representatives of the shareholders, and that these shareholder representatives have the ultimate authority and responsibility to select, evaluate, and where appropriate, replace the outside auditors (or to nominate the outside auditors to be proposed for shareholder approval in any proxy statement)."

• Develop a formal calendar of activities related to those areas of responsibility prescribed in the committee charter, including a meeting plan that is reviewed and agreed to by the entire board. The meeting plan should include communications between the committee chair or full committee and the auditor before the release of interim or year-end financial data. In addition, the Panel recommends a minimum of two face-to-face meetings during the year with the external auditor and at least one executive session with the internal and external auditors without management's presence.

• Take charge of their agenda and ensure, in particular, that it focuses on, among other matters, risks directly affecting the financial statements, key controls, interim financial information, policies and practices for management's communications with analysts, and the qualitative aspects of financial reporting.

• Inquire about time pressures on the auditor, including pressures on the timing of audit procedures; the degree of management's cooperation with the auditor; and their potential effects on audit effectiveness.

• Review the internal and external auditors' performance on an annual basis; exercise responsibility, as the external auditor's primary client, to assess the auditor's responsiveness to the committee's and board of directors' expectations; and be satisfied that the auditor is appropriately compensated for performing a thorough audit.

• Require the auditor and management to advise the committee of the entity's plans to hire any of the audit firm's personnel into high-level positions, and the actions, if any, that the auditor and management intend to take to ensure that the auditor maintains independence [pp. 68–69].

**3.54** The Panel recommends that audit committees:

• Request management to report on the control environment within the entity and how that environment and the entity's policies and procedures (including management's monitoring activities) serve to prevent and detect financial statement fraud. Such reporting should acknowledge, in explicit terms, that fraud prevention and detection are primarily the responsibility of management. It also should help audit committees assess the strength of management's commitment to a culture of intolerance for improper conduct. Furthermore, audit committees should seek the views of auditors on their assessment of the risks of financial statement fraud and their understanding of the controls designed to mitigate such risks.

- Accept responsibility for ascertaining that the auditors receive the necessary cooperation from management to carry out their duties in accordance with the strengthened auditing standards to be developed by the ASB [Accounting Standards Board] [p. 94].

**5.30** The Panel recommends that audit committees pre-approve non-audit services that exceed a threshold determined by the committee. This recommendation is consistent with the recommendations of the Blue Ribbon Committee on Improving the Effectiveness of Corporate Audit Committees regarding auditors' services. The threshold should be at a level that ensures that significant services are pre-approved, but not so low that the committee assumes a management function.

When audit committees determine whether to approve specific non-audit services, the Panel recommends that they consider the same guiding principle and the factors suggested above for use by the ISB. [p. 117][13]

In addition to the panel's recommendations, Arthur Levitt issued a letter to the chairmen of audit committees of the top 5,000 corporations. The letter is shown in Exhibit 1.5.

In May 2002, the Business Roundtable issued a white paper, *Principles of Corporate Governance*, explaining how boards of directors perform their oversight function through the audit committee. The Business Roundtable provides these guidelines:

- Every publicly owned corporation should have an audit committee comprised solely of independent directors.
- Audit committees typically consist of three to five members. The listing standards of the major securities markets require audit committees and require that an audit committee have at least three members and that all members of the audit committee qualify as independent under the applicable listing standards, subject to limited exceptions.
- Audit committee members should meet minimum financial literacy standards, and at least one of the committee members should have accounting or financial management expertise, as required by the listing standards of the major securities markets. However, more important than financial expertise is the ability of audit committee members, as with all directors, to understand the corporation's business and risk profile and to apply their business experience

---

[13] Panel on Audit Effectiveness, *Panel on Audit Effectiveness Report and Recommendations* (Stamford, CT: POB, 2000).

---

**EXHIBIT 1.5**   Chairman Arthur Levitt's Letter to Audit Committees

---

*Washington, DC, January 5, 2001*—Securities and Exchange Commission Chairman Arthur Levitt today sent the following letter to the audit committee chairmen of the top 5,000 public companies.

Dear Members of the Audit Committee:

Almost a year ago, the Commission, our major markets and standard setters—building on the work of the Blue Ribbon Committee on Audit Committee Effectiveness—adopted rules that strengthen the audit committee's independence, and give its members the tools and the wherewithal to fulfill their duty to the investing public. In addition, the rules improve communications, through greater disclosure, among the board, outside auditors and management.

When auditors and the board engage in frank and meaningful discussions about the significant, but sometimes gray areas of accounting, both the company's and its shareholders' interests are served. In this way, the board, including the audit committee, management, and outside auditors, form a "three-legged stool" of responsible disclosure and active oversight.

In recent months, the Commission and the accounting profession have been engaged in a discussion on the vital issue of auditor independence. Among other reasons, increased economic pressures on the profession, coupled with greater competition and consolidation, mandated that we modernize and further clarify independence requirements. This discussion has led to a combination of rules and disclosures that establish clear guidelines on the non-audit services an auditor may provide to an audit client, as well as the meaningful involvement of the audit committee in consideration of consulting services that may impair independence. More specifically, the Commission's rules require companies to state in their proxy statement whether the audit committee has considered whether the provision of non-audit services is compatible with maintaining the auditor's independence.

In August, the Panel on Audit Effectiveness issued its final report recommending that, among other things, audit committees obtain annual reports from management assessing the company's internal controls, specify in their charters that the outside auditor is ultimately accountable to the board of directors and audit committee, inquire about time pressures on the auditor, and pre-approve non-audit services provided by the auditor.

The Panel, more specifically, provided guidance an audit committee can use to determine the appropriateness of a service. This guidance includes:

1. Whether the service is being performed principally for the audit committee.
2. The effects of the service, if any, on audit effectiveness or on the quality and timeliness of the entity's financial reporting process.
3. Whether the service would be performed by specialists (e.g., technology specialists) who ordinarily also provide recurring audit support.
4. Whether the service would be performed by audit personnel, and if so, whether it will enhance their knowledge of the entity's business and operations.
5. Whether the role of those performing the service would be inconsistent with the auditors' role (e.g., a role where neutrality, impartiality, and auditor skepticism are likely to be subverted).
6. Whether the audit firm personnel would be assuming a management role or creating a mutual or conflicting interest with management.
7. Whether the auditors, in effect, would be "auditing their own numbers."
8. Whether the project must be started and completed very quickly.
9. Whether the audit firm has unique expertise in the service.
10. The size of the fee(s) for the non-audit service(s).

(*continued*)

---

**EXHIBIT 1.5**  *(Continued)*

---

I encourage your audit committee to discuss the Panel's recommendations as well as these ten factors and consider them in relevant discussions with your auditor. The Panel's report can be found at *www.pobauditpanel.org/*. I also encourage you to read the Commission's rule release at *www.sec.gov.rules/final/33-7919.htm*.

During my almost eight years at the Commission, I have come to believe that one of the most reliable guardians of the public interest is a competent, committed, independent and tough-minded audit committee. The audit committee stands to protect and preserve the integrity of America's financial reporting process. I encourage your committee to take every step possible to ensure that the integrity of the financial statements, and by extension, the interest of shareholders, remains second to none.

Sincerely,

*Arthur Levitt*

---

*Source:*www.sec.gov/news/digest/2001/dig010501.pdf.

---

and judgment to the issues for which the committee is responsible with an independent and critical eye.

- The audit committee is responsible for oversight of the corporation's financial reporting process. The primary functions of the audit committee are the following:

  - *Risk profile.* The audit committee should understand the corporation's risk profile and oversee the corporation's risk assessment and management practices.

  - *Outside auditor.* The audit committee is responsible for supervising the corporation's relationship with its outside auditor, including recommending to the full board the firm to be engaged as the outside auditor, evaluating the auditor's performance, and considering whether it would be appropriate to rotate senior audit personnel or for the corporation periodically to change its outside auditor. The selection of an outside auditor should involve an annual due diligence process in which the audit committee reviews the qualifications, work product, independence, and reputation of the proposed outside auditor. The audit committee should base its decisions about selecting and possibly changing the outside auditor on its assessment of what is likely to lead to more effective audits. Based on its due diligence, the audit committee should make an annual recommendation to the full board about the selection of the outside auditor.

  - *Auditor independence.* The audit committee should consider the independence of the outside auditor and should develop policies concerning the provision of non-audit services by the outside auditor. The provision of some types of audit-related and consulting services by the outside auditor may not be inconsistent with independence or the attestation function. In considering whether the outside auditor should provide certain types of non-audit services, the audit committee should consider the degree of review and oversight that may be appropriate for new and existing services. When making independence judgments, the audit committee should consider the nature and dollar amount of all services provided by the outside auditor.

- *Critical accounting policies, judgments, and estimates.* The audit committee should review and discuss with management and the outside auditor the corporation's critical accounting policies and the quality of accounting judgments and estimates made by management.
- *Internal controls.* The audit committee should understand and be familiar with the corporation's system of internal controls and on a periodic basis should review with both internal and outside auditors the adequacy of this system.
- *Compliance.* Unless the full board or another committee does so, the audit committee should review the corporation's procedures addressing compliance with the law and important corporate policies, including the corporation's code of ethics or code of conduct.
- *Financial statements.* The audit committee should review and discuss the corporation's annual financial statements with management and the outside auditor and, based on these discussions, recommend that the board approve the financial statements for publication and filing. Most audit committees also find it advisable to implement processes for the committee or its designee to review the corporation's quarterly financial statements prior to release.
- *Internal audit function.* The audit committee should oversee the corporation's internal audit function, including review of reports submitted by the internal audit staff, and should review the appointment and replacement of the senior internal auditing executive.
- *Communication.* The audit committee should provide a channel of communication to the board for the outside auditor and internal auditors and may also meet with and receive reports from finance officers, compliance officers, and the general counsel.
- *Hiring auditor personnel.* Under audit committee supervision, some corporations have implemented "revolving door" policies covering the hiring of auditor personnel. For example, these policies may impose "cooling off" periods prohibiting the corporation from employing members of the audit engagement team in senior financial management positions for some period of time after their work as auditors for the corporation. The audit committee should consider whether to adopt such a policy. Any policy on the hiring of auditor personnel should be flexible enough to allow exceptions, but only when specifically approved by the audit committee.

- Audit committee meetings should be held frequently enough to allow the committee to appropriately monitor the annual and quarterly financial reports. For many corporations, this means four or more meetings a year. Meetings should be scheduled with enough time to permit and encourage active discussions with management and the internal and outside auditors. The audit committee should meet with the internal and outside auditors, without management present, at every meeting and communicate with them between meetings as necessary. Some audit committees may decide that specific functions, such as quarterly review meetings with the outside auditor or management, can be delegated to the audit committee chairman or other members of the audit committee.[14]

In addition to the Business Roundtable's *Principles of Corporate Governance*, both the NYSE and NASDAQ proposed new changes to their corporate governance listing standards. The NYSE's rule changes are:

*6. Add to the "independence" requirement for audit committee membership the requirements of Rule 10A-3(b)(1) under the Exchange Act, subject to the exemptions provided for in Rule 10A-3(c).*

Commentary Applicable to All Companies: While it is not the audit committee's responsibility to certify the company's financial statements or to guarantee the auditor's report, the committee stands at the crucial intersection of management, independent auditors, internal auditors and the board of directors. The Exchange supports additional directors' fees to compensate audit committee members for the significant time and effort they expend to fulfill their duties as audit committee members, but does not believe that any member of the audit committee should receive any compensation other than such director's fees from the company. If a director satisfies the definition of "independent director" set out in Section 303A(2), then his or her receipt of a pension or other form of deferred compensation from the company for prior service (provided such compensation is not contingent in any way on continued service) will not preclude him or her from satisfying the requirement that director's fees are the only form of compensation he or she receives from the company.

An audit committee member may receive his or her fee in cash and/or company stock or options or other in-kind consideration ordinarily available to directors, as well as all of the regular benefits that other directors receive. Because of the significantly greater commitment of audit committee members, they may receive reasonable compensation greater than that paid to the other directors (as may other directors for other committee work). Disallowed compensation for an audit committee member includes fees paid directly or indirectly for services as a consultant or a legal or financial advisor, regardless of the amount. Disallowed compensation also includes compensation paid to such a director's firm for such consulting or advisory services even if the director is not the actual service provider. Disallowed compensation is not intended to include ordinary compensation paid in another customer or supplier or business relationship that the board has already determined to be immaterial for purposes of its basic director independence analysis. To avoid any confusion, note that this requirement pertains only to audit committee qualification and not to the independence determinations that the board must make for other directors.

Commentary Applicable to All Companies Other than Foreign Private Issuers: Each member of the committee must be financially literate, as such qualification is interpreted by the company's board in its business judgment, or must become financially literate within a reasonable period of time after his or her appointment to

---

[14] Business Roundtable, *Principles of Corporate Governance* (Washington, DC: Business Roundtable, May 2002), 12–16.

the audit committee. In addition, at least one member of the audit committee must have accounting or related financial management expertise, as the company's board interprets such qualification in its business judgment. A board may presume that a person who satisfies the definition of audit committee financial expert set out in Item 401(e) of Regulation S-K has accounting or related financial management expertise.

Because of the audit committee's demanding role and responsibilities, and the time commitment attendant to committee membership, each prospective audit committee member should evaluate carefully the existing demands on his or her time before accepting this important assignment. Additionally, if an audit committee member simultaneously serves on the audit committee of more than three public companies, and the listed company does not limit the number of audit committees on which its audit committee members serve, then in each case, the board must determine that such simultaneous service would not impair the ability of such member to effectively serve on the listed company's audit committee and disclose such determination in the annual proxy statement or, if the company does not file an annual proxy statement, in the company's annual report on Form 10-K filed with the SEC.

7. *(a) Each company is required to have a minimum three person audit committee composed entirely of independent directors that meet the requirements of Section 303A(6).*

  *(b) The audit committee must have a written charter that addresses:*

  *(i) the committee's purpose—which, at minimum, must be to:*

  *(A) assist board oversight of (1) the integrity of the company's financial statements, (2) the company's compliance with legal and regulatory requirements, (3) the independent auditor's qualifications and indepen-dence, and (4) the performance of the company's internal audit function and independent auditors; and*

  *(B) prepare the report required by the SEC's proxy rules to be included in the company's annual proxy statement, or, if the company does not file a proxy statement, in the company's annual report filed on Form 10-K with the SEC;*

  *(ii) the duties and responsibilities of the audit committee set out in Section 303A (7)(c) and (d); and*

  *(iii) an annual performance evaluation of the audit committee.*

  *(c) As required by Rule 10A-3(b)(2), (3), (4) and (5) of the Securities Exchange Act of 1934, and subject to the exemptions provided for in Rule 10A-3(c), the audit committee must:*

  *(i) directly appoint, retain, compensate, evaluate and terminate the company's independent auditors;*

Commentary: In connection with this requirement, the audit committee must have the sole authority to approve all audit engagement fees and terms, as well as all significant non-audit engagements with the independent auditors. In addition, the independent auditor must report directly to the audit committee. This requirement does not preclude the committee from obtaining the input of management, but these responsibilities may not be delegated to management. The audit committee must be directly responsible for oversight of the independent auditors, including resolution of disagreements between management and the independent auditor and pre-approval of all non-audit services.

    *(ii) establish procedures for the receipt, retention and treatment of complaints from listed company employees on accounting, internal accounting controls or auditing matters, as well as for confidential, anonymous submissions by listed company employees of concerns regarding questionable accounting or auditing matters;*

    *(iii) obtain advice and assistance from outside legal, accounting or other advisors as the audit committee deems necessary to carry out its duties; and*

Commentary: In the course of fulfilling its duties, the audit committee may wish to consult with independent counsel and other advisors. The audit committee must be empowered to retain and compensate these advisors without seeking board approval.

    *(iv) receive appropriate funding, as determined by the audit committee, from the listed company for payment of compensation to the outside legal, accounting or other advisors employed by the audit committee.*

*(d) In addition to the duties set out in Section 303(A)(7)(c), the duties of the audit committee must be, at a minimum, to:*

    *(i) at least annually, obtain and review a report by the independent auditor describing: the firm's internal quality-control procedures; any material issues raised by the most recent internal quality-control review, or peer review, of the firm, or by any inquiry or investigation by governmental or professional authorities, within the preceding five years, respecting one or more independent audits carried out by the firm, and any steps taken to deal with any such issues; and (to assess the auditor's independence) all relationships between the independent auditor and the company;*

Commentary: After reviewing the foregoing report and the independent auditor's work throughout the year, the audit committee will be in a position to evaluate the auditor's qualifications, performance and independence. This evaluation should include the review and evaluation of the lead partner of the independent auditor. In making its evaluation, the audit committee should take into account the opinions of management and the company's internal auditors (or other personnel responsible for the internal audit function). In addition to assuring the regular rotation of the lead audit partner as required by law, the audit committee should further consider whether, in order to assure continuing auditor independence, there should be regular rotation of the audit firm itself. The audit committee should present its conclusions with respect to the independent auditor to the full board.

    *(ii) discuss the annual audited financial statements and quarterly financial statements with management and the independent auditor, including the company's disclosures under "Management's Discussion and Analysis of Financial Condition and Results of Operations";*

    *(iii) discuss earnings press releases, as well as financial information and earnings guidance provided to analysts and rating agencies;*

Commentary: The audit committee's responsibility to discuss earnings releases as well as financial information and earnings guidance may be done generally (i.e., discussion of the types of information to be disclosed and the type of presentation to be made). The audit committee need not discuss in advance each earnings release or each instance in which a company may provide earnings guidance.

*(iv) discuss policies with respect to risk assessment and risk management;*

Commentary: While it is the job of the CEO and senior management to assess and manage the company's exposure to risk, the audit committee must discuss guidelines and policies to govern the process by which this is handled. The audit committee should discuss the company's major financial risk exposures and the steps management has taken to monitor and control such exposures. The audit committee is not required to be the sole body responsible for risk assessment and management, but, as stated above, the committee must discuss guidelines and policies to govern the process by which risk assessment and management is undertaken. Many companies, particularly financial companies, manage and assess their risk through mechanisms other than the audit committee. The processes these companies have in place should be reviewed in a general manner by the audit committee, but they need not be replaced by the audit committee.

*(v) meet separately, periodically, with management, with internal auditors (or other personnel responsible for the internal audit function) and with independent auditors;*

Commentary: To perform its oversight functions most effectively, the audit committee must have the benefit of separate sessions with management, the independent auditors and those responsible for the internal audit function. As noted herein, all listed companies must have an internal audit function. These separate sessions may be more productive than joint sessions in surfacing issues warranting committee attention.

*(vi) review with the independent auditor any audit problems or difficulties and management's response;*

Commentary: The audit committee must regularly review with the independent auditor any difficulties the auditor encountered in the course of the audit work, including any restrictions on the scope of the independent auditor's activities or on access to requested information, and any significant disagreements with management. Among the items the audit committee may want to review with the auditor are: any accounting adjustments that were noted or proposed by the auditor but were "passed" (as immaterial or otherwise); any communications between the audit team and the audit firm's national office respecting auditing or accounting issues presented by the engagement; and any "management" or "internal control" letter issued, or proposed to be issued, by the audit firm to the company. The review should also include discussion of the responsibilities, budget, and staffing of the company's internal audit function.

*(vii) set clear hiring policies for employees or former employees of the independent auditors; and*

Commentary: Employees or former employees of the independent auditor are often valuable additions to corporate management. Such individuals' familiarity with the business, and personal rapport with the employees, may be attractive qualities when filling a key opening. However, the audit committee should set hiring policies taking into account the pressures that may exist for auditors consciously or subconsciously seeking a job with the company they audit.

*(viii) report regularly to the board of directors.*

Commentary: The audit committee should review with the full board any issues that arise with respect to the quality or integrity of the company's financial statements, the company's compliance with legal or regulatory requirements, the performance and independence of the company's independent auditors, or the performance of the internal audit function.

General Commentary to Section 303A(7)(d): While the fundamental responsibility for the company's financial statements and disclosures rests with management and the independent auditor, the audit committee must review: (A) major issues regarding accounting principles and financial statement presentations, including any significant changes in the company's selection or application of accounting principles, and major issues as to the adequacy of the company's internal controls and any special audit steps adopted in light of material control deficiencies; (B) analyses prepared by management and/or the independent auditor setting forth significant financial reporting issues and judgments made in connection with the preparation of the financial statements, including analyses of the effects of alternative GAAP methods on the financial statements; (C) the effect of regulatory and accounting initiatives, as well as off–balance sheet structures, on the financial statements of the company; and (D) the type and presentation of information to be included in earnings press releases (paying particular attention to any use of "pro forma," or "adjusted" non-GAAP, information), as well as review any financial information and earnings guidance provided to analysts and rating agencies.

General Commentary to Section 303A(7): To avoid any confusion, note that the audit committee functions specified in Section 303A(7) are the sole responsibility of the audit committee and may not be allocated to a different committee.

*(e) Each listed company must have an internal audit function.*

Commentary: Listed companies must maintain an internal audit function to provide management and the audit committee with ongoing assessments of the company's risk management processes and system of internal control. A company may choose to outsource this function to a firm other than its independent auditor.[15]

## CORPORATE ACCOUNTABILITY AND THE AUDIT COMMITTEE

### The Role of the Audit Committee

The audit committee has a critical role within the framework of corporate accountability since the jurisdiction of the committee is to oversee and monitor the activities of the corporation's financial reporting system and the internal and external audit processes. The audit committee assists the board of directors with the development and maintenance of the corporate accountability framework and helps create an environment conducive to exemplary financial reporting.

As Harold M. Williams, former chairman of the SEC, asserted:

It should be evident, but perhaps bears repeating, that integrity in reporting financial data is vital both to an efficient and effective securities market and to capital formation. One key to increasing public confidence in that data long advocated by many segments of the financial community, including public accounting firms, is

---

[15] Securities and Exchange Commission Release No. 34-47672, File No. SR-NYSE-2002-33, *Proposed Rule Change Relating to Corporate Governance* (Washington DC: April 11, 2003). See also SEC Release No. 34-47672, File No. SR-NASD-2002-141, for FINRA, *Proposed Rule Change Relating to Corporate Governance.*

**EXHIBIT 1.6** The Audit Committee's Accountability Relationship

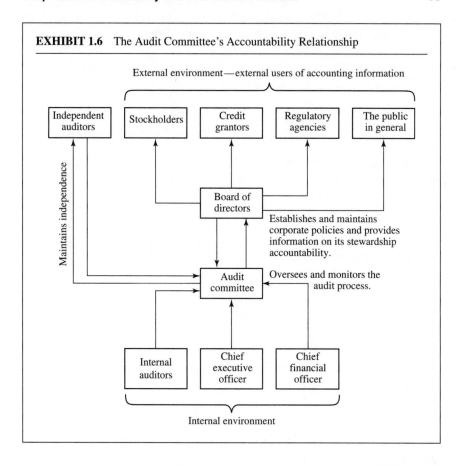

more direct involvement by boards of directors in the auditing process and the integrity of reported financial information. The vehicle which the Securities and Exchange Commission, the New York Stock Exchange and an increasing number of public corporations have turned to has been the independent audit committee.[16]

As a standing committee appointed by the board of directors, the audit committee is directly accountable for its actions to the board. The audit committee operates in an advisory capacity. Thus the audit committee has limited authority because a final decision concerning its recommendations is made by the board. The board seeks guidance from the audit committee in formulating or amending the financial accounting policies to service properly the needs of its various constituencies.

To further illustrate the role of the audit committee, Exhibit 1.6 diagrams the direct relationship between the committee and its constituencies in the internal corporate environment.

---

[16] Harold M. Williams, "Audit Committees—The Public Sector's View," *Journal of Accountancy* 144, no. 3 (September 1977), 71.

***The Audit Committee and the Chief Executive Officer***   The chief executive officer has an obligation not only to the board but also to the standing committees of the board. The chief CEO is responsible primarily for recommending major policy decisions to the board of directors. Since CEOs participate in the decisions concerning the financial accounting policies, they should have direct communication with the audit committee.

However, it is essential that the audit committee be totally independent from the CEO because he is a "managing director." As a managing director, the CEO participates in the general administration of the corporation as well as assuming ultimate responsibility for the decisions.

Based on a close examination of the audit committees of 13 corporations listed on the NYSE, Michael L. Lovdal found:

> Effective audit committees permit the chief executive to attend by invitation only
> . . . After all, he is the best source concerning questions related to the business and
> he can ensure quick action on committee requests. In achieving the appropriate
> relationship with the chief executive, a key ingredient is the quality of the audit
> committee chairman. He must have both the sensitivity to know when to bring the
> CEO into the group's deliberations and the strength to stand up to him when the
> committee wants to pursue an inquiry or change policy.[17]

In short, the audit committee should determine its own agenda items, which should not be based on the chief executive officer's prerogatives. As Ivan Bull observed,

> Concern about other environmental factors, such as legal liability, also may have
> influenced board agendas and operating practices. The board's practice of allowing
> and listening to dissent and advice from outside members is healthier than the
> popular belief that CEOs dominate passive boards.[18]

***The Audit Committee and the Chief Financial Officer***[19]   In most corporations, the chief financial officer (CFO) is responsible for the functions of the controller. In turn, the CFO is accountable to the CEO for the conduct of the various administrative functions of the controller. Although the controller is responsible for the general administration and supervision of the accounting operations, the CFO has executive responsibility for the financial accounting policies.

Since the audit committee is responsible for assuring that management fulfills its responsibilities in the preparation of the financial statements, the CFO should consult with the committee in order to coordinate the financial accounting activities. Thus the audit committee should have a dialogue with

---

[17] Michael L. Lovdal, "Making the Audit Committee Work," *Harvard Business Review* 55 (March–April 1977): 110.

[18] Bull, "Board of Director Acceptance," 71. Also see J. Michael Cook, "The CEO and the Audit Committee," *Chief Executive* no. 76 (April 1993): 44–47.

[19] For further discussion, see Louis Braiotta, Jr., and Jay R. Olson, "Guiding the Audit Committee: A CFO's Concern," *Financial Executive* 51, no. 9 (September 1983): 52–54. See also Chapter 13 for a discussion of the audit committee's review of the quarterly reporting process.

the CFO to consider any questions concerning the financial reporting practices. For example, if the CFO has certain reservations or exceptions to certain accounting policies and practices, the audit committee would recommend the necessary course of action subsequent to its consultation with the independent auditors.

**The Audit Committee and the Internal Audit Group**  The internal audit executive is essentially responsible for the establishment and maintenance of an effective and efficient system of internal auditing. With respect to the audit committee's involvement with the internal audit group, Lovdal points out:

> The internal audit group can be an avenue for the committee in reaching the source of a variety of problems. One committee I examined uses internal auditors regularly for investigations in such areas as computer security, transfer pricing, and capital budgeting. For these activities, the committee should deal directly with the head of internal audit, rather than solely through other finance or control executives, and should make itself knowledgeable about the organization, staffing, and budgets of the internal audit department.[20]

The reporting responsibility of the internal audit group varies from one organization to the next. For example, the director of internal auditing may report to the controller or CFO and meet with the audit committee on a separate or joint basis. Whatever the reporting arrangement, the director of internal auditing should have access to the audit committee to provide for a forum whereby the internal audit group can resolve questionable matters between the audit staff and corporate management. (See Chapter 9.)

**The Audit Committee and the External Auditor**  One of the major provisions of the Sarbanes-Oxley Act was to create the Public Company Accounting Oversight Board (PCAOB), which now is the regulator of auditors of public companies. Previously, public company auditors were self-regulated through the Public Oversight Board (POB), a private organization that worked in concert with the American Institute of Certified Public Accountants to regulate the quality control aspects of public company audits through a private sector, firm-on-firm, peer review process. While the POB was a distinct body from the AICPA, the AICPA administered peer review and created the quality control standards that formed the basis for a peer review. Another unit of the AICPA, the Auditing Standards Board (ASB), was the source of generally accepted auditing standards (GAAS) for virtually all financial statement audits performed in the country.

For the audits of public companies only, the creation of the PCOAB removed from the private sector at the AICPA the auditing standards, quality control standards, ethics standards, peer review monitoring, and enforcement activities. Audits of other entities remain the subject of standards, monitoring, and enforcement of the AICPA, other private-sector bodies such as state CPA organizations, and state

---

[20] Lovdal, "Making the Audit Committee Work," 111.

governments. Of course, audit failures in the non-public company sector can be litigated in state courts. Because of this dual system of control that is determined by the status of the auditee as an issuer subject to SEC regulation, an audit firm is subject to PCOAB oversight for its public company audits and to a collection of private sector and state governments for its non-public company audits.

The PCAOB has five board members appointed by the SEC, one of whom serves as the chair. Up to two of the board members can be CPAs from the audit profession, but to chair the board a CPA must not have been associated with a CPA firm for at least five years. Board members serve five-year terms. The PCAOB is organized as a not-for-profit in the District of Columbia. The PCAOB's budget, along with that of the FASB, is approved annually by the SEC. The Sarbanes-Oxley Act authorizes the PCAOB to collect fees from public companies and their auditors to fund the budgets of the PCAOB and FASB. Any of the rules of the PCAOB are approved by the SEC after appropriate exposure and comment periods. If the SEC does not approve a PCAOB rule, then it is returned to the PCAOB for additional work.

The PCAOB is organized into two divisions and a number of offices. The Division of Registration and Inspections registers CPA firms that audit U.S. public companies, or that aspire to audit U.S. public companies. On September 1, 2009, 2,146 audit firms from around the world were registered with the PCAOB. This Division also conducts the annual or triennial inspections of registered firms. Firms that audit 100 or more U.S. public companies are inspected annually. Firms auditing between five and 99 U.S. public companies are inspected every three years. Firms auditing fewer than five U.S. public companies have each of their audits inspected. PCAOB inspections cover the quality control of the firms and selected audit issues for selected clients. The inspections are meant to be risk-based, so inspectors deliberately choose the riskiest companies and riskiest transactions for their examinations. The inspection reports have two parts. Part A is publicly available at the PCAOB Web site (www.pcaobus.org) and focuses on accounting or auditing issues that the PCAOB inspectors consider problematic. Part B, which is not public by statute, is the PCAOB's assessment of a firm's quality control. The Sarbanes-Oxley Act provides that as long as a firm makes satisfactory progress in addressing quality control concerns, Part B of the report remains private between the firm and the PCAOB.

The Division of Enforcement and Investigations is the disciplinary arm of the PCAOB. Its investigations and actions can lead to disciplinary actions against individual auditors or audit firms. Disciplinary actions range from remedial activities to complete bars from audits of U.S. public companies. The authority to subpoena, conduct investigations, and discipline is well beyond the power that previously had been held by the POB. The inspection process at the PCAOB also has much more authority than the peer review process previously conducted by the AICPA.

The office of the PCAOB that likely is of most interest to audit committee members is the Office of the Chief Auditor, which is responsible for the development of professional standards for auditing, quality control, and indepen-dence and ethics. The PCAOB adopted interim standards that had been developed previously by various bodies at the AICPA. The PCAOB has extended the standards for independence beyond the interim standards and has developed two standards related to integrated audits of financial statements and internal control over financial reporting. The second standard simplified the original standard in order to focus auditors' attention more clearly on risk issues and to reduce overall costs on implementing the internal control requirements of the Sarbanes-Oxley Act. The debates and disagreements about how to implement Section 404 of the Act consumed enormous time and energy between 2004 and 2007, the time between the first standard on integrated audits, Standard 2, and the new standard, Standard 5.

Auditors of U.S. non-public companies participate in a peer review program that is a cooperative effort between the AICPA, the state CPA societies, and those states that require a quality review of CPA firms registered with them. This private-sector-run program has been in existence since the late 1970s. Firms could be part of several distinct peer review programs, depending on which program they entered and when. Many of the firms will be part of a program with a public file, which is available at www.aicpa.org under the peer review program tab. Some firms will participate in a program that does not have a public file, in which case the results of peer review are available only from the firm itself. The quality control standards for the peer review are the same regardless of the program, and the AICPA's standards have functioned well for the PCAOB as interim standards, so the standards are consistent with those used by PCAOB inspections.

Auditors subject to PCAOB oversight have formed the Center for Audit Quality (CAQ) as a public interest forum for public company auditors. The CAQ's Web site, at www.thecaq.org, frequently has material of interest to audit committee members about public company auditing and current developments. The CAQ also has acted as the organizing body for public company auditors when the federal government forms commissions or blue ribbon committees studying the audit industry. The U.S. Treasury formed such a committee in 2007, the Advisory Committee on the Auditing Profession (ACAP), which issued its report in October 2008. The ACAP report is available at www.treas.gov. Among other things, the report suggests that public company audit firms publish an annual "transparency report" with metrics about audit quality variables and financial information. The PCAOB, CAQ, and audit firms currently are studying how to implement this recommendation.

Such reports already are published by audit firms in the EU.

To see an example of such a transparency report, visit the Grant Thornton International Web site, which can be accessed at www.gt.com, the public Web site for Grant Thornton LLP, the U.S. member firm of Grant Thornton International. This transparency report covers topics such as legal structure and ownership, membership criteria, governance and management, client acceptance and reacceptance, quality control systems, independence practices, people and culture, financial information, partner remuneration, public interest entities audited, and member firms of Grant Thornton International. Other firms have similar reports about their operations.

Public transparency reports, the public section of PCAOB inspections, and public peer review files can provide audit committees with insights into different audit firms and be of assistance in conducting a constructive dialog with incumbent and prospective auditors. Audit committees should discuss such

**EXHIBIT 1.7**   Summaries of Research Studies

DeZoort, F. Todd, Dana R. Hermanson, and Richard W. Houston, "Audit Committee Support for Auditors: The Effects of Materiality Justification and Accounting Precision." *Journal of Accounting and Public Policy* 22, (2003), pp. 175–199.

> Summary: The authors find that, in the context of auditor-management disagreements, independent auditors and audit committees need to discuss the qualitative aspects of materiality with respect to unrecorded adjustments. Additionally, the authors conclude that both accounting and auditing standard setters should consider approaches to enhance accounting estimates in the financial reporting process, including communications with audit committees. Finally, they find that audit committees with CPAs provide greater support for independent auditors.

Klein, April, "Audit Committees, Board of Director Characteristics, and Earnings Management." *Journal of Accounting & Economics* 33 (2002), pp. 375–400.

> Summary: Klein concludes that reductions in the independence of boards of directors or audit committees cause large increases in abnormal accruals. The results suggest that boards of directors that are more independent of the CEO are more effective in monitoring earnings management in the financial reporting process.

Beasley, Mark S., and Steven E. Salterio, "The Relationship between Board Characteristics and Voluntary Improvements in Audit Committee Composition and Experience." *Contemporary Accounting Research* 18, No. 4 (Winter 2001), pp. 539–570.

> Summary: Beasley and Salterio find that Canadian firms that voluntarily include more outside directors on the audit committee than the minimum mandated by Canadian corporate law have larger boards of directors with more outside directors and thus are more likely to segregate the board chair and CEO/president positions. Likewise, audit committees with financial reporting knowledge and experience and larger boards with outside members are less likely to be chaired by the CEO/president. Thus the researchers conclude that one person serving as both chairman and CEO/president increases the potential for less effective monitoring by the audit committee.

Klein, April, "Economic Determinants of Audit Committee Independence." *Accounting Review* 77, No. 2 (April 2002), pp. 435–452.

> Summary: Klein reports that audit committee independence increases with board size and the percentage of outsiders on the board of directors. However, audit committee independence decreases with an increase in a firm's growth opportunities or when a firm reports net losses. Klein confirms the findings of the Blue Ribbon Committee on Improving the Effectiveness of Corporate Audit Committees that "one size doesn't fill all" when it comes to audit committees. The results suggest that the stock exchanges should allow boards flexibility with respect to audit committee composition.

Carcello, Joseph V., and Terry L. Neal, "Audit Committee Composition and Auditor Reporting." *Accounting Review* 75, No. 4 (October 2000), pp. 453–467.

> Summary: Carcello and Neal find that the greater the percentage of affiliated directors on the audit committee, the lower the probability the auditor will issue a going-concern report. Thus their evidence supports the proposition that the audit committee should be composed of independent, outside directors.

Beasley, Mark S., Joseph V. Carcello, Dana R. Hermanson, and Paul D. Lapides, "Fraudulent Financial Reporting: Consideration of Industry Traits and Corporate Governance Mechanisms." *Accounting Horizons* 14, No. 4 (December 2000), pp. 441–454.

Summary: The authors confirm earlier findings that fraudulent firms and no-fraud firms differ to the extent that audit committees exist and such committees are independent, including the board's independence from management. With the identification of no-fraud industry benchmarks (e.g., number of audit committee meetings and internal audit experience), they find that the sample fraud firms have weak governance mechanisms. Moreover, independent auditors should consider the industry context with respect to their fraud risk assessment on client audit engagements.

Abbott, Lawrence J., and Susan Parker, "Auditor Selection and Audit Committee Characteristics." *Auditing: A Journal of Practice and Theory* 19, No. 2 (Fall 2000), pp. 47–66.

Summary: The authors conclude that the requirement for financial experts on audit committees is more likely to change the structure and focus of audit committee discussions about the quality of the financial reporting process. Their results suggest that audit committee members who are financially literate are more likely to focus on reporting treatments that are prominent in the press and nonrecurring, while financial experts are more likely to focus on the relevance of reporting treatments as well as recurring activities.

Abbott, Lawrence J., and Susan Parker, "Auditor Selection and Audit Committee Characteristics." *Auditing: A Journal of Practice and Theory* 19, No. 2 (Fall 2000), pp. 47–66.

Summary: Abbott and Parker find that independent and active audit committee members are more likely to select an industry-specialist auditor because they demand a high level of audit quality. Their results suggest that an industry-specialist auditor helps minimize the client's reputational or monetary losses.

McDaniel, Linda, Roger D. Martin, and Laureen A. Maines, "Evaluating Financial Reporting Quality: The Effects of Financial Expertise vs. Financial Literacy." *Accounting Review* 77 (Supplement 2002), pp. 139–167.

Summary: The authors conclude that the requirement for financial experts on audit committees is more likely to change the structure and focus of audit committee discussions about the quality of the financial reporting process. Their results suggest that audit committee members who are financially literate are more likely to focus on reporting treatments that are prominent in the press and nonrecurring, while financial experts are more likely to focus on the relevance of reporting treatments as well as recurring activities.

Carcello, Joseph V., and Terry L. Neal, "Audit Committee Characteristics and Auditor Dismissals Following 'New' Going-Concern Reports." *Accounting Review* 78, No. 1 (January 2003), pp. 95–117.

Summary: Carcello and Neal find as a follow-on to their 2000 study that the higher the percentage of affiliated directors on the audit committee, the more likely a client will dismiss its independent auditors because of a going-concern audit report. Moreover, they report that the probability of client dismissal of the independent auditors

(*continued*)

**EXHIBIT 1.7**   *(Continued)*

subsequent to the going-concern report increases as audit committee ownership of client stock increases. In contrast, audit committee members with more governance expertise are less likely to dismiss their independent auditors after receiving a going-concern report. Likewise, the turnover rate of independent audit committee members who retain their independent auditors is less significant compared to audit committee members who dismiss their independent auditors.

Zaman, Mahbub, "The Corporate Governance Effects of Audit Committees." *Journal of Management and Governance,* Vol. 8, No. 3 (2004), pp. 305–332.

Summary: This paper synthesizes previous empirical research on the governance effects of audit committees in several countries. It finds that most of the existing evidence has focused on factors associated with audit committee existence, characteristics, and measures of activities. There is very little evidence about audit committee processes and operations and other ways that they might impact corporate behavior. The evidence suggests that there is no automatic relationship between the existence of an audit committee with certain characteristics and achievement of desirable corporate effects. The author cautions against excessive codification of specific requirements until more is understood about the interactions of audit committees and effective governance.

Yang, Joon S., and Jagan Krishnan, "Audit Committees and Quarterly Earnings Management." *International Journal of Auditing*, Vol. 9, No. 3 (November 2005), pp. 201–219.

Summary: The authors collected a sample of 896 observations for the years 1996-2000, prior to the reforms generated by the Sarbanes-Oxley Act of 2002, to test the association between audit committee characteristics and measures of quarterly earnings management. They found that (1) quarterly earnings management is lower for companies whose audit committee members have greater governance experience, (2) stock ownership by audit committee members is positively associated with measures of quarterly earnings management, and (3) the average tenure of audit committee members is negatively associated with measures of quarterly earnings management.

Baxter, Peter, and Julie Cotter, "Audit Committees and Earnings Quality." *Accounting & Finance*, Vol. 49, Issue 2 (June 2009), pp. 267–290.

Summary: The authors investigate whether audit committees are associated with improvements in earnings quality for a sample of Australian listed companies before the introduction of mandatory audit committees in 2003, while audit committees were still voluntary. The results indicate that audit committee formation reduces intentional earnings management, but does not affect accrual estimation errors. Audit committees with more accounting expertise are associated statistically with higher earnings-quality measures.

Goh, Beng Wee, "Audit Committees, Boards of Directors, and Remediation of Material Weaknesses in Internal Control." *Contemporary Accounting Research*, Vol, 26, No. 2 (Summer 2009).

Summary: This study correlates board and audit committee characteristics with the speed of remediation of material weaknesses in internal control of accelerated filers in

*(continued)*

the U.S. that disclosed at least one material weakness between July 2003 and December 2004 as described in section 302 of the Sarbanes-Oxley Act. Companies with larger audit committees composed of individuals with financial expertise but not accounting expertise, in the context of boards with more independent members, are more likely to remediate material weaknesses rapidly.

Skaife, Hollis Ashbaugh, Daniel W., Collins, William R., Jr., Kinney, and Ryan, LaFond, "The Effect of SOX Internal Control Deficiencies on Firm Risk and Cost of Equity." *Journal of Accounting Research*, Vol. 47, Issue 1 (March 2009), pp. 1–43.

Summary: The authors use unaudited pre-Sarbanes-Oxley disclosures and Sarbanes-Oxley Section 404 audit opinions to assess how changes in internal control quality affect company risk and cost of equity. After controlling for other risk factors, they find that companies with internal control deficiencies have significantly higher idiosyncratic risk (company specific risk), higher systematic risk, and higher cost of equity. Auditor-confirmed improvements in internal control effectiveness, including remediation of previously disclosed control deficiencies, are followed by significant decreases in the cost of equity ranging from 50 to 150 basis points.

**EXHIBIT 1.8** Summary of Sections of the Sarbanes-Oxley Act of 2002 Impacting Audit Committees

| Sections | Title |
|---|---|
| 2 | Definitions |
| 101 | Public Company Accounting Oversight Board |
| 201 | Services Outside the Scope of Practice of Auditors |
| 202 | Preapproval Requirements (audit and non-audit services) |
| 203 | Audit Partner Rotation (5-year rotation period) |
| 204 | Auditor Reports to Audit Committees |
| 206 | Conflicts of Interest (1-year cooling-off period) |
| 207 | Study of Mandatory Rotation of Registered Public Accounting Firms |
| 301 | Public Company Audit Committees |
| 302 | Corporate Responsibility for Financial Reports |
| 303 | Improper Influence on Conduct of Audits |
| 307 | Rules of Professional Responsibility for Attorneys |
| 401 | Disclosure in Periodic Reports |
| 402 | Enhanced Conflict of Interest Provisions (Personal Loans to Executives) |
| 403 | Disclosures of Transactions Involving Management and Principal Stockholders |
| 404 | Management Assessment of Internal Controls |
| 406 | Code of Ethics for Senior Financial Officers |
| 407 | Disclosure of Audit Committee Financial Expert |
| 409 | Real Time Issues Disclosures |
| 906 | Corporate Responsibility for Financial Reports (Failure of Corporate Officers to Certify Financial Reports and Criminal Penalties) |

*Source:* The act is contained in Public Law No. 107-204, July 30, 2002.

**EXHIBIT 1.9**   Corporate Accountability: Self-Assessment Checklist

| Audit Committee Practice Area | Management | Internal Auditors | External Auditors | Legal Counsel | Bd of Directors | Sarbanes-Oxley | SEC | SROs | ASB | Comments |
|---|---|---|---|---|---|---|---|---|---|---|
| **Services available from:** | | | | | | | | | | |
| Legal liabilities under, | | | | | | | | | | |
|   State statutes | | | | | | | | | | |
|     Fiduciary liability | | | | ✓ | | | | | | |
|     Business judgment rule | | | | ✓ | | | | | | |
|     Standards of conduct | | | | ✓ | | | | | | |
|   Federal Statutes* | | | | | | | | | | |
|     Sarbanes-Oxley Act of 2002 | | | | ✓ | | ✓ | ✓ | | | |
|     Private Securities Litigation Reform Act of 1995 | | | | ✓ | | | ✓ | | | |
|     Securities Act of 1933 | | | | ✓ | | | ✓ | | | |
|     Securities Exchange Act of 1934 | | | | ✓ | | | ✓ | | | |
|   Legal Cases | | | | ✓ | | | | | | |
| Corporate Governance Principles and Rules | | | | | ✓ | ✓ | ✓ | ✓ | | |
| Formation† | | | | | | ✓ | ✓ | | | |
| Membership | | | | | | | | | | |
|   Number of members (size) | | | | | | ✓ | ✓ | | | |
|   Appointments | | | | | | ✓ | | | | |
|   Term of Service | | | | | | ✓ | | | | |
|   Qualifications | | | | | | ✓ | ✓ | | | |
|   Composition | | | | | | ✓ | ✓ | | | |
| Meetings, frequency and type | | | | | | | ✓ | | | |
| Knowledge Areas | | | | | | | | | | |
|   Type of business and industry | ✓ | | | | | | | | | |
|   Internal audit process | | ✓ | | | | | | | | |
|   External audit process | | | ✓ | | | | | | | |
|   Internal control concepts‡ | | ✓ | ✓ | | | | | | | |
|   Management's risk assessment | ✓ | ✓ | ✓ | | | | | | | |
|   Industry accounting practices | ✓ | ✓ | ✓ | | | | | | | |
|   Complex business transactions | ✓ | ✓ | ✓ | ✓ | | | | | | |
|   Financial reporting process | ✓ | ✓ | ✓ | | | | | | | |
|   Internal communication process§ | ✓ | ✓ | ✓ | ✓ | ✓ | ✓ | ✓ | ✓ | | |
|   External communication process | | | | | ✓ | ✓ | ✓ | ✓ | ✓ | |

* See Chapter 4 for other acts. † Board resolution or corporate bylaws and a format written charter. ‡ Includes conflicts of interest (e.g., code of conduct, related party transactions). § Related to the above areas.

reports with their auditors and understand how their auditors are trying to manage and improve their delivery of high-quality audits.

## CONCLUSION

The purpose of this chapter is to orient audit committee members to their governance responsibilities as directors and committee members. Chapter 1 has drawn some samples from the rich literature that is available about audit committees. In addition, Exhibit 1.7 presents summaries of selected academic research studies concerning audit committees. Summarizing the wisdom distilled from that research, to the extent that the audit committee maintains an independent posture in the corporate environment, the committee will act as a check on corporate management with respect to its corporate power and as a supporter of corporate stewardship accountability. The committee's primary objective is to foster the accountability relationship between the audit committee and the representatives of management and thereby create an environment in which management will be positively responsive in fulfilling its financial reporting responsibilities to its constituencies.

Because the Sarbanes-Oxley Act has had such a seminal impact on corporate governance, especially on the role of the audit committee, Exhibit 1.8 presents a summary of selected sections and titles of the Act. Each section is presented in Chapter 2. Exhibit 1.9 contains a corporate accountability self-assessment checklist.

## SOURCES AND SUGGESTED READINGS

American Assembly. *Corporate Governance in America,* Pamphlet 54. New York: Columbia University, April 1978.

American Institute of Certified Public Accountants. *Audit Committees, Answers to Typical Questions about Their Organization and Operations.* New York: AICPA, 1978.

Barlas, Stephen. "Blue Ribbon Panel Focus: Audit Committees." *Management Accounting* 80, no. 6 (December 1998): 10.

Bean, James W. "The Audit Committee's Readings." *Journal of Accountancy* 187, no. 1 (January 1999): 47–54.

Beresford, Dennis R. "After Enron: Let's Not Throw Out the Baby." *CPA Journal* 72, no. 7 (July 2002): 10–13.

Bishop, William G., Dana R. Hermanson, Paul D. Lapides, and Larry E. Rittenberg. "The Year of the Audit Committee." *Internal Auditor* 57, no. 2 (April 2000): 46–51.

Blue Ribbon Committee on Improving the Effectiveness of Corporate Audit Committees. *Report and Recommendations of the Blue Ribbon Committee on Improving the Effectiveness of Corporate Audit Committees.* New York: NYSE; and Washington DC: National Association of Securities Dealers, 1999.

Braiotta, Louis, and Jay R. Olson. "Guiding the Audit Committee: A CFO's Concern." *Financial Executive* 51, no. 9 (September 1983): 52–54.

Bull, Ivan. "Board of Directors Acceptance of Treadway Responsibilities." *Journal of Accountancy* 171, no. 2 (February 1991): 67–72, 74.

The Business Roundtable. *Corporate Governance and American Competitiveness.* New York: The Business Roundtable, 1990, 2002.

The Business Roundtable. *Principles of Corporate Governance.* Washington, DC: The Business Roundtable, 2002.

DiPiazza, Samuel A., and Robert G. Eccles. *Building Public Trust: The Future of Corporate Reporting.* New York: John Wiley & Sons, 2002.

Fleming, John M. "Audit Committees: Roles, Responsibilities, and Performance." *Pennsylvania CPA Journal* 73, no. 2 (Summer 2002): 29–32.

Goodman, Amy L., and Michael J. Scanlon. "Enhanced Audit Committee Responsibilities." *Insights, The Corporate & Securities Law Advisor* 15, no. 2 (February 2001): 12–17.

Hermanson, Dana R. "Does Corporate Governance Really Matter? What the Research Tells Us." *Internal Auditing* 18, no. 2 (March/April 2003): 44–45.

Hills, Roderick M. "Restoring Faith with Audit Process." *Directors & Boards* 26, no. 3 (Spring 2002): 26–37.

Hnatt, Kelly M. "Forge the Right Relationship." *Journal of Accountancy* 191, no. 5 (May 2001): 49–54.

Kirk, Donald J. "Experiences with the Public Oversight Board and Corporate Audit Committees." *Accounting Horizons* 14, no. 1 (March 2000): 103–111.

Levitt, Arthur. "Letter to Audit Committees Chairmen of the Top 5000 Public Companies." Washington, DC: SEC, January 5, 2001.

Levitt, Arthur. "The Numbers Game," speech presented at the NYU Center for Law and Business. Washington, DC: SEC, September 28, 1998.

Lovdal, Michael L. "Making the Audit Committee Work." *Harvard Business Review* 55 (March–April 1977): 108–114.

Miller, Richard I., and Paul H. Pashkoff. "Regulations under the Sarbanes-Oxley Act." *Journal of Accountancy* 194, no. 4 (October 2002): 33–36.

Morrissey, John. "Corporate Responsibility and the Audit Committee," speech presented at the General Audit Management Conference. Washington, DC: SEC, March 21, 2000.

Olson, John F., Ronald O. Mueller, Stephanie Tsacoumis, and Amy L. Goodman. "After Enron: Issues for Boards and Audit Committees to Consider." *Insights* 16, no. 4 (April 2002): 2–8.

Panel on Audit Effectiveness. *Panel on Audit Effectiveness Report and Recommendations.* Stamford, CT: POB, 2000.

Pearson, Mark W. "Where Was the Audit Committee?" *Financial Executive* 17, no. 8 (November 2001): 44–47.

Read, William J., and Kannass Raghunandan. "The State of Audit Committees." *Journal of Accountancy* 191, no. 5 (May 2001): 57–60.

Rouse, Robert W., and Mark R. Borrelli. "Audit Committees in an Era of Increased Scrutiny." *CPA Journal* 70, no. 6 (June 2000): 26–32.

Sarbanes-Oxley Act of 2002. H.R. Rep. No. 107-610, July 25, 2002. Title 1 of Public Law No. 107-204, July 30, 2002.

Securities and Exchange Commission Release No. 34-47672, File No. SR-NYSE-2002-03. *Proposed Rule Changes Relating to Corporate Governance.* Washington, DC, April 11, 2003.

Sweeney, Paul. "Audit Committees Bracing for Shakeys." *Financial Executive* 18, no. 9, (December 2002): 16–18.

Terrill, Mark C., and Timothy J. Zanni. "CFOs and Audit Committees: Mutual Expectations." *CPA Journal* 72, no. 2 (February 2002): 54.

Turley, James S. "The Future of Corporate Reporting: From the Top." *Financial Executive* 70 (December 2002): 2.

Turner, Lynn E. "Audit Committees: A Roadway for Establishing Accountability." *Insights, the Corporate & Securities Law Advisor* 15, no. 5 (May 2001): 17–24.

Whitehead, John C. "A Healthy 'Self-Cleaning': What Can and Should Be Done Now to Restore Confidence in the System." *Directors & Boards* 26, no. 3 (Spring 2002): 88–91.

Williams, Harold M. "Audit Committees—The Public Sector's View." *Journal of Accountancy* 144, no. 3 (September 1977): 71–74.

# Chapter 2

# Audit Committees

## Basic Roles and Responsibilities

The major purpose of this chapter is not only to examine the organizational and functional characteristics of the audit committee but also to introduce the nature and importance of the external and internal auditing processes. Conceptually, one should understand the following:

- The basic considerations in forming the audit committee
- The basic audit committee functions
- The role of the audit committee with respect to the external and internal auditing processes

As far back as July 20, 1967, the Executive Committee of the American Institute of Certified Public Accountants (AICPA) issued a statement recommending:

> . . . that publicly owned corporations appoint committees composed of outside directors (those who are not officers or employees) to nominate the independent directors of the corporations' financial statements and to discuss the auditors' work with them.[1]

Soon afterward, in a landmark study based on survey research published in 1970, Mautz and Neumann presciently observed:

> Corporate audit committees, in practice, can contribute significantly to corporate governance and discipline, but their mere establishment by board resolution does not guarantee any significant degree of success.[2]

More recently, former SEC Chairman Arthur Levitt, in his seminal "The Numbers Game" speech at New York University, asserted that ". . . qualified, committed, independent and tough-minded audit committees represent the most reliable guardians of the public interest."[3]

---

[1] American Institute of Certified Public Accountants, "Executive Committee Statement on Audit Committees of Boards of Directors." *Journal of Accountancy* 124 (September 1967):10.

[2] Mautz, R. K. and F. L. Neumann. 1970. *Corporate Audit Committees.* Urbana, IL: University of Illinois.

[3] www.sec.gov/news/speech/speecharchive/1998/spch220.txt. (Levitt was then chairman of the Securities and Exchange Commission, so the speech was quite influential, including spurring the formation of a Blue Ribbon Commission to Improve the Effectiveness of Audit Committees.)

## ORGANIZATION OF THE AUDIT COMMITTEE

### Nature of the Audit Committee

In view of the complexity of the modern corporation and the increased demands for corporate accountability, the audit committee's role has become an increasingly important consideration in the conduct of corporate affairs. As defined by the American Institute of Certified Public Accountants (AICPA), "An audit committee should be organized as a standing committee of the board composed mainly of nonofficer directors."[4] In Section 2 (a)(3) of the Sarbanes-Oxley Act of 2002, the U.S. Congress reaffirmed AICPA's definition of the audit committee, stating:

> (3) AUDIT COMMITTEE—The term "audit committee" means—
>
> (A) a committee (or equivalent body) established by and amongst the board of directors of an issuer for the purpose of overseeing the accounting and financial reporting processes of the issuer and audits of the financial statements of the issuer; and
>
> (B) if no such committee exists with respect to an issuer, the entire board of directors of the issuer.[5]

In contrast to the other standing committees of the board, such as the executive or finance committees, the audit committee is unique because it consists of outside or independent directors. Independent directors are individuals who are not directly involved in managing the corporation. For example, the chief executive officer and chief financial officer are considered management directors because not only are they intimately involved in managing corporate affairs, they are also employees of the corporation. Thus the independent audit committee is composed of individuals who are nonmanagement directors.

The Corporate Organization Policy Committee of the Business Roundtable concluded that the board of directors should be served by an audit committee because it would allow committee members to focus their attention on corporate matters in greater depth than would be practical for the full board. Tracing the historical development of audit committees, a 1978 Conference Board study on audit committees found that "93 percent of the surveyed companies have such a committee. The recent action of the New York Stock Exchange requiring the 1,200 or so listed companies to establish by mid-1978 such a committee made up solely of directors independent of management reinforces this development."[6]

A decade later, the Conference Board found a significant increase in the audit committee's involvement in such activities as reviewing the internal audit function and the independent status of the outside auditors, approving

---

[4] American Institute of Certified Public Accountants, *Audit Committees, Answers to Typical Questions about Their Organization and Operations* (New York: AICPA, 1978): 11.

[5] The act is contained in Title 1 of Public Law No. 107-204, July 30, 2002.

[6] Business Roundtable, *The Role and Composition of the Board of Directors of the Large Publicly Owned Corporation* (New York: Business Roundtable, 1978), 21–22.

both audit and nonaudit services and related fees, and preparing a written agenda in advance of the meetings. They concluded that:

> Audit committees are larger: median sizes are now 4 members for manufacturing and nonfinancial services companies—up from 3 in 1978—and 4.5 for financial firms, up from 4.

> Their members include fewer directors with relationships that might interfere with the exercise of independent judgment, especially former executives of the company and directors affiliated with banks serving the company. Ninety percent of the committees have no members with such a potential conflict of interest.[7]

Around the same time, the National Commission on Fraudulent Financial Reporting (NCFFR) endorsed the principle that "the board of directors of all public companies should be required by SEC rule to establish audit committees composed solely of independent directors."[8] The Commission recommended that senior management set the tone for the corporation's control environment, which includes an effective audit committee of the board of directors. The Commission asserted: "Audit Committees should be informed, vigilant, and effective over-seers of the financial reporting process and the company's internal controls."[9]

Ray Bromark and Ralph Hoffman note that the role of the audit committee is expanding because of its value to the board of directors and to management and because of the need to meet the challenges of constantly changing business conditions. They point out that the audit committee has the following primary responsibilities:

- Assisting the board to fulfill its oversight responsibilities as they relate to the financial reporting process and the internal structure
- Maintaining, by way of regularly scheduled meetings, direct lines of communication between the board, financial management, the independent accountant, and internal audit

Additional responsibilities include:

- Reviewing corporate policies relating to compliance with laws and regulations, ethics, conflict of interests, and the investigation of misconduct and fraud
- Conducting periodic reviews of current pending litigation of regulatory proceedings bearing on corporate governance in which the corporation is a party
- Coordinating annual reviews of compliance with corporate governance policies through internal audit or the company's independent accountants
- Performing or supervising special investigations

---

[7] Jeremy Bacon, *The Audit Committee: A Broader Mandate*, Report No. 914 (New York: Conference Board, 1988), vii.

[8] National Commission on Fraudulent Financial Reporting, Report of the National Commission on Fraudulent Financial Reporting (Washington, DC: NCFFR, 1987), 40. This principle has become statutory law under the Sarbanes-Oxley Act and the federal securities laws.

[9] NCFFR Report, 41.

- Reviewing executive expenses
- Reviewing policies on sensitive payments
- Reviewing past or proposed transactions between the corporation and members of management
- Reviewing the corporation's benefits programs
- Assessing the performance of financial management[10]

In 2000, the Report of the National Association of Corporate Directors (NACD)'s Blue Ribbon Commission on Audit Committees provided the following rationale for why corporations need audit committees:

> The independent audit committee fulfills a vital role in corporate governance. The audit committee can be a critical component in ensuring quality reporting and controls, as well as the proper identification and management of risk.[11]

## Making the Audit Committee Effective

To organize an effective and efficient audit committee, consideration should be given to the proper delegation of responsibility and authority as well as to its written charter, membership, and size.

*Delegation of Responsibility and Authority* As a prerequisite to the effective performance of the committee, the board of directors should formulate a clear definition of the committee's responsibilities and authority. Moreover, the board should either pass a formal resolution or amend the bylaws of the corporation in order to document the establishment of the committee. An audit committee can best serve a corporation when it is a viable, independent group with a definite mission and it has full access to the company's financial information. One study noted that 51 companies with financial reporting problems, namely Securities and Exchange Commission (SEC) enforcement actions and/or material misstatements of quarterly earnings, were much less likely to have audit committees consisting solely of outside directors. Additionally, the researchers found that accounting and finance knowledge as well as frequent meetings are minimum steps needed to improve the quality in financial reporting.[12] In addition to both the internal and

---

[10] Ray Bromark and Ralph Hoffman, "An Audit Committee for Dynamic Times," *Directors and Boards* 16, no. 3 (Spring 1992): 52, 53, 60.

[11] National Association of Corporate Directors, *Report of the Blue Ribbon Commission on Audit Committees.* Washington, DC: NACD, 2000.

[12] See Dorothy A. McMullen and K. Raghunandan, "Enhancing Audit Committee Effectiveness," *Journal of Accountancy* 182, no. 2 (August 1996): 79–81. Also see Eugene M. Katz, "Keys to an Effective Audit Committee," *Credit World* 86, no. 4 (March/April 1998): 21–23; Krishnagopal Menon and Joanne D. Williams, "The Use of Audit Committees for Monitoring," *Journal of Accounting & Public Policy* 13, no. 2 (Summer 1994): 121–139; F. Todd De Zoort, "An Investigation of Audit Committees' Oversight Responsibilities," *Abacus* 33, no. 2 (September 1997): 208–227; Robert Lear, "The Decline of the Audit Committee," *Chief Executive* no. 111 (March 1996): 10; William W. Warrick and Duncan J. Galloway, "The Governance Audit: How Can We Make Sure We Don't Get Surprised?" *Directorship* 22, no. 5 (May 1996): 1–4.

external auditors' guidance and assistance, the chief financial officer must educate and guide the audit committee to enable it to serve the company effectively.

## Audit Committee Charter

As noted in Chapter 1, both the Securities and Exchange Commission (SEC) and self-regulatory organizations (SROs) require that the audit committee adopt and annually reassess its written charter, which describes the scope of the committee's responsibilities and how it fulfills these responsibilities. Moreover, the rules require that the audit committee charter be included in the proxy statement at least every three years.

Exhibit 2.1 presents two examples—the audit committee charter of Wal-Mart Stores, Inc. and that of Dow Chemical, Inc.

---

**EXHIBIT 2.1a**   Wal-Mart Stores, Inc., Audit Committee Charter (Example 1)

---

**WAL-MART STORES, INC. AUDIT COMMITTEE CHARTER**

**Committee Members**
Arne Sorenson
Christopher J. Williams
James I. Cash, Jr.
Aida M. Alvarez

*Purpose*
The Audit Committee is appointed by the Board to: (1) assist the Board in monitoring (a) the integrity of the financial reporting process, systems of internal controls and financial statements and reports of the Company, (b) the performance of the Company's internal audit function, and (c) the compliance by the Company with legal and regulatory requirements; and (2) be directly responsible for the appointment, compensation and oversight of the Company's independent auditor employed by the Company for the purpose of preparing or issuing an audit report or related work (the "Outside Auditor").

*Committee Membership*
The Audit Committee should consist of no fewer than three members, as determined annually by the Board on the recommendation of the Compensation, Nominating and Governance Committee; provided, however, that the Committee may operate with fewer than three members as long as such composition complies with applicable laws, rules, regulations, and securities exchange listing standards. The members of the Audit Committee shall meet the independence and expertise requirements of the New York Stock Exchange, any other exchange on which the Company's securities are traded, Section 10A(m)(3) of the Securities Exchange Act of 1934, as amended (the "Exchange Act") and the rules and regulations of the Securities and Exchange Commission (the "Commission"). Audit Committee members shall not serve simultaneously on the audit committees of more than two other public companies without the approval of the full Board.

The members of the Audit Committee shall be appointed annually by the Board on the recommendation of the Compensation, Nominating and Governance Committee. Audit

Committee members may be replaced by the Board at any time. The Board shall designate the Chairman or Chairwoman (the "Chairperson") of the Audit Committee.

### Committee Authority and Responsibilities

The basic responsibility of the members of the Audit Committee is to exercise their business judgment to act in what they reasonably believe to be in the best interests of the Company and its shareholders. In discharging that obligation, members should be entitled to rely on the honesty and integrity of the Company's senior executives and its outside advisors and auditors, to the fullest extent permitted by law.

The Audit Committee shall prepare the report required by the rules of the Commission to be included in the Company's annual proxy statement.

The Audit Committee shall be responsible directly for the appointment (subject, if applicable, to shareholder ratification), retention, termination, compensation and terms of engagement, evaluation, and oversight of the work of the Outside Auditor (including resolution of disagreements between management and the Outside Auditor regarding financial reporting). The Outside Auditor shall report directly to the Audit Committee.

The Audit Committee shall oversee the integrity of the audit process, financial reporting and internal accounting controls of the Company, oversee the work of the Company's management, internal auditors (the "Internal Auditors") and the Outside Auditor in these areas, oversee management's development of, and adherence to, a sound system of internal accounting and financial controls, review whether the Internal Auditors and the Outside Auditor objectively assess the Company's financial reporting, accounting practices and internal controls, and provide an open avenue of communication among the Outside Auditor, the Internal Auditors and the Board. It is the responsibility of: (i) management of the Company and the Outside Auditor, under the oversight of the Audit Committee and the Board, to plan and conduct financial audits and to determine that the Company's financial statements and disclosures are complete and accurate in accordance with generally accepted accounting principles ("GAAP") and applicable rules and regulations and fairly present, in all material respects, the financial condition of the Company; (ii) management of the Company, under the oversight of the Audit Committee and the Board, to assure compliance by the Company with applicable legal and regulatory requirements; and (iii) the Internal Auditors, under the oversight of the Audit Committee and the Board, to review the Company's internal transactions and accounting which do not require involvement in the detailed presentation of the Company's financial statements.

The Audit Committee shall pre-approve all audit services and non-audit services (including the fees and terms thereof) to be performed for the Company by the Outside Auditor to the extent required by and in a manner consistent with applicable law.

The Audit Committee shall meet as often as it determines necessary or appropriate, but not less frequently than quarterly. The Chairperson shall preside at each meeting and, in the absence of the Chairperson, one of the other members of the Audit Committee shall be designated as the acting chair of the meeting. The Chairperson (or acting chair) may direct appropriate members of management and staff to prepare draft agendas and related background information for each Audit Committee meeting. The draft agenda shall be reviewed and approved by the Audit Committee Chairperson (or acting chair) in advance of distribution to the other Audit Committee members. Any background materials, together with the agenda, should be distributed to the Audit Committee members in advance of the meeting. All meetings of the Audit Committee shall be held pursuant to the amended and restated bylaws of the Company with regard to notice and waiver thereof,

*(continued)*

---

**Exhibit 2.1a**  *(Continued)*

---

and written minutes of each meeting, in the form approved by the Audit Committee, shall be duly filed in the Company records. Reports of meetings of the Audit Committee shall be made to the Board at its next regularly scheduled meeting following the Audit Committee meeting accompanied by any recommendations to the Board approved by the Audit Committee.

The Audit Committee may form and delegate authority to subcommittees consisting of one or more members when appropriate.

The Audit Committee shall have the authority, to the extent it deems necessary or appropriate, to retain independent legal, accounting or other advisers. The Company shall provide for appropriate funding, as determined by the Audit Committee, for payment of compensation to the Outside Auditor for the purpose of rendering or issuing an audit report and to any advisers employed by the Audit Committee, subject only to any limitations imposed by applicable rules and regulations. The Audit Committee may request any officer or associate of the Company or the Company's outside counsel or Outside Auditor to attend a meeting of the Audit Committee or to meet with any members of, or consultants to, the Audit Committee. The Audit Committee shall meet with management, the Internal Auditors and the Outside Auditor in separate executive sessions at least quarterly to discuss matters for which the Audit Committee has responsibility.

The Audit Committee shall make regular reports to the Board. The Audit Committee shall review and reassess the adequacy of this Charter annually and recommend any proposed changes to the Board for approval. The Audit Committee shall annually review its own performance.

In performing its functions, the Audit Committee shall undertake those tasks and responsibilities that, in its judgment, would contribute most effectively to and implement the purposes of the Audit Committee. In addition to the general tasks and responsibilities noted above, the following are the specific functions of the Audit Committee:

*Financial Statement and Disclosure Matters*

1. Review and discuss with management, and to the extent the Audit Committee deems necessary or appropriate, the Internal Auditors and the Outside Auditor, the Company's disclosure controls and procedures that are designed to ensure that the reports the Company files with the Commission comply with the Commission's rules and forms.
2. Review and discuss with management, the Internal Auditors and the Outside Auditor the annual audited financial statements, including disclosures made in management's discussion and analysis, and recommend to the Board whether the audited financial statements should be included in the Company's Form 10-K.
3. Review and discuss with management, the Internal Auditors and the Outside Auditor the Company's quarterly financial statements, including disclosures made in management's discussion and analysis, prior to the filing of its Form 10-Q, including the results of the Outside Auditor's reviews of the quarterly financial statements.
4. Review and discuss quarterly reports from the Outside Auditor on:
    a. All critical accounting policies and practices to be used;
    b. All alternative treatments within GAAP for policies and practices related to material items that have been discussed with management, including ramifications of the use of such alternative disclosures and treatments, and the treatment preferred by the Outside Auditor;

    c. The internal controls adhered to by the Company, management, and the Company's financial, accounting and internal auditing personnel, and the impact of each on the quality and reliability of the Company's financial reporting; and

    d. Other material written communications between the Outside Auditor and management, such as any management letter or schedule of unadjusted differences.

5. Discuss in advance with management the Company's practice with respect to the types of information to be disclosed and the types of presentations to be made in earnings press releases, including the use, if any, of "pro forma" or "adjusted" non-GAAP information, as well as financial information and earnings guidance provided to analysts and rating agencies.

6. Review and discuss with management, the Internal Auditors and the Outside Auditor:

    a. Significant financial reporting issues and judgments made in connection with the preparation of the Company's financial statements;

    b. The clarity of the financial disclosures made by the Company;

    c. The development, selection and disclosure of critical accounting estimates and the analyses of alternative assumptions or estimates, and the effect of such estimates on the Company's financial statements;

    d. Potential changes in GAAP and the effect such changes would have on the Company's financial statements;

    e. Significant changes in accounting principles, financial reporting policies and internal controls implemented by the Company;

    f. Significant litigation, contingencies and claims against the Company and material accounting issues that require disclosure in the Company's financial statements;

    g. Information regarding any "second" opinions sought by management from an independent auditor with respect to the accounting treatment of a particular event or transaction;

    h. Management's compliance with the Company's processes, procedures and internal controls;

    i. The adequacy and effectiveness of the Company's internal accounting and financial controls and the recommendations of management, the Internal Auditors and the Outside Auditor for the improvement of accounting practices and internal controls; and

    j. Any difficulties encountered by the Outside Auditor or the Internal Auditors in the course of their audit work, including any restrictions on the scope of activities or access to requested information, and any significant disagreements with management.

7. Discuss with management and the Outside Auditor the effect of regulatory and accounting initiatives as well as off-balance sheet structures and aggregate contractual obligations on the Company's financial statements.

8. Discuss with management the Company's major financial risk exposures and the steps management has taken to monitor and control such exposures, including the Company's risk assessment and risk management policies.

9. Discuss with the Outside Auditor the matters required to be discussed by Statement on Auditing Standards ("SAS") No. 61 relating to the conduct of the audit. In particular, discuss:

    a. The adoption of, or changes to, the Company's significant internal auditing and accounting principles and practices as suggested by the Outside Auditor, Internal Auditors or management; and

    b. The management letter provided by the Outside Auditor and the Company's response to that letter.

10. Receive and review disclosures made to the Audit Committee by the Company's Chief Executive Officer and Chief Financial Officer during their certification process

*(continued)*

---
**Exhibit 2.1a**  *(Continued)*
---

for the Company's Form 10-K and Form 10-Q about (a) any significant deficiencies in the design or operation of internal controls or material weakness therein, (b) any fraud involving management or other associates who have a significant role in the Company's internal controls and (c) any significant changes in internal controls or in other factors that could significantly affect internal controls subsequent to the date of their evaluation.

11. Review and discuss with management (including the senior internal audit executive) and the Outside Auditor the Company's internal controls report and the Outside Auditor's attestation of the report prior to the filing of the Company's Annual Report on Form 10-K.

*Oversight of the Company's Relationship with the Outside Auditor*

12. Review the experience and qualifications of the senior members of the Outside Auditor team.

13. Obtain and review a report from the Outside Auditor at least annually regarding (a) the Outside Auditor's internal quality-control procedures, (b) any material issues raised by the most recent internal quality-control review, or peer review, of the firm, or by any inquiry or investigation by governmental or professional authorities, within the preceding five years respecting one or more independent audits carried out by the firm, (c) any steps taken to deal with any such issues, and (d) all relationships between the Outside Auditor and the Company, including the written disclosures and the letter required by applicable independence standards, rules and regulations.

14. Evaluate the qualifications, performance and independence of the Outside Auditor, including considering whether the Outside Auditor's quality controls are adequate and the provision of non-audit services is compatible with maintaining the Outside Auditor's independence, and taking into account the opinions of management and the Internal Auditor. The Audit Committee shall present its conclusions to the Board.

15. Oversee the rotation of the lead (or coordinating) audit partner having primary responsibility for the audit and the audit partner responsible for reviewing the audit at least once every five years, and oversee the rotation of other audit partners, in accordance with the rules of the Commission.

16. Develop and periodically review policies for the Company's hiring of present and former employees of the Outside Auditor.

17. To the extent the Audit Committee deems necessary or appropriate, discuss with the national office of the Outside Auditor issues on which they were consulted by the Company's audit team and matters of audit quality and consistency.

18. Discuss with management, the Internal Auditors and the Outside Auditor any accounting adjustments that were noted or proposed by the Outside Auditor, but were not adopted or reflected.

19. Meet with management, the Internal Auditors and the Outside Auditor prior to the audit to discuss and review the scope, planning and staffing of the audit.

20. Obtain from the Outside Auditor the information required to be disclosed to the Company by generally accepted auditing standards in connection with the conduct of an audit, including topics covered by SAS 54, 60, 61 and 82.

21. Require the Outside Auditor to review the financial information included in the Company's Form 10-Q in accordance with Rule 10-01(d) of Regulation S-X of the Commission prior to the Company filing such reports with the Commission and to

provide to the Company for inclusion in the Company's Form 10-Q any reports of the Outside Auditor required by Rule 10-01(d).

### *Oversight of the Company's Internal Audit Function*

22. Ensure that the Company has an internal audit function.
23. Review and concur in the appointment, replacement, reassignment or dismissal of the senior internal auditing executive, and the compensation package for such person.
24. Review the significant reports to management prepared by the internal auditing department and management's responses.
25. Communicate with management and the Internal Auditors to obtain information concerning internal audits, accounting principles adopted by the Company, internal controls of the Company, management, and the Company's financial and accounting personnel, and review the impact of each on the quality and reliability of the Company's financial statements.
26. Evaluate the internal auditing department and its impact on the accounting practices, internal controls and financial reporting of the Company.
27. Discuss with the Outside Auditor the internal audit department's responsibilities, budget and staffing and any recommended changes in the planned scope of the internal audit.

### *Compliance Oversight Responsibilities*

28. Obtain from the Outside Auditor the reports required to be furnished to the Audit Committee under Section 10A of the Exchange Act and obtain from the Outside Auditor any information with respect to illegal acts in accordance with Section 10A.
29. Discuss with management and the Outside Auditor, and advise the Board with respect to, the Company's policies, processes and procedures regarding compliance with applicable laws and regulations and the Statement of Ethics, and instances of non-compliance therewith. Obtain and review reports and disclosures of insider and affiliated party transactions.
30. Establish procedures for (a) the receipt, retention and treatment of complaints received by the Company regarding accounting, internal accounting controls or auditing matters, and (b) the confidential, anonymous submission by associates of the Company of concerns regarding questionable accounting or auditing matters.
31. Discuss with management and the Outside Auditor any correspondence between the Company and regulators or governmental agencies and any associate complaints or published reports that raise material issues regarding the Company's financial statements or accounting policies.
32. Discuss with the Company's Chief Legal Officer legal matters that may have a material impact on the financial statements or the Company's compliance policies.

### *Additional Responsibilities*

33. Prepare annually a report for inclusion in the Company's proxy statement relating to its annual shareholders meeting. In that report, the Audit Committee will state whether it has: (a) reviewed and discussed the audited financial statements with management; (b) discussed with the Outside Auditor the matters required to be discussed by SAS No. 61, as that statement may be modified or supplemented from time to time; (c) received from the Outside Auditor the written disclosures and the letter required, by applicable independence standards, rules and regulations, and has discussed with the Outside Auditor, the Outside Auditor's independence; and

(*continued*)

**Exhibit 2.1a**   *(Continued)*

(d) based on the review and discussions referred to in clauses (a), (b) and (c) above, recommended to the Board that the audited financial statements be included in the Company's Annual Report on Form 10-K for the last fiscal year for filing with the Commission.

34. Conduct or authorize investigations into any matters within the Audit Committee's scope of responsibilities.

35. Review the Company's Transaction Review Policy and recommend any changes to the Compensation, Nominating and Governance Committee and then to the Board for approval. Review and determine whether to approve or ratify transactions covered by such policy, as appropriate.

---

*Source*: http://walmartstores.com/Investors/7852.aspx?p=7822.

---

**EXHIBIT 2.1b**   Dow Chemical, Inc., Audit Committee Charter (Example 2)

**DOW CHEMICAL AUDIT COMMITTEE**

*Members*
Barbara H. Franklin, Chair
James A. Bell
Jeff M. Fettig
Dennis H. Reilley
Paul G. Stern
Charter of the Audit Committee

*Purpose*
The Audit Committee is appointed by the Board to assist the Board in monitoring:

1. The integrity of the financial statements of the Company
2. The independent auditors' qualifications, independence, and performance
3. The performance of the Company's internal audit function
4. The compliance by the Company with legal and regulatory requirements.

The Audit Committee shall prepare the report required by the rules of the Securities and Exchange Commission (the "Commission") to be included in the Company's annual meeting proxy statement.

*Committee Membership*
The Audit Committee shall consist of no fewer than three members. The members of the Audit Committee shall meet the independence and experience requirements of the New York Stock Exchange, Section 10A(m)(3) of the Securities Exchange Act of 1934 (the "Exchange Act") and the rules and regulations of the Commission. The Company shall disclose as required by the Commission whether at least one member of the Audit Committee is an "audit committee financial expert" as defined by the Commission. The simultaneous service on the audit committees of more than two other public companies requires a Board determination that such simultaneous service does not impair the ability of such member to effectively serve on the Company's Audit Committee.

The members of the Audit Committee shall be appointed by the Board on the recommendation of the Governance Committee. Audit Committee members may be replaced by the Board.

*Meetings*

The Audit Committee shall meet as often as it determines, but not less frequently than quarterly. The Audit Committee shall meet at each in-person meeting with the controller, general counsel, internal auditor and the independent auditors in separate executive sessions, and also in executive session with only the Committee members. The Audit Committee may request any officer or employee of the Company or the Company's outside counsel or independent auditors to attend a meeting of the Audit Committee or to meet with any members of, or consultants to, the Audit Committee.

*Committee Authority and Responsibilities*

The Audit Committee shall perform the duties assigned to it by Section 4.3 of the Company's Bylaws and by the Board of Directors.

The Audit Committee shall have the sole authority to appoint or replace the independent auditors (subject to shareholder ratification). The Audit Committee shall be directly responsible for the compensation and oversight of the work of the independent auditors (including resolution of disagreements between management and the independent auditors regarding financial reporting) for the purpose of preparing or issuing an audit report or related work. The independent auditors shall report directly to the Audit Committee.

The Audit Committee shall preapprove all auditing services and permitted non-audit services (including the fees and terms thereof) to be performed for the Company by its independent auditors, subject to the de minimis exceptions for non-audit services described in Section 10A(i)(1)(B) of the Exchange Act, which should be approved by the Audit Committee prior to the completion of the audit. The Audit Committee may form and delegate authority to subcommittees consisting of one or more members when appropriate, including the authority to grant preapprovals of audit and permitted non-audit services, provided that decisions of such subcommittee to grant preapprovals shall be presented to the full Audit Committee at its next scheduled meeting.

The Audit Committee shall have the authority, to the extent it deems necessary or appropriate, to retain independent legal, accounting or other advisors. The Company shall provide for appropriate funding, as determined by the Audit Committee, for payment of compensation to the independent auditors for the purpose of rendering or issuing an audit report and to any advisors employed by the Audit Committee.

The Audit Committee shall make regular reports to the Board. The Audit Committee shall review and reassess the adequacy of this Charter annually and recommend any proposed changes to the Board for approval. The Audit Committee shall annually review the Audit Committee's own performance.

The Audit Committee, to the extent it deems necessary or appropriate, shall:

*As to Financial Statement and Disclosure Matters*

1. Review and discuss with management and the independent auditors the annual audited financial statements, including disclosures made in management's discussion and analysis, and recommend to the Board whether the audited financial statements should be included in the Company's Form 10-K.
2. Review and discuss with management and the independent auditors the Company's quarterly financial statements prior to the filing of its Form 10-Q, including the results of the independent auditors' review of the quarterly financial statements.
3. Discuss with management and the independent auditors significant financial reporting issues and judgments made in connection with the preparation of the Company's

(*continued*)

---

**Exhibit 2.1b** *(Continued)*

---

financial statements, including any significant changes in the Company's selection or application of accounting principles, any major issues as to the adequacy of the Company's internal controls and any special steps adopted in light of material control deficiencies.

4. Review and discuss quarterly reports from the independent auditors on:
   a. All critical accounting policies and practices to be used.
   b. All alternative treatments of financial information within generally accepted accounting principles that have been discussed with management, ramifications of the use of such alternative disclosures and treatments, and the treatment preferred by the independent auditors.
   c. Other material written communications between the independent auditors and management, such as any management letter or schedule of unadjusted differences.

Discuss with management the Company's earnings press releases, including the use of "pro forma" or "adjusted" non-GAAP information, as well as financial information and earnings guidance provided to analysts and rating agencies. Such discussion may be done generally (consisting of discussing the types of information to be disclosed and the types of presentations to be made) rather than specifically as to individual press releases, analysts, and rating agencies.

Discuss with management and the independent auditors the effect of applicable regulations and accounting profession initiatives as well as off-balance sheet structures on the Company's financial statements.

Discuss with management the Company's major financial risk exposures and the steps management has taken to monitor and control such exposures, including the Company's risk assessment and risk management policies.

Discuss with the independent auditors the matters required to be discussed by Statement on Auditing Standards No. 61 relating to the conduct of the audit, including any difficulties encountered in the course of the audit work, any restrictions on the scope of activities or access to requested information, and any significant disagreements with management.

Review disclosures made to the Audit Committee by the Company's CEO and CFO during their certification process for the Form 10-K and Form 10-Q about any significant deficiencies in the design or operation of internal controls or material weaknesses therein and any fraud involving management or other employees who have a significant role in the Company's internal controls.

### As to Oversight of the Company's Relationship with the Independent Auditors

Review and evaluate the lead partner of the independent auditors team.

Obtain and review a report from the independent auditors at least annually regarding (a) the independent auditors' internal quality-control procedures, (b) any material issues raised by the most recent internal quality-control review, or peer review, of the firm, or by any inquiry or investigation by governmental or professional authorities within the preceding five years respecting one or more independent audits carried out by the firm, (c) any steps taken to deal with any such issues, and (d) all relationships between the independent auditors and the Company. Evaluate the qualifications, performance and independence of the independent auditors, including considering whether the auditors' quality controls are adequate and the provision of permitted non-audit services is compatible with maintaining the auditors' independence, and taking into account the opinions of management and internal auditors. The Audit Committee shall present its conclusions with respect to the independent auditors to the Board.

Ensure the rotation of the lead (or coordinating) audit partner having primary responsibility for the audit and the audit partner responsible for reviewing the audit as required by law. Consider whether, in order to assure continuing auditor independence, it is appropriate to adopt a policy of rotating the independent auditing firm on a regular basis.

Recommend to the Board policies for the Company's hiring of employees or former employees of the independent auditors who participated in any capacity in the audit of the Company.

Discuss with the independent auditors matters of audit quality and consistency and any significant auditing or accounting issues presented by the audit engagement on which the audit team has consulted with their national office.

Meet with the independent auditors prior to the audit to discuss the planning and staffing of the audit.

### As to Oversight of the Company's Internal Audit Function

Review the appointment and replacement of the senior internal auditing executive. Review the significant issues raised in reports to management prepared by the internal auditing department and management's responses.

Review at least annually the internal audit department and its mission, responsibilities, independence, budget and staffing and any recommended changes in the planned scope of the internal audit.

### As to Compliance Oversight Responsibilities

Obtain from the independent auditors assurance that Section 10A(b) of the Exchange Act has not been implicated. Section 10A(b) relates to illegal acts that have come to the attention of the independent auditors during the course of the audit.

Obtain reports from management, the Company's senior internal auditing executive and the independent auditors concerning whether the Company and its subsidiary/foreign affiliated entities are in conformity with applicable legal requirements and the Company's Code of Business Conduct and Ethics. Review reports and disclosures of insider and affiliated party transactions. Advise the Board with respect to the Company's policies and procedures regarding compliance with applicable laws and regulations and with the Company's Code of Business Conduct and Ethics.

Establish and implement procedures for the receipt, retention and treatment of complaints received by the Company regarding accounting, internal accounting controls or auditing matters, and the confidential, anonymous submission by employees of concerns regarding questionable accounting or auditing matters.

Discuss with management and the independent auditors any correspondence with regulators or governmental agencies and any published reports which raise material issues regarding the Company's financial statements or accounting policies.

Discuss with the Company's General Counsel legal matters that may have a material impact on the financial statements or the Company's compliance policies.

*(continued)*

**Exhibit 2.1b**   *(Continued)*

*Limitation of Audit Committee's Role*

While the Audit Committee has the responsibilities and powers set forth in this Charter, it is not the duty of the Audit Committee to plan or conduct audits or to determine that the Company's financial statements and disclosures are complete and accurate and are in accordance with generally accepted accounting principles and applicable rules and regulations. These are the responsibilities of management and the independent auditors.

*Source:* http://www.dow.com/corpgov/board/audit.htm.

***Membership and Size of the Audit Committee***   The effectiveness of the audit committee depends on the backgrounds of the members and of the chairman.

## Audit Committee Independence

Under Section 301 of the Sarbanes-Oxley Act of 2002, Section 10A of the Securities Exchange Act of 1934 is amended by adding (m) Standards Relating to Audit Committees, which states in part:

(2) RESPONSIBILITIES RELATING TO REGISTERED PUBLIC ACCOUNT-ING FIRMS—The audit committee of each issuer, in its capacity as a committee of the board of directors, shall be directly responsible for the appointment, compensation, and oversight of the work of any registered public accounting firm employed by that issuer (including resolution of disagreements between management and the auditor regarding financial reporting) for the purpose of preparing or issuing an audit report or related work, and each such registered public accounting firm shall report directly to the audit committee.

(3) INDEPENDENCE—

    (A) IN GENERAL—Each member of the audit committee of the issuer shall be a member of the board of directors of the issuer, and shall otherwise be independent.

    (B) CRITERIA—In order to be considered to be independent for purposes of this paragraph, a member of an audit committee of an issuer may not, other than in his or her capacity as a member of the audit committee, the board of directors, or any other board committee—

        (i) accept any consulting, advisory, or other compensatory fee from the issuer; or

        (ii) be an affiliated person of the issuer or any subsidiary thereof.

    (C) EXEMPTION AUTHORITY—The Commission may exempt from the requirements of subparagraph (B) a particular relationship with respect to audit committee members, as the Commission determines appropriate in light of the circumstances.

(4) COMPLAINTS—Each audit committee shall establish procedures for—

    (A) the receipt, retention, and treatment of complaints received by the issuer regarding accounting, internal accounting controls, or auditing matters; and

(B) the confidential, anonymous submission by employees of the issuer of concerns regarding questionable accounting or auditing matters.

(5) AUTHORITY TO ENGAGE ADVISERS—Each audit committee shall have the authority to engage independent counsel and other advisers, as it determines necessary to carry out its duties.

(6) FUNDING—Each issuer shall provide for appropriate funding, as determined by the audit committee, in its capacity as a committee of the board of directors, for payment of compensation—

(A) to the registered public accounting firm employed by the issuer for the purpose of rendering or issuing an audit report; and

(B) to any advisers employed by the audit committee under paragraph (5).[13]

The standard of independence is also disclosed in the Federal Deposit Insurance Corporation Improvement Act (FDICIA) as noted in the historical perspective. To discuss additional SEC and SRO audit committee independence requirements, the next section of this chapter contains the Standards Relating to Listing Company Audit Committees.

In addition to those outlined in the Sarbanes-Oxley Act, other basic qualifications of the audit committee are:

- A general understanding of the company's industry and the social, political, economic, and legal forces that affect the industry
- A knowledge of the company with respect to its history, organization, and operational policies
- An understanding of the fundamental problems of planning and control, as well as the fundamentals of the functional aspects of the company

In short, the membership of the committee should consist of both financial and nonfinancial people so that the board can draw on members from various professions, such as accounting, economics, education, psychology, and sociology. (See the ensuing discussion about the Sarbanes-Oxley Act Section 407 requirement for a public company audit committee to have at least one "audit committee financial expert.") Having members with diverse backgrounds is advantageous since it provides the audit committee with the kind of perspective and experience that is desirable in assessing both the internal and external audit functions.

Equally important, the chairman has a critical role in coordinating the committee's task. The success or failure of the operation may depend on the chairman, and therefore such an individual should be chosen with great care. Specifically, the chairman should possess the same basic qualifications listed earlier, as well as:

---

[13] Sarbanes-Oxley Act of 2002, H.R. Rep. No. 107-610, July 25, 2002. See also remarks by Commissioner Paul S. Atkins, Securities and Exchange Commission, "The Sarbanes-Oxley Act of 2002: Goals, Content, and Status of Implementation," University of Cologne, Germany, February 5, 2003 (www.sec.gov/news/speech/spch020503psa.htm).

- The ability to stimulate the audit directors' thinking without dominating the meeting
- The ability to sustain not only each member's personal interest in the work of the committee, but also the member's willingness to contribute to its objectives
- A general understanding of the committee's objectives and jurisdictional aspects
- The ability to plan the agenda and to coordinate and disseminate information to the committee and the board members

## Financial Expert

Section 407 of the Sarbanes-Oxley Act provides that:

(a) RULES DEFINING "FINANCIAL EXPERT"—The Commission shall issue rules, as necessary or appropriate in the public interest and consistent with the protection of investors, to require each issuer, together with periodic reports required pursuant to sections 13(a) and 15(d) of the Securities Exchange Act of 1934, to disclose whether or not, and if not, the reasons therefor, the audit committee of that issuer is comprised of at least 1 member who is a financial expert, as such term is defined by the Commission.

(b) CONSIDERATIONS—In defining the term "financial expert" for purposes of subsection (a), the Commission shall consider whether a person has, through education and experience as a public accountant or auditor or a principal financial officer, comptroller, or principle accounting officer of an issuer, or from a position involving the performance of similar functions—

(1) an understanding of generally accepted accounting principles and financial statements;

(2) experience in—

(A) the preparation or auditing of financial statements of generally comparable issuers; and

(B) the application of such principles in connection with the accounting for estimates, accruals, and reserves;

(3) experience with internal accounting controls; and

(4) an understanding of audit committee functions.[14]

## Audit Committee Meetings

Although the Sarbanes-Oxley Act does not address audit committee meetings, the New York Stock Exchange issued a proposed rule change that states:

Meet separately, periodically, with management, with internal auditors (or other personnel responsible for the internal audit function) and with independent auditors.[15]

---

[14] Sarbanes-Oxley Act of 2002, H.R. Rep. No. 107-610, July 25, 2002. See also SEC Release No. 33-8177, January 23, 2003.

[15] Securities and Exchange Commission Release No. 34-47672, File No. SR-NYSE-2002-33 Proposed Rule Change Relating to Corporate Governance (April 11, 2003), 13.

Furthermore, the National Commission on Fraudulent Financial Reporting recommended the "audit committee oversight responsibilities undertaken on behalf of the board of directors extend to the quarterly reporting process. The audit committee should review the controls that management has established to protect the integrity of the quarterly reporting process. This review should be ongoing."[16]

## THE AUDIT COMMITTEE FUNCTIONS

### Audit Committee Functions as Defined by the American Bar Association

The Committee on Corporate Laws of the American Bar Association has defined the functions of the audit committee in this way:

In its capacity as the communication link between the board of directors as representative of stockholders, on the one hand, and the independent auditors, on the other hand, the audit committee should have prime responsibility for the discharge of at least the following four functions:

1. To recommend the particular persons or firm to be employed by the corporation as its independent auditors;
2. To consult with the persons so chosen to be the independent auditors with regard to the plan of audit;
3. To review, in consultation with the independent auditors, their report of audit, or proposed report of audit, and the accompanying management letter, if any; and
4. To consult with the independent auditors (periodically, as appropriate, out of the presence of management) with regard to the adequacy of internal controls, and if need be, to consult also with the internal auditors (since their product has a strong influence on the quality and integrity of the resulting independent audit).[17]

Subsequently, the Committee on Corporate Laws expanded its definitions to include in substantial part the American Law Institute's Principles of Corporate Governance:

1. Recommend which firm to engage as the corporation's external auditor and whether to terminate that relationship.
2. Review the external auditor's compensation, the proposed terms of its engagement, and its independence.
3. Review the appointment and replacement of the senior internal auditing executive, if any.
4. Serve as a channel of communication between the external auditor and the board and between the senior internal auditing executive, if any, and the board.

---

[16] National Commission on Fraudulent Financial Reporting, Report of the National Commission on Fraudulent Reporting (Washington, DC: NCFFR, 1987), 48.

[17] American Bar Association, *Corporate Director's Guidebook* (Chicago: ABA, 1978), 32–33.

5. Review the results of each external audit, including any qualifications in the external auditor's opinion, any related management letter, management's responses to recommendations made by the external auditor in connection with the audit, reports submitted to the Audit Committee by the internal auditing department that are material to the corporation as a whole, and management's responses to those reports.

6. Review the corporation's annual financial statements and any significant disputes between management and the external auditor that arose in connection with the preparation of those financial statements.

7. Consider, in consultation with the external auditor and the senior internal auditing executive, if any, the adequacy of the corporation's internal financial controls. Among other things, these controls must be designed to provide reasonable assurance that the corporation's publicly reported financial statements are presented fairly in conformity with generally accepted accounting principles.

8. Consider major changes and other major questions of choice regarding the appropriate auditing and accounting principles and practices to be followed when preparing the corporation's financial statements.

9. Review the procedures employed by the corporation in preparing published financial statements and related management commentaries.

10. Meet periodically with management to review the corporation's major financial risk exposures.[18]

In addition to the American Bar Association's definition on the function of the audit committee, the National Commission on Fraudulent Financial Reporting recommends these functions:[19]

As part of its ongoing oversight of the effectiveness of internal controls, a company's audit committee should review annually the program management establishes to monitor compliance with the code of conduct (p. 35).

All public companies should develop a written charter setting forth the duties and responsibilities of the audit committee. The board of directors should approve the charter, review it periodically, and modify it as necessary (p. 42).

Audit committees should have adequate resources and authority to discharge their responsibilities (p. 43).

Audit committees should oversee the quarterly reporting process (p. 47).

Management and the audit committee should ensure that the internal auditors' involvement in the audit of the financial reporting process is appropriate and properly coordinated with the independent public accountant (p. 39).

---

[18] American Bar Association, *Corporate Director's Guidebook* (Chicago: ABA, 1994), 28–29.
[19] NCFFR, "Report of the National Commission on Fraudulent Financial Reporting, 1987." For further discussion, see the Committee of Sponsoring Organizations of the Treadway Commission (COSO), International Control-Integrated Framework 4, COSO of the Treadway Commission (1992): 8–10.

The audit committee should review management's evaluation of factors related to the independence of the company's public accountant. Both the audit committee and management should assist the public accountant in preserving his independence (p. 43).

Before the beginning of each year, the audit committee should review management's plans for engaging the company's independent public accountant to perform management advisory services during the coming year, considering both the types of services that may be rendered and the projected fees (p. 43).

All public companies should be required by SEC rule to include in their annual report to stockholders a letter signed by the chairman of the audit committee describing the committee's responsibilities and activities during the year (p. 46).

Management should advise the audit committee when it seeks a second opinion on a significant accounting issue (p. 47).

More recently, the National Association of Corporate Directors' "Report of the Blue Ribbon Commission on Audit Committees: A Practical Guide" (2000) makes the following recommendations as to the nature, scope, and functions of the audit committee (in a sample charter):

Committee Role

The committee's role is to act on behalf of the board of directors and oversee all material aspects of the company's reporting, control, and audit functions, except those specifically related to the responsibilities of another standing committee of the board. The audit committee's role includes a particular focus on the qualitative aspects of financial reporting to shareholders and on company processes for the management of business/financial risk and for compliance with significant applicable legal, ethical, and regulatory requirements. The role also includes coordination with other board committees and maintenance of strong, positive working relationships with management, external and internal auditors, counsel, and other committee advisors.[20]

## Basic Audit Committee Functions

In addition to the preceding conclusions on the functions of the audit committee, the basic functions should include:

- The planning function
- The monitoring function
- The reporting function

***The Planning Function***  Since the primary objective of the committee is to oversee and monitor the financial accounting and auditing processes, it should adopt its own coordinated plan of administration, one that is consistent with this

---

[20] National Association of Corporate Directors, "Report of the Blue Ribbon Commission on Audit Committees." Washington, DC: NACD, 2000.

objective. Such a plan should be designed to provide assurance to the full board of directors that both the internal and external resources allocated to the audit function are adequate and are being used effectively. The Committee on Corporate Organization Policy of The Business Roundtable agreed on two core functions of the board that are related directly to the committee's planning function:

1. Although the board cannot effectively conduct day-to-day operations, the board does have a major role in, and a major accountability for, the financial performance of the enterprise. This clearly requires a continuing check on corporate financial results and prospects.
2. Directors and top management cannot be the guarantors of the lawful conduct of every employee or manager in a large organization. . . . Policies and procedures should be designed to promote corporate law compliance.[21]

Thus, in view of the committee's oversight and advisory capacity, its plan should include:

- A review and appraisal of the overall purpose, objectives, and resources available for the entity's overall audit plan in accordance with the committee's charter, as well as the committee's recommendation of the audit goals and objectives for the board's approval
- A review and consolidation of the audit plans of the internal and external auditing groups
- An annual appraisal of the corporate audit plan[22]

Furthermore, the committee should consider an integrated approach so that its plan is oriented toward the segments of the auditing cycle, which are (1) initial planning segment, (2) preaudit segment, and (3) postaudit segment. For example, during the initial planning segment, the committee should develop a basic understanding of the entity's business and its industry. Such an understanding of the qualitative characteristics of the entity and its position in the industry will enhance the committee's ability to discharge its responsibilities effectively. In addition, during the preaudit and postaudit segments, it should develop an understanding of management's business risk assessment process and the audit risk assessment process related to financial reporting risk, as well as the analytical review process with respect to the financial statements.

---

[21] Business Roundtable, *The Role and Composition of the Board of Directors of the Large Publicly Owned Corporations*, 10–13.

[22] See Chapters 6 and 7 for more information on the committee's role in the planning function. It should be noted that the chairman of the audit committee usually will ask the audit engagement partner, the director of internal audit, and the chief financial officer to suggest agenda items for the committee meetings. These individuals are a major source of guidance and information to the committee. In addition, it is essential that agenda and supporting documents be prepared and distributed in advance for each meeting.

## Responsibilities under the Sarbanes-Oxley Act of 2002 (Sarbanes-Oxley)
### Section 201—Services Outside the Scope of Practice of Auditors

(a) PROHIBITED ACTIVITIES—Section 10A of the Securities Exchange Act of 1934 (15 U.S.C. 78j-1) is amended by adding at the end the following:

(g) PROHIBITED ACTIVITIES—Except as provided in subsection (h), it shall be unlawful for a registered public accounting firm (and any associated person of that firm, to the extent determined appropriate by the Commission) that performs for any issuer any audit required by this title or the rules of the Commission under this title or, beginning 180 days after the date of commencement of the operations of the Public Company Accounting Oversight Board established under section 101 of the Sarbanes-Oxley Act of 2002 (in this section referred to as the "Board"), the rules of the Board, to provide to that issuer, contemporaneously with the audit, any non-audit service, including—

(1) bookkeeping or other services related to the accounting records or financial statements of the audit client;

(2) financial information systems design and implementation;

(3) appraisal or valuation services, fairness opinions, or contribution-in-kind reports;

(4) actuarial services;

(5) internal audit outsourcing services;

(6) management functions or human resources;

(7) broker or dealer, investment adviser, or investment banking services;

(8) legal services and expert services unrelated to the audit; and

(9) any other service that the Board determines, by regulation, is impermissible.[23]

(h) PREAPPROVAL REQUIRED FOR NON-AUDIT SERVICES—A registered public accounting firm may engage in any non-audit service, including tax services, that is not described in any of paragraphs (1) through (9) of subsection (g) for an audit client, only if the activity is approved in advance by the audit committee of the issuer, in accordance with subsection (i).

(b) EXEMPTION AUTHORITY—The Board may, on a case-by-case basis, exempt any person, issuer, public accounting firm, or transaction from the prohibition on the provision of services under section 10A(g) of the Securities Exchange Act of 1934 (as added by this section), to the extent that such exemption is necessary or appropriate in the public interest and is consistent with the protection of investors, and subject to review by the Commission in the same manner as for rules of the Board under section 107.[24]

### Section 202—Preapproval of Audit and Nonaudit Services

Section 10A of the Securities Exchange Act of 1934 (15 U.S.C. 78j-1), as amended by this Act, is amended by adding at the end the following:

---

[23] See the broader discussion of nonaudit services in Chapter 9.
[24] Sarbanes-Oxley Act of 2002, H.R. Rep. No. 107-610, July 25, 2002.

(i) PREAPPROVAL REQUIREMENTS—

(1) IN GENERAL—

(A) AUDIT COMMITTEE ACTION—All auditing services (which may entail providing comfort letters in connection with securities underwritings or statutory audits required for insurance companies for purposes of State law) and non-audit services, other than as provided in subparagraph (B), provided to an issuer by the auditor of the issuer shall be preapproved by the audit committee of the issuer.

(B) DE MINIMIS EXCEPTION—The preapproval requirement under subparagraph (A) is waived with respect to the provision of non-audit services for an issuer, if—

(i) the aggregate amount of all such non-audit services provided to the issuer constitutes not more than 5 percent of the total amount of revenues paid by the issuer to its auditor during the fiscal year in which the non-audit services are provided;

(ii) such services were not recognized by the issuer at the time of the engagement to be non-audit services; and

(iii) such services are promptly brought to the attention of the audit committee of the issuer and approved prior to the completion of the audit by the audit committee or by 1 or more members of the audit committee who are members of the board of directors to whom authority to grant such approvals has been delegated by the audit committee.

(2) DISCLOSURE TO INVESTORS—Approval by an audit committee of an issuer under this subsection of a non-audit service to be performed by the auditor of the issuer shall be disclosed to investors in periodic reports required by section 13(a).

(3) DELEGATION AUTHORITY—The audit committee of an issuer may delegate to 1 or more designated members of the audit committee who are independent directors of the board of directors, the authority to grant preapprovals required by this subsection. The decisions of any member to whom authority is delegated under this paragraph to preapprove an activity under this subsection shall be presented to the full audit committee at each of its scheduled meetings.

(4) APPROVAL OF AUDIT SERVICES FOR OTHER PURPOSES—In carrying out its duties under subsection (m)(2), if the audit committee of an issuer approves an audit service within the scope of the engagement of the auditor, such audit service shall be deemed to have been preapproved for purposes of this subsection.[25]

## *Section 203—Audit Partner Rotation*

Section 10A of the Securities Exchange Act of 1934 (15 U.S.C. 78j-1), as amended by this Act, is amended by adding at the end the following:

(j) AUDIT PARTNER ROTATION—It shall be unlawful for a registered public accounting firm to provide audit services to an issuer if the lead (or coordinating) audit partner (having primary responsibility for the audit), or the audit partner

---

[25] Ibid., Sec. 202.

responsible for reviewing the audit, has performed audit services for that issuer in each of the 5 previous fiscal years of that issuer.[26]

## Section 204—Auditors' Reports to Audit Committees

Section 10A of the Securities Exchange Act of 1934 (15 U.S.C. 78j-1), as amended by this Act, is amended by adding at the end the following:

(k) REPORTS TO AUDIT COMMITTEES—Each registered public accounting firm that performs for any issuer any audit required by this title shall timely report to the audit committee of the issuer—

(1) all critical accounting policies and practices to be used;

(2) all alternative treatments of financial information within generally accepted accounting principles that have been discussed with management officials of the issuer, ramifications of the use of such alternative disclosures and treatments, and the treatment preferred by the registered public accounting firm; and

(3) other material written communications between the registered public accounting firm and the management of the issuer, such as any management letter or schedule of unadjusted differences.[27]

## Section 206—Conflicts of Interest

Section 10A of the Securities Exchange Act of 1934 (15 U.S.C. 78j-1), as amended by this Act, is amended by adding at the end the following:

(l) CONFLICTS OF INTEREST—It shall be unlawful for a registered public accounting firm to perform for an issuer any audit service required by this title, if a chief executive officer, controller, chief financial officer, chief accounting officer, or any person serving in an equivalent position for the issuer, was employed by that registered independent public accounting firm and participated in any capacity in the audit of that issuer during the 1-year period preceding the date of the initiation of the audit.[28]

## Section 403—Disclosure of Transactions Involving Management and Principal Stockholders

(a) AMENDMENT—Section 16 of the Securities Exchange Act of 1934 (15 U.S.C. 78p) is amended by striking the heading of such section and subsection (a) and inserting the following:

**SEC. 16. DIRECTORS, OFFICERS, AND PRINCIPAL STOCKHOLDERS.**

(a) DISCLOSURES REQUIRED—

(1) DIRECTORS, OFFICERS, AND PRINCIPAL STOCKHOLDERS REQUIRED TO FILE—Every person who is directly or indirectly the beneficial owner of more than 10 percent of any class of any equity security (other than an exempted security) which is registered pursuant to section 12, or who is a director or an officer of the issuer of such security, shall file the statements

---

[26] Ibid., Sec. 203.

[27] Ibid., Sec. 204.

[28] Ibid., Sec. 206.

required by this subsection with the Commission (and, if such security is registered on a national securities exchange, also with the exchange).

(2) TIME OF FILING—The statements required by this subsection shall be filed—

(A) at the time of the registration of such security on a national securities exchange or by the effective date of a registration statement filed pursuant to section 12(g);

(B) within 10 days after he or she becomes such beneficial owner, director, or officer;

(C) if there has been a change in such ownership, or if such person shall have purchased or sold a security-based swap agreement (as defined in section 206(b) of the Gramm-Leach-Bliley Act (15 U.S.C. 78c note)) involving such equity security, before the end of the second business day following the day on which the subject transaction has been executed, or at such other time as the Commission shall establish, by rule, in any case in which the Commission determines that such 2-day period is not feasible.

(3) CONTENTS OF STATEMENTS—A statement filed—

(A) under subparagraph (A) or (B) of paragraph (2) shall contain a statement of the amount of all equity securities of such issuer of which the filing person is the beneficial owner; and

(B) under subparagraph (C) of such paragraph shall indicate ownership by the filing person at the date of filing, any such changes in such ownership, and such purchases and sales of the security-based swap agreements as have occurred since the most recent filing under such subparagraph.

(4) ELECTRONIC FILING AND AVAILABILITY—Beginning not later than 1 year after the date of enactment of the Sarbanes-Oxley Act of 2002—

(A) a statement filed under subparagraph (C) of paragraph (2) shall be filed electronically;

(B) the Commission shall provide each such statement on a publicly accessible Internet site not later than the end of the business day following that filing; and

(C) the issuer (if the issuer maintains a corporate Web site) shall provide that statement on that corporate Web site, not later than the end of the business day following that filing.

(b) EFFECTIVE DATE—The amendment made by this section shall be effective 30 days after the date of the enactment of this Act.[29]

## Section 404—Management Assessment of Internal Controls

(a) RULES REQUIRED—The Commission shall prescribe rules requiring each annual report required by section 13(a) or 15(d) of the Securities Exchange Act of 1934 (15 U.S.C. 78m or 78o(d)) to contain an internal control report, which shall—

(1) state the responsibility of management for establishing and maintaining an adequate internal control structure and procedures for financial reporting; and

---

[29] Ibid., Sec. 403.

(2) contain an assessment, as of the end of the most recent fiscal year of the issuer, of the effectiveness of the internal control structure and procedures of the issuer for financial reporting.

(b) INTERNAL CONTROL EVALUATION AND REPORTING—With respect to the internal control assessment required by subsection (a), each registered public accounting firm that prepares or issues the audit report for the issuer shall attest to, and report on, the assessment made by the management of the issuer. An attestation made under this subsection shall be made in accordance with standards for attestation engagements issued or adopted by the Board. Any such attestation shall not be the subject of a separate engagement.[30]

To better understand the requirements of Section 404 and how it is being implemented in practice, both by management and by external auditors, it is valuable to refer to the Public Company Accounting Oversight Board (PCAOB) Auditing Standard No. 5: *An Audit of Internal Control Over Financial Reporting That Is Integrated with An Audit of Financial Statements* that was issued on June 12, 2007 (replacing the earlier PCAOB AS No. 2), and the PCAOB's 2009 Staff View, *An Audit of Internal Control Over Financial Reporting That Is Integrated with An Audit of Financial Statements: Guidance for Auditors of Smaller Public Companies*. (Available via free download from www.pcaobus.org.)

### Section 406—Code of Ethics for Senior Financial Officers

(a) CODE OF ETHICS DISCLOSURE—The Commission shall issue rules to require each issuer, together with periodic reports required pursuant to section 13(a) or 15(d) of the Securities Exchange Act of 1934, to disclose whether or not, and if not, the reason therefor, such issuer has adopted a code of ethics for senior financial officers, applicable to its principal financial officer and comptroller or principal accounting officer, or persons performing similar functions.

(b) CHANGES IN CODES OF ETHICS—The Commission shall revise its regulations concerning matters requiring prompt disclosure on Form 8-K (or any successor thereto) to require the immediate disclosure, by means of the filing of such form, dissemination by the Internet or by other electronic means, by any issuer of any change in or waiver of the code of ethics for senior financial officers.

(c) DEFINITION—In this section, the term "code of ethics" means such standards as are reasonably necessary to promote—

(1) honest and ethical conduct, including the ethical handling of actual or apparent conflicts of interest between personal and professional relationships;

(2) full, fair, accurate, timely, and understandable disclosure in the periodic reports required to be filed by the issuer; and

(3) compliance with applicable governmental rules and regulations.

(d) DEADLINE FOR RULEMAKING—The Commission shall—

(1) propose rules to implement this section, not later than 90 days after the date of enactment of this Act; and

(2) issue final rules to implement this section, not later than 180 days after that date of enactment.[31]

---

[30] Ibid., Sec. 404.
[31] Ibid., Sec. 406.

***The Monitoring Function***   Obviously, the audit committee cannot participate in the accounting and auditing functions on a day-to-day basis, because such a task is contrary to its overall purpose. However, since the board of directors has the ultimate responsibility for these functions, the audit directors should monitor the corporation's activities based on their jurisdiction. The monitoring function should be administered so that the planning function is accomplished. Consequently, the committee can assist the board by obtaining information from the accounting and auditing executives in order to discharge the board's responsibility. The consensus seems to be that the audit directors should monitor:

- The internal auditing function
- The internal control system and related business risks
- The financial reporting disclosures
- Conflicts of interest, ethics audit, and fraud audit activities
- Corporate perquisites
- Corporate contributions
- Information technology systems
- Other tasks as requested by the board

In administering the monitoring function, it may be advisable for the committee to retain necessary professional expertise, such as the corporation's outside legal counsel or outside data processing experts. In this connection, COSO's 2009, *Guidance on Monitoring Internal Control Systems* also provides useful perspectives on how the Board plays a critical role in monitoring activities and follow-up. (See www.coso.org/guidance.htm.)

### Section 806—Protection for Employees of Publicly Traded Companies Who Provide Evidence of Fraud

(a) IN GENERAL—Chapter 73 of title 18, United States Code, is amended by inserting after section 1514 the following:

Sec. 1514A. Civil action to protect against retaliation in fraud cases

(a) WHISTLEBLOWER PROTECTION FOR EMPLOYEES OF PUBLICLY TRADED COMPANIES—No company with a class of securities registered under section 12 of the Securities Exchange Act of 1934 (15 U.S.C. 78l), or that is required to file reports under section 15(d) of the Securities Exchange Act of 1934 (15 U.S.C. 78o (d))), or any officer, employee, contractor, subcontractor, or agent of such company, may discharge, demote, suspend, threaten, harass, or in any other manner discriminate against an employee in the terms and conditions of employment because of any lawful act done by the employee—

(1) to provide information, cause information to be provided, or otherwise assist in an investigation regarding any conduct which the employee reasonably believes constitutes a violation of section 1341, 1343, 1344, or 1348, any rule or regulation of the Securities and Exchange Commission, or any provision of Federal law relating to fraud against shareholders, when the information or assistance is provided to or the investigation is conducted by—

(A) a Federal regulatory or law enforcement agency;

(B) any Member of Congress or any committee of Congress; or

(C) a person with supervisory authority over the employee (or such other person working for the employer who has the authority to investigate, discover, or terminate misconduct); or

(2) to file, cause to be filed, testify, participate in, or otherwise assist in a proceeding filed or about to be filed (with any knowledge of the employer) relating to an alleged violation of section 1341, 1343, 1344, or 1348, any rule or regulation of the Securities and Exchange Commission, or any provision of Federal law relating to fraud against shareholders.

(b) ENFORCEMENT ACTION—

1. IN GENERAL—A person who alleges discharge or other discrimination by any person in violation of subsection (a) may seek relief under subsection (c), by—

   (A) filing a complaint with the Secretary of Labor; or

   (B) if the Secretary has not issued a final decision within 180 days of the filing of the complaint and there is no showing that such delay is due to the bad faith of the claimant, bringing an action at law or equity for de novo review in the appropriate district court of the United States, which shall have jurisdiction over such an action without regard to the amount in controversy.

2. PROCEDURE—

   (C) IN GENERAL—An action under paragraph (1)(A) shall be governed under the rules and procedures set forth in section 42121(b) of title 49, United States Code.

   (D) EXCEPTION—Notification made under section 42121(b)(1) of title 49, United States Code, shall be made to the person named in the complaint and to the employer.

   (E) BURDENS OF PROOF—An action brought under paragraph (1)(B) shall be governed by the legal burdens of proof set forth in section 42121(b) of title 49, United States Code.

   (F) STATUTE OF LIMITATIONS—An action under paragraph (1) shall be commenced not later than 90 days after the date on which the violation occurs.

(c) REMEDIES—

1. IN GENERAL—An employee prevailing in any action under subsection (b)(1) shall be entitled to all relief necessary to make the employee whole.

2. COMPENSATORY DAMAGES—Relief for any action under paragraph (1) shall include—

   (A) reinstatement with the same seniority status that the employee would have had, but for the discrimination;

   (B) the amount of back pay, with interest; and

   (C) compensation for any special damages sustained as a result of the discrimination, including litigation costs, expert witness fees, and reasonable attorney fees.

3. RIGHTS RETAINED BY EMPLOYEE—Nothing in this section shall be deemed to diminish the rights, privileges, or remedies of any employee

under any Federal or State law, or under any collective bargaining agreement.

(b) CLERICAL AMENDMENT—The table of sections at the beginning of chapter 73 of title 18, United States Code, is amended by inserting after the item relating to section 1514 the following new item:

"1514A. Civil action to protect against retaliation in fraud cases."[32]

## Section 303—Improper Influence on Conducts of Audits

(a) RULES TO PROHIBIT—It shall be unlawful, in contravention of such rules or regulations as the Commission shall prescribe as necessary and appropriate in the public interest or for the protection of investors, for any officer or director of an issuer, or any other person acting under the direction thereof, to take any action to fraudulently influence, coerce, manipulate, or mislead any independent public or certified accountant engaged in the performance of an audit of the financial statements of that issuer for the purpose of rendering such financial statements materially misleading.

(b) ENFORCEMENT—In any civil proceeding, the Commission shall have exclusive authority to enforce this section and any rule or regulation issued under this section.

(c) NO PREEMPTION OF OTHER LAW—The provisions of subsection (a) shall be in addition to, and shall not supersede or preempt, any other provision of law or any rule or regulation issued thereunder.

(d) DEADLINE FOR RULEMAKING—The Commission shall—

(1) propose the rules or regulations required by this section, not later than 90 days after the date of enactment of this Act; and

(2) issue final rules or regulations required by this section, not later than 270 days after that date of enactment.[33]

## Section 402—Enhanced Conflict of Interest Provisions

(a) PROHIBITION ON PERSONAL LOANS TO EXECUTIVES—Section 13 of the Securities Exchange Act of 1934 (15 U.S.C. 78m), as amended by this Act, is amended by adding at the end the following:

(k) PROHIBITION ON PERSONAL LOANS TO EXECUTIVES—

(1) IN GENERAL—It shall be unlawful for any issuer (as defined in section 2 of the Sarbanes-Oxley Act of 2002), directly or indirectly, including through any subsidiary, to extend or maintain credit, to arrange for the extension of credit, or to renew an extension of credit, in the form of a personal loan to or for any director or executive officer (or equivalent thereof) of that issuer. An extension of credit maintained by the issuer on the date of enactment of this subsection shall not be subject to the provisions of this subsection, provided that there is no material modification to any term of any such extension of credit or any renewal of any such extension of credit on or after that date of enactment.

(2) LIMITATION—Paragraph (1) does not preclude any home improvement and manufactured home loans (as that term is defined in section 5 of the Home

---

[32] Ibid., Sec. 806.
[33] Ibid., Sec. 303.

Owners' Loan Act (12 U.S.C. 1464)), consumer credit (as defined in section 103 of the Truth in Lending Act (15 U.S.C. 1602)), or any extension of credit under an open end credit plan (as defined in section 127(c)(4)(e) of the Truth in Lending Act (15 U.S.C. 1637(c)(4)(e)), or any extension of credit by a broker or dealer registered under section 15 of this title to an employee of that broker or dealer to buy, trade, or carry securities, that is permitted under rules or regulations of the Board of Governors of the Federal Reserve System pursuant to section 7 of this title (other than an extension of credit that would be used to purchase stock of that issuer), that is—

> (A) made or provided in the ordinary course of the consumer credit business of such issuer;

> (B) of a type that is generally made available by such issuer to the public; and

> (C) made by such issuer on market terms, or terms that are no more favorable than those offered by the issuer to the general public for such extensions of credit.

(3) RULE OF CONSTRUCTION FOR CERTAIN LOANS—Paragraph (1) does not apply to any loan made or maintained by an insured depository institution (as defined in section 3 of the Federal Deposit Insurance Act (12 U.S.C. 1813)), if the loan is subject to the insider lending restrictions of section 22(h) of the Federal Reserve Act (12 U.S.C. 375b)."[34]

With respect to the internal audit function, the NYSE's proposed listing standards (Section 303A(7)(e)) provide that:

> Each listed company must have an internal audit function.

> Commentary: Listed companies must maintain an internal audit function to provide management and the audit committee with ongoing assessments of the company's risk management processes and system of internal control. A company may choose to outsource this function to a firm other than its independent auditor.[35]

***The Reporting Function*[36]** The audit committee should report directly to the board of directors—not to the chief executive officer. Since the members are independent or nonmanagement directors, they provide an objective appraisal of management's accounting and auditing performance. Furthermore, the reporting function is related directly to both the planning and monitoring functions. The general content of the audit directors' report should be based on the review programs regarding the planning function. Although the minutes of the committee meetings are a record of the proceedings, the nature of its function warrants a formal report. The report should contain a summary of its findings and recommendations with the appropriate figures and narrative remarks. In developing the reports for the board, the committee should focus its attention on the board's interests in such matters as the following:

---

[34] Ibid., Sec. 402.

[35] Securities and Exchange Commission, Release No. 34-47672; File No. SR-NYSE-2002-33, Proposed Rule Change Relating to Corporate Governance (Washington, DC: SEC, April 11, 2003), 13.

[36] For further discussion, see Chapter 14.

- The financial accounting policies and the related industry accounting practices (e.g., depreciation methods, inventory pricing, basis for consolidation)
- The reports of the independent auditors and the internal auditors (e.g., the auditors' opinion on the system of internal control)
- The reports of legal counsel with respect to significant commitments, contingencies, and governmental compliance
- The reports of a special investigation concerning the review of the corporation's financial affairs, such as political contributions

In short, the report of the audit committee may vary in form; however, the committee should render a concise report that fulfills the needs and interests of the board.

### *Section 302—Corporate Responsibility for Financial Reports*

(a) REGULATIONS REQUIRED—The Commission shall, by rule, require, for each company filing periodic reports under section 13(a) or 15(d) of the Securities Exchange Act of 1934 (15 U.S.C. 78m, 78o(d)), that the principal executive officer or officers and the principal financial officer or officers, or persons performing similar functions, certify in each annual or quarterly report filed or submitted under either such section of such Act that—

(1) the signing officer has reviewed the report;

(2) based on the officer's knowledge, the report does not contain any untrue statement of a material fact or omit to state a material fact necessary in order to make the statements made, in light of the circumstances under which such statements were made, not misleading;

(3) based on such officer's knowledge, the financial statements, and other financial information included in the report, fairly present in all material respects the financial condition and results of operations of the issuer as of, and for, the periods presented in the report;

(4) the signing officers—

(A) are responsible for establishing and maintaining internal controls;

(B) have designed such internal controls to ensure that material information relating to the issuer and its consolidated subsidiaries is made known to such officers by others within those entities, particularly during the period in which the periodic reports are being prepared;

(C) have evaluated the effectiveness of the issuer's internal controls as of a date within 90 days prior to the report; and

(D) have presented in the report their conclusions about the effectiveness of their internal controls based on their evaluation as of that date;

(5) the signing officers have disclosed to the issuer's auditors and the audit committee of the board of directors (or persons fulfilling the equivalent function)—

(A) all significant deficiencies in the design or operation of internal controls which could adversely affect the issuer's ability to record, process, summarize, and report financial data and have identified for the issuer's auditors any material weaknesses in internal controls; and

(B)  any fraud, whether or not material, that involves management or other employees who have a significant role in the issuer's internal controls; and

(6) the signing officers have indicated in the report whether or not there were significant changes in internal controls or in other factors that could significantly affect internal controls subsequent to the date of their evaluation, including any corrective actions with regard to significant deficiencies and material weaknesses.

(b) FOREIGN REINCORPORATIONS HAVE NO EFFECT—Nothing in this section 302 shall be interpreted or applied in any way to allow any issuer to lessen the legal force of the statement required under this section 302, by an issuer having reincorporated or having engaged in any other transaction that resulted in the transfer of the corporate domicile or offices of the issuer from inside the United States to outside of the United States.

(c) DEADLINE—The rules required by subsection (a) shall be effective not later than 30 days after the date of enactment of this act.[37]

## Section 906—Corporate Responsibility for Financial Reports

(a) IN GENERAL—Chapter 63 of title 18, United States Code, is amended by inserting after section 1349, as created by this Act, the following:

Sec. 1350. Failure of corporate officers to certify financial reports

(a) CERTIFICATION OF PERIODIC FINANCIAL REPORTS—Each periodic report containing financial statements filed by an issuer with the Securities Exchange Commission pursuant to section 13(a) or 15(d) of the Securities Exchange Act of 1934 (15 U.S.C. 78m(a) or 78o(d)) shall be accompanied by a written statement by the chief executive officer and chief financial officer (or equivalent thereof) of the issuer.

(b) CONTENT—The statement required under subsection (a) shall certify that the periodic report containing the financial statements fully complies with the requirements of section 13(a) or 15(d) of the Securities Exchange Act of 1934 (15 U.S.C. 78m or 78o(d)) and that information contained in the periodic report fairly presents, in all material respects, the financial condition and results of operations of the issuer.

(c) CRIMINAL PENALTIES—Whoever—

(1) certifies any statement as set forth in subsections (a) and (b) of this section knowing that the periodic report accompanying the statement does not comport with all the requirements set forth in this section shall be fined not more than $1,000,000 or imprisoned not more than 10 years, or both; or

(2) willfully certifies any statement as set forth in subsections (a) and (b) of this section knowing that the periodic report accompanying the statement does not comport with all the requirements set forth in this section shall be fined not more than $5,000,000, or imprisoned not more than 20 years, or both.

(b) CLERICAL AMENDMENT—The table of sections at the beginning of chapter 63 of title 18, United States Code, is amended by adding at the end the following:

1350. Failure of corporate officers to certify financial reports.[38]

---

[37] Sarbanes-Oxley Act of 2002, H.R. Rep. No. 107-610, July 25, 2002.
[38] Ibid., Sec. 906.

See Chapter 9 (especially the Reporting Requirements section and Exhibits 8.3–8.4) for further discussion of the quarterly certification and annual assertion requirements under Sarbanes-Oxley.

## Section 401: Disclosure of Periodic Reports

(a) DISCLOSURES REQUIRED—Section 13 of the Securities Exchange Act of 1934 (15 U.S.C. 78m) is amended by adding at the end the following:

(i) ACCURACY OF FINANCIAL REPORTS—Each financial report that contains financial statements, and that is required to be prepared in accordance with (or reconciled to) generally accepted accounting principles under this title and filed with the Commission shall reflect all material correcting adjustments that have been identified by a registered public accounting firm in accordance with generally accepted accounting principles and the rules and regulations of the Commission.

(j) OFF-BALANCE SHEET TRANSACTIONS—Not later than 180 days after the date of enactment of the Sarbanes-Oxley Act of 2002, the Commission shall issue final rules providing that each annual and quarterly financial report required to be filed with the Commission shall disclose all material off-balance sheet transactions, arrangements, obligations (including contingent obligations), and other relationships of the issuer with unconsolidated entities or other persons, that may have a material current or future effect on financial condition, changes in financial condition, results of operations, liquidity, capital expenditures, capital resources, or significant components of revenues or expenses.

(b) COMMISSION RULES ON PRO FORMA FIGURES—Not later than 180 days after the date of enactment of the Sarbanes-Oxley Act of 2002, the Commission shall issue final rules providing that pro forma financial information included in any periodic or other report filed with the Commission pursuant to the securities laws, or in any public disclosure or press or other release, shall be presented in a manner that—

(1) does not contain an untrue statement of a material fact or omit to state a material fact necessary in order to make the pro forma financial information, in light of the circumstances under which it is presented, not misleading; and

(2) reconciles it with the financial condition and results of operation of the issuer under generally accepted accounting principles.

(c) STUDY AND REPORT ON SPECIAL PURPOSES ENTITIES—

(1) STUDY REQUIRED—The Commission shall, not later than 1 year after the effective date of adoption of off-balance sheet disclosure rules required by section 13(j) of the Securities Exchange Act of 1934, as added by this section, completes a study of filings by issuers and their disclosures to determine—

(A) the extent of off-balance sheet transactions, including assets, liabilities, leases, losses, and the use of special purpose entities; and

(B) whether generally accepted accounting rules result in financial statements of issuers reflecting the economics of such off-balance sheet transactions to investors in a transparent fashion.

(2) REPORT AND RECOMMENDATIONS—Not later than 6 months after the date of completion of the study required by paragraph (1), the Commission shall

submit a report to the President, the Committee on Banking, Housing, and Urban Affairs of the Senate, and the Committee on Financial Services of the House of Representatives, setting forth—

(A) the amount or an estimate of the amount of off-balance sheet transactions, including assets, liabilities, leases, and losses of, and the use of special purpose entities by, issuers filing periodic reports pursuant to section 13 or 15 of the Securities Exchange Act of 1934;

(B) the extent to which special purpose entities are used to facilitate off-balance sheet transactions;

(C) whether generally accepted accounting principles or the rules of the Commission result in financial statements of issuers reflecting the economics of such transactions to investors in a transparent fashion;

(D) whether generally accepted accounting principles specifically result in the consolidation of special purpose entities sponsored by an issuer in cases in which the issuer has the majority of the risks and rewards of the special purpose entity; and

(E) any recommendations of the Commission for improving the transparency and quality of reporting off-balance sheet transactions in the financial statements and disclosures required to be filed by an issuer with the Commission.[39]

In this regard, it may be useful to access both the AICPA's Audit Committee Effectiveness Center (available at www.aicpa.org/audcommctr/homepage.htm) and the Center for Audit Quality (CAQ) (www.thecaq.org/). Both of these Web sites contain useful resources and references to current materials that are directly relevant to members of audit committees.

### Section 409—Real-Time Issuer Disclosures

Section 13 of the Securities Exchange Act of 1934 (15 U.S.C. 78m), as amended by this Act is amended by adding at the end the following:

(l) REAL TIME ISSUER DISCLOSURES—Each issuer reporting under section 13 (a) or 15(d) shall disclose to the public on a rapid and current basis such additional information concerning material changes in the financial condition or operations of the issuer, in plain English, which may include trend and qualitative information and graphic presentations, as the Commission determines, by rule, is necessary or useful for the protection of investors and in the public interest.[40]

### SEC Final Rules—Standards Relating to Listing Company Audit Committee

On April 9, 2003, the SEC issued a release that mandates changes in the SROs' listing standards. As directed by the Sarbanes-Oxley Act of 2002, the SEC issued a directive to the SROs to prohibit the listing of any security of an issuer that is not in compliance with the audit committee requirements mandated by the Sarbanes-Oxley Act. These requirements relate to the following matters:

---

[39] Ibid., Sec. 401.
[40] Ibid., Sec. 409.

- The independence of audit committee members
- The audit committee's responsibility to select and oversee the issuer's independent accountant
- Procedures for handling complaints regarding the issuer's accounting practices
- The authority of the audit committee to engage advisors
- Funding for the independent auditor and any outside advisors engaged by the audit committee[41]

**Audit Committee Member Independence**   In an effort to tighten the independence requirements for audit committee members, the SEC final rules contained two criteria:[42]

1. Audit committee members are barred from accepting any consulting, advisory, or other compensatory fee from the issuer or any subsidiary thereof, other than in the member's capacity as a member of the board of directors and any board committees.[43]
2. Audit committee members of an issuer that is not an investment company may not be an affiliated person of the issuer or any subsidiary of the issuer apart from his or her capacity as a member of the board and any board committee.[44]

**Responsibilities Relating to Registered Public Accounting Firms**   To increase investor confidence in the audit process, the SEC adopted the requirement that the audit committee of a listed issuer will be directly responsible for the appointment, compensation, retention, and oversight of the work of any registered public accounting firm engaged for the purpose of preparing or issuing an audit report or performing other audits, or review or attest services. The independent auditor will report directly to the audit committee.[45]

**Procedures for Handling Complaints**   Each audit committee must establish procedures for the following matters:

[41] Securities and Exchange Commission, Release No. 38-8220, Standards Relating to Listing Company Audit Committee (Washington, DC: SEC, April 9, 2003).

[42] For further information regarding the SRO's proposed additional standards, see SEC Release No. 34-47672.

[43] More specifically, disallowed payments to an audit committee member include payments made directly or indirectly. See SEC Release No. 33-8220 for examples of relationships. Also, a de minimis exception for independence is nonexistent and will be removed from the listing requirements.

[44] The SEC defines "affiliate" and "affiliated person" as a person who directly or indirectly, through one or more intermediaries, controls, or is controlled by, or is under common control with, the person specified. Under the final rule, only executive officers, directors who are also employees of an affiliate, general partner, and managing members of an affiliate will be deemed to be affiliates. Moreover, the limitation on directors will exclude outside directors of an affiliate as well as individuals with passive, noncontrol positions, and nonpolicymaking functions. For further information on investment company issuers and new issuers, see the aforementioned release number.

[45] With respect to clarifications regarding possible conflicts with other requirements, see the release for such matters as the application of noncountry laws or listing requirements for the appointment of laws or listing requirements for the appointment of the independent auditors. However, if the issuer provides a recommendation or nomination for the independent auditors, then the audit committee (or body performing similar functions) must be responsible for making the recommendation on nomination.

- The receipt, retention, and treatment of complaints received by the issuer regarding accounting, internal controls, or auditing matters
- The confidential, anonymous submission by employees of the issuer of concerns regarding questionable accounting or auditing matters
- The SEC pointed out that audit committees should be provided with flexibility to develop and utilize procedures appropriate for their circumstances.

**Authority to Engage Advisors**  The SEC's final rule requires that audit committees have authority to engage outside advisors, including accounting and legal experts. This rule supports the SEC's position that the audit committee must have the necessary resources to fulfill its function.

**Funding**  The SEC's final rule on funding requires the issuer to provide for payment of compensation to the following:

- Any registered public accounting firm engaged for the purpose of preparing or issuing an audit report or performing other audit, review, or attest services
- Any advisor employed by the audit committee

The final rule does not set funding limits. Finally, the final rule provides that the issuer must provide funding for the ordinary administrative expenses of the audit committee.

**Compliance and Curing Defects**  In addition to the listing or delisting requirement, for issuers not in compliance with the standards, the SEC adopted a final rule stating that the SROs must require a listed issuer to notify the applicable SRO of any material noncompliance with the audit committee requirements.

With respect to the SEC's final rule on curing defects, the SROs are required to establish procedures before they prohibit the listing of or delist any security of an issuer. The SEC believes that the SRO's existing continued listing procedures will suffice.[46]

**Disclosure Changes Regarding Audit Committees—Disclosure Regarding Exemptions**  The SEC requires issuers to disclose their reliance on an exemption and their assessment of whether, and if so how, such reliance will materially adversely affect the ability of their audit committee to act independently and to satisfy the other requirements. Such disclosure will need to appear in, or be incorporated by reference into, annual reports filed with the Commission. The disclosure also will need to appear in proxy statements or information statements for shareholders' meetings at which elections for directors are held.[47]

**Identification of the Audit Committee in Annual Reports**  In an effort to readily determine basic information about the composition of a listed issuer's

---

[46] See the text of the release regarding rare situations that may occur when the audit committee member ceases to be independent as well as SRO implanting rules.

[47] The SEC's final rule on listed issuers that are not required to provide disclosure on their reliance on one of the exemptions to the rule, such as a subsidiary relying on multiple listing exemption, a foreign government issuer, or an asset-backed issuer are excluded from the requirement to disclose, whether they have a separate audit committee or not.

audit committee, the SEC requires that the disclosure of audit committee members be included or incorporated by reference in the issuer's annual report. Additionally, if a listed issuer does not have an audit committee, then it must disclose that the entire board of directors is acting as the audit committee.

**Updates to Existing Audit Committee Disclosure**    Regarding the independence disclosure for audit committees, all national exchanges and national securities associations will need to have independence standards for audit committee members, not just the NYSE, AMEX, and NASDAQ.

Nonlisted issuers that have separately designated audit committees will still be required to disclose whether their audit committee members are independent. Such issuers may choose any definition for audit committee independence of a national securities exchange or national securities association that has been approved by the Commission.

## THE EXTERNAL AND INTERNAL AUDITING PROCESS

### The Nature of External Auditing

External auditing is the process not only of examining the financial statements but also of testing the underlying accounting records of the company. The examination is conducted by the independent auditors, who express an objective opinion regarding the fairness of presentation of the financial statements. The audit examination is conducted within a predetermined set of generally accepted auditing standards that are promulgated by the Auditing Standards Board, formerly named the Auditing Standards Executive Committee of the American Institute of Certified Public Accountants (AICPA).[48] Since the audit examination is performed by certified public accountants (CPAs) who are independent of the company's management, the objective opinion of the independent auditing firm strengthens the reliability and credibility of the company's financial reporting practices.

More specifically, corporate management has full responsibility for the financial statements because such statements represent a report on management's stewardship accountability to its outside constituencies. The Auditing Standards Board of the AICPA asserts:

> The financial statements are management's responsibility. The auditor's responsibility is to express an opinion on the financial statements. Management is responsible for adopting sound accounting policies and for establishing and maintaining internal control that will, among other things, record, process, summarize, and report transactions (as well as events and conditions) consistent with management's assertions embodied in the financial statements. The entity's transactions and the related assets, liabilities, and equity are within the direct knowledge and control of management. The auditor's knowledge of these matters and internal control is limited to that acquired through the audit. Thus, the fair presentation of financial statements in conformity with

---

[48] As noted in Chapter 13, the name of this committee has been changed to the Auditing Standards Board. However, the former name of this group will be used in connection with the appropriate Statements on Auditing Standards as discussed in the text.

generally accepted accounting principles is an implicit and integral part of management's responsibility. The independent auditor may make suggestions about the form or content of the financial statements or draft them, in whole or in part, based on information from management during the performance of the audit. However, the auditor's responsibility for the financial statements he or she has audited is confined to the expression of his or her opinion on them.[49]

**Role of the Audit Committee**    The work of the audit committee and the independent auditors is very closely related because both groups have common objectives regarding the financial affairs. The audit committee members are responsible for overseeing the independent audit examination as well as the recommendations of the independent auditors. The audit committee members must assure themselves that the financial statements and the system of internal accounting controls are based on acceptable accounting principles and procedures. Moreover, they need assurance that the executives and their staff are reasonably competent and trustworthy.

Although the extent of the audit committee's activities has led to some controversy, it is clearly evident that its effectiveness has been increased by the U.S. Securities and Exchange Commission, the U.S. Congress (FDICIA, Sarbanes-Oxley Act of 2002), and other private-sector initiatives (National Commission on Fraudulent Financial Reporting, the MacDonald Commission (Canada), and the Cadbury Committee, Hampel Committee, and Committee on Corporate Governance (U.K.), as well as self-regulatory organizations. The reality of the situation is that the Foreign Corrupt Practices Act, the Private Securities Litigation Reform Act, and the aforementioned initiatives place greater responsibilities on the audit committee. For this reason, it is important that the committee keep a perspective and focus on its oversight role for the system of internal control and financial reporting areas of the company. If the audit committee becomes too deeply involved in management's operational activities, its effectiveness will be diluted.

In a survey dealing with the effectiveness of audit committees as perceived by both external auditors and audit committee members of 34 publicly held companies, Lawrence P. Kalbers found that practicing audit committees are not uniformly effective and that, with respect to responsibilities, attributes, and effectiveness, the auditors rate committee members significantly lower than members do. He concludes that the audit committee, management, and auditors need to work toward the right balance of the committee's involvement with audit fees, audit scope, audit results, and internal controls. He believes that training and educating the committee members can help them meet their responsibilities.[50]

---

[49] AICPA, *Professional Standards, U.S. Auditing Standards/Attestation Standards*, vol. 1 (New York: AICPA, 2003), AU Sec. 110.03.

[50] Lawrence P. Kalbers, "An Examination of the Relationship between Audit Committees and External Auditors," *Ohio CPA Journal* 51, no. 6 (December 1992): 27. Similarly, Price Waterhouse noted: "The single most important findings, and the key to audit committee effectiveness, is: background information and training." See The Institute of Internal Auditor's, *Improving Audit Committee Performance: What Works Best* (Altamonte Springs, FL: IIA, 1993), p. 2. For further discussion on training and educating audit committee members, see Chapter 5 and Chapter 7 of the second edition, 2000.

## The Nature of Internal Auditing

As defined by the Institute of Internal Auditors:

> Internal auditing is an independent, objective assurance and consulting activity designed to add value and improve an organization's operations. It helps an organization accomplish its objectives by bringing a systematic, disciplined approach to evaluate and improve the effectiveness of risk management, control, and governance processes.[51]

For example, internal auditors may evaluate the internal control of a company as well as review management's adherence to the company's policies. They can also help the audit committee with special investigations and compliance audits.

However, it is important to recognize that the internal auditing group is not completely independent from corporate management because the members of the group are employees of the company. To strengthen their independence and objectivity, the Institute of Internal Auditors recommends that the chief audit executive should be responsible to an individual whose authority is sufficient to promote independence and provide the necessary internal auditing coverage.[52]

***Role of the Audit Committee***   The interface between the audit committee and the internal auditing group provides a logical relationship because these groups have common goals.[53] It is important that both groups establish a working relationship that is not counterproductive. The internal audit function and its reporting relationship is discussed more extensively in Chapters 7 and 9.

As noted in Chapter 1, audit committees have become a key institution in the corporate accountability process. Given the Congressional enactment of the Sarbanes-Oxley Act of 2002, many audit committee-related guidelines of professional and regulatory organizations have become law. Thus the role and responsibilities of audit committees are now dealt with in a federal statute by which such committees measure their performance.

To assist audit committees with their roles and responsibilities, Exhibit 2.2 contains a summary of the sections of the Sarbanes-Oxley Act, SRO's listing standards, and SEC final rules on audit committee disclosures. Clearly, boards of directors and their audit committees need to reexamine and update their charters to reflect the laws and regulations. Exhibit 2.3 discusses an approach to continuous improvement for audit committees.

---

[51] Institute of Internal Auditors, *The Professional Practice Framework* (Altamonte Springs, FL: IIA, 2009), p. 3.

[52] Institute of Internal Auditors, *Professional Practice Framework*, 7.

[53] For further discussion of the audit committee's role, see *Internal Auditing and the Audit Committee: Working Together toward Common Goals* (Altamonte Springs, FL: IIA, 1987); and Barbara A. Apostolou and Raymond Jeffords, *Working with the Audit Committee* (Altamonte Springs, FL: IIA, 1990). Also see the video, *Audit Committees and Internal Auditing: An Essential Alliance for Effective Governance* (Altamonte Springs, FL.: IIA, 1994), and Timothy J. Fogarty, Organizational and Economic Explanations of Audit Committee Oversight (*Journal of Managerial Issues*, June, 1998).

**EXHIBIT 2.2**  Audit Committees Roles and Responsibilities under the Sarbanes-Oxley Act of 2002, SROs, and SEC

| Audit Committee Practice Area | Section[a] | Applicability | | |
| --- | --- | --- | --- | --- |
| | | SOA[a] | SROs[b] | SEC[c] |
| Organization of the audit committee | | | | |
| • Charter | | | ✔ | ✔ |
| • Membership | | | ✔ | ✔ |
| • Meetings | | | ✔ | |
| • Independence | 301 | ✔ | ✔ | ✔ |
| • Financial literacy/expertise | 407 | ✔ | ✔[f] | ✔[f] |
| **Activities** | | | | |
| Internal control | 404 | ✔ | ✔[d] | ✔ |
| Annual and interim financial statements, CEO/CFO certification | 302/906 | ✔ | ✔[d] | ✔ |
| Loans to directors or officers | 402 | ✔ | | |
| Corporate code of conduct | | | ✔ | |
| Code of ethics for CFOs | 406 | ✔ | | |
| **Auditors** | | | | |
| Internal auditors | | | ✔[d] | |
| External auditors | | | | |
| • Retention and fees | 301 | ✔ | ✔ | |
| • Hiring | 206 | ✔ | ✔[d] | |
| • Non-audit services | 202 | ✔ | ✔ | |
| • Auditor rotation | 203/207 | ✔ | ✔[d] | |
| • Disagreements | 301 | ✔ | ✔[d] | |
| • Critical accounting policies and disclosures | 204, 401, 409 | ✔ | ✔ | |
| **Communication** | | | | |
| • Opinions from legal counsel and other advisers | 301, 307 | ✔ | ✔ | |
| • Whistleblowing protection | 301, 307, 806 | ✔ | ✔[e] | |
| • Stock exchange listing requirements (annual certification) | | | ✔[d] | |
| • Stock exchange listing requirements (one-time certification) | | | ✔ | |
| • Education and training | | | ✔ | |

[a] Sarbanes-Oxley Act of 2002.
[b] NYSE, NASDAQ, AMEX Listing Standards.
[c] SEC Final Rules, Audit Committee Disclosures.
[d] NYSE Listing Standards only; see also SEC Release No. 34-47672.
[e] NASDAQ Listing Standards only.
[f] At least one member must have accounting or related financial management expertise.

**EXHIBIT 2.3**   Corporate Audit Committees: An Approach to Continuous Improvement

Audit committees today are faced with the sizable task of overseeing both the auditing and financial reporting processes. The final rules of the SEC, national stock exchanges, and the AICPA's Auditing Standards Board cover corporate governance of audit committees, including independence, qualifications, charters, external auditor involvement, and reports.

Nonetheless, it remains up to audit committees to ensure that they continuously improve their oversight role. Continuous improvement requires a constructive relationship between audit committees and management, internal auditors, external auditors, and legal counsel. Audit committees should function as team members and be empowered by their boards to ask tough-minded questions about the audit and financial reporting processes as well as to probe into the entity's affairs. Continuous improvement helps minimize the costs of achieving quality in both financial management services and audit services. Thus, boards of directors are assured that such resources are allocated efficiently and effectively to prevent the costs of poor quality in the board's corporate accountability process.

**Continuous improvement approach.** To achieve continuous improvement, audit committees should consider the following three-step approach:

(1) Complete a profile worksheet with details of the committee's role, responsibilities, and organization;
(2) Develop a customized review and action plan to achieve the committee's goals in the board-approved charter; and
(3) Develop a quality assurance review based on the elements that guide the committee in adopting quality assurance policies and procedures.

**Audit Committee's Profile Worksheet**

Audit committees are now required to disclose their written charter in the entity's annual proxy statement. This document provides a clear presentation of the committee's oversight role, responsibilities, and organization. It defines the jurisdictional charge to the committee, minimizing potential litigation risk as well as avoiding the dilution of the committee's activities. See Exhibit 2.3.1 for a suggested format for a profile worksheet.

Audit committees need knowledge about—

• the entity's business and industry,
• significant risks,
• internal control concepts,
• industry accounting practices, and
• complex business transactions.

Likewise, audit committees need to review the following:

• Industry and business data in terms of vulnerability of the industry to changing economic conditions and operating characteristics of the business. Such a review would usually include the annual stockholders' report, SEC filings, (10Qs, 10Ks, annual proxy statement), the entity's Web site, analytical review procedures, absolute data comparisons, and financial ratio data.
• Management's risk assessment process
• The components of COSO's Internal Control-Integrated Framework (control environment, risk assessment, information and communication, control activities, and monitoring)

**EXHIBIT 2.3.1**   Audit Committee's Profile Worksheet

| Services available from: | Management | Internal Auditors | External Auditors | Legal Counsel | Board of Directors | Compliance with SEC, SROs, ASB | |
|---|:---:|:---:|:---:|:---:|:---:|:---:|---|
| Audit Committee Practice Area | | | | | | | Comments |
| **Organizational Structure and Composition** | | | | | | | |
| **Formation*** | | | | | | | |
| **Membership** | | | | | | | |
|   Number of members (size) | | | | | ✔ | ✔ | |
|   Appointments | | | | | ✔ | | |
|   Term of Service | | | | | ✔ | | |
|   Qualification | | | | | ✔ | ✔ | |
|   Composition | | | | | ✔ | ✔ | |
| **Meetings** | | | | | | | |
|   Frequency | | | | | ✔ | | |
|   Type | | | | | ✔ | | |
| **Knowledge Areas** | | | | | | | |
|   Type of business and industry | ✔ | | | | | | |
|   Internal audit process | | ✔ | | | | | |
|   External audit process | | | ✔ | | | | |
|   Internal control concepts | | ✔ | ✔ | | | | |
|   Management's risk assessment | ✔ | ✔ | ✔ | | | | |
|   Industry accounting practices | ✔ | ✔ | ✔ | | | | |
|   Complex business transactions | ✔ | ✔ | ✔ | ✔ | | | |
|   Financial reporting process | ✔ | ✔ | ✔ | | | | |
|   Internal communication process** | ✔ | ✔ | ✔ | ✔ | ✔ | ✔ | |
|   External communication process | | | | | ✔ | ✔ | |

*Board resolution or corporate by-laws and a formal written charter.
**Related to the above areas.

- Industry accounting practices, with particular emphasis on the appropriateness of accounting principles
- Complex business transactions (e.g., restructuring charges and pre-acquisition audits).

Additionally, audit committees should perform a review in connection with other matters, such as:

- code of conduct;
- conflict of interest statements (related party transactions);
- corporate perquisites;
- computer security, business continuity plan, and planned systems modifications; and
- biographical information on senior management and financial management.

### Audit Committee's Action Plan

Based on the audit committee's profile worksheet, the chair can develop a customized review and action plan (Exhibit 2.3.2). This plan serves as an oversight compass for the financial management, audit, legal, and communication process.

**Financial management.** Responsibility for the integrity and objectivity of the information in financial reports rests with the entity's management. Audit committees should review background information on the competence and integrity of important members of the financial management group.

**EXHIBIT 2.3.2**   Audit Committee's Review and Action Plan

| Services available from: | Management | Internal Auditors | External Auditors | Legal Counsel | Board of Directors | Compliance with SEC, SROs, ASB | |
|---|---|---|---|---|---|---|---|
| **Audit Committee Practice Area** | | | | | | | **Comments** |
| **Agendas** | | | | | | | |
| **Pre-audit Meeting (Audit Scope)** | | | | | | | |
| Audit plan | ✔ | ✔ | ✔ | | | | |
| Analytical review | | | ✔ | | | | |
| Accounting and auditing developments | ✔ | ✔ | ✔ | | | | |
| Financial reporting matters | ✔ | ✔ | ✔ | | | | |
| Risk assessment | ✔ | ✔ | ✔ | | | | |

| Services available from: | Management | Internal Auditors | External Auditors | Legal Counsel | Board of Directors | Compliance with SEC, SROs, ASB | |
|---|---|---|---|---|---|---|---|
| Risk control processes | ✔ | ✔ | ✔ | | | | |
| **Interim meeting (optional)** | | | | | | | |
| Problem areas | ✔ | ✔ | ✔ | | | | |
| Audit progress | | | ✔ | | | | |
| **Post-audit Meeting** | | | | | | | |
| Audit findings | | ✔ | ✔ | | | | |
| Analytical review | | | | | | | |
| Annual financial statements | ✔ | | ✔ | | | | |
| SEC Form 10-K Report | ✔ | | ✔ | | | | |
| **Other Concerns** | | | | | | | |
| Unresolved matters | ✔ | ✔ | ✔ | ✔ | | | |
| Disagreements with management | | ✔ | ✔ | | | | |
| Significant audit adjustments | | ✔ | ✔ | | | | |
| Completeness of disclosure and risks and uncertainties | ✔ | ✔ | ✔ | ✔ | | | |
| Appropriateness of accounting policies | ✔ | ✔ | ✔ | | | | |
| Management's representations (client representation letter) | ✔ | | | ✔ | | | |
| Lawyer's letter | | | ✔ | ✔ | | | |
| **Follow-up Meeting** | | | | | | | |
| Management letter | ✔ | ✔ | ✔ | | | | |
| Evaluation of the external auditors | ✔ | ✔ | | | | | |
| Appointment of the external auditors | | | | | ✔ | | |

(*continued*)

**EXHIBIT 2.3.2** *(Continued)*

| Services available from: | Management | Internal Auditors | External Auditors | Legal Counsel | Board of Directors | Compliance with SEC, SROs, ASB | |
|---|---|---|---|---|---|---|---|
| Audit and non-audit fees | | | ✔ | | ✔ | ✔ | |
| Auditor's independence letter | | | ✔ | | | ✔ | |
| Evaluation of the internal auditors and selection or reappointment | ✔ | | ✔ | | | | |
| Internal audit plan for the next fiscal year | | ✔ | | | | | |
| Outsourcing activities | | ✔ | ✔ | | | | |
| Evaluation of financial management | | ✔ | ✔ | | | | |
| Compliance with laws and regulations (disclosure matters) | | | ✔ | ✔ | | | |
| Impact of proposed legislation on the financial statements | | | ✔ | ✔ | | | |
| **Other Matters** | | | | | | | |
| Special investigations | | | | ✔ | ✔ | | |
| Information technology (computer security, EDI, business continuity plan) | ✔ | ✔ | ✔ | | | | |
| **Conflict of Interest** | | | | | | | |
| Corporate perquisites (officers' expense accounts, etc.) | | ✔ | ✔ | ✔ | | | |
| Corporate contributions | ✔ | ✔ | ✔ | ✔ | | | |
| Code of conduct | ✔ | ✔ | | ✔ | | | |
| Related party transactions | ✔ | ✔ | ✔ | ✔ | | | |

| Services available from: | Management | Internal Auditors | External Auditors | Legal Counsel | Board of Directors | Compliance with SEC, SROs, ASB | |
|---|---|---|---|---|---|---|---|
| Illegal, improper or sensitive payments | | | ✔ | ✔ | ✔ | | |
| **Quarterly Reporting Process** | | | | | | | |
| Quality of earnings and disclosures | ✔ | | ✔ | | | | |
| Income tax assessments | | | ✔ | | | | |
| Pre-acquisition audits | ✔ | | ✔ | | | | |
| Material transactions and contracts (e.g., restructuring charges, etc.) | ✔ | | ✔ | | | | |
| **Reporting to the Board of Directors** | | | | | | | |
| Formal report | | | | | ✔ | | |
| **Reporting to the Stockholders** | | | | | | | |
| Proxy-statement disclosures | | | | ✔ | | ✔ | |
| **Reporting to the national stock exchange(s)** | | | | ✔ | | ✔ | |

Likewise, management is responsible for a system of internal control. Audit committees may request management and auditors to present a review of the COSO components of internal control in order to ensure that internal controls provide a reasonable assurance that the financial accounts are maintained and accounted for under the entity's policies. For financial reporting purposes, audit committees need assurance that management is managing identified risks so that financial statement assertions will not be misstated. Reference should also be made to the newly issued COSO Guidance on Monitoring Internal Control Systems (2009) that contains many pointers for management, audit committees as well as internal auditors on how to ensure that the internal controls put in are continuing to function effectively over time.

**Exhibit 2.3.2**   *(Continued)*

**Internal auditing.** As part of the monitoring component of the entity's system of internal control, the scope of the internal audit effort extends to several types of audits: financial, operational, compliance, ethics and fraud, systems, and risk audits. Audit committees should review the internal audit plan as well as the organizational structure and composition of the internal audit group. Audit committees want assurance that the entity's comprehensive internal audit program evaluates the adherence to management's policies and procedures.

**External auditing.** The audit committee's meetings and agendas should be directly linked to the auditing cycle, consisting of a pre-audit interview, an optional interim audit interview, a post-audit interview, and a follow-up interview.

During the pre-audit interview, the agenda ordinarily includes a review and discussion of matters such as the audit plan, accounting and auditing developments that impact the financial statements, risk assessment and related risk control processes, an analytical review, the personnel assigned to the audit team, an internal financial audit plan, and estimated audit and non-audit fees.

Audit committees or external auditors might request an interim audit interview to address problem areas and discuss the progress of the audit.

The major objective of the post-audit interview is to review the audit findings and the draft of the annual stockholders' report. Typically, audit committees focus on deviations from the audit plan, the analytical review, significant discoveries, resolved and unresolved matters, and disagreements with management, and material audit adjustments as well as immaterial uncorrected misstatements. Additionally, audit committees should review the appropriateness of accounting policies (e.g., conformity with industry practice and alternative accounting principles) and any changes in accounting principle.

During the follow-up interview, audit committees generally focus on recommendations for improvement in internal control, approving the internal audit plan for the following year, and recommending the appointment of the external auditors. They might also engage in a performance review of management, the internal audit group, or the external auditors. Audit committees might also review the external audit and non-audit fees that must now be disclosed in the annual proxy statement.

**Legal process.** Both in-house general counsel and outside legal counsel interact with audit committees on various issues:

- The standard of independence for the audit committee members
- The committee's written charter, as described in the entity's annual proxy statement
- Significant litigation, claims, and assessments against the entity
- Any pending litigation against the external auditors, as well as any impairment of their independence
- Compliance with key legislative acts (e.g., the Foreign Corrupt Practices Act, the Private Securities Litigation Reform Act)
- Proposed special investigations
- Material contracts, related party transactions, and contingencies
- Compliance with the entity's code of conduct and conflict of interest statements.

**Communications.** During the audit committee's audit cycle interviews, the internal communication process consists of both executive and joint sessions. Executive sessions may be used for the audit committee's performance reviews of management, the internal auditing group, and the external auditors, as well as a discussion of external audit and non-audit fees, and any disagreements with management.

With respect to external communications, audit committees are required to disclose the following items in the entity's annual proxy statement:

- A review and discussion of the entity's consolidated financial statements with management and the independent auditors
- A review of management's representations that the consolidated financial statements were prepared in accordance with GAAP
- Discussion with the independent auditors about SAS 114 matters (i.e., required communications)
- Written disclosures and the ISB 1 letter from the external auditor regarding their independence from the entity
- A consideration of whether the external auditors' provision of non-audit services is consistent with independence
- A recommendation of whether the audited financial statements should be included in SEC filings
- A recommendation as to the selection of the audit firm
- Presentation of an audit committee charter
- A letter to the appropriate stock exchange certifying the number and qualifications of independent audit committee members.

### Audit Committee's Quality Assurance Review

The major objective of this third step in the evaluative process is to effectively strive for zero defects in performing the first two steps. The audit committee's oversight role is to ensure efficiency and effectiveness in these processes, which, in turn, should lead to a high level of assurance of the board's corporate accountability. Given the demand for strong boards and audit committees, the audit committee should reflect and assess their overall operating performance and that of each committee member. This assessment process may be accomplished through a series of targeted questions that effectively address financial accounting and auditing issues affecting the financial statements. For example, audit committees might benchmark their performance review against their formal written charter. Exhibit 2.3.3 contains six quality assurance elements that enable the committee to develop an effective oversight strategy. Comprehensive reporting, combined with an ongoing dialogue between audit committee members and all interested parties, is the key to effective performance.

**EXHIBIT 2.3.3** Audit Committee's Quality Assurance Elements, Policies, and Procedures

| Quality Assurance Elements | Purpose | Quality Assurance Policies and Procedures |
| --- | --- | --- |
| Independence | Avoid a relationship with the entity that would interfere with the director's exercise of independent judgment | A |
| Financial knowledge | Directors need to be financially literate | B |

(*continued*)

**EXHIBIT 2.3.3**   (*Continued*)

| Quality Assurance Elements | Purpose | Quality Assurance Policies and Procedures |
|---|---|---|
| Written charter | Provides a clear understanding of the committee's oversight role, responsibilities, and organization | C |
| Performance review | Work performed meets the audit committee's charter | D |
| Continuing education | Directors need an ongoing program of additional courses | E |
| Monitoring | Annual review for each of the above elements | F |

Examples of related policies and procedures that an audit committee might implement include:

A: Provide for legal counsel's monitoring compliance with independent rules.
B: Establish review procedures for information about new accounting and auditing standards.
C: Communicate the scope of oversight responsibilities to audit committee members.
D: Establish procedures for benchmarking the audit committee's performance review.
E: Establish review procedures for a continuing education program.
F: Provide for reporting monitoring activities to the full board of directors.

---

*Source:* This discussion is adapted from an article by Louis Braiotta, Jr., "Corporate Audit Committees: An Approach to Continuous Improvement," *CPA Journal* 72, no. 7 (July 2002): 48–51. Reprinted with permission from *CPA Journal*, Copyright © 2002, New York State Society of Certified Public Accountants, 530 Fifth Avenue, New York, NY 10036-5101. All rights reserved.

In this overview of the audit committee's role in the auditing process, it is interesting to note some general observations:

- The audit committee has become an integral part of the corporate framework to help fulfill the board of directors' stewardship accountability to its outside constituencies.
- The work of the audit committee is dynamic since the accounting and auditing processes are subject to change.
- Authoritative bodies at home and abroad, such as the U.S. Congress, the national stock exchanges, the Cadbury Committee, the Hampel Committee, and the Committee on Corporate Governance (U.K.), have established standards for both the board of directors and the auditors to improve the financial reporting process.
- The audit committee is fundamental to the concept of corporate accountability.

## SOURCES AND SUGGESTED READINGS

American Bar Association. *Corporate Director's Guidebook* (Chicago: ABA, 1978).
American Bar Association. *Corporate Director's Guidebook* (Chicago: ABA, 1994).

American Institute of Certified Public Accountants. "Executive Committee Statement on Audit Committees of Boards of Directors." *Journal of Accountancy* 124 (September 1967):10.

American Institute of Certified Public Accountants. *Audit Committees, Answers to Typical Questions about Their Organization and Operations* (New York: AICPA, 1978).

American Institute of Certified Public Accountants. *Professional Standards, U.S. Auditing Standards/Attestation Standards*, vol. 1. New York, 2003.

American Society of Corporate Secretaries, *Current Board Practices* (New York: ASCD, 1996).

American Society of Corporate Secretaries. *Current Board Practices*, 2nd Study (New York: ASCD, 1998).

Atkins, Paul S. "The Sarbanes-Oxley Act of 2002: Goals, Content, and Status of Implementation." (Washington, DC: SEC, February 5, 2003).

Bacon, Jeremy. *The Audit Committee: A Broader Mandate*, Report no. 914 (New York: The Conference Board, Inc., 1988).

Barlas, Stephen. "Auditors Must State Independence." *Management Accounting* 80 no. 7 (January 1999): 10.

The Business Roundtable. *The Role and Composition of the Board of Directors of the Large Publicly Owned Corporation* (New York: The Business Roundtable, January 1978).

Carcello, Joseph V., Dana R. Hermanson, and Terry L. Neal, "Disclosure in Audit Committee Charters and Reports." *Accounting Horizons* 16, no. 4 (December 2002: 291–304.

Committee of Sponsoring Organizations of the Treadway Commission. *Internal Control-Integrated Framework* (New York: AICPA, 1992).

Ferrara, Ralph C., and Philip S. Khinda, "A Workable Audit Committee Charter." *Directors and Boards* 25, no. 1 (Fall 2000): 14.

Fleming, John M. "Audit Committees: Roles, Responsibilities, and Performance." *Pennsylvania CPA Journal* 73, no. 2 (Summer 2002): 29–32.

Goodman, Amy L., and Michael J. Scanlon. "Survey of Audit Committee Charters and Audit Committee Reports." *Insights: The Corporate & Securities Law Advisor* 15, no. 8 (August 2001): 13–18.

Hoffman, Ralph. and Ray Bromark. "An Audit Committee for Dynamic Times." *Directors & Boards* 16, no. 3 (Spring 1992): 51–53, 60.

Institute of Internal Auditors. *Improving Audit Committee Performance: What Works Best* (Altamonte Springs, FL: The IIA, 1993).

Institute of Internal Auditors. *The Professional Practice Framework* (Altamonte Springs, FL: The IIA, 2009).

Kalbers, L.P. "An Examination of the Relationship Between Audit Committees and External Auditors." *Ohio CPA Journal* 51, no. 6 (December 1992): 19–27.

Katz, Eugene M. "Keys to an Effective Audit Committee." *Credit World* 86, no. 4 (March/April 1998): 21–23.

Leanby, Bruce A., Paul R. Grazina, and John D. Zook. "Improving the Effectiveness of Corporate Audit Committees." *Pennsylvania CPA Journal* 70 no. 2 (Summer 1999): 37–40.

Levitt, A. "The Numbers Game." Speech delivered on September 28, 1998, at New York University. (www.sec.gov/news/speech/speecharchive/1998/spch220.txt).

Livingston, Philip. "Financial Experts on Audit Committees—An Overdue Implementation." *Financial Executive* 19, no. 1 (January/February 2003): 6–7.

Livingston, Philip. "Test From Financial Literacy." *Directors and Boards* 26 no. 2 (Winter 2002): 21–23.

National Association of Corporate Directors. *Report of the Blue Ribbon Commission on Audit Committees.* Washington, D.C.: NACD, 2000.

National Commission on Fraudulent Financial Reporting. *Report of the National Commission on Fraudulent Financial Reporting.* Washington, DC: NCFFR, 1987.

Quinn, Lawrence Richber. "Strengthening the Role of the Audit Committee." *Strategic Finance* 84, no. 6 (December 2002): 42–47.

Richardson, Robert C., and Charles P. Baril. "Can Your Audit Committee Withstand the Market's Scrutiny of Independence?" *Financial Executive* 19, no. 1 (January/February 2003): 35–38.

Sarbanes-Oxley Act of 2002. H.R. Rep. No. 107-610, July 25, 2002.

Securities and Exchange Commission. *Proposed Rule Change Relating to Corporate Governance.* Release No. 34-47672, File No. SR-NYSE-2002-33 (April 11, 2003).

Spangler, William D. and Louis Braiotta, Jr. "Leadership and Audit Committee Effectiveness." *Group and Organization Studies* 15, no. 2 (June 1990): 134–157.

*Statement on Auditing Standards No. 58.* "Reports on Audited Financial Statements." New York: AICPA, 1988.

Sweeney, Paul, and Cynthia Wallace Vallario. "NYSE Sets Audit Committees on New Road." *Journal of Accountancy* 194, no. 5 (November 2002): 51–59.

Title 1 of Public Law no. 107-204, July 30, 2002.

Verschoor, Curtis C., Michael Barry, and Larry E. Rittenberg. "Reflections on the Audit Committee's Role." *Internal Auditor* 59, no. 2 (April 2002): 26–35.

# Chapter 3

# The External Users of Financial Reporting Information

The information demands of groups external to the enterprise have become fundamental to the financial reporting environment. Because management and other internal users control the information systems that produce financial and operating reports for an enterprise, there are few constraints on their ability to get relevant and timely information except the costs to produce it. Outsiders to the organization are limited to information that the enterprise makes public voluntarily, files in compliance with regulatory requirements, or discloses by contract. The audit committee, through its oversight of the financial reporting process, plays an important mediating role between management and the various external users of financial reports. Unfortunately, users have differing information demands, and their information needs are not always easy to predict or to satisfy. In the past few years, institutional investors through the Council for Institutional Investors, and financial analysts through the Chartered Financial Analysts Institute, have become increasingly active and engaged in the process for creating financial accounting standards. Likewise, proxy advisors such as the Risk Metrics Group and Glass Lewis have increased their influence through reports used by institutional investors to determine their votes on annual corporate proposals, including directors and audit committee concerns.

## INTRODUCTION

Since the board of directors, through the audit committee, is responsible for ensuring that management fulfills its financial reporting obligations, audit committees share accountability to the external users of accounting information. According to the Financial Accounting Standards Board (FASB),

> Members and potential members of some groups—such as owners, creditors, and employees—have or contemplate having direct economic interests in particular business enterprises . . . Members of other groups—such as financial analysts and advisors, regulatory authorities, and labor unions—have derived or indirect interests

because they advise or represent those who have or contemplate having direct interests.[1]

The FASB has developed a conceptual framework consisting of six Statements of Financial Accounting Concepts (SFAC) on financial reporting for business enterprises and one SFAC on financial reporting for nonbusiness enterprises. The SFACs are intended to serve the public interest by setting the objectives, qualitative characteristics, and other concepts that guide selection of the economic phenomena to be recognized and measured for financial reporting, and their display in financial statements or related information. SFACs guide the FASB in developing sound accounting principles and provide its members and constituents with an understanding of the appropriate content and inherent limitations of financial reporting. SFACs themselves do not establish generally accepted accounting standards.

The six SFACs on business enterprises cover the following topics:

*SFAC No. 1:* "Objectives of Financial Reporting by Business Enterprises" (November 1978)

*SFAC No. 2:* "Qualitative Characteristics of Accounting Information" (May 1980)

*SFAC No. 3:* "Elements of Financial Statements of Business Enterprises" (December 1980)

*SFAC No. 5:* "Recognition and Measurement in Financial Statements of Business Enterprises" (December 1984)

*SFAC No. 6:* "Elements of Financial Statements" (December 1985)[2]

*SFAC No. 7:* "Using Cash Flow Information and Present Value in Accounting Measurements" (February 2000)

The FASB and the International Accounting Standards Board (IASB) began discussing updates to their conceptual frameworks early in the 2000s. Their conceptual framework project has progressed at a slow and deliberate pace for several years. Conceptual framework exposure documents usually generate many comment letters with various perspectives and viewpoints that differ both from the Boards' proposals and from one another. The Boards have subdivided their work into eight phases, several of which are now inactive:

1. Objective and Qualitative Characteristics
2. Elements and Recognition
3. Measurement
4. Reporting Entity
5. Presentation and Disclosure, including Financial Reporting Boundaries (Inactive)

---

[1] Financial Accounting Standards Board, *Statement of Financial Accounting Concepts, No. 1* (Stamford, CT.: FASB, 1978), 11.

[2] SFAC No. 4, "Objectives of Financial Reporting by Nonbusiness Organizations," December 1980. It should be noted that SFACs No. 2 and No. 6 apply to nonbusiness enterprises.

**6.** Framework Purpose and Status in GAAP Hierarchy (Inactive)
**7.** Applicability to the Not-for-Profit Sector (Inactive)
**8.** Remaining Issues (Inactive)

Some of the areas in the conceptual framework that have generated the most discussion and debate among the Boards' constituencies involve whether financial reporting is solely for market information purposes or also for stewardship purposes; whether recognition should be oriented to assets and liabilities, to income and expense, or to some balance; whether measurement should be completely at "fair value," "transaction value," or some combination of the two; whether unrealized gains and losses should be considered income; and whether the orientation of accounting standards should be transactional or organizational. Needless to say, there are numerous viewpoints on these issues. Importantly for audit committee members, during the process of considering changes, the FASB and IASB make public at www.fasb.org and at www.iasb.org the comment letters that are written in response to exposure documents. Reading the comment letters from institutional investors, credit rating agencies, and financial analysts can help audit committee members understand and appreciate more fully the substance of users' informational issues and concerns. Audit committee members may also find reading the comment letters filed by their external auditors helpful and may encourage management of the organizations they serve to write comment letters on standards that may affect them.

While the FASB and IASB use the SFACs as a means of determining the appropriateness and quality of specific accounting standards, the auditing profession has developed and continues to promulgate principles and procedures that address the interplay between the expectations of outsiders and the requirements of GAAP. Both internal accountants and external auditors exercise judgment in the selection of accounting standards for a fair presentation of the financial statements in order to satisfy the objective of complete and accurate information. In regard to the audit committee's role in this process, the PCAOB's interim audit standards state in part:

> 11. In connection with each SEC engagement . . . , the auditor should discuss with the audit committee the auditor's judgments about the quality, not just the acceptability, of the entity's accounting principles as applied in its financial reporting. Since the primary responsibility for establishing an entity's accounting principles rests with management, the discussion generally would include management as an active participant. The discussion should be open and frank and generally should include such matters as the consistency of the entity's accounting policies and their application, and the clarity and completeness of the entity's financial statements, which include related disclosures. The discussion should also include items that have a significant impact on the representational faithfulness, verifiability, and neutrality of the accounting information included in the financial statements.[*] Examples of items that may have such an impact are the following:

---

[*] These characteristics of accounting information are discussed in the Financial Accounting Standards Board (FASB) Statement of Financial Accounting Concepts No. 2, Qualitative characteristics of Accounting Information. FASB Concepts Statement No. 2 notes that consistently understating results or overly optimistic estimates of realization are inconsistent with these characteristics.

- Selection of new or changes to accounting policies
- Estimates, judgments, and uncertainties
- Unusual transactions
- Accounting policies relating to significant financial statement items, including the timing of transactions and the period in which they are recorded

Objective criteria have not been developed to aid in the consistent evaluation of the quality of an entity's accounting principles as applied in its financial statements. The discussion should be tailored to the entity's specific circumstances, including accounting applications and practices not explicitly addressed in the accounting literature, for example, those that may be unique to an industry.[3]

While SFACs are not considered authoritative in terms of accounting practice, in the absence of authoritative accounting literature concerning the accounting treatment of a particular item, account, or transaction, the SFACs may provide insights that assist in understanding and solving accounting dilemmas.[4] In an article dealing with the subjects of minority interest, stock issues, and legally enforceable contracts, Steven Rubin indicated how the conceptual framework could be used for the appropriate accounting treatment, and he concluded that

> Concepts statements can provide helpful guidance in resolving knotty practice problems involving liabilities and other matters. Consult them as you would other sources of established accounting principles. You may be surprised to find that these basic statements will provide the help you need.[5]

One way of classifying the external users is to divide them into groups of investors, credit grantors, regulatory agencies, and other outside constituencies. Such classification is useful from the audit committee's point of view, because each constituent has different informational needs and objectives. Thus, the four-way classification of the users is a useful framework for discharging the board of directors' financial accountability. To the extent that the audit committee can monitor the accounting information as well as understand the perceived needs of the outside constituencies, it can provide a balance in the corporate financial reporting process.

---

[3] Statement on Auditing Standards, No. 90, *Audit Committee Communications* (New York: AICPA, 1999), par. 1.

[4] Statement on Auditing Standards, No. 69, *The Meaning of Present Fairly in Conformity with Generally Accepted Accounting Principles in the Independent Auditor's Report* (New York: AICPA, 1992), par. 11.

[5] Steven Rubin, "How Concepts Statements Can Solve Practice Problems," *Journal of Accountancy* 166, no. 4 (October 1988), 126. Two authors have developed a flow chart, "An Overview of FASB's Concepts Statements." See Gwen Richardson Pate and Keith G. Stanga, "A Guide to the FASB's Concepts Statements," *Journal of Accountancy* 168, no. 2 (August 1989): 28–31.

## THE INVESTORS

### Importance of the Investors

Investors are the largest users of accounting information. As a group, investors include both current and potential shareholders. For many years the Federal Reserve Board statistics have tracked in Release Z1 (www.federalreserve.gov) changes in the proportions of U.S. corporate equities held by different sectors of the economy. In 1950, more than 90 percent of U.S. corporate equities were held by households, but by 2002 that proportion had dropped to under 50 percent and has held steady since then. The statistics show that over time, institutional investors have begun to hold more equities on behalf of their beneficiaries. Institutional investors include government and private pension funds, mutual funds, insurance companies, and financial institutions. Many institutional investors hold and trade securities on behalf of individuals who, either by circumstance or preference, place their savings with institutional investors to invest on their behalf. Many participants in defined contribution pension plans, such as 401(k) and 403(b) plans, save for retirement through investment accounts with institutional investors. These institutional investors represent a dominant force in daily stock trading. Their influential role is important because they can concentrate their investments in large corporations and thus increase their power to influence those companies. In addition, audit committee members should be aware that hedge funds and sovereign investment funds have also grown in significance in terms of ownership positions in U.S. public companies.

Many assessments of the corporation's role in society have made the point that corporations have responsibility beyond the short-term return to their current shareholders. For example, the Business Roundtable concluded:

> Corporations are chartered to serve both their shareholders and society as a whole. The interests of the shareholders are primarily measured in terms of economic return over time. The interests of others in society (other stakeholders) are defined by their relationship to the corporation.

> The other stakeholders in the corporation are its employees, customers, suppliers, creditors, the communities where the corporation does business, and society as a whole. The duties and responsibilities of the corporation to the stakeholders are expressed in various laws, regulations, contracts, and custom and practice.[6]

More recently, between 2006 and 2009 the Committee for Economic Development (www.ced.org) issued a series of three reports on corporate governance that focus on directors' responsibilities for long-term performance and for linking long-term performance with public goals.

> Directors have a legal obligation and duty to address the long-term performance of the corporation. Directors' fiduciary responsibilities include broader societal

---

[6] The Business Roundtable, *Corporate Governance and American Competitiveness* (New York: Business Roundtable, 1990), 4.

concerns that affirmatively affect the corporation's performance and long-term sustainability. To meet that duty, directors must consider the concerns of all entities—not just current shareholders, managers, or other powerful constituents—that are in a position to affect a company's long-term performance.[7]

In addition to their significance in capital markets, investors have an impact on corporate policies through their voting activities and proxy access. For example, stockholders can influence corporate policies through their votes at the annual stockholders' meeting. They can vote on such issues as the following:

- The election and removal of the board of directors
- Amendments to the corporate charter and bylaws
- Proposals of the stockholders to corporate management
- The board of directors' proposals
- The authorization of a new stock or bond issue
- Corporate management's conduct with respect to corporate affairs
- The selection of the independent auditing firm

In 2009 the SEC addressed several issues related to corporate governance and shareholder votes. For companies receiving aid through the Troubled Asset Relief Program (TARP), the Commission voted to give shareholders better proxy information about executive compensation and a vote on executive compensation in companies' proxy solicitations. The commission also voted to approve a New York Stock Exchange rule that stops brokers from voting proxies for which they do not receive instructions from their customers (i.e., the owners). The Commission has issued proposals for comment that would facilitate the rights of shareholders to nominate directors. The SEC also has formed for the first time a standing advisory body composed of investors and analysts. In addition, as of the date of this writing, several bills were pending in the U.S. Congress that would give shareholders greater access to proxies, eliminate staggered board terms, require majority votes in board elections, and provide shareholders with advisory votes executive compensation.

As a result of the new powers likely to be given to investors, it is essential that the audit committee have access to stockholder profiles that identify stockholders and their stockholdings in order to analyze their degree of voting power. Voting power may be concentrated in a family group, or it could be concentrated in an institutional investor. An activist hedge fund or venture capital fund could have a large stake. Such groups can greatly influence corporate policies through their percentages of stock ownership. Although the board has other demands from its outside constituencies, the audit committee can aid the board through its understanding and familiarity with investors' interests and of their investments in the corporation. In short, the primary concern of the audit committee is to give

---

[7] Committee for Economic Development, *Rebuilding Corporate Leadership: How Directors Can Link Long-Term Performance with Public Goals* (Washington, DC, 2009), 2.

consideration to the stockholders' interests because of their relationship to corporate policy decisions.

In the past two decades, efforts have accelerated to improve communications between shareholders and corporations. In 1992, Richard C. Breeden, former chairman of the SEC, stated in his annual report to Congress:

> The Commission adopted significant revisions of the proxy rules to facilitate effective communications among shareholders and between shareholders and their corporations. The reforms will encourage greater participation by shareholders in corporate governance by removing unnecessary regulatory barriers, reducing the costs of complying with the proxy rules and improving disclosure.

> In addition, the Commission revised its rules to ensure that shareholders receive better information about executive compensation. Among other things, the new executive compensation disclosure rules require new tables that will disclose clearly and concisely the compensation received by a corporation's highest paid executives.[8]

> The Commission adopted important amendments to its executive compensation disclosure requirements. The amendments are designed to (1) ensure that shareholders receive comprehensible, relevant, and complete information about compensation paid to executives upon which to base their voting and investment decisions; and (2) foster accountability of directors to shareholders by permitting shareholders to vote on the proposals of other shareholders with regard to executive and director compensation, and thereby advise the board of directors of the shareholders' assessment of the compensation policies and practices applied by the board.

> After three years of study, two releases for public comment, a two-day public conference, and more than 1,700 public comment letters, the Commission substantially revised its rules governing proxy solicitations. The revisions were adopted to (1) facilitate effective communications among shareholders and between shareholders and their corporations, as well as participation by shareholders in corporate governance, by removing unnecessary regulatory barriers, (2) reduce the costs of complying with the proxy rules, (3) improve disclosures to shareholders, and (4) restore a balance between the free speech rights of shareholders and Congress' concern that solicitation of proxy voting authority be conducted on a fair, honest and informed basis.[9]

Of particular interest to audit committees is the concern raised in 1998 by Arthur Levitt, then SEC chairman:

> An area of great concern to the Commission is inappropriate earnings management. While this is not a new problem, it has risen in a market unforgiving of companies that miss Wall Street's estimates. During the year, our staff issued guidance on various issues relating to the presentation of earnings per share."[10]

---

[8] Securities and Exchange Commission, *1992 Annual Report*, viii.
[9] Ibid., p. 53.
[10] Securities and Exchange Commission, *1998 Annual Report* (Washington, DC: U.S. Government Printing Office, 1998), vi.

Likewise, in 1999, Levitt stated:

An area of continued concern to the Commission is inappropriate earnings management. Abusive earnings management involves the use of various forms of gimmickry to distort a company's true financial performance in order to achieve a desired result. Staff Accounting Bulletin 99 reemphasizes that the exclusive reliance on any percentage or numerical threshold in assessing materiality for financial reporting has no basis in the accounting literature or in the law. The staff also issued two other bulletins to provide guidance on the criteria necessary to recognize restructuring liabilities and asset impairments and the conditions prerequisite to recognizing revenue.[11]

One aspect of audit committees' concern for the quality of financial reporting is reflected in the number of SEC actions and class-action litigation. Often such regulatory actions by an investor protection agency and shareholder litigation concern issues that come under the oversight of the audit committee. NERA Economic Consulting has reported SEC settlements and federal class action lawsuit settlements over recent years:

| Settlements | 2003 | 2004 | 2005 | 2006 | 2007 | 2008 |
|---|---|---|---|---|---|---|
| SEC Actions | 898 | 859 | 771 | 663 | 702 | 739 |
| Class-Actions | 238 | 248 | 189 | 131 | 195 | 255 |

*Sources:* "SEC Settlements: A New Era Post-SOX," NERA Economic Consulting, Jan Larsen with Elaine Buckley and Dr. Baruch Lev, Nov. 10, 2008; and "2008 Trends in Securities Class Actions," Stephanie Plancich, Ph.D., and Svetlana Statykh, December 2008.

In addition, restated financial statements are sometimes an indicator of the overall quality of a company's financial reporting process. Obviously, it's appropriate for a company to restate its previously issued financial statement when previously issued statements are found to be misleading or do not comply with GAAP. In considering whether a restatement is needed, audit committee members should seek the advice of management and their accounting and legal professional advisors. Whether a restatement is needed will depend on whether the error would have affected decisions by a reasonable investor in the context of the totality of information available.

Susan Scholz, an associate professor of accounting at the University of Kansas, was commissioned by the Treasury Department to study the restatement phenomenon. Her report, "The Changing Nature and Consequences of Public Company Restatements 1997–2006," was completed in April 2008. Restatements grew from 90 in 1997 to 1,577 in 2006. Of the 90 in 1997, 26 (29 percent) of the restatements were made because fraud had been discovered. In 2006, 31 (2 percent) were the

---

[11] Securities and Exchange Commission, *1999 Annual Report* (Washington, DC: U.S. Government Printing Office, 1999), vi. For further discussion, see Chapter 5.

result of a subsequent discovery of fraud. Nearly half of the restatements were made each year by companies not traded on exchanges. Professor Scholz reported the incidence of restatements from 2000 forward as follows:

| 2000 | 2001 | 2002 | 2003 | 2004 | 2005 | 2006 |
|------|------|------|------|------|------|------|
| 224  | 484  | 640  | 847  | 979  | 1468 | 1577 |

Stockholders and potential investors realize that if a company does not meet or beat Wall Street expectations, then investors will punish the market price of company's stock. Consequently, management has an incentive to manage current and expected earnings because net income is used to measure earnings per share and return on equity as well as the value of management's stock options. Therefore, the quality of earnings may be affected by management's choice of accounting methods and estimates, including those for nonoperating and financial items affecting the income statement.

As a case in point, the SEC reported:

> *In the Matter of W.R. Grace & Co.* Former senior management of W.R. Grace & Co. and its main health care subsidiary, National Medical Care, Inc., falsely reported results of operations and made false and misleading statements in press releases and at teleconferences with analysts. The managers deferred reporting income, by improperly increasing or establishing reserves, to bring reported earnings into line with targeted earnings. Grace consented to the entry of a cease and desist order, and agreed to establish a $1 million fund for programs to further awareness and education about financial statements and generally accepted accounting principles.[12]

This case illustrates management's use of cookie jar reserves through which management makes unrealistic assumptions to estimate liabilities, which in turn can be reduced in the future to increase net income.

## The Need for Accounting Information

As a principal constituency of the corporation, investors make decisions based on financial accounting information. Although regulatory agencies, such as the SEC, can establish the form and general content of their reports, investors must rely on such reports' details provided by corporate management. Investors use these reports (which are based on management's financial accounting representations) not only to evaluate the effectiveness of management, but also to decide whether to increase or decrease their stockholding in a corporation.

More important, because of its stewardship accountability, corporate management must periodically communicate its financial accounting information to its constituencies. The corporate financial statements are the principal reports that

---

[12] Securities and Exchange Commission, *1999 Annual Report*, 5. For further discussion, see Securities and Exchange Commission, *In the Matter of W.R. Grace & Co.*, Release No. 34-41578, Accounting and Auditing Enforcement Release No. 1140 (June 30, 1999). See also Ann Davis, "SEC Case Claims Profit 'Management' by Grace," *Wall Street Journal*, April 7, 1999.

are used to communicate accounting data. In November 1978, the FASB released its first statement as part of its conceptual framework project for financial accounting and reporting. The board concluded the following on objectives of financial reporting:

> Financial reporting should provide information that is useful to present and potential investors and creditors and other users in making rational investment, credit, and similar decisions. The information should be comprehensible to those who have a reasonable understanding of business and economic activities and are willing to study the information with reasonable diligence.

> Financial reporting should provide information to help present and potential investors and creditors and other users in assessing the amounts, timing, and uncertainty of prospective cash receipts from dividends or interest and the proceeds from the sale, redemption, or maturity of securities or loans. Since investors' and creditors' cash flows are related to enterprise cash flows, financial reporting should provide information to help investors, creditors, and others assess the amounts, timing, and uncertainty of prospective net cash inflows to the related enterprise.

> Financial reporting should provide information about the economic resources of an enterprise, the claims to those resources (obligations of the enterprise to transfer resources to other entities and owners' equity), and the effects of transactions, events, and circumstances that change its resources and claims to those resources.[13]

For public companies that are combined in an annual filing with the SEC on Form 10-K or in a quarterly filing on Form 10-Q, financial reporting consists of three distinct items: the financial statements, the notes to financial statements, and numerous other disclosures related to the performance of the entity. Generally, the financial statements and their notes are audited by an external auditor, while the other disclosures are not. Investors and analysts generally are consistent in their advocacy for audited numbers, so they tend to give greater weight to those parts of the financial report that are audited. This preference for audited information also drives in part their desires to see more pieces of corporations' financial picture covered by the financial statements rather than in general unaudited disclosures. This focus on "rational investment, credit, and similar decisions" also has led to additional concern about the recognition and measurement of financial assets and liabilities, along with extensive disclosures about the risks associated with them.

The second objective of financial reporting means that investors need financial information in order to evaluate their investment opportunities and objectives. Obviously, investors wish to safeguard the principal amount of their investment and maximize the income and capital appreciation. Furthermore, investors must assess their willingness and ability to accept risk. Similarly, management must effectively use the economic resources of the enterprise in order to generate a monetary return to its investors. Thus, "since an enterprise's ability to generate favorable cash flows affects both its ability to pay dividends and interest and the

---

[13] Financial Accounting Standards Board, *Statement of Financial Accounting Concepts, No. 1*, viii.

market prices of its securities, expected cash flows to investors and creditors are related to expected cash flows to the enterprise."[14]

Finally, the third objective of financial reporting relates to the enterprise's financial condition and operating performance. Investors need information on the current and future financial strength of the corporation to appraise the soundness of their investment. Such information is critical. Not only does it indicate the ability of the enterprise to meet its short-term and long-term financial commitments, but it allows investors to evaluate their risk and return on investment. Furthermore, investors need information regarding the uses of economic resources in the operations. Although the enterprise may have an adequate financial position, such a position may deteriorate because of poor operational performance. In short, investors want financial information on the use and disposition of the enterprise's economic resources in order to assess their own investment policy.[15]

## Role of the Audit Committee

In order to discharge effectively their responsibilities in the area of financial reporting, the audit committee should establish operational objectives for the financial reporting process that consider and incorporate investors' need for financial information. Such operational objectives should be consistent with the FASB's objectives of financial reporting in order to fulfill the stewardship responsibility of the committee to provide assurance regarding the usefulness of the information in financial reports.

In addition to the quantitative representations in the financial statements, the committee should use the following qualitative characteristics to assess the corporation's financial reporting policies and practices:

> The qualitative characteristics of financial statements, like objectives, should be based largely upon the needs of users of the statements. Information is useless unless it is relevant and material to a user's decision. Information should be as free as possible from any biases of the preparer. In making decisions, users should not only understand the information presented, but also should be able to assess its reliability and compare it with information about alternative opportunities and previous experience. In all cases, information is more useful if it stresses economic substance rather than technical form.[16]

The preceding discussions on the operational objectives and the criteria for evaluating the usefulness of the financial statements provide guidelines for

---

[14] Financial Accounting Standards Board, *Statement on Financial Accounting Concepts, No. 1*, 19.

[15] For further discussion, see SRI International, *Investor Informational Needs and the Annual Report* (Morristown, NJ: Financial Executive Research Foundation, 1987).

[16] American Institute of Certified Public Accountants, *Report of the Study Group on the Objectives of Financial Statements* (New York: AICPA, 1973), 60. For further discussion, see Financial Accounting Standards Board, *Statement of Financial Accounting Concepts No. 2*, "Qualitative Characteristics of Accounting" (Stamford, CT: FASB, May 1980).

evaluating management's responsibilities in the preparation of the financial statements. In addition, the audit committee should give consideration to the following criteria, which were used by the Financial Analysts Federation in its Awards for Excellence in Corporate Reporting program:

1. Responsiveness of management to analysts' and investors' desire for information prerequisite to real understanding of companies and their problems.
2. Efforts by companies to supply financial and other information going well beyond the level of disclosure required by the SEC, the exchanges, and the FASB.
3. A coordinated and consistent program of personal contact with investors and their representatives—both through provision of experienced and helpful officials in the investor relations function and via regular management presentations to analyst groups, company-sponsored field trips, and so on.
4. A high "candor quotient" in both oral and written communications to the investment community. Too many managements prejudice an otherwise creditable information program by ignoring or glossing over unfavorable developments with a thick patina of corporate optimism.[17]

In 2004, the CFA Center for Financial Market Integrity (www.cfainstitute.org) and the National Investors Relations Institute (www.niri.org) cooperated in developing best practice guidelines for appropriate information transfer between corporate issuers and analysts. The guidelines can be downloaded from either organization's Web site under the title "Best Practice Guidelines Governing Analyst/Corporate Issuer Relations." The guidelines cover such topics as information flow between analysts and corporate issuers; analysts' conduct in preparing and publishing research reports and making investment recommendations; corporate issuers' conduct in providing analysts with access to corporate management; review of analysts' reports by corporate issuers; and research that is solicited, paid, or sponsored by an issuer.

These guidelines were crafted after the SEC adopted Regulation FD (fair disclosure) on August 15, 2000. Regulation FD changed the practices of selective disclosure of information to certain analysts by publicly traded companies and other issuers. Regulation FD provides that when an issuer discloses material nonpublic information to certain individuals or entities—generally, securities market professionals such as stock analysts, or holders of the issuer's securities who may well trade on the basis of the information—the issuer must make public disclosure of that information. In this way, the new rule aims to promote full and fair disclosure of material information to all market participants.

Finally, the audit committee should be aware of the independent auditing firm's quality control policies and procedures, which provide reasonable

---

[17] Financial Analysts Federation, "Awards for Excellence in Corporate Reporting," Financial Analysts Federation News Release (New York: FAF, January 1978), 1.

assurance that the firm has followed professional standards.[18] The Auditing Standards Board's *Statements on Quality Control Standards*, which serve as the interim standards for quality control of the PCAOB (public companies) and as the standards for AICPA members (private companies and other nonpublic entities), identify five elements of quality control:

1. Independence, integrity, and objectivity
2. Personnel management
3. Acceptance and continuance of clients and engagements
4. Engagement performance
5. Monitoring

The quality control standards provide a framework for an audit firm's quality review program. For example, firms registered with the PCAOB are required to rotate engagement partners at least every five years, and audit engagements are subject to a second-partner review process. As noted in Chapter 2, Section 203 of the Sarbanes-Oxley Act limits both the lead partner and concurring partners to a maximum of five consecutive years of service with a five-year time-out.

It's not enough that audit committees simply be aware of auditors' quality control standards. They should take serious interest in how their auditors comply with the requirements of the PCAOB, AICPA, and other applicable regulatory bodies. In the United States most states also require CPA firms providing assurance services (audits, reviews, compilations and other attestations) to participate in a quality control program acceptable to the state, usually the AICPA Peer Review Program. In particular, the committees should discuss each year with their auditor ways that the auditor is improving their quality control. In their survey of 42 audit partners and managers on issues related to the content and form of audit committee activities, Ganesh Krishnamoorthy, Arnie Wright, and Jeffrey Cohen concluded:

> One must go beyond just determining whether the committees comply with existing regulations. In fact, 81% of the respondents believe that you need to look at the substance (the actual effectiveness of the audit committee) and not just the form of audit committees. Thus, an audit committee might comply with all existing regulations, but if they are not providing active oversight to the quality and integrity of the financial reporting process, they cannot be relied upon.[19]

---

[18] Statement on Auditing Standards No. 25, *The Relationship of Generally Accepted Auditing Standards to Quality Control Standards* (New York: AICPA, 1979). For further discussion, see Statement on Quality Control Standards No. 2, "System of Quality Control for a CPA Firm's Accounting and Auditing Practice"; Statement on Quality Control Standards No. 3, "Monitoring a CPA Firm's Accounting and Auditing Practice"; and AICPA Peer Review Board, *Standards for Performing and Reporting on Peer Reviews* (New York: AICPA, 1996). The audit committee's knowledge and understanding of the independent accounting firm's quality control policies and procedures is important to provide assurance to the full board of directors that the independent auditors are discharging their responsibilities to the client company and the general public.

[19] Ganesh Krishnamoorthy, Arnie Wright, and Jeffrey Cohen, "Auditors' Views on Audit Committees and Financial Reporting Quality," *CPA Journal* 75, no. 10 (October 2002): 56.

## CREDIT GRANTORS

### Importance of the Credit Grantors

Obviously, credit grantors are a significant group since they are a source of funds to the enterprise. The group consists of both short-term and long-term lenders of credit, such as banks, insurance companies, trade creditors, and bondholders. Short-term creditors are concerned principally with the corporation's ability to maintain an adequate cash position because they expect to be paid in a short period of time. Hence, they focus their attention on the working capital position of the enterprise, which represents the relationship between cash and near-cash assets, such as short-term securities, receivables, inventories, and short-term liabilities. Such information is central to this group's decision-making process because the particular assets may be converted readily into cash. Conversely, long-term creditors are concerned not only with the corporation's ability to generate cash but also with its potential profitability. For example, they are interested in the ability of the enterprise to secure a loan with the necessary assets in relationship to its commitments and contingencies, such as a pending lawsuit. Thus, credit grantors are primarily interested in the current solvency position of the corporation and its adherence to the loan covenants. In short, the major objective of the creditors is not only to safeguard their claim against the assets of the enterprise but also to obtain assurance with respect to the debt-paying ability of the corporation.

### The Need for Accounting Information

Credit grantors need information on the financial and operational conditions of the enterprise. To judge a credit risk or establish a line of credit, they focus their attention on the financial statements as well as other sources of information, such as Dun & Bradstreet or National Credit Office credit reports.

George Cox and associates report that "the recent spate of corporate disasters almost defies understanding." Such companies have "credit lines with premier lending institutions and yet, disaster struck without much warning to investors, creditors, or employees." They believe that "the audit committee should meet with investment and commercial bankers, as well as rating agency personnel, about the health of the organization." For example, "are bank loans and credit lines competitive, meeting ordinary and customary market terms? Strong oversight and control are the best prescription for company health."[20]

### Role of the Audit Committee

Although the finance committee is responsible for the financial policies and program, the audit committee should give attention to the financial reporting matters concerning the credit lenders. The audit committee members are in a

---

[20] George Cox, H. Stephen Grace, Jr., John E. Haupert, Peter Howell, and Ronald H. Wilcomes, "A Prescription for Company Health," *CPA Journal* 72, no. 7 (July 2002): 62–63.

unique position because they must monitor the accounting information that is related to the corporation's financial policies. In approaching the financial reporting task, the committee should consult with the chairperson of the finance committee as well as the chief financial officer. For example, the committee's review of loan agreements and other commitments should be made in view of the preceding discussion of the objectives of financial reporting and the information needs of the credit grantors. Thus the audit committee should be concerned primarily with such matters as the following:

- The proper disclosure of the short-term and long-term obligations and any outstanding commitments of the corporation
- The adherence to the loan covenants regarding the necessary working capital ratios
- A summary of the sources of creditors' equity and the related cost of debt
- A forecast of the proposed debt financing activities and repayment schedule and its relationship to the stockholders' equity

In his article entitled "The Enron Affair from a Lender's View," Neville Grusd, executive vice president of Merchant Factors, points out that "no one has mentioned the loss sustained by the creditors of Enron." He notes that "most credit grantors, however, rely upon the very financial statements" that the parties in the public sector (the President, SEC, and Congress) are worrying about.[21]

Grusd suggests the following to credit grantors:

- "Become more active in accounting rule making through the American Bankers Association and Commercial Finance Association."
- "If a lender knows the client is a major account of the CPA firm issuing its financials, the lender should take the necessary steps to ensure the quality of the financial reporting."
- With respect to review engagements, "lenders and accountants should discuss the accountant's procedures, then decide the extent to which the lender's own field exam should be extended to cover weak areas."
- Lenders should insist that the financial statements are prepared by "competent and independent CPAs."[22]

In addition to the issues already discussed, several Financial Accounting Standards Board Statements are relevant to credit grantors:[23]

---

[21] Neville Grusd, "The Enron Affair from a Lender's View," *CPA Journal* 72, no. 12 (December 2002): 8.

[22] Ibid., 8–10.

[23] In 2009 the FASB completed a project to codify all of its authoritative accounting literature, resulting in a new codification framework. The new codification is organized by Accounting Standards Codification (ASC) numbers. That project is discussed more fully in Chapter 5. The accounting standards above reflect the original accounting standard reference with parenthetical notation of the primary ASC number.

- *SFAS No. 95 (ASC 230):* "Statement of Cash Flows" (November 1987)
- *SFAS No. 107 (ASC 825):* "Disclosure About Fair Value of Financial Instruments" (December 1991)
- *SFAS No. 133 (ASC 815):* "Accounting for Derivative Instruments and Hedging Activities" (June 1998)
- *SFAS No. 157 (ASC 820):* "Fair Value Measurements" (September 2006)

These accounting standards are summarized in the following paragraphs.

**Reporting Cash Flows**    In November 1987, the FASB issued SFAS No. 95, "Statement of Cash Flows." The board recognized that a presentation of a company's cash flows is an important measure of liquidity for the users of financial statements. Prior to the issuance of SFAS No. 95, companies could present their funds flow statement on either a working capital or a cash basis. Under the new accounting standard, companies are required to classify cash flows as operating, investing, or financial activities.[24] Management is required to provide additional information on cash flows in its presentation of management's discussion and analysis of financial condition and results of operations. Although the FASB has encouraged management to report cash flows from operating activities by the direct method, which consists of classes of cash transactions, the indirect method is commonly used. The FASB will reconsider during 2009 and 2010 whether to require presentation of the cash flow statement by the direct method. As in the past, some analysts and preparers are negative about moving from the indirect method. Some analysts have decades of proprietary data collected from adaptations of the indirect method, and they are concerned that it will become less valuable for their analyses if they are no longer able to produce similar data in the future. Some preparers express concerns about the additional costs of creating new systems to support the indirect method when analysts as a group may not necessarily prefer the change.

**Financial Instruments**    In the late 1980s, the accounting treatment associated with financial instruments and transactions received a great deal of attention because of the lack of financial accounting and disclosure standards.

In June 1998, the Financial Accounting Standards Board issued SFAS No. 133, "Accounting for Derivative Instruments and Hedging Activities." In summary, this accounting standard requires:

- All derivatives must be measured at fair value and recognized in the balance sheet as assets or liabilities.
- With the exception for derivatives that qualify as hedges (fair value hedge, cashflow hedge, and foreign currency hedge), changes in the fair value of derivatives must be recognized in income.

With respect to derivatives that qualify as hedges, management may elect to use hedge accounting to defer gains or losses; however, it should be noted that the deferral of such gains or losses depends on the effectiveness of the derivative in

---

[24] Financial Accounting Standards Board, *Statement of Financial Accounting Standards No. 95,* "Statement of Cash Flows" (Stamford, CT.: FASB, 1987). See SFAS Nos. 102 and 104 for amendments.

offsetting changes in the fair value of the hedged item or changes in future cash flows. In addition, the changes in the fair value of asset, liability, or firm commitment being hedged must be recognized in income to the extent of offsetting gains or losses on the hedged instrument.[25]

The use of market value accounting and the estimate of fair values may cause positive or negative variability in income because of changes in the market values and inaccurate estimates of fair values of financial instruments.

***Reporting and Disclosing Fair Values*** In September 2006, the FASB issued SFAS 157, "Fair Value Measurements," which provided definitions of fair value and guidance for the implementation of a number of previous standards that required fair value measurements for financial instruments. SFAS 157 treats fair value as an "exit value," the amount for which an asset can be sold or a liability can be settled in the normal course of business in a market advantageous to the reporting entity. It creates a three-tier hierarchy of fair value measurements. Tier one is a closing market price from an active market on the date of the balance sheet. Tier two comes into play when a tier-one market does not exist, and consists of estimating fair value of a financial instrument by using other market data. Tier three is used when neither tier-one nor tier-two measurements are possible (such as when no active exit market exists) and consists of probability-weighted net present value calculations based on internal data supplied by management. The standard's hierarchy places a preference on tier one, followed by tier two, and then tier three. SFAS 157 itself does not require fair value accounting for any particular asset or liability, but it does establish the preferred implementation of fair value accounting required by other standards.

The financial crisis of 2008 and 2009 focused considerable attention on fair value accounting. The FASB and the IASB have issued several clarifications and amendments to address some of the issues that arose during the crisis—in particular, how to determine whether an active market exists for a specific financial instrument. As part of this reconsideration, there has also been discussion related to the interplay of management's intentions with regard to a financial instrument and the appropriate accounting. Should different accounting apply depending on whether management intends to hold the financial instrument until it matures, to hold it for trading, or to hold it for potential future resale? What fair value concept should apply to each of the three categories, and what should be done with any unrealized gain or loss from applying the fair value? Should gains and losses be reflected in income, comprehensive income, or equity?

## Role of the Credit Raters

When providing a rating on a bond issue, the major credit rating agencies use accounting information and other financial disclosures as important inputs to their

---

[25] Financial Accounting Standards Board, Statement of Financial Accounting Standards No. 133, "Accounting for Derivatives Instruments and Hedging Activities" (Norwalk, CT.: FASB, 1998). With respect to the different types of hedges, disclosure, and transition requirements, see SFAS No. 133. This statement is effective for all fiscal quarters of fiscal years beginning after June 15, 1999. Also see SFAS Nos. 138, 149, and 150 for amendments.

rating processes. The three major credit raters—Moody's, Standard & Poor's, and Fitch Ratings—all issue public and private reports about the entities they rate. Each credit rater also periodically publishes, for its own purposes, the adjustments it makes to published financial statements. All of the credit raters issue periodic accounting issues reports that audit committee members would find helpful to read, for the reports provide insights into the credit raters' use of accounting information. Reading a credit report about a company or the industry within which it operates can also be highly informative.

Because of public concerns about the conflicts of interest between bond raters and their financial institution clients that arose over the ratings of mortgage securitizations (the subprime crisis), the federal government has been considering a number of alternative regulatory approaches that would change the institutional practices of the bond rating industry. The SEC has regulated the major credit rating agencies for a number of years, but the perceived poor performance of the credit raters in the subprime crisis has called into question the business model by which entities wanting ratings for their offerings pay for the ratings. Many people have expressed concerns that the credit raters were not appropriately incentivized to look skeptically at many of the financial instruments that later failed.

Audit committees should be aware that small changes in their company's credit rating can have significant impacts on the company's debt covenants and on its ability to borrow. Careful monitoring of the company's relationship with its bond raters is an important piece of the audit committee's responsibility.

## REGULATORY AGENCIES

### Importance of Regulatory Agencies

In a private enterprise economy, corporate management is engaged in the ultimate economic decisions regarding the use of the enterprise's economic resources. Such economic decisions are influenced by the various regulatory agencies, such as the Securities and Exchange Commission (SEC) and the Federal Trade Commission (FTC), so that management is not totally free from oversight. Regulatory agencies provide a comprehensive set of rules and regulations in order to control the enterprise and to safeguard the interests of investors and the general public. For example, the objective of the FTC is to prevent monopolistic practices and price discrimination in American industry. Also, several commissions supervise certain industries, such as the utility and transportation industries, as well as the area of labor-management relations. Particularly important is the government's regulation of the securities and futures markets, and the federal taxation process. Because such regulation is an essential part of the economic landscape within which companies operate, audit committees often spend a great deal of their time and effort in oversight of management's compliance with the reporting requirements of government regulatory agencies.

## The Need for Accounting Information

In order to formulate sound public policies, the regulatory commissions need accounting information concerning the economic activities of the enterprise. In addition, they need accounting information to monitor the corporation's compliance with government rules and regulations. Although there are many regulatory agencies, of particular importance are the SEC and the FTC.

***Securities and Exchange Commission*** The principal purpose of the SEC laws is to provide public disclosure of the relevant facts with respect to new securities and securities listed on the stock exchanges.[26] In particular, the SEC requires a registration statement that contains background information, such as the size and competitive position of the corporation. Moreover, a prospective investor must be furnished a prospectus, which is a summary of the registration statement. For example, the prospectus will contain such matters as the offering price of the security, the intended use of the proceeds by the registrant, and the financial statements.[27] Furthermore, the SEC requires periodic reports from the corporations in order to update its files on each corporation. Such periodic reports include the annual report (Form 10-K) and interim reports (Forms 10-Q and 8-K).[28]

The SEC annual Form 10-K report is used to update the information that is included in the registration statement. This report must be filed within 60 days of the end of a registrant's fiscal year if the registrant is a large accelerated filer, within 75 days if it is an accelerated filer, and within 90 days if it is a nonaccelerated filer. Large accelerated filers have common equity with market values of over $700 million; accelerated filers have market values of common equity between $75 million and $700 million; and nonaccelerated filers have market values of common equity of less than $75 million. The report contains this information:

Part I—Item
  1. Business
  1a. Risk factors
  2. Properties
  3. Legal proceedings
  4. Submission of matters to a vote of security holders

Part II—Item
  5. Market for the registrant's common stock and related stockholder matters
  6. Selected financial data
  7. Management's discussion and analysis of financial condition and results of operations

---

[26] Such rules of law are contained in the Accounting Series Releases, Staff Accounting Bulletins, and Financial Reporting Releases of the SEC.

[27] For a complete description of all the items in the prospectus, see Part I of Form S-1.

[28] For further details and description of all forms, see Regulation S-X and Regulation S-K. Copies may be obtained from the U.S. Government Printing Office.

    **7a.** Quantitative and qualitative disclosure about market risk
    **8.** Financial statements and supplementary data
    **9.** Changes in and disagreements with accountants on accounting and financial disclosure
    **9a.** Controls and procedures

Part III—Item
    **10.** Directors and executive officers of the registrant
    **11.** Executive compensation
    **12.** Security ownership of certain beneficial owners and management
    **13.** Certain relationships and related transactions
    **14.** Principal accounting fees and services

Part IV—Item
    **15.** Exhibits, financial statement schedules, and reports on Form 8-K

Signatures
Certification (Sarbanes-Oxley Act, Section 302)
Certification (Sarbanes-Oxley Act, Section 906)

The SEC quarterly Form 10-Q report is used to report interim changes in the financial position and the results of operating the corporation. This particular report must be filed within 45 days after the close of each of the first three quarters for nonaccelerated filers and accelerated filers (market capitalization of $700 million or less). Large accelerated filers must file their 10-Q within 35 days of their quarter-end.

With respect to the financial information, the report contains information on its preparation, reviews by the independent public accountants, and other financial information. Concerning other information, the report discloses information on such matters as legal proceedings, changes in securities, and other materially important events.

The SEC Form 8-K report is an interim or current report that contains information with respect to certain significant special events. For example, a change in the independent accounting firm must be reported within two business days subsequent to the change. Other events include such items as a change in control of the registrant or significant legal proceedings. This report is particularly important since it provides timely information regarding the disclosure of material events. Consequently, the SEC needs accounting information not only to monitor management's compliance with its rules but also to protect the investing public.

## SEC Topical Developments

The SEC has focused on a number of financial reporting areas that relate to the audit committee's oversight responsibility. The more significant developments in these reporting areas are discussed in the next paragraphs.

*Management's Discussion and Analysis* The quality of information reported to the SEC concerning Management's Discussion and Analysis (MD&A) of Financial Condition and Results of Operations in the registrant's filings has been of major concern to the investing public and to the SEC. In response, the SEC issued Financial Reporting Release No. 36, which is an interpretive release regarding disclosures required by Item 303 of Regulation S-K with respect to the registrants' filings containing Management's Discussion and Analysis of Financial Condition and Results of Operations.[29] Based on a review project of such filings, the Commission found that several key disclosure matters, namely, prospective information, liquidity and capital resources analysis, material changes in financial statement line items, and business segment analysis, should be considered by registrants in preparing MD&A disclosures.

The SEC requires management to discuss favorable or unfavorable trends, significant events, and uncertainties that impact the various reporting areas. Given that MD&A reporting is highly subjective and that management must comply with Item 303 of Regulation S-K, the question is frequently asked: Is the objective of the MD&A disclosure requirement being accomplished? Clearly, the MD&A narrative discussion is the appropriate vehicle to provide early warning signals or red flags to the investing public.

In addition to management's involvement with the preparation of MD&A, independent auditors must review this information to ensure that the narrative discussion is consistent with their findings and conclusions as expressed in their opinion in the audit report. For example, if management knows of events, trends, or uncertainties that are reasonably likely to occur, then such information should be reported under prospective information. Conversely, if management concludes that events, trends, or uncertainties are not reasonably likely to occur, then no disclosure is required. Thus the reasonably likely standard, and whether management knows of the trends, events, or uncertainties, determines whether such information is disclosed. If management anticipates such trends, events, or uncertainties, then disclosure is optional under prospective information. In addition, SAS No. 59 requires that the independent auditors evaluate, in every audit engagement, whether there is substantial doubt about the entity's ability to continue as a going concern.

Given the continuing debate over business failure versus audit failure and the continued number of lawsuits against well-known publicly held companies and public accounting firms, it is imperative that the audit committee focus its attention on MD&A disclosures in the financial reporting process. The committee should (1) review and discuss the SEC's regulations concerning MD&A reporting and (2) evaluate management's compliance with the SEC's required disclosures and its interpretive releases. Clearly, one would expect the audit committee to improve the quality of MD&A disclosures in light of the SEC's interpretive release.

---

[29] Securities and Exchange Commission, "Management's Discussion and Analysis of Financial Condition and Results of Operations; Interpretive Release," Title 17, Code of Federal Regulations, Secs. 211, 231, 241, and 271 (June 1989), pp. 1–44. See Chapter 10 for additional discussion about the application of critical accounting policies.

***XBRL*** eXtensible Business Reporting Language allows the tagging and electronic submission of a wide range of data and narrative associated with paper-based financial reports. Executives, regulators, investors, and analysts can extract and use the information they desire for their decision making by identifying electronically the relevant tags. XBRL reduces the information management problems resulting from multiple reports covering financial, environmental, social accountability, and governance issues as filed in a paper-based system. The SEC released in 2008 a final rule requiring that the 500 largest filers start reporting in an XBRL format in the second quarter of 2009, followed by all accelerated files in 2010 and all filers in 2011.

XBRL software, which is becoming widely available in the United States from a number of vendors, may also be of interest to audit committees because of potential cost savings in periodic accounting closings related to the aggregation and adjustment processes. Essentially, correctly tagging transactions at the point of entry to the accounting system could eliminate some of the time now needed for internal review of aggregated data. It could also improve the integrity of the data aggregation process in many situations and provide additional strength to internal control over financial reporting. As public companies use XBRL-based systems in fulfilling the SEC requirements, more will become known about the internal and external costs and benefits associated with them.[30]

***Disagreements with the Independent Auditors***[31] As noted in Part II, Item 9, of the SEC annual 10-K report, a registrant is required to disclose accounting and financial disclosure disagreements between management and the independent auditors. In addition, the SEC requires a registrant to file a Form 8-K and the independent auditors' response with respect to reporting the reasons for changes in independent auditors. The original purpose of the SEC's requirement in 1972 for such disclosure concerned audit opinion shopping. In a consent decree with the FTC in 1968, the audit firms had just begun to compete for clients. There was considerable concern that unscrupulous managements would fire auditors that disagreed with their accounting treatments and shop for those that would permit what they desired. Hence, the SEC in 1972 required 8-K disclosure of disagreements with auditors when there was an auditor change. At about the same time, the AICPA also issued Statement on Auditing Standards No. 50, "Reports on the Application of Accounting Principles," to allay concerns about opinion shopping. Thus, when the principal auditor's client company requests from another accounting firm a report on the application of an accounting principle, the reporting auditor is required to consult with the principal auditor.[32] Such an auditing standard helps ensure the independent auditor's independence.

---

[30] See more about XBRL and its implications for the audit committee in Chapter 7.

[31] See Jerry E. Serlin, "Shopping Around: A Closer Look at Opinion Shopping," *Journal of Accounting, Auditing & Finance* 9, no. 1 (Fall 1985): 74–80.

[32] Statement on Auditing Standards, No. 50, *Reports on the Application of Accounting Principles* (New York: AICPA, 1986), par 1.

Because the audit committee, in the United States, has specific responsibility under the Sarbanes-Oxley Act of 2002 for the relationship with the independent auditor, committee members should be aware of the SEC notification requirements around auditor changes. Times have changed somewhat since 1972, and the incidence of auditor switches has increased, frequently for positive reasons unrelated to opinion shopping. The company must file with the SEC—within two days of the event—an 8-K report that its incumbent auditor has either been fired or has resigned. The company must indicate whether an accounting or auditing disagreement with the incumbent auditor was involved in the decision, or whether the audit firm had communicated any one of four "reportable conditions" about the company or its management. A very small proportion of 8-Ks communicating an auditor change contain indications of one of these problems, typically between 2 and 4 percent a year. The majority of 8-Ks provide no reason for the change, simply a notification. An increasing number, 29 percent in 2008 according to data from Audit Analytics (www.auditanalytics.com), gave specific reasons for the switch even though the reasons did not involve a disagreement or reportable condition. Some investor advocates, such as the Council of Institutional Investors and proxy advisor Glass Lewis, have adopted resolutions that every auditor change should be accompanied with a rationale, with some discussion of the positive and negative reasons. Likewise, major credit raters, such as Standard & Poor's, Moody's, and Fitch, often request more information when auditor changes take place.

**Environmental Liabilities**[33]   The board of directors has oversight responsibility to determine that management is complying with environmental laws. In some industries with significant environmental exposure, board committees may be appointed to deal with the issue. Whether the full board or a committee is assigned this responsibility, the audit committee should determine that environmental costs and liabilities are properly reflected in the financial statements and related disclosure.

The committee may recommend to the board the establishment and monitoring of an environmental auditing program. In many parts of the world in 2008 and 2009, accounting for sustainability has become a major focus of a number of commissions. Both the Aspen Institute (www.aspeninstitute.org) and the International Corporate Governance Network (www.icgn.org) have developed programs to promote corporate sustainability and accounting for it. See Chapter 10 for further discussion of this subject.

**Executive Compensation Disclosure**   On October 15, 1992, the SEC adopted amendments to the executive officer and director compensation disclosure requirements applicable to proxy statements, registration statements, and periodic reports (e.g., 10-Qs and 10-K) under the Securities Act of 1933 and the

---

[33] A National Priority List of potentially responsible parties (PRPs) is issued by the U.S. Environmental Protection Agency on an annual basis. See also the SEC's SAB No. 92, "Accounting and Disclosures Relating to Loss Contingencies," and the AICPA's Accounting Standard Executive Committee, Statement of Position (SOP) No. 96-1, "Environmental Remediation Liabilities" (New York: AICPA, 1996).

Securities Exchange Act of 1934 (Release Nos. 33-6962, 34-31327, and IC-19032 applicable to Regulation S-K).[34]

In 2006, the SEC changed significantly the disclosure requirements related to executive compensation. These new SEC rules require the preparation of a thorough discussion and analysis of executive compensation and the disclosure of more quantitative information than was required previously. The rules also broaden the scope of the narratives to the extent that these new disclosures are referred to as Compensation Discussion and Analysis (CD&A), which puts it on footing similar to Management Discussion and Analysis (MD&A). Although the compensation committee generally has the responsibility to prepare the executive compensation disclosures, the audit committee should review such disclosures carefully because of the importance of executive compensation in both the disclosure process and in its significance to the financial reports. A clear understanding of the effect of executives' compensation packages on the current and future financial statements, and of the disclosures that must be made about them, lies within the responsibility of the audit committee. Director compensation is also covered in the required disclosures. Finally, the intent of the SEC rules change was to make compensation easier to understand by the use of "plain English." The SEC publishes a guide to "plain English" use in annual reports at www.sec.gov/pdf/handbook.pdf.

**Federal Trade Commission**   The major objective of the FTC is to police the business community to eliminate unfair methods of competition. Essentially, the FTC is involved with the enforcement of the antitrust laws, such as the Sherman and Clayton acts. Furthermore, the FTC administers the laws concerning the Robinson-Patman Act, which prohibits big businesses from exploiting their small competitors through price discrimination and quantity discounts. Thus, the FTC needs accounting information regarding distribution costs and related prices to ensure that the corporation is not engaged in unlawful pricing practices.

## Role of the Audit Committee

Since the corporate annual report and the SEC annual 10-K report must be examined by the independent public accountants, the audit committee should review these reports with the accountants from a compliance perspective. For example, the audit committee should be concerned with the protection of the corporation's interest against penalties or fines regarding any noncompliance with the laws, such as environmental protection laws. Such penalties can be very costly and reduce the earnings performance of the enterprise. Indeed, there are myriad complex laws and regulations affecting the corporation. The members of the committee may not have the necessary legal expertise to determine whether the firm is complying with the laws. Accordingly, it may be advisable for the

---

[34] Securities and Exchange Commission, "Executive Compensation Disclosure," Title 17, Code of Federal Regulations, Parts 228, 299, 240, and 249 (October 1992). In November 1993, the SEC amended its executive compensation disclosure rules to address such matters as executives covered, restricted stock holdings, option valuations, and peer group index. See the Federal Register 58, no. 227 (November 29, 1993), 63010 and 63017, for further details.

committee to retain the corporation's in-house counsel or outside legal counsel to gain assurance regarding management's compliance. Such assistance will enable the committee to be aware of the effect of certain laws on the corporation and thus avoid expensive or embarrassing fines or penalties. More specifically, the audit committee must make an informed judgment on management's efforts to comply with the laws through a review of the corporation's history of compliance and the necessary managerial corrective actions. Thus the committee can minimize the firm's noncompliance liability based on the above procedures.

## OTHER OUTSIDE CONSTITUENCIES

### Importance of Other Outside Constituencies

With respect to the significance of the other external users of accounting information, the American Assembly concluded:

> Employees should be regarded as a crucial part of the constituency of the corporation. Employee interests will be better served by various means, such as collective bargaining, direct communications, and participative management approaches rather than by direct employee representation on boards of directors.
>
> Consumers have large roles to play. They act as advance guideposts to the needs and expectations of the marketplace. Corporations which enhance their long-term profitability should build relationships with future customers.[35]

Thus, it may be appropriate for corporate management to share the accounting information with the above groups, since such groups not only provide services but also receive the goods and services from the enterprise. Because such groups are vital to the successful operation of the corporation, management should consider sharing its accounting information concerning the economic performance of the enterprise. Although there is no uniform pattern in communicating financial accounting information to employees, it may be desirable to consider a special annual report for employees. Similarly, some organizations may consider making available a copy of the annual report to special consumer interest groups.

Through an overview of the importance and the need for accounting information, the audit directors can contribute to improving the effectiveness of the audit function in society. Moreover, the Business Roundtable noted:

> The central corporate governance point to be made about a corporation's stakeholders beyond the shareholder is that they are vital to the long-term successful economic performance of the corporation. Some argue that only the interests of the shareholders should be considered by directors. The thrust of history and law strongly supports the broader view of the directors' responsibility to carefully weigh the interests of all stakeholders as part of their responsibility to the corporation or to the long-term interests of its shareholders.

---

[35] The American Assembly, *Corporate Governance in America*, pamphlet 54 (New York: The American Assembly, 1978), 6.

Resolving the potentially differing interests of various stakeholders and the best long-term interest of the corporation and its shareholders involves compromises and tradeoffs which often must be made rapidly. It is important that all stakeholder interests be considered, but impossible to assure that all will be satisfied because competing claims may be mutually exclusive.[36]

## The Need for Accounting Information

A corporation's stakeholders need accounting information in order to judge management's economic decisions and performance. For example, employees are interested in the solvency position of the corporation since they expect to receive wages in return for their services. Moreover, they are interested in the enterprise's image as a corporate citizen of society. Similarly, consumers need accounting information regarding the present and future economic status of the corporation because they rely on the enterprise to provide necessary goods and services to the community.

## Role of the Audit Committee

To improve the communication process between the enterprise and stakeholder groups, the committee should consult with the executive in charge of the public relations program. For example, the audit directors should satisfy themselves that the information in any special annual reports to employees is consistent with the financial information in the annual or quarterly reports. In addition, the audit committee should review management's commentary in the special reports in view of the quantitative characteristics of financial reporting. As a participative management approach, the committee may suggest an employee report whereby the financial information is related to each employee. Such reports enhance not only the employees' perception of the organization but also their work attitude since both corporate management and the employees are contributing to the organizational goals.

Furthermore, the audit directors should determine that adequate management controls exist with respect to the release of special financial reports to the general public, such as newspaper and other releases, to ensure that such releases are appropriate and consistent with the company's policies and plans. In some instances, it may be desirable to clear such distribution of financial information with the audit committee.

## IMPORTANT DEVELOPMENTS IN BUSINESS REPORTING AND ASSURANCE SERVICES

This section briefly highlights and discusses the findings and conclusions of two major studies conducted by the AICPA Special Committee on Financial Reporting (Jenkins Committee) and the AICPA Special Committee on Assurance

---

[36] Business Roundtable, *Corporate Governance and American Competitiveness*, 4.

Services (Elliott Committee). The major objective of this review discussion is to provide an understanding of the issues and emerging trends impacting the public accounting profession that, in turn, are of particular concern to audit committees in the latter half of the 1990s.

In 1991, a Special Committee on Financial Reporting (Jenkins Committee) was established by the AICPA to study the need for a new financial reporting model in response to the information needs of users. After completing a three-year study of the financial reporting system in the United States, in 1994 the AICPA Special Committee on Financial Reporting issued its final comprehensive report (202 pages) and summary report (20 pages), entitled *Improving Business Reporting— A Customer Focus: Meeting the Information Needs of Investors and Creditors*. As part of the AICPA's broad initiative to improve the value of business information and the public's confidence in the financial reporting process, the study examined the relevance and usefulness of business reporting and the independent auditors' association with that type of reporting. The Committee set forth these recommendations with respect to four broad categories:

1. Improving the Types of Information in Business Reporting

   Recommendation 1: Standard setters should develop a comprehensive model of business reporting indicating the types and timing of information that users need to value and assess the risk of their investments.

   Recommendation 2: Improve understanding of costs and benefits of business reporting, recognizing that definitive quantification of costs and benefits is not possible.

2. Financial Statements and Related Disclosures

   Recommendation 1: Improve disclosure of business segment information.

   Recommendation 2: Address the disclosures and accounting for innovative financial instruments.

   Recommendation 3: Improve disclosures about the identity, opportunities, and risks of off-balance-sheet financing arrangements and reconsider the accounting for those arrangements.

   Recommendation 4: Report separately the effects of core and non-core activities and events, and measure at fair value non-core assets and liabilities.

   Recommendation 5: Improve disclosures about the uncertainty of measurements of certain assets and liabilities.

   Recommendation 6: Improve quarterly reporting by reporting on the fourth quarter separately and including business segment data.

   Recommendation 7: Standard setters should search for and eliminate less relevant disclosures.

3. Auditor Association with Business Reporting

   Recommendation 1: Allow for flexible auditor association with business reporting, whereby the elements of information on which auditors report and the level of auditor involvement with those elements are decided by agreement between a company and the users of its business reporting.

Recommendation 2: The auditing profession should prepare to be involved with all the information in the comprehensive model, so companies and users can call on it to provide assurance on any of the model's elements.

Recommendation 3: The newly formed AICPA Special Committee on Assurance Services should research and formulate conclusions on analytical commentary in auditors' reports within the context of the Committee's model, focusing on users' needs for information.

Recommendation 4: The profession should continue its projects on other matters related to auditor association with business reporting.

4. Facilitating Change in Business Reporting

Recommendation 1: National and international standard setters and regulators should increase their focus on the information needs of users, and users should be encouraged to work with standard setters to increase the level of their involvement in the standard-setting process.

Recommendation 2: U.S. standard setters and regulators should continue to work with their non-U.S. counterparts and international standard setters to develop international accounting standards, provided the resulting standards meet users' needs for information.

Recommendation 3: Lawmakers, regulators, and standard setters should develop more effective deterrents to unwarranted litigation that discourages companies from disclosing forward-looking information.

Recommendation 4: Companies should be encouraged to experiment voluntarily with ways to improve the usefulness of reporting consistent with the Committee's model. Standard setters and regulators should consider allowing companies that experiment to substitute information specified by the model for information currently required.

Recommendation 5: Standard setters should adopt a longer term focus by developing a vision of the future business environment and users' needs for information in that environment. Standards should be consistent directionally with that long-term vision.

Recommendation 6: Regulators should consider whether there are any alternatives to the current requirement that public companies make all disclosures publicly available.

Recommendation 7: The AICPA should establish a Coordinating Committee charged to ensure that the recommendations in this report are given adequate consideration by those who can act on them.[37]

As a result of the Special Committee's report, standard setters, regulators, professional organizations, professional practitioners, and academics need to focus their attention on the points of view on the Committee's recommendations.

---

[37] American Institute of Certified Public Accountants, *Improving Business Reporting—A Customer Focus, Meeting the Information Needs of Investors and Creditors* (New York: AICPA, 1994), 123–127.

This report has a wealth of information concerning the business reporting model and a comprehensive illustration of the Committee's recommendations. Audit committees should review these recommendations, with particular emphasis on the elements of the Committee's model of business reporting relative to the current model of financial reporting. Additionally, they should discuss the implications for independent auditors.

Recognizing that audit committees have oversight responsibilities for the external audit process, it is desirable to review the Special Committee's form of report that would be issued by the independent auditors. To improve the independent auditors' communications about their role and responsibility, the Committee attempted to articulate an illustrative audit report. This type of report is shown in Exhibit 3.1.

The Committee's proposed audit report is different in several ways from the standard independent auditors' report. First, the introductory paragraph mentions "core earnings" and the audit of the five-year summary of business data and other descriptions. Additionally, the auditors are expressing their opinion on these presentations as opposed to only financial statements. Second, the auditors would be required to substitute the word *presentation* for *financial statement* in the scope paragraph. Finally, the auditors would be required to express two opinions with respect to both financial and nonfinancial data.

Notwithstanding the FASB's current model of financial reporting, the Special Committee has offered 20 recommendations and a comprehensive model of business reporting. In fact, the Committee goes beyond the full disclosure principle with a requirement for disclosure of nonfinancial data. Of course, the major objective is to minimize information overload within the cost-benefit constraint. Moreover, the Committee has broadened the attest function with respect to seven sections of the annual report, as noted in the proposed auditors' report. Regarding flexible auditors' association with business reporting, the Special Committee recommends that the AICPA Special Committee on Assurance Services and the Auditing Standards Board pursue the subject of alternative levels of assurance within the Committee's reporting framework. In sum, the Committee's report is a significant step in the continuous process of improving financial reporting; however, many preparers of financial statements would argue that the cost of implementing the recommendations would be prohibitive. Moreover, it is reasonable to expect that many nonpublic companies, particularly small companies, would have difficulty with the Committee's proposals.

In 1995, the AICPA established the Financial Reporting Coordinating Committee to coordinate actions taken on the recommendations made by the Jenkins Committee. Although the Coordinating Committee held a symposium (fall 1996) to continue the discussion of Jenkins Committee's Comprehensive Model for Business Reporting, the debate between the financial statement preparers and users about the aforementioned recommendations continues. However, the Auditing Standards Board has issued a Statement on Standards for Attestation Engagements (SSAE) No. 8, *Management's Discussion and Analysis* (March 1998), in response to the Jenkins Committee's recommendations. Therefore, financial statement preparers and users can engage the accounting profession to provide

**EXHIBIT 3.1**   Report of Independent Accountants

This example illustrates the form of report that would be issued if the independent accountant had been engaged to render an opinion on the entire FauxCom annual report, although this may not always be the case.

We have audited the accompanying consolidated balance sheet of FauxCom, Inc. as of December 31, 1993, and 1992, and the related consolidated statements of core earnings and net income, cash flows, and stockholders' equity for each of the two years in the period ended December 31, 1993. We also audited the five-year summary of business data, the description of information about management and shareholders, and the scope and description of the Company's businesses accompanying the financial statements. These financial statements, five-year summary and descriptions are the responsibility of the Company's management. Our responsibility is to express an opinion on these presentations based on our audits.

We conducted our audits in accordance with generally accepted auditing standards. Those standards require that we plan and perform the audit to obtain reasonable assurance about whether the information presented is free of material misstatement. An audit includes examining, on a test basis, evidence supporting the amounts and disclosures presented. An audit also includes assessing the accounting principles used and significant estimates made by management, as well as evaluating the overall presentation. We believe that our audits provide a reasonable basis for our opinion.

In our opinion, the financial statements referred to above present fairly, in all material respects, the financial position of FauxCom, Inc. as of December 31, 1993, and 1992, and the results of its operations and its cash flows for each of the two years in the period ended December 31, 1993, in conformity with generally accepted accounting principles. It is also our opinion that the five-year summary and descriptions referred to above are fairly presented, in all material respects, in conformity with the applicable standards.

As part of the audit, we also performed such audit procedures as we considered necessary to evaluate management's assumptions and analyses and the preparation and presentation of the information in the following sections of the annual report:

• Current year review
• Management's analysis of financial and non-financial data
• Opportunities and risks, including those resulting from key trends
• Management's plans, including critical success factors
• Comparison of actual business performance to previously disclosed forward-looking information
• Broad objectives and strategies
• Impact of industry structure on the Company

In our opinion, the accompanying sections described above are presented in conformity with the respective standards of presentation, and management has a reasonable basis for the underlying assumptions and analyses reflected in the aforementioned sections.

February 15, 1994
Boston, Massachusetts

---

*Source:* American Institute of Certified Public Accountants, *Comprehensive Report of the Special Committee on Financial Reporting* (New York: AICPA, 1994), 184.

assurance on the elements of the Comprehensive Model for Business Reporting.[38] Since 2003, the Enhanced Business Reporting Consortium (EBRC) has picked up where the Jenkins Committee left off in studying and promoting a range of enhancements to the general reporting model. EBRC's focus has centered on the measurement and disclosure of key performance indicators (KPIs), which would supplement the financial statements and their notes by providing measurements of value drivers such as innovation, intangibles, customer loyalty, management systems, people, market share, and R&D results. Supporters of KPIs argue that disclosing them will assist investors in assessing the quality, sustainability, and variability of a company's earnings and cash flows. KPIs would differ by industry, but EBRC and others have engaged to create private sector standards to ensure understandable, consistent, relevant, and comparable KPIs.[39]

In October 2002, the General Accounting Office (GAO) issued a report entitled *Financial Statement Restatements: Trends, Market Impacts, Regulatory Responses, and Remaining Challenges.* The GAO reported that a number of well-publicized announcements about financial statement restatements by large, well-known public companies have erased billions of dollars of previously reported earnings and raised questions about the credibility of accounting practices and the quality of corporate final disclosure and oversight in the United States.[40]

In sum, the GAO's principal findings were:

- The number of restatements due to accounting irregularities grew significantly— by 145 percent—from January 1997 through June 2002.

- The 845 restating companies identified by the GAO had restated their financial statements to adjust revenues, costs, or expenses or to address securities-related issues.

- Issues involving revenue recognition accounted for almost 38 percent of the restatements.

- Of the 845 restating companies, 689 companies lost billions of dollars in market capitalization in the days around the initial reinstatement announcement.[41]

Recognizing that these losses have shaken investors' confidence in the nation's financial reporting system, the GAO believes that the Sarbanes-Oxley Act of 2002 addresses concerns about the financial statement restatements,

---

[38] For further discussion regarding an examination, review, or an agreed-on procedure engagement, see SSAE No. 8. Also see James L. Craig, "The CPA Journal Symposium on Recommendations for Improving Business Reporting," *CPA Journal* 65, no. 1 (January 1995):18–27; Daniel J. Noll and Jerry J. Weygandt, "Business Reporting: What Comes Next?" *Journal of Accountancy* 183, No. 2 (February 1997): 59.

[39] For further research on the future of financial reporting and KPIs see Robert H. Eccles and Michael P. Krzus, *One Report: Integrated Reporting for a Sustainable Strategy and a Sustainable Society* (Hoboken, NJ: John Wiley & Sons, 2009)

[40] U.S. General Accounting Office, Financial Statement Restatements: Trends, Market Impact, Regulatory Responses, and Remaining Challenges, GAO-03-138, October 4, 2002. GAO-03-138 available at www.gao.gov/new.items/d03138.pdf.

[41] Ibid., 1.

including strengthening corporate governance and improving transparency and accountability to help ensure the accuracy and integrity of its financial reporting system. In 2007 the GAO produced another study on restatements, with similar results, and the U.S. Treasury commissioned research on this topic that was published in 2008 (see earlier section reporting on the research of Susan Scholz).

Given the recent failures of major corporations, such as Enron, WorldCom, Adelphia, and Global Crossing, the government's increased scrutiny of the accounting profession and the enactment of the Sarbanes-Oxley Act of 2002 have triggered many new legal and regulatory reforms, as discussed in Chapters 1 and 2. Notwithstanding the demise of the AICPA's Independence Standards Board, Public Oversight Board, and the Auditing Standards Board, for publicly held companies the new Public Company Accounting Oversight Board not only will have oversight and enforcement authority, but will also promulgate auditing, quality control, and independence standards for the accounting profession. Historically, many of the AICPA's Special Committees on financial reporting and POB's blue ribbon panels and committees have served as platforms for the issuance of standards and rules.

It is not known to what extent the new PCAOB will promulgate standards and rules to close the expectations gap. However, the need for reliable and relevant financial information remains of utmost importance to ensure an efficient capital market system.

In an effort to enhance financial reporting and provide guidance for the participants in the financial reporting process (financial statement preparers, auditors, and audit committees), the five largest accounting firms in the United States and the American Institute of Certified Public Accountants set forth as common goals the following recommended actions. They remain relevant for audit committees seeking to minimize problems with their published financial reports:

**Management**

- Ensure the proper tone at the top and an expectation that only the highest-quality financial reporting is acceptable.
- Review all elements of the company's internal control—control environment, risk assessment, control activities, information and communication, and monitoring— in light of changes in the company's business environment and with particular attention to significant financial statement areas.
- Ensure the appropriate levels of management involvement and review exist over key accounting policy and financial reporting decisions.
- Establish a framework for open, timely communication with the auditors and the audit committee on all significant matters.
- Strive for the highest quality, most transparent accounting and disclosure—not just what is acceptable—in both financial statements and MD&A.
- Make sure estimates and judgments are supported by reliable information and the most reasonable assumptions in the circumstances, and that processes are in place to ensure consistent application from period to period.

- Record identified audit differences.
- Base business decisions on economic reality rather than accounting goals.
- Expand the depth and disclosure surrounding subjective measurements used in preparing the financial statements, including the likelihood and ramifications of subsequent changes.
- When faced with a "gray" area, consult with others, consider the need for SEC pre-clearance, and focus on the transparency of financial reporting.

## Auditors

- Understand how a company is affected by changes in the current business environment.
- Understand the stresses on the company's internal control over financial reporting, and how they may impact its effectiveness.
- Identify key risk areas, particularly those involving significant estimates and judgments.
- Approach the audit with objectivity and skepticism, notwithstanding prior experiences with or belief in management's integrity.
- Pay special attention to complex transactions, especially those presenting difficult issues of form versus substance.
- Consider whether additional specialized knowledge is needed on the audit team.
- Make management aware of identified audit differences on a timely basis.
- Question the unusual and challenge anything that doesn't make sense.
- Foster open, ongoing communications with management and the audit committee, including discussions about the quality of financial reporting and any pressure to accept less than high-quality financial reporting.
- When faced with a "gray" area, perform appropriate procedures to test and corroborate management's explanations and representations, and consult with others as needed.

## Audit Committees

- Evaluate whether management exhibits the proper tone at the top and fosters a culture and environment that promotes high-quality financial reporting, including addressing internal control issues.
- Question management and auditors about how they assess the risk of material misstatement, what the major risk areas are, and how they respond to identified risks.
- Challenge management and the auditors to identify the difficult areas (e.g., significant estimates and judgments) and explain fully how they each made their judgments in those areas.
- Probe how management and the auditors have reacted to changes in the company's business environment.
- Understand why critical accounting principles were chosen and how they were applied and changed, and consider the quality of financial reporting and the transparency of disclosures about accounting principles.

- Challenge management for explanations of any identified audit differences not recorded.

- Understand the extent to which related parties exist and consider the transparency of the related disclosures.

- Read the financial statements and MD&A to see if anything is inconsistent with your own knowledge.

- Consider whether the readers of the financial statements and the MD&A will be able to understand the disclosures and the risks of the company without the access to management that the committee enjoys.

- Ask the auditors about pressure by management to accept less than high-quality financial reporting.

- When faced with a "gray" area, increase the level of communication with management and the auditors.

Management, auditors, and audit committees each must diligently fulfill its own role and effectively work together with the others through proactive communication and information sharing. In working together, we can collectively improve the financial reporting process. This requires renewed commitment by each of the parties to the needs of financial statement users.[42]

## BENCHMARKING

This chapter has covered a wide range of external factors that affect the activities and responsibilities of an audit committee. Most of these factors are connected to pressures that come to bear on an audit committee because of the demands of a variety of external constituencies, many of which have conflicting goals, desires, and concerns. An obvious question arises: How can an audit committee reassure itself that company management and the external auditors are doing a good job in the financial reporting area? Because financial reports are either publicly available, or often are widely available for larger nonpublic companies and for virtually all not-for-profit entities, comparing a company to others similarly situated is often possible.

We have deliberately not provided financial reporting examples in the text of this chapter because any that we might choose may not be applicable to the situation faced by a given audit committee. We suggest a different approach. Audit committees should identify a small number of companies that bear similarities to theirs—perhaps 5 to 10—and monitor the financial reports and other disclosures of that peer group. Audit committees of companies trying to move up in their industry should also identify another group of companies that represent what they aspire to be, and they should monitor the financial reports and disclosures of that aspirant group. Other things to monitor include the background and expertise of the accounting personnel, the characteristics of the external auditors, and what can be discovered about the peer or aspirant group's approach

---

[42] American Institute of Certified Public Accountants, "Impact of the Current Economic and Business Environment on Financial Reporting" (2000), 10–11. Available at www.aicpa.org.

to internal control over financial reporting and about the processes, workload, and structures of the groups' audit committees. Management and the external auditors could be excellent sources of information in choosing peer and aspirant groups, and in collecting and summarizing the benchmarking information for monitoring purposes. Monitoring implies more than careful study; it includes appropriate actions to maintain parity with a peer group or to upgrade in order to join an aspirant group.

## SOURCES AND SUGGESTED READINGS

American Assembly. *Corporate Governance in America,* Pamphlet 54. New York: Columbia University, April 1978.

American Assembly. *The American Assembly Report 1991–1992.* New York: American Assembly, 1992.

American Institute of Certified Public Accountants. *Accounting Trends and Techniques—1990.* New York: AICPA, 1990.

American Institute of Certified Public Accountants. *Improving Business Reporting—A Customer Focus, Meeting the Information Needs of Investors and Creditors.* New York: AICPA, 1994.

American Institute of Certified Public Accountants. "Impact of the Current Economic and Business Environment on Financial Reporting" (2000), 1–11. Available at www.aicpa.org.

American Institute of Certified Public Accountants. *Report of the Study Group on the Objectives of Financial Statements.* New York: AICPA, 1973.

American Stock Exchange, *American Stock Exchange Fact Book 1991.* New York: ASE, 1991.

Association for Investment Management and Research. *Corporate Information Committee Report 1995–1996.* New York: Association for Investment Management and Research, 1997.

Barlas, Stephen. "SEC Cracks Down on MD&A Sections." *Management Accounting* 73, no. 12 (June 1992): 8.

Billings, Anthony B., and Larry D. Crumbley. "Financial Difficulties of Governmental Units." *CPA Journal* 58, no. 7 (October 1988): 52–61.

BSB Bancorp, Inc. *2002 Annual Report.*

Business Roundtable. *Corporate Governance and American Competitiveness.* New York: Business Roundtable, 1990.

Cox, George, H. Stephen Grace Jr., John E. Haupert, Peter Howell, and Ronald H. Wilcomes. "A Prescription for Company Health." *CPA Journal* 72, no. 7 (July 2002): 62–63.

Davis, Ann., "SEC Case Claims Profit 'Management' by Grace." *Wall Street Journal* (April 7, 1999): C1.

Eccles, Robert H., and Michael P. Krzus. *One Report: Integrated Reporting for a Sustainable Strategy.* Hoboken, NJ: John Wiley & Sons, forthcoming.

Financial Accounting Standards Board. *Statement of Financial Accounting Concepts No. 1.* Stamford, CT: FASB, 1978.

Financial Accounting Standards Board. *Statement of Financial Accounting Concepts No. 7,* "Using Cash Flow Information and Present Value in Accounting Measurement." Stamford, CT: FASB, 2000.

Financial Accounting Standards Board. *Statement of Financial Accounting Standards No. 95.* "Statement of Cash Flows." Stamford,CT: FASB, 1987.

Financial Accounting Standards Board. *Statement of Financial Accounting Standards No. 107.* "Disclosures About Fair Value of Financial Instruments." Norwalk, CT: FASB, 1991.

Financial Accounting Standards Board. *Statement of Financial Accounting Standards, No. 133.* "Accounting for Derivative Instruments and Hedging Activities." Norwalk, CT: FASB, 1998.

Financial Analysts Federation. "Awards for Excellence in Corporate Reporting." *Financial Analysts Federation News Release* (January 1978).

Grusd, Neville. "The Enron Affair from a Lender's View." *CPA Journal* 72, no. 12 (December 2002): 8–10.

Investor Responsibility Research Center. *Annual Report 1992.* Washington, DC: Investor Responsibility Research Center, 1992.

Krishnamoorthy, Ganesh, Arnie Wright, and Jeffrey Cohen. "Auditors' Views on Audit Committees and Financial Reporting Quality." *CPA Journal* 72, no. 10, (October 2002): 56–57.

Lubow, Nathan M. "New Disclosures FASB No. 105." *Secured Lender* 48, no. 6 (November/December 1992): 112, 114.

MacIver, Brian H., James Welch, and Priscilla A. Burnaby. "Quality Review—Observations of a Team Captain." *Ohio CPA Journal* 50, no. 1 (January–April 1991): 54–55.

Most, Kenneth S., and Lucia S. Chang. "An Empirical Study of Investor Views Concerning Financial Statements and Investment Decisions." *Collected Papers of the American Accounting Association's Annual Meeting* (Sarasota, FL: American Accounting Association, August 20–23, 1978): 241–260.

National Association of Corporate Directors. *Report of the NACD Blue Ribbon Commission on Executive Compensation: Guidelines for Corporate Directors.* Washington, DC: NACD, 1993.

New York Stock Exchange. *New York Stock Exchange Fact Book 1992.* New York: NYSE, 1992.

Pate, Gwen Richardson, and Keith G. Stanga. "A Guide to the FASB's Concepts Statements." *Journal of Accountancy* 168, no. 2 (August 1989): 28–31.

Rubin, Steven. "How Concepts Statements Can Solve Practice Problems." *Journal of Accountancy* 166, no. 4 (October 1988): 123–124, 126.

Securities and Exchange Commission. *1992 Annual Report.* Washington, DC: U.S. Government Printing Office, 1992.

Securities and Exchange Commission. *1997 Annual Report.* Washington, DC: U.S. Government Printing Office, 1997.

Securities and Exchange Commission. *1998 Annual Report.* Washington, DC: U.S. Government Printing Office, 1998.

Securities and Exchange Commission. *1999 Annual Report.* Washington, DC: U.S. Government Printing Office, 1999.

Securities and Exchange Commission. *2002 Annual Report*. Washington, DC: U.S. Government Printing Office, 2002.

Securities and Exchange Commission. *Acceleration of Periodic Report Filing Dates and Disclosure Concerning Web site Access to Reports* (August 27, 2002) Available at www. sec.gov.

Securities and Exchange Commission. *Accounting and Auditing Enforcement Release no. 363* (March 31, 1992), 51 SEC Docket 300.

Securities and Exchange Commission. "Executive Compensation Disclosure." Title 17 Code of Federal Regulations, Parts 228, 229, 240, and 249 (October 1989). See Rules and Regulations, Federal Register, 57, no. 204 (October 21, 1992): 48126–48159.

Securities and Exchange Commission. *In the Matter of W.R. Grace & Co., Release no. 34-41578*. Accounting and Auditing Enforcement Release No. 1140 (June 30, 1999).

Securities and Exchange Commission. "Management's Discussion and Analysis of Financial Condition and Results of Operations: Interpretive Release." Title 17 *Code of Federal Regulations,* Sec. 211, 231, 241, and 271 (June 1989): 1–44.

SRI International. *Investor Informational Needs and the Annual Report,* Financial Executive Research Foundation. Morristown, NJ: Financial Executive Institute, 1987.

Stanga, Keith G., and James J. Benjamin. "Information Needs of Bankers." *Management Accounting* 59, no. 12 (June 1978): 17–21.

*Statement on Auditing Standards No. 25.* "The Relationship of Generally Accepted Auditing Standards to Quality Control Standards." New York: AICPA, 1979.

*Statement on Auditing Standards No. 50.* "Reports on the Application of Accounting Principles." New York: AICPA, 1986.

*Statement on Auditing Standards No. 59.* "The Auditor's Consideration of an Entity's Ability to Continue as a Going Concern." New York: AICPA, 1988.

*Statement on Auditing Standards No. 69.* "The Meaning of Present Fairly in Conformity with Generally Accepted Accounting Principles in the Independent Auditor's Report." New York: AICPA, 1992.

*Statement on Auditing Standards No. 90.* "Audit Committee Communications." New York: AICPA, 1999.

U.S. General Accounting Office. "Financial Statement Restatements: Trends, Market Impacts, Regulatory Responses, and Remaining Challenges." GAO-03-138 (October 4, 2002). Available at www.gao.gov/cgi-bin/getrpt?GAO-03-138.

# Chapter 4

# The Legal Environment of the Audit Committee

The Sarbanes-Oxley Act of 2002 and the subsequent SEC final regulations regarding the composition, roles, and responsibilities of audit committees have established a specific body of federal law and regulation that governs audit committees. Likewise, state corporation laws specify the rights and obligations of corporate directors, including audit committee members, and certain other federal statutes address directorate responsibilities. This chapter discusses the general legal responsibilities of audit committees and reviews several legal cases that have affected audit committee processes and responsibilities. In addition, an overview of securities litigation (see Exhibit 4.1) and some guidelines for minimizing the committee's possible legal liability provide a perspective on understanding and managing the legal exposure of directors serving on audit committees.[1]

The contents of this chapter are not intended to represent a legal document or legal advice. The chapter's purpose is to inform generally about the legal environment in which audit committees function. Audit committees should seek competent and appropriate legal counsel when faced with issues having legal implications.

Three points should be kept in mind when considering the information in this chapter:

1. In the United States, the Sarbanes-Oxley Act significantly increased the audit committee's responsibilities and the cost of directors' and officers' liability insurance. It also has prompted boards of directors to manage their directors' and officers' liability insurance more carefully. While some people have warned that perceptions of greater personal liability for outside directors would dampen the enthusiasm of qualified individuals for such positions, the evidence thus far does not indicate that outside directors have been exposed to greater than normal out-of-pocket costs in litigation.
2. To help boards of directors fulfill their fiduciary responsibilities, audit committees should consider their use of authority under Sarbanes-Oxley Section 301 to engage independent counsel and other advisors. While state laws generally permit directors to rely on management, professionals, and

---

[1] Although reference is made to both the federal and state statutes, such references provide only a description of the law. One should have recourse to legal counsel for the appropriate legal interpretation.

---

**EXHIBIT 4.1**   Securities Litigation and Preventing Fraudulent Reporting

---

When Kirschner Medical Corp., a Baltimore-based manufacturer of orthopedic equipment, went public in 1986, President Bruce Hegstad planned to go from $6.5 million to $100 million in revenues. They did indeed skyrocket, reaching $55 million in 1989. Naturally, stock prices soared as well.

But the investors who flocked to Kirschner now claim that the company duped them. During the third quarter of 1989, the company lost $488,000. Despite its assurances of a quick rebound, Kirschner lost $2.5 million in the next quarter and wrote off an additional $13.2 million in losses.

During this time, the company allegedly failed to disclose information about defective products, obsolete inventories, and an unprofitable European plant. When the bad news finally came out, stock prices dove $17 a share, causing a lost market value of $35.7 million. Claiming fraudulent financial reporting, over 1,000 investors have filed a class-action suit against Kirschner and three of its executives in the U.S. District Court in Baltimore.

In recent years, corporate boards of directors and their audit committees have faced great vulnerability to such litigation.

According to William R. McLucas, the Security and Exchange Commission's enforcement director, "The agency has a hefty backlog of cases, many focusing on financial fraud and accounting problems."

In 1989, the SEC filed enforcement actions against the officers and directors of 30 public companies and 12 public accounting firms, alleging improper financial reporting practices.

Two years earlier, the National Commission on Fraudulent Financial Reporting, established by accounting associations and chaired by former SEC Commissioner James Treadway, reported that it had "reviewed 119 enforcement actions against public companies and 42 cases against independent public accounting firms by the SEC from 1981–1986."

The commission asserted that "public companies should maintain internal controls that provide reasonable assurance that fraudulent financial reporting will be prevented or subject to early detection."

What is fraudulent financial reporting? The commission defines it "as intentional or reckless conduct, whether act or omission, that results in materially misleading financial statements."

Generally speaking, fraudulent reporting occurs when management intentionally overstates assets and improperly recognizes revenue. These actions clearly differ from unintentional errors.

The irregularities are shown by the misapplication of generally accepted accounting principles, inappropriate valuations, and/or omissions of material information from financial statements. For example, the deliberate distortion of accounting records to overstate inventory, along with falsified transactions to increase sales and overstate earnings, is clearly fraudulent financial reporting.

These activities, often referred to as "cooked books" and "cute accounting," cause management to restate the financial statements, which, in turn, causes a decrease in the market price of the stock. Such misleading representations in the company's annual and quarterly figures can be the basis of a class-action lawsuit.

Typically in this type of litigation, a class of stockholders alleges that the board of directors, the officers and the independent auditing firm have prepared and distributed materially false and misleading financial statements and reports to existing stockholders and potential investors.

Plaintiffs accuse defendants of violating Section 10(b) of the Securities Exchange Act, SEC Rule 10(b)-5 and common law. Relief claims are based on fraud, deceit, and negligence by the directors, officers, employees, and the independent auditors.

Questions of law and fact commonly arising in these cases are:

- Whether defendants knowingly or recklessly disseminated untrue statements of material fact and/or omitted material facts relating to the sales and earnings during the class period;
- Whether the market prices of securities were artificially inflated by reason of the defendants' conduct, constituting a fraud on the market;
- Whether defendants violated Section 10(b) of the 1934 Act and Rule 10(b)-5 and/or perpetrated common law fraud or negligent misrepresentations upon the members of the class;
- Whether the defendant's SEC Form 10-Q, 10K, annual and quarterly reports, and public announcements of expected earnings and growth during the class period were materially false and misleading.

Failure on the part of the audit committee to review and evaluate the financial statements and related accounting policies in accordance with generally accepted accounting principles is clearly malfeasance.

A case in point is Crazy Eddie Inc., which, like many public companies, had audit committees. According to the SEC, Eddie Antar, founder and former chairman of the East Coast electronics chain, directed activities that resulted in overstating the company's 1985 pretax income by $2 million, or 18.9 percent; by approximately $6.7 million, or 33.8 percent, in 1986; and by "tens of millions of dollars" in 1987.

Peter Martosella, who was brought in to run Crazy Eddie after the fraudulent reporting was discovered, told Forbes magazine, "You have to be careful how much you expect of the audit committee. You're talking about people brought in by the CEO, and you're telling them they shouldn't necessarily listen to him. It's not realistic, especially when the chief executive is a charismatic person, a darling of the securities world, like Eddie Antar was."

Antar allegedly made $60 million from the sale of his Crazy Eddie stock; investors allegedly lost $200 million. In 1989 the SEC filed a complaint against Antar and other company officials and employees. Last summer the U.S. District Court for New Jersey entered a $73.5 million judgment against Antar, who is currently a fugitive. (It should be noted that Antar was recently apprehended by the authorities.)

Moreover, a group of about 10,000 shareholders have filed a lawsuit in the federal district court in New York against Crazy Eddie's former officers and directors, as well as its external auditor and several Wall Street brokerage firms.

In another case, Sundstrand Corp. pleaded guilty to a criminal defense procurement fraud of overbilling the Defense Department. Sundstrand agreed to pay a $115 million settlement to the federal government. In addition, the liability insurance carrier for Sundstrand's board of directors and officers agreed to pay $15 million to settle shareholder litigation.

An academic research study found that Sundstrand's audit committee was ineffective since it had too few meetings and too many changes in membership.[a]

As a result of the committee's performance, there were management-imposed scope limitations on the internal audit department, which ultimately caused the company to defraud the federal government.

As the Crazy Eddie and Sundstrand cases demonstrate, merely having an audit committee isn't always enough. So what exactly is this committee supposed to do?

The major impetus for establishing and maintaining audit committees occurred in 1978 when the New York Stock Exchange adopted a policy requiring all of its listed companies to have such a committee, composed solely of independent outside directors.

---

**EXHIBIT 4.1**   (*Continued*)

---

Of course, the NYSE's intent was to increase the investing public's confidence in the quality of financial reporting.

Before the NYSE's mandate, the SEC required companies to establish and maintain independent audit committees.

Thus, a consent injunction and ancillary relief against respondents charged with fraudulent financial reporting issues—for example, in cases against Lum's Inc. and Mattel Inc. in 1974—provided a framework for defining the duties and functions of audit committees.

Lum's agreed not to commit any proxy fraud in connection with future acquisitions of businesses or business assets. Mattel was charged with overstating sales by $14 million. These sales were subject to customer cancellation.

The question of what constitutes proper standards and practices for the audit committee has emerged through settlements, with the courts dictating the audit committee's responsibilities. In particular, the courts in Lum's and Mattel required the following general responsibilities:

- Recommend or approve appointment or independent auditors.
- Review internal accounting control policies and procedures.
- Oversee the duties and results of the internal audit department.
- Review with the independent auditors the proposed scope and general extent of their audit.
- Review, prior to issuance, financial statements and significant press releases concerning financial results.
- Act as a mediator between management and the independent auditors for any disagreements over accounting issues.

Recognizing the SEC enforcement actions, court decisions, and the national stock exchange listing requirements for audit committees, the National Commission on Fraudulent Financial Reporting has fully supported and endorsed implementation of audit committees.

In particular, the commission recommended that "the boards of directors of all public companies should be required by SEC rule to establish audit committees composed solely of independent directors. Such committees should be informed, vigilant, and effective overseers of the financial reporting process and the company's internal controls."

Today, both the American Stock Exchange and the National Association of Securities Dealers[b] have listing requirements for audit committees that are modeled after the NYSE's requirements. The U.S. House of Representatives is currently considering legislation, sponsored by Rep. John Dingell, D-Mich., requiring all public companies to create audit committees.

Given that the audit committee is a part-time operation, the commission's call for vigilance requires committee members to be willing to make a significant commitment of their time.

The audit committee should be informed about the financial and operational aspects of the company and, therefore, should receive sufficient and timely information. If the audit committee meeting is scheduled to coincide with the regular full board meetings, then the committee must receive written information well in advance of the meetings.

To be vigilant, the audit committee should ask probing questions about the propriety of the company's financial reporting process and the quality of its internal controls. This task requires the committee to keep abreast of financial reporting developments affecting the company.

(*continued*)

**EXHIBIT 4.1**   *(Continued)*

To be an effective independent overseer, the audit committee must be positioned between senior management and the external auditors. This organizational structure allows the audit committee to question management's judgments about financial reporting matters and to suggest improvements in the internal control systems. Finally, the committee should develop a charter that defines its mission, duties and responsibilities; plans its annual agenda; and documents its findings and conclusions.

Through audit committees, boards of directors can meet their oversight responsibilities in the internal and external auditing processes and the financial reporting process.

And, since in-house legal counsel and outside counsel frequently interact with audit committees, these lawyers are in an excellent position to help the committees develop a constructive relationship between their function and the activities of the full board and, ultimately, minimize the potential for class-action suits by recognizing the warning signals that lead to fraudulent reporting.[c]

For example, corporate legal counsel can assist the audit committees with the following matters:

• Review and approve the standard of independence for the audit committee members as required by the national stock exchanges and the SEC.
• Review the audit committee's charter, which is disclosed in part in the company's annual proxy statement.
• Review significant litigation, claims and assessments with both in-house and outside legal counsel.
• Advise the committee with respect to any pending litigation against the external auditors and any impairment of their independence.
• Advise the committee on proposed investigations and compliance with regulations.

Of course, outside legal counsel may be asked to serve on the audit committee, in which case he or she would address the warning signals directly.

Given the audit committee's critical role in the company's internal control structure, the committee must obtain reasonable assurances from the internal and external auditors that management's assertions in the financial statements are fairly presented. Moreover, the external auditors are required by generally accepted auditing standards to communicate certain matters to the audit committee.

In particular, the auditors are required to report material misstatements in the financial statements or omissions of material information.

It should be emphasized that audit committees should be highly attuned to potential situations of fraudulent financial reporting.

Failure on the part of an audit committee to question management's representations may be the basis for audit committee malfeasance, since the audit committee and the board may be held liable for their failure to know what they were responsible for recognizing.

---

*Source:* This discussion is adapted from an article by Louis Braiotta, Jr., "Auditing for Honesty," *American Bar Association Journal* 78, no. 5 (May 1992): 76–79. Copyright © 1992 by Louis Braiotta, Jr.

[a]For further reading, see Curtis C. Verschoor, "A Case Study of Audit Committee Effectiveness at Sundstrand," *Internal Auditing* 4, No. 4 (Spring 1989), pp. 11–19. Also see Verschoor's article, "Miniscribe: A New Example of Audit Committee Ineffectiveness," *Internal Auditing* 5, No. 4 (Spring 1990), pp. 13–19.

[b]Now the Financial Industry Regulatory Authority (FINRA)

[c]See Exhibit 4.2 for further details.

subject matter experts when acting in good faith, Sarbanes-Oxley establishes a primary responsibility for external and internal audit oversight, for oversight over financial reporting and internal control over financial reporting, and for whistle blowing that may require counsel that is independent of management and its advisors. As practice evolves, engaging independent counsel or experts could be indicative of appropriate due diligence, while not doing so could be considered an act of malfeasance.

3. Finally, the roles, responsibilities, and functions of audit committees, as documented in charters, policies, and guidelines, should comply specifically with laws and regulations. A major objective in organizing and managing the workload of audit committees is to avoid exposing its members unnecessarily to claims of breach of fiduciary responsibilities. The vast majority of litigation in which outside directors have been named as defendants has involved oversight failures rather than duty of loyalty failures or actions beyond their power.

## GENERAL LEGAL RESPONSIBILITIES

### State Statutes

Although the board of directors has the statutory power to establish standing committees of the board, state corporation laws often limit the board's powers to delegate authority and responsibility. Boards of directors usually have authority and corresponding responsibility as an indivisible whole rather than by parts. Whereas boards can establish committees to subdivide the work effort, they generally cannot shed responsibility for decisions. For example, the New York State incorporation statute provides that:

No such committee shall have authority as to the following matters:

1. The submission to shareholders of any action that needs shareholder's authorization under this chapter

2. The filling of vacancies in the board of directors or in any committee

3. The fixing of compensation of the directors for serving on the board or on any committee

4. The amendment or repeal of the bylaws, or the adoption of new bylaws

5. The amendment or repeal of any resolution of the board which by its terms shall not be so amendable or repealable[2]

Some state statutes require audit committees for corporations with certain characteristics. For example, the state of Connecticut has enacted legislation that requires companies incorporated with at least 100 stockholders to establish an audit committee. In Sections 33-318(b)(1) and 33-318(b)(2), the statute defines

---

[2] New York Business Corporation Law, Sec. 712, *McKinney's Consolidated Laws of New York Annotated, Book 6* (Brooklyn, NY: Edward Thompson Company, 1963).

the standard of independence and the functions of the audit committee. See the Connecticut General Statutes Annotated in West 1960 and Supplement 1985 (Eagan, MN.: West Publishing Corporation) for further details. New York State has adopted an approach for school boards that either requires an audit committee with financially literate members or an explanation of why a school district has chosen not to have such an audit committee. The same legislation also requires school districts to demonstrate oversight of independent auditors in a variety of ways, including five-year reviews with presumptive requests for proposals from new auditors.

Each member of the board of directors and its standing committees has statutory duties of care and loyalty because of the fiduciary relationship, which is established in state incorporation statutes, between the directors and the corporation. With respect to the duties of the directors and officers, the New York State statute (for purposes of illustration) indicates:

> Directors and officers shall discharge the duties of their respective positions in good faith and with that degree of diligence, care and skill which ordinarily prudent men would exercise under similar circumstances in like positions. In discharging their duties, directors and officers, when acting in good faith, may rely upon financial statements of the corporation represented to them to be correct by the president or the officer of the corporation having charge of its books of accounts, or stated in a written report by an independent public or certified public accountant or firm of such accountants fairly to reflect the financial condition of such corporations.[3]

Since the directors serve the corporation in a fiduciary capacity, their statutory duties cannot be delegated because of the personal nature of the director's relationship with the corporation. Although the audit committee can make recommendations to the entire board, the final decisions are made by the board because it has overall responsibility for the committee's actions. In short, because of the corporate fiduciary principle, the standing committees of the board cannot eliminate each director's duties and obligations, or those of the board as a whole.

Particularly important to the concept of the duty of care is the degree of care. To measure its reasonableness, several state corporation laws provide a business judgment rule. Because so many corporations are chartered in Delaware, cases before the Delaware Court of Chancery regarding its business judgment rule are of particular importance. Such a rule protects the directors against personal liability on the presumption that not only do they act in good faith, but they also exercise reasonable care and prudence regarding their decisions. Thus, in the absence of fraud, bad faith, or negligence, a director, under most state laws, cannot be held personally liable concerning matters of corporate policy and business judgment.[4] (For further information regarding such matters as the business judgment rule, see the Delaware Court of Chancery, *In Re Caremark International Inc. Derivative Litigation*, 698 A. 2d 959 (Del. Ch. 1996), and the section on legal cases in this chapter. Also see William C. Powers, *Report of Investigation*

---

[3] Ibid., Sec. 717.
[4] Ibid.

*by the Special Investigative Committee of the Board of Directors of Enron Corporation* (February 1, 2002), available at www.news.findlaw.com/hdocs/docs/enron/sicreport/.

Directors may be personally liable for negligence with respect to losses suffered by the corporation.[5] Directors can be held jointly and severally liable to the corporation whereby an injured stockholder or creditor can recover a loss from an individual director, several directors, or the full board. For example, if the directors vote to declare dividends from the corporation's capital rather than from its retained earnings, then they are liable because their actions constitute an unauthorized dividend distribution.[6]

Directors also have a duty of loyalty to the corporation. They cannot exploit the corporation for personal gain because of their fiduciary relationship. For example, if a director has a personal interest in a particular corporate transaction, then the director should disassociate herself from the transaction because of the apparent conflict of interest. Thus, each director has an "undivided loyalty and an allegiance" with respect to the interests of the corporation and stockholders.[7]

In 1978, the American Bar Association amended Section 35 of its Model Business Corporation Act, which, when adopted as part of the state corporation statutes, increases a director's ability to rely on the board's standing committees. Specifically, the amendment provides that a director may rely on the information that is presented by a committee although the director is not a member of this group. Such reliance on the board committee is based on the director's confidence in the committee. When relying on the committee, the director must adhere to the duty-of-care principle whereby the director should be familiar with the committee's activities. In short, the amendment allows a director to rely on the work of a committee that has an oversight or supervisory responsibility, such as the audit committee. Accordingly, the amendment poses certain questions regarding the legal implications of the committee since it appears that a non–committee director may be exonerated from any potential liability provided that he has exercised his duty of care.[8]

In 1984, the American Bar Association adopted a Revised Model Business Corporation Act. In 1998, the American Bar Association adopted the Model Business Corporate Act. Section 8.25 of the act stipulates that a board of directors may create standing committees, such as an audit committee. This stipulation is consistent with the statutory provisions at the state level. In

---

[5] For example, if it can be proven that a director has breached her fiduciary duty to the corporation, then the director may be held personally liable for the losses suffered by the corporation.

[6] New York Business Corporation Law, Sec. 719.

[7] Ibid., Sec. 717.

[8] American Bar Association, *Corporate Director's Guidebook* (Chicago: ABA, 1978), 42. Also see American Bar Association, *Corporate Director's Guidebook*, 2nd ed. (Chicago: ABA, 1994). Finally, the reader may wish to review *Escott v. BarChris Construction Corp.*, 283 F, Supp. 643 (S.D.N.Y. 1968), which deals with the standard of differential liability. In short, the court states that a director with a particular expertise and access to information may be held to a higher standard of liability. Of course, the performance of individual audit committee members is based on his skills and qualifications and access to information. Thus a member with an accounting background would be more aware of the accounting and auditing implications than would be a member without this expertise.

addition, Section 8.3(0), which deals with the standards of conduct for directors, indicates that a director is entitled to rely on information, opinions, reports, or statements—including financial statements—prepared by officers of the corporation and public accountants. A director is also entitled to rely on the opinions of legal counsel as well as on the work of a standing committee of the board of which she is not a member. Subsequent revisions to the ABA's Model Corporation Act have continued to affirm its position with respect to good-faith reliance on officers, public accountants, legal counsel, and committee members of the board.

## Federal Statutes—Key Sections

In addition to the legal responsibilities created by states' corporation statutes, the directors may face legal liability associated with federal statutes. The federal statutes that are particularly important are summarized below.

***Securities Act of 1933***    Although this particular act provides financial information regarding the public sale of securities, it is needed "to prohibit misrepresentation, deceit, and other fraudulent acts and practices in the sale of securities."[9] In particular, this act provides for civil liability of the directors with respect to fraud in the registration statement and the right for legal action by private parties. Litigation under Section 11 of the Securities Act of 1933 accounts for the largest number of cases in which outside directors are named. Section 11(a) of the act provides:

(1) In case any part of the registration statement, when such part became effective, contained an untrue statement of a material fact or omitted to state a material fact required to be stated therein or necessary to make the statement therein not misleading, any person acquiring such security (unless it is proved that at the time of such acquisition he knew of such untruth or omission) may, either at law or in equity, in any court of competent jurisdiction, sue– . . .

(2) every person who was a director of . . . the issuer at the time of the filing of the part of the registration statement . . . .[10]

In order to avoid any liability, Sections 11(b) and 11(c) of the act provide:

Notwithstanding the provisions of subsection (a) of this section no person, other than the issuer, shall be liable as provided therein who shall sustain the burden of proof–

(1) that before the effective date of the part of the registration statement with respect to which his liability is asserted (A) he had resigned from or had taken such steps as are permitted by law to resign from, or ceased or refused to act in, every office, capacity, or relationship in which he was described in the registration

---

[9] Securities and Exchange Commission, *The Work of the Securities and Exchange Commission* (Washington, DC: U.S. Government Printing Office, 1974), 1.
[10] U.S. Code, Title 15, Sec. 77k.

statement as acting or agreeing to act, and (B) he had advised the Commission and the issuer in writing that he had taken such action and that he would not be responsible for such part of the registration statement; or

(2) that if such part of the registration statement became effective without his knowledge, upon becoming aware of such fact he forthwith acted and advised the Commission, in accordance with paragraph (1) of this subsection, and, in addition, gave reasonable public notice that such part of the registration statement had become effective without his knowledge, or

(3) that (A) as regards any part of the registration statement not purporting to be made on the authority of an expert, and not purporting to be a copy of or extract from a report or valuation of an expert, and not purporting to be made on the authority of a public official document or statement, he had, after reasonable investigation, reasonable ground to believe and did believe, at the time such part of the registration statement became effective, that the statements therein were true and that there was no omission to state a material fact required to be stated therein or necessary to make the statements therein not misleading; and (B) as regards any part of the registration statement purporting to be made upon his authority as an expert or purporting to be a copy of or extract from a report or valuation of himself as an expert, (i) he had, after reasonable investigation, reasonable ground to believe and did believe at the time such part of the registration statement became effective, that the statements therein were true and that there was no omission to state a material fact required to be stated therein or necessary to make the statements therein not misleading, or (ii) such part of the registration statement did not fairly represent his statement as an expert or was not a fair copy of or extract from his report or valuation as an expert; and (C) as regards any part of the registration statement purporting to be made on the authority of an expert (other than himself) or purporting to be a copy of or extract from a report or valuation of an expert (other than himself), he had no reasonable ground to believe and did not believe, at the time such part of the registration statement became effective, that the statements therein were untrue or that there was an omission to state a material fact required to be stated therein or necessary to make the statements therein not misleading, or that such part of the registration statement did not fairly represent the statement of the expert or was not a fair copy of or extract from the report of valuation of the expert; and (D) as regards any part of the registration statement purporting to be a statement made by an official person or purporting to be a copy of or extract from a public official document, he had no reasonable ground to believe and did not believe, at the time such part of the registration statement became effective, that the statements therein were untrue, or that there was an omission to state a material fact required to be stated therein or necessary to make the statements therein not misleading, or that such part of the registration statement did not fairly represent the statement made by the official person or was not a fair copy of or extract from the public official document.

In determining what constitutes reasonable investigation and reasonable ground for belief, for the purpose of paragraph (3) of subsection (b) of this section, the standard of reasonableness shall be that required of a prudent man in the management of his property.[11]

---

[11] Ibid., Sec. 77k.

In January 2005, settlements involving out-of-pocket payments by members of boards of directors were reached in two important cases—*WorldCom* and *Enron*. In both cases, the directors of the two companies made payments from their own pockets rather than being indemnified by the corporations either directly or through insurance. The primary legal issue at stake in both cases was whether there was director liability under Section 11 of the 1933 Act in connection with the issuance of securities. Both Enron and WorldCom offered billions of dollars of debt and equity securities to investors. Section 11 makes the company liable for material misstatements or omissions relied on by investors in prospectuses and offering documents. A company has no defense in the case of a demonstrated material misstatement or omission in an offering statement. Officers, directors, and underwriters can avoid personal liability if they can demonstrate that their performance of due diligence was appropriate and not only *did not* lead to their knowledge of the misstatement or omission, but also *could not* have done so. In the case of both Enron and WorldCom, special investigations led by prominent individuals (a former SEC chairman and a former attorney general) had already delivered reports that indicated a fairly clear lack of due diligence by members of both boards before the private class action suits were filed. Although this was not the first time that corporate directors had been held personally liable for corporate malfeasance, the Enron and WorldCom settlements made an impression throughout the community of corporate directors that has led to a far greater focus on board processes.

Further, Section 12 of the act provides additional liability regarding any transactions that are false or misleading in connection with the issuance of the securities. Thus a director has not only a potential liability with respect to the registration statement but also a liability concerning the written and/or oral representations in the offering prospectus.[12]

Section 13 of the act establishes a limitation in order to enforce a civil action against the wrongdoers.

> No action shall be maintained to enforce any liability created under section 77k or 77l (2) of this title unless brought within one year after the discovery of the untrue statement or the omission, or after such discovery should have been made by the exercise of reasonable diligence, or, if the action is to enforce a liability created under section 77l (1) of this title, unless brought within one year after the violation upon which it is based. In no event shall any such action be brought to enforce a liability created under section 77k or 77l (1) of this title more than three years after the security was bona fide offered to the public, or under section 77l (2) of this title more than three years after the sale.[13]

Finally, the penalties that may be assessed under the Securities Act of 1933 consist of the following:

> Any person who willfully violates any of the provisions of this subchapter, or the rules and regulations promulgated by the Commission under authority thereof, or

---

[12] U.S. Code, Title 15, Sec. 77l.
[13] U.S. Code, Title 15, Sec. 77m.

any person who willfully, in a registration statement filed under this subchapter, makes any untrue statement of a material fact or omits to state any material fact required to be stated therein or necessary to make the statements therein not misleading, shall upon conviction be fined not more than $5,000 or imprisoned not more than five years, or both.[14]

**Securities Exchange Act of 1934**   The primary purpose of this act is to regulate the public sales of the securities through the securities exchanges or brokers after the original sale of the securities. This act also established the Securities and Exchange Commission. More specifically, Section 18 of the act provides this liability for misleading statements:

(a) Any person who shall make or cause to be made any statement in any application, report, or document filed pursuant to this chapter or any rule or regulation thereunder or any undertaking contained in a registration statement as provided in subsection (d) of section 780 of this title, which statement was at the time and in the light of the circumstances under which it was made false or misleading with respect to any material fact, shall be liable to any person (not knowing that such statement was false or misleading) who, in reliance upon such statement, shall have purchased or sold a security at a price which was affected by such statement, for damages caused by such reliance, unless the person sued shall prove that he acted in good faith and had no knowledge that such statement was false or misleading. A person seeking to enforce such liability may sue at law or in equity in any court of competent jurisdiction. In any such suit the court may, in its discretion, require an undertaking for the payment of the costs of such suit, and assess reasonable costs, including reasonable attorney's fees, against either party litigant.

(c) No action shall be maintained to enforce any liability created under this section unless brought within one year after the discovery of the facts constituting the cause of action and within three years after such cause of action accrued.[15]

In contrast to the 1933 Act, a plaintiff must prove that she relied on a misstatement of fact or omission of fact in the financial statements and as a result suffered a loss.

Litigation under Section 10(b) of the Securities and Exchange Act of 1934 gives rise to the second highest number of cases naming outside directors. Section 10(b) of the act establishes an antifraud provision, which indicates that it is illegal "to use or employ . . . any manipulative or deceptive devices" regarding security transactions.[16] Equally important, the SEC enacted Rule 10 (b)-5, which provides the following:

It shall be unlawful for any person, directly or indirectly, by the use of any means . . .

(a) to employ any device, scheme, or artifice to defraud,

---

[14] U.S. Code, Title 15, Sec. 77x.

[15] U.S. Code, Title 15, Sec. 78r.

[16] U.S. Code, Title 15, Sec. 78j.

(b) to make any untrue statement of a material fact or to omit to state a material fact necessary in order to make the statements made, in the light of the circumstances under which they were made, not misleading, or,

(c) to engage in any act, practice, or course of business which operates or would operate as a fraud or deceit upon any person, in connection with purchase or sale of any security.[17]

Thus Rule 10 (b)-5 can hold directors liable primarily because of clause (b). In short, this particular rule increases the director's liability, which did not exist under the provisions of the act.

In addition, the 1934 act provides these penalties:

(a) Any person who willfully violates any provision of this chapter, or any rule or regulation thereunder the violation of which is made unlawful or the observance of which is required under the terms of this chapter, or any person who willfully and knowingly makes, or causes to be made, any statement in any application, report, or document required to be filed under this chapter or any rule or regulation thereunder or any undertaking contained in a registration statement as provided in subsection (d) of section 78o of this title, which statement was false or misleading with respect to any material fact, shall upon conviction be fined not more than $10,000, or imprisoned not more than two years, or both, except that when such person is an exchange, a fine not exceeding $500,000 may be imposed; but no person shall be subject to imprisonment under this section for the violation of any rule or regulation if he proves that he had no knowledge of such rule or regulation.[18]

A general perception exists that events associated with the Sarbanes-Oxley Act and the settlements in the Enron and WorldCom class action suits have increased the risk for audit committee members and board members in general. Such perceptions can lead qualified individuals to conclude that service on boards is too risky if their personal wealth is at stake, especially where their oversight of a large company's management cannot possibly be detailed enough to ensure knowledge of all potentially dangerous actions, and where the damages could be large enough to wreak financial ruin on even a wealthy individual.

In an article published in 2006 in the *Stanford Law Review*,[19] Bernard Black, Brian Cheffins, and Michael Klausner analyze the degree to which outside directors of public companies are exposed to out-of-pocket liability risk—the risk of paying legal expenses or damages, as part of a court judgment or settlement agreement, that are not paid by the company or another source (such as a large shareholder) or that are not covered by directors' and officers' liability insurance. The analysis revealed that, between 1980 and 2005, directors of public companies made out-of-pocket payments in 13 cases in corporate and security law.

---

[17] Code of Federal Regulations, Sec. 240, 10(b)-5.

[18] U.S. Code, Title 15, Sec. 78ff.

[19] Bernard Black, Brian Cheffins, and Michael Klausner, "Outside Director Liability," *Stanford Law Review* 58 (2006: 1055–1060.)

Trials in which outside directors are named as defendants are quite rare, with only one case involving out-of-pocket costs, and it affected only one outside director. Settlements of cases are much more common, and over the 25 years analyzed by Black, Ceffins, and Klausner, outside directors paid settlements from their own pockets on 12 occasions. Only three of the settlements in which outside directors incurred out-of-pocket payments were widely covered by the financial media—Enron, WorldCom, and Tyco. As a group, 10 of Enron's outside directors made out-of-pocket payments of $13 million to settle federal securities private class actions under Section 11 of the 1933 Act, and 11 outside directors paid $1.5 million to settle ERISA actions. Twelve of WorldCom's outside directors paid $24.75 million to settle a federal securities private class action under Section 11. One Tyco director paid a $22.5 million settlement as a disgorgement and criminal fine in an SEC and criminal enforcement action related to self-dealing and the duty of loyalty. The other nine settlements involved lesser amounts and received little or no media attention.

Ten of the cases analyzed by Black, Ceffins, and Klausner involved failures of oversight by outside directors (failures of the duty of care)—failures that usually would not occur if appropriate due diligence had been followed. Two cases involved self-dealing and one involved a transaction setting directors' own compensation (failure of the duty of loyalty). Black, Ceffins, and Klausner conclude:

> . . . [G]oing forward, if a company has a D&O policy with appropriate coverage and sensible limits, outside directors will be potentially vulnerable to out-of-pocket liability only when (1) the company is insolvent and the expected damage awards exceed those limits, (2) the case includes a substantial claim under Section 11 of the Securities Acts or an unusually strong Section 10(b) claim, and (3) there is an alignment between outside directors' or other defendants' culpability and their wealth. Absent facts that fit or approach this 'perfect storm' scenario, directors with state-of-the-art insurance policies face little out-of-pocket liability risk, and even in a perfect storm they may not face out-of-pocket liability. The principal threats to outside directors who perform poorly are the time, aggravation, and potential harm to reputation that a lawsuit can entail, not direct financial loss.[20]

## The Private Securities Reform Act of 1995

During the latter half of 1995, Congress enacted the Private Securities Litigation Reform Act of 1995 based on House Bill 1058 and Senate Bill 240. The major objective of this reform legislation was to curb the number of abusive securities class action suits. Of particular interest to audit committees is Section 301, "Fraud Detection and Disclosure," and Section 10A, "Audit Requirements." While Section 10A does not expand the auditors' responsibility to detect fraud or illegal acts, it does require auditors who detect illegal acts to report their findings to the Securities and Exchange Commission if the client company fails to take appropriate remedial action on such acts that have a material effect on the financial

---

[20] Ibid. 1060.

statements. If the necessary remedial action has not been taken, the auditors are required to notify the board of directors in writing. Based on these events, the board is required to submit such written reports from auditors to the SEC within one business day. If the board fails to notify the SEC, then the auditors are required to submit their report to the SEC the next business day.[21]

Before 1995, court-created precedents and the Securities Act of 1933 and the Securities Exchange Act of 1934 formed the basis for securities lawsuits. During Congressional hearings in the mid-1990s, several individuals testified about an excessive number of lawsuits, alleging violations of the federal securities laws in the hope that defendants would settle quickly to avoid the expense of litigation. These suits often were filed on the announcement of bad news rather than on evidence of fraud or other wrongdoing. The plaintiffs' bar and the defendants' bar have long debated, and continue to debate, the legitimacy and purpose of "pleading requirements" for securities cases. Congress enacted the Private Securities Litigation Reform Act of 1995 (PSLRA) (overriding two presidential vetoes), whose express purposes were to reduce perceived abuses and to encourage meritorious legal actions.

After 1995, plaintiffs' lawyers began to file class action securities suits in state courts in order to avoid the provisions of the PSLRA. In response, Congress passed the Securities Litigation Uniform Standards Act (SLUSA) in 1998, signed without veto, which restricts securities class actions to federal courts.

The U.S. Supreme Court has decided three important cases related to the scope, pleading standards, and damage calculations in the context of PSLRA and SLUSA. In *Merrill Lynch, Pierce, Fenner & Smith, Inc. v. Dabit* (547 U.S. 71 (2006)), the Supreme Court decided on March 21, 2006, that SLUSA did not allow litigation based on state law when shareholders lose money because of holding a stock instead of selling or purchasing it. Federal securities laws provide for a private litigation action to individuals with losses caused by the purchase or sale of stock. This decision resolved a split among the federal circuit courts and affirmed that securities litigation would take place in federal rather than state courts. In *Dura Pharmaceuticals, Inc. v. Broudo* (544 U.S. 366 (2005)), the Supreme Court on April 19, 2005, narrowed the ways in which plaintiffs can prove loss causation and the amount of damages. The Court rejected the notion that, in cases brought under Section 10(b) of the 1934 Act, it was sufficient to demonstrate loss causation by alleging that a security had an inflated price on the date of purchase because of the misrepresentation. Rather, the loss causation criteria recognized by the Court interpret the proximate causation concept in PLSRA as restricted to identified price

---

[21] The act is contained in Title 1 of Public Law No. 104-67, December 22, 1995. Sections 301 and 10A are contained in Title 3 of Public Law No. 104-67, December 22, 1995. For further discussion, see the act with respect to such matters as proportionate liability, safe harbor for forward-looking statements, and the loss causation principle. Also see the U.S. Federal Sentencing Commission's *Federal Sentencing Guidelines for Organizations* (Washington, DC: U.S. Federal Sentencing Commission, 1990) for an expanded discussion on encouraging effective programs to prevent and detect violations of law; Edward J. Boyle and Fred N. Knopf, "The Private Securities Litigation Reform Act of 1995, *CPA Journal* 66, no. 4 (April 1996): 44–47; and Daniel L. Goldwasser, "The Private Securities Act of 1995: Impact on Accountants," *CPA Journal* 67, no. 6 (June 1997):72–75.

declines that specifically can be traced to the disclosure of an alleged fraud. This decision also requires sorting out the factors causing large predisclosure declines in share prices and attributing the losses across multiple potential loss causes, such as market, industry, firm, and alleged fraud impacts, rather than just to the fraud. In *Tellabs v. Makor Issues & Rights, Ltd.*, a case decided on June 21, 2007, the Supreme Court held that "in determining whether the pleaded facts give rise to a 'strong' inference (that a company intended to commit fraud), the court must take into account plausible opposing inferences" (551 U.S. 308 (2007)). As a consequence, federal district courts will have to consider at the motion-to-dismiss stage whether plaintiffs have alleged particular facts sufficiently to support a strong inference of the intent to commit fraud, or whether there are other equally plausible inferences from the alleged facts.

## OTHER FEDERAL PROVISIONS RELATED TO FRAUD

The federal government has addressed various other aspects of fraud that may apply to audit committee members. The following four sections quote federal legislations related to fraud and false statements, use of the federal postal system to commit fraud, conspiring to commit fraud, and fraud related to income taxes.

### Fraud and False Statements Act

Whoever, in any matter within the jurisdiction of any department or agency of the United States knowingly and willfully falsifies, conceals or covers up by any trick, scheme, or device a material fact, or makes any false, fictitious or fraudulent statements or representations, or makes or uses any false writing or document knowing the same to contain any false, fictitious or fraudulent statement or entry, shall be fined not more than $10,000 or imprisoned not more than five years, or both.[22]

### Mail Fraud Act

Whoever, having devised or intending to devise any scheme or artifice to defraud, or for obtaining money or property by means of false or fraudulent pretenses, representations, or promises, or to sell, dispose of, loan, exchange, alter, give away, distribute, supply, or furnish or produce for unlawful use any counterfeit or spurious coin, obligation, security, or other article, or anything represented to be or intimated to or held out to be such counterfeit or spurious articles, for the purpose of executing such scheme or artifice or attempting so to do, places in any post office or authorized depository for mail matter, any matter or thing whatever to be sent or delivered by the Postal Service, or takes or receives therefrom, any such matter or thing, or knowingly causes to be delivered by mail according to the direction thereon, or at the place at which it is directed to be delivered by the person to whom it is addressed, any such matter or thing, shall be fined not more than $1,000 or imprisoned not more than five years, or both.[23]

---

[22] U.S. Code, Title 18, Sec. 1001.

[23] Ibid., Sec. 1341.

Whoever, having devised or intending to devise any scheme or artifice to defraud, or for obtaining money or property by means of false or fraudulent pretenses, representations, or promises, transmits or causes to be transmitted by means of wire, radio, or television communication in interstate or foreign commerce, any writings, signs, signals, pictures, or sounds for the purpose of executing such scheme or artifice, shall be fined not more than $1,000 or imprisoned not more than five years, or both.[24]

## Conspiracy Act

If two or more persons conspire to commit any offense against the United States, or to defraud the United States, or any agency thereof in any manner or for any purpose, and one or more of such persons do any act to effect the object of the conspiracy, each shall be fined not more than $10,000 or imprisoned not more than five years, or both.

If, however, the offense, the commission of which is the object of the conspiracy, is a misdemeanor only, the punishment for such conspiracy shall not exceed the maximum punishment provided for such misdemeanor.[25]

## Income Taxes[26]

Any person who:

1. *Declaration under penalties of perjury* Willfully makes and subscribes any return, statement or other document, which contains or is verified by a written declaration that it is made under the penalties of perjury, and which he does not believe to be true and correct as to every material matter; or

2. *Aid or assistance* Willfully aids or assists in, or procures, counsels or advises the preparation or presentation under, or in connection with any matter arising under, the internal revenue laws, of a return, affidavit, claim or other document, which is fraudulent or is false as to any material matter, whether or not such falsity or fraud is with the knowledge or consent of the person authorized or required to present such return, affidavit, claim or document; or

3. *Fraudulent bonds, permits, and entries* Simulates or falsely or fraudulently executes or signs any bond, permit, entry, or other document required by the provisions of the internal revenue laws, or by any regulation made in pursuance thereof, or procures the same to be falsely or fraudulently executed or advises, aids in, or connives at such execution thereof; or

4. *Removal or concealment with intent to defraud* Removes, deposits, or conceals, or is concerned in removing, depositing, or concealing any goods or commodities for or in respect whereof any tax is or shall be imposed, or any property upon which levy is authorized by section 6331, with intent to evade or defeat the assessment or collection of any tax imposed by this title; or

---

[24] Ibid., Sec. 1343.

[25] Ibid., Sec. 371.

[26] It may be advisable to request the outside auditors to remind executives that tax returns must be filed. The audit committee should make certain that the returns were filed appropriately through discussions with the auditors.

5. *Compromises and closing agreements* In connection with any compromise under section 7122, or offer of such compromise, or in connection with any closing agreement under section 7121, or offer to enter into any such agreement, willfully—

   A. *Concealment of property* Conceals from any officer or employee of the United States any property belonging to the estate of a taxpayer or other person liable in respect of the tax, or

   B. *Withholding, falsifying, and destroying records* Receives, withholds, destroys, mutilates, or falsifies any book, document, or record, or makes any false statement, relating to the estate or financial condition of the taxpayer or other person liable in respect of the tax; shall be guilty of a felony and, upon conviction thereof, shall be fined not more than $5,000, or imprisoned not more than 3 years, or both, together with the cost of prosecution.[27]

Any person who willfully delivers or discloses to the Secretary or his delegate any list, return, account, statement, or other document, known by him to be fraudulent or to be false as to any material matter, shall be fined not more than $1,000, or imprisoned not more than 1 year, or both. Any person required pursuant to sections 6047 (b) or (c), 6056, or 6104 (d) to furnish any information to the Secretary or any other person who willfully furnishes to the Secretary or such other person any information known by him to be fraudulent or to be false as to any material matter shall be fined not more than $1,000, or imprisoned not more than 1 year, or both.[28]

## Anti–Money Laundering Issues

The USA Patriot Act, passed in the aftermath of the September 11, 2001, terrorist attacks, elevated concerns related to money laundering by terrorist organizations. A number of federal statutes cover aspects of money laundering, as do the laws of many other countries. "Anti–money laundering" describes the legal and other controls that require financial institutions and other regulated entities to prevent, monitor, or report money laundering activities. Audit committees of most financial institutions will have to deal with oversight of the controls required to identify and report transactions of a suspicious nature to the financial intelligence unit in the affected country. Banks generally have due diligence requirements in determining customers' identities and in monitoring transactions for suspicious activity. Anti–money laundering requirements also extend to nonfinancial institutions to the extent of requiring companies to report suspicious activity that comes to their attention.

## LESSONS FOR THE AUDIT COMMITTEE FROM LITIGATION

During the 1970s and 1980s, litigation involving the audit committee exemplified the significance of the audit director's role. The Securities and Exchange Commission's elevated enforcement of the provisions of the federal securities laws has imposed greater professional responsibilities on the committee. As one

---

[27] Internal Revenue Code, Sec. 7206.
[28] Ibid., Sec. 7207.

notable conservative columnist and editor stated, "The evolution of the director's responsibility is running ahead of inflation . . . The contemporary director is supposed to know more about accounting . . . and more about the law."[29] Several legal cases are briefly reviewed in order to demonstrate the philosophy of the courts and the SEC with respect to the audit committee.

## The Penn Central Case

On August 3, 1972, the SEC released its study regarding the financial collapse of the Penn Central Company to a Special Subcommittee on Investigations of the House of Representatives. With respect to the role of the directors, the SEC found that the directors had a passive role in company affairs. They avoided confrontation with management on issues that were critical to testing the integrity of management and to providing adequate disclosure to the stockholders. For example, the company's CFO was involved in a lawsuit that claimed improper, unlawful conduct in connection with a subsidiary and a private investment club. Although the board authorized an investigation, it later cancelled the investigation because the CFO threatened to resign. As a result, the financial management was permitted to operate without any effective review of control by the board.[30] In particular, the Commission noted that the directors have a responsibility to obtain from management information that is adequate in both "quantity and quality" in order to discharge their state corporate legal liability. For example, a new director indicated that "lists of new equipment did not particularly help him discharge his responsibilities and thus information regarding the corporate objectives and plans was necessary to do the job."[31] Furthermore, the Commission emphasized the "critical importance" of the director's responsibility as well as "greater utilization of public and independent directors." Such independent directors should be judged on the "reasonableness of their judgment."[32] The Commission's findings and conclusions point toward the need for an advisory committee of outside directors. The audit committee would fulfill this particular purpose.

## Lum's, Inc. Case

On April 11, 1974, the SEC obtained a consent injunction from the U.S. District Court against Lum's, Inc. whereby the registrant "agreed not to employ any manipulative scheme to defraud and not to commit any proxy fraud in connection with future acquisitions of businesses or business assets." More specifically, the court ordered that the registrant had to include this information in its registration or proxy statement:

1. The identity of the individuals who control the acquired business
2. Any material consideration to be paid for the acquiring business in addition to the purchase price

---

[29] "Firing Line," *Time*, February 19, 1979.
[30] Commerce Clearing House, Federal Securities Law Reporter, par. 78,931.
[31] Ibid.
[32] Ibid.

3. Any material information known indicating that the earnings of an acquired business were affected by the failure of management to maintain proper accounting records and internal controls

Furthermore, the registrant had to establish a standing audit committee to review the accountant's evaluations of the system of internal controls and to review other casino activities in terms of personnel and security. The court required that the audit committee consist of two or more members of the board of directors who are not officers or employees of the company.[33] The Lum's consent injunction is of particular importance because it was the impetus toward the establishment of a standing audit committee through court action.

## Mattel, Inc. Case

In the Mattel case of *SEC v. Mattel, Inc.* (October 1, 1974), the Commission sought a consent injunction against the registrant for false financial reporting. The Commission charged not only that the registrant's financial statements for 1971 were overstated by $14 million in sales that were subject to customer cancellation but also that the pretax income was overstated by $10.5 million due to inadequate accounting provisions. As a result, the U.S. District Court ordered Mattel to establish and maintain a financial controls and audit committee whereby three of the four members must be unaffiliated directors. In particular, the court required that the committee have these five duties and functions:

1. Review the financial controls and accounting procedures and recommend improvements to management.
2. Review the quarterly financial statements to determine whether such reports are in conformity with generally accepted accounting principles.
3. Review all releases and other information to the news media, general public, and stockholders with respect to the financial condition of the company and approve or disapprove such dissemination.
4. Review the results of the independent audit examination of the financial statements.
5. Approve or disapprove any change of the independent auditors.[34]

Thus, through a consent injunction against Mattel, it is clearly evident that the SEC continued to rely more heavily on the independent audit committee to review and monitor the company's financial controls, accounting procedures, and financial statements. Also, this particular legal action provided an initial framework for the duties and functions of the committee. Indeed, the question of what constitutes proper standards and practices for the committee was emerging through a court settlement; as a consequence the court was dictating the responsibilities of the audit directors. Such an approach is further evidenced by the results of the *Killearn Properties* case.

---

[33] Ibid., par. 94,504.
[34] Ibid., par. 94,807.

## Killearn Properties, Inc. Case

In the *SEC v. Killearn Properties, Inc.* case (May 1977), the SEC outlined its directives concerning the audit committee as part of a consent judgment. The defendants were enjoined from directly or indirectly making use of the mails or other communication to transmit any prospectus regarding the stock since the prospectus must meet the requirement of the securities laws. More specifically, the court ordered the defendants to observe the following policies and practices with respect to the audit committee:

B. The Board of Directors shall continue to maintain an Audit Committee ("Committee") of the Board consisting of at least Three (3) persons who shall be members of the Board and outside directors of Killearn. The Committee shall assume, upon the entering of this Order, the following duties, functions and responsibilities:

i. It should review the engagement of the independent accountants, including the scope and general extent of their review, the audit procedures which will be utilized, and the compensation to be paid.

ii. It should review with the independent accountants, and with the company's chief financial officer (as well as with other appropriate company personnel) the general policies and procedures utilized by the company with respect to internal auditing, accounting, and financial controls. The members of the committee should have at least general familiarity with the accounting and reporting principles and practices applied by the company in preparing its financial statements.

iii. It should review with the independent accountants, upon completion of their audit, (a) any report or opinion proposed to be rendered in connection therewith; (b) the independent accountants' perceptions of the company's financial and accounting personnel; (c) the cooperation which the independent accountants received during the course of their review; (d) the extent to which the resources of the company were and should be utilized to minimize time spent by the outside auditors; (e) any significant transactions which are not a normal part of the company's business; (f) any change in accounting principles; (g) all significant adjustments proposed by the auditor; (h) any recommendations which the independent accountants may have with respect to improving internal financial controls, choice of accounting principles, or management reporting systems.

iv. It should inquire of the appropriate company personnel and the independent auditors as to any instances of deviations from established codes of conduct of the company and periodically review such policies.

v. It should meet with the company's financial staff at least twice a year to review and discuss with them the scope of internal accounting and auditing procedures then in effect; and the extent to which recommendations made by the internal staff or by the independent accountants have been implemented.

vi. It should prepare and present to the company's board of directors a report summarizing its recommendation with respect to the retention (or discharge) of the independent accountants for the ensuing year.

vii. It should have a power to direct and supervise an investigation into any matter brought to its attention within the scope of its duties (including the power to retain outside counsel in connection with any such investigation).

In addition, the Audit Committee shall have the following special duties, functions and responsibilities:

viii. review, either by the Committee as a whole or by a designated member, all releases and other information to be disseminated by Killearn to press media, the public, or shareholders of Killearn which concern disclosure of financial conditions of and projections of financial conditions of Killearn and its subsidiaries;

ix. review of the activities of the officers and directors of Killearn as to their future dealing with the company and take any action the Committee may deem appropriate with regard to such activities;

x. approve any settlement or disposition of any claims or actions from causes of action arising after the date hereof or any litigation now pending which Killearn may have against any past or present officers, directors, employees or controlling persons.[35]

## U.S. Surgical Corporation

In February 1984, the SEC filed an action against U.S. Surgical Corporation and six of its senior executives, alleging numerous improper financial reporting practices from 1979 to 1981. The corporation's pretax earnings were overstated by more than $18 million. This overstatement amounted to 56 percent of the pretax earnings reported during 1979 and 1981. In addition, the improper accounting practices continued during 1982 and 1983. In the final consent order, the corporation agreed to appoint two new independent directors to the audit committee and define new responsibilities of the audit committee. In particular, the committee was required to:

Review for a period of at least five years, prior to release, all earnings reports and the financial statements that accompany the annual audit and quarterly review reports of the external auditors and reports of the internal audit department;

Engage the external auditors to review and report to the committee on accounting policies concerning review recognition, capitalization of certain costs, inventories, R&D expenses, and accruals; and

Engage an accounting firm (advisory accountants) for a period of three years to review the services performed by the external auditors, and to assist the committee on other matters as requested.[36]

This case demonstrated the need for the board of directors through its audit committee to exercise its oversight responsibility for the internal and external auditing processes and financial reporting disclosures.

Based on a review of the court actions, it is apparent that the audit committee has been established to oversee and monitor the conduct of the corporate officials. Although the committee is not directly involved with the day-to-day management affairs, the SEC and the courts forced the registrants to establish committees in

---

[35] Ibid., par. 96,256.
[36] Ibid., par. 105,124.

order to comply with the requirements of the federal securities laws. Such legal enforcement of the courts has augmented not only the audit directors' legal obligations but also their standard of duty and loyalty to the enterprise.

The critical involvement of audit committees is highlighted by such companies as California Life Corporation, Playboy Enterprises, Inc., and H.J. Heinz Co. Some of the excerpts from the *Wall Street Journal* involving these companies are used to illustrate the audit committee's involvement.

## California Life Corporation

When the audit committee learned that Cal Life was late in filing its 1978 annual financial statements with the SEC, the committee began an investigation. The late filing was the result of a dispute between management and its independent auditors. As Lancaster reported: "Certainly, the committee had some mitigating problems: a new, inexperienced committee chairman, a chief executive who was hard to deal with, and complex and unanticipated accounting issues." With a high expected loss rate on insurance premiums, the auditors lacked confidence that the deferred costs related to new policies could be recovered from future profits. As a result of this disagreement, the company reported a $3.2 million loss rather than an anticipated $2.6 million profit. Given the situation at Cal Life, a number of actions were taken to improve the financial reporting process. In particular, the senior executives of the firm were replaced and the membership of the audit committee increased to five from three. The committee had convened six times as opposed to two meetings and assumed an active role in overseeing the audit processes.[37]

Clearly, this case demonstrated that the audit committee is a viable mechanism in helping boards of directors discharge their oversight responsibilities for the financial reporting process. There is little question that the committee has assumed greater responsibilities.

## Playboy Enterprises, Inc.

In the *Playboy Enterprises* case, the audit committee requested that Hugh Hefner, chief executive officer of *Playboy*, and four other executives return to the company more than $900,000. The amounts owed by these parties involved perquisites (perks), such as the use of the DC-9 plane and the value of benefits (lodging, meals, valet, etc.) received from the company. As a result, the aforementioned parties repaid their perks and the board also established a compensation committee.[38] Thus the audit committee's close scrutiny of these activities did unearth a significant problem area before it impaired the integrity of the company.

---

[37] Hal Lancaster, "Fuss at Cal Life Shows Audit Committee Role Is Critical," *Wall Street Journal*, March 17, 1980.

[38] *Wall Street Journal*, "Playboy Audit Committee Bares Details of Hefner's High Living on Firm's Tab," *Wall Street Journal*, April 4, 1980.

## H.J. Heinz

From 1972 to 1979, Heinz was involved in profit-juggling practices at several divisions. More specifically, the audit committee reported that "the practices, designed to give the appearance of smooth profit growth of the divisions, stemmed partly from inadequate internal accounting controls, poor internal communications, the autonomy of division accountants and careless review of division reports by the Heinz corporate staff."[39] To correct these practices, the audit committee recommended more internal auditors, more corporate supervision of division accountants, and a tougher corporate code of conduct. In addition, the audit committee recommended changing the outside auditing firm, and, as a result, another multinational accounting firm is now the auditor. Furthermore, the company hired an outside law firm and another large accounting firm to assist in the special investigation.[40] Clearly, Heinz's audit committee proved to be a very strong and effective operating tool of the company. Its involvement established a high degree of confidence in the quality of the financial reports and disclosures to stockholders, underwriters, and financial analysts. Exhibits 4.1 and 4.2 contain a discussion of possible warning signals and red flags.

As Hugh L. Marsh and Thomas E. Powell assert:

> It would be a misconception to believe the possibility of fraud is the only reason for establishing a chartered audit committee. While the primary role has been to oversee management's financial and reporting responsibilities, the Treadway Commission's investigations indicated that audit committees could serve very effectively to reduce the incidence of fraud.[41]

## Livent, Inc.

This case relates to securities class actions brought by investors against Livent and associated individuals and entities. In addition to other defendants, three directors who served on Livent's audit committee were named as defendants. The audit committee members were charged with violating federal securities laws, namely Section 10(b), and Section 20(a) claims of the 1934 act. The case involved fraudulent revenue-generating transactions and manipulation of books and records. The shareholders alleged that the audit committee failed to discover the aforementioned schemes. In the decision, the judge dismissed the Section 10(a) and Section 20(a) violations since the audit committee was not a culpable participant in the fraud schemes. Likewise, the Section 10(a) and Section 20(a) violations were not sufficient to plead scienter as well as the criteria for control person liability.[42]

---

[39] Thomas Petziner, Jr., "Heinz Senior Officials Didn't Participate in Profit-Juggling Practices, Panel Says," *Wall Street Journal,* May 9, 1980.

[40] Ibid.

[41] Hugh L. Marsh and Thomas E. Powell, "The Audit Committee Charter: Rx for Fraud Prevention," *Journal of Accountancy* 167, no. 2 (February 1989): 56.

[42] *In Re Livent, Inc. Securities Litigation,* 148 F. Supp. 2d 331 (S.D.N.Y. 2001). For additional court cases, see *Haltman, et al. v. Aura Systems, Inc., et al.,* 844 F. Supp. 544 (C.D. C.A. 1993); and *Bomarko, Inc. v. Hemodynamics, Inc.,* 848 F. Supp. 1335 (W.D. M.I. 1993).

**EXHIBIT 4.2** Warning Signals for the Possible Existence of Fraudulent Financial Reporting

| Symptom | Problem | Solution |
| --- | --- | --- |
| **I. Industry Matters** | | |
| Competitive and economic conditions | Overoptimistic news releases with respect to earnings. Capital investment in a rapidly changing industry. | Analyze annual and interim earnings trends to avoid increased opportunities for managing earnings. |
| Competitive foreign businesses | Foreign competitors have significant advantages. | Discuss management's strategy as it relates to financial matters. |
| Government regulations | The industry is subject to new regulations that increase the cost of compliance. | Obtain assurance on the entity's compliance affecting financial matters. |
| Industry accounting practices | Unusual revenue recognition policies and/or deferred expenses to increase earnings. | Access significant accounting policies that are industry specific from the NAARS data base, and review and discuss this information with the independent auditors. |
| **II. Entity's Business Matters** | | |
| Organizational structure | High turnover in key accounting personnel (e.g., controller). Complex corporate structure that is not warranted. | Determine the reasons for such personnel turnover. |
| Lines of business and product segments | Rapid expansion of business lines in excess of industry averages. | Investigate the reasons for this rapid expansion. |
| Lack of security over computer operations | Control procedures over computer operations are weak. | Inquire of management as to key security problems. |
| Accounting policies | Significant changes in accounting practices and estimates by management with an excessive interest in earnings. Unusual year-end transactions that increase earnings. Inconsistencies between financial statements, MDA, and the president's letter. | Compare the entity's policies with the industry norms and determine the reasons for the changes. Raise questions on issues that support these transactions; determine the reasons for the inconsistent disclosures. |

| | | |
|---|---|---|
| Conflict-of-interest | Significant contracts that affect financial statements. Frequent related-party transactions. Failure to enforce the corporate code of conduct. | Determine management intent to disclose such contracts; determine how the company addresses possible conflict-of-interest situations; determine how management monitors compliance with the code. |
| Frequent change of legal counsel | Disagreements on asserted or unasserted claims and contingencies. | Discuss disclosures with general counsel and outside counsel. |
| Unexplained significant fluctuations in account balances | Material physical inventory variances. | Focus on the analytical review procedures. |

### III. External Auditing Matters

| | | |
|---|---|---|
| Frequent change of auditors | Disagreement on GAAP, which causes opinion shopping. | Investigate the reasons for frequent changes in auditors. |
| Quantity of lawsuits against the CPA firm | Firm has violated the securities laws. | Review the latest peer review report and the number of lawsuits against the firm. |
| Nonacceptance of recommendations in the management letter | Breakdowns in the internal control structures. | Obtain assurance from the auditors that management has evaluated the weaknesses and that corrective action has been taken. |

### IV. Internal Auditing Matters

| | | |
|---|---|---|
| Departmental organization | The size of the internal audit department is not compatible with the size of the company. | Discuss this matter with chief internal auditor and independent auditor. |
| Reporting responsibility | Scope restrictions. | Direct access to the audit committee. |

## Manzo v. Rite Aid Corporation

The plaintiffs brought a class action lawsuit against the officers, directors, and outside accounting firm. With respect to the audit committee, they alleged a breach of fiduciary duty with respect to fraudulent financial statements during the class period. The defendants denied any wrongdoing with regard to misleading financial statements. They contended good faith reliance on the officers' reports. The court ruled for the defendants, saying that the complaint failed to adequately allege reliance and damages and failed to establish a direct claim and a derivative claim.[43]

## Guttman v. Nvidia Corporation

In this case, the plaintiffs alleged that the defendants issued materially misstated financial statements. They contend the defendants used cookie jar reserves to smooth earnings in bad times. The court ruled in favor of the defendants because the audit committee did not commit any culpable failure of oversight under the *Caremark* standard.[44]

As William T. Allen, chancellor of the Court of Chancery of Delaware stated in his decision:

> In order to show that the Caremark directors breached their duty of care by failing adequately to control Caremark's employees, plaintiffs would have to show either (1) that the directors knew or (2) should have known that violations of law were occurring and, in either event, (3) that the directors took no steps in a good faith effort to prevent or remedy that situation, and (4) that such failure proximately resulted in the losses complained of, although under *Cede & Co. v. Technicolor, Inc.*, Del. Supr., 636 A.2d 956 (1994) this last element may be thought to constitute an affirmative defense.
>
> 1. Knowing violation for statute: Concerning the possibility that the Caremark directors knew of violations of law, none of the documents submitted for review, nor any of the position transcripts appear to provide evidence of it. Certainly the board understood that the company had entered into a variety of contracts with physicians, researchers, and health care providers and it was understood that some of these contracts were with persons who had prescribed treatments that Caremark partici-pated in providing. The board was informed that the Company's reimbursement for patient care was frequently from government funded sources and that such services were subject to the ARPL. But the Board appears to have been informed by experts that the company's practices while contestable, were lawful. There is no evidence that reliance on such reports was not reasonable. Thus, this case presents no occasion to apply a principle to the effect that knowingly causing the corporation to violate a criminal statute constitutes a breach of a director's fiduciary duty. See *Roth v. Robertson*, N.Y. Sup. Ct., 64 Misc. 343, 18 N.Y. 351 (1909); *Miller v. American Tel. & Tel. Co.*, 507 F.2d 759 (3rd ci. 1974). It is not clear that the Board knew the detail found, for example, in the indictments arising from the Company's payments. But,

---

[43] Manzo v. Rite Aid Corporation, C.A. No. 18451-NC (Del. Ch. 2002).

[44] *Guttman v. Jen-Hsun Huang et al. Nvidia Corporation*, C.A. No. 19571-N.C. (Del. Ch. 2003).

of course, the duty to act in good faith to be informed cannot be thought to require directors to possess detailed information about all aspects of the operation of the enterprise. Such a requirement would simply be inconsistent with the scale and scope of efficient organization size in this technological age.

2. Failure to monitor: Since it does appears that the Board was to some extent unaware of the activities that led to liability, I turn to a consideration of the potential avenue to director liability that the pleadings take: director inattention or "negligence." Generally where a claim of directorial liability for corporate loss is predicated upon ignorance of liability creating activities within the corporation, as in Graham or in this case, in my opinion only a sustained or systematic failure of the board to exercise oversight—such as an utter failure to attempt to assure a reasonable information and reporting system exists—will establish the lack of good faith that is a necessary condition to liability. Such a test of liability—lack of good faith as evidenced by sustained or systematic failure of a director to exercise reasonable oversight—is quite high. But, a demanding test of liability in the oversight context is probably beneficial to corporate shareholders as a class, as it is in the board decision context, since it makes board service by qualified persons more likely, while continuing to act as a stimulus to good faith performance of duty by such directors.

Here the record supplies essentially no evidence that the director defendants were guilty of a sustained failure to exercise their oversight function. To the contrary, insofar as I am able to tell on this record, the corporation's information systems appear to have represented a good faith attempt to be informed of the relevant facts. If the directors did not know the specifics of the activities that lead to the indictments, they cannot be faulted.

The liability that eventuated in this instance was huge. But the fact that it resulted from a violation of criminal law alone does not create a breach of fiduciary duty by directors. The record at this stage does not support the conclusion that the defendants either lacked good faith in the exercise of their monitoring responsibilities or conscientiously permitted a known violation of law by the corporation to occur. The claims asserted against them must be viewed at this stage as extremely weak.[45]

## Stoneridge Investment Partners, LLC v. Scientific-Atlanta, Inc.

This case involved "scheme liability" and whether a private action under Section 10(b) of the 1934 Act could be brought against alleged aiders and abettors. Stoneridge alleged losses after purchasing shares of common stock of Charter Communications, Inc. Scientific-Atlanta, a customer and supplier of Charter, agreed to a transaction that Charter used to mislead its auditor and to issue misleading financial statements. Scientific-Atlanta had no role in preparing or disseminating the financial statements of Charter. The Supreme Court held in its January 15, 2008, decision that, because Stoneridge and other investors in Charter had not relied on statements or representations by Scientific-Atlanta, they could not bring a Section 10(b) suit against Scientific-Atlanta. The Court also affirmed

---

[45] See *In Re Caremark International Inc. Derivative Litigation*, 698 A.2d 959 (Del. Ch. 1996).

Section 104 of PLSRA, which specifically directed the SEC to prosecute aiders and abettors rather than permitting private 10(b) suits against them. This decision clarified what "reliance" means, tying reliance to causation and whether acts are immediate or remote to an injury.[46]

## Developments at the SEC Related to Audit Committees

In 2003 and 2004, the SEC adopted final rules to fulfill the demands of a number of Sections of the Sarbanes-Oxley Act of 2002. Many of those rules pertain to the responsibilities that fall under the audit committee's work program.

In Release No. 34-47890 in 2003, the SEC adopted final rules concerning improper influence on the conduct of audits. As directed by Section 303 of the Sarbanes-Oxley Act of 2002, the rule prohibits officers and directors of an issuer, and persons acting under their direction, from taking any action to coerce, manipulate, mislead, or fraudulently influence the auditor of the issuer's financial statements if it were known or should have been known that such actions, if successful, could result in materially misleading financial statements.

In Release No. 33-8220, adopted in 2003, the SEC adopted a new rule that directs the national securities exchanges and national securities associations not to list companies that do not comply with the audit committee requirements of Sarbanes-Oxley in Section 301. These requirements concern the independence of audit committee members, the responsibility to select and oversee the independent accountant, procedures for handling complaints about accounting practices (whistle blowing notification systems), the authority to engage advisors, and the authorization to fund the independent auditor and outside advisors.

SEC Release No. 33-8176 in 2003 laid down the conditions for the use of non-GAAP financial measures through the adoption of Regulation G, which requires public companies that disclose or release non-GAAP financial measures to include in their disclosure or release a presentation of the most directly comparable GAAP financial measure and a reconciliation of the non-GAAP measure to the GAAP measure.

Sections 406 and 407 of Sarbanes-Oxley directed the SEC to issue rules about audit committee financial experts and company codes of ethics. In Release No. 33-8177, issued in January 2003, the SEC required companies to disclose whether they have at least one financial expert serving on the audit committee and, if so, the name of the individual and whether the individual is independent of management. If a company does not have such an independent financial expert, then it must disclose that fact and explain why it does not have such an expert. The rules also require the disclosure of whether a company has adopted a code of ethics for the principal executive officer, principal financial officer, principal accounting officer or controller, or persons performing similar functions. If such a code has not been adopted, that fact must be disclosed along with an explanation as to why.

In Release No. 33-8180, the SEC adopted final rules requiring accounting firms to retain for seven years certain records associated with their audits and

---

[46] Note, as of the date of this writing, legislation was pending in the U.S. Senate (S.1551) that, if passed, would nullify the *Stoneridge* decision.

reviews of public company financial statements. Accounting firms have to retain their working papers and certain documents containing conclusions, opinions, analyses, or financial data pertaining to the audit or review engagement.

As directed by Section 401(a) of Sarbanes-Oxley, the SEC issued Release No. 33-8182 to require in a separate section of Management's Discussion and Analysis disclosure and explanation of off-balance sheet arrangements.

In 2003 SEC Release No. 33-8133 strengthened requirements regarding auditor independence as directed by Section 208(a) of Sarbanes-Oxley. Audit committees are given substantial responsibilities in the financial reporting process and in assuring auditor independence. Audit committees must know whether their audit firms are in conformity with these provisions:

- The rules prohibiting nonaudit services that impair an accounting firm's independence.
- Pre-approval by the audit committee of all audit and permitted nonaudit services.
- Five (seven) consecutive years' limitation on audit engagement (concurring) partners, depending on their role.
- Prohibition on auditing if certain members of management were members of the accounting firm's audit engagement team for the company during the previous year.
- Certain matters related to management's integrity and the financial reporting process that come to the attention of the auditor must be reported to the audit committee, including critical accounting policies adopted by management.
- Required disclosures to investors of audit and permitted nonaudit services performed, along with the fees for such services.
- Auditors lose their independence from an audit client if part of their compensation is based on selling to that client services other than audit, review, and attest services.

SEC Release 33-8185, prompted by Section 307 of Sarbanes-Oxley and issued in 2003, addresses the implementation of standards of professional conduct for attorneys. The final rule indicates that standards of professional conduct for attorneys must include a rule requiring an attorney to report to the chief legal counsel or the chief executive officer evidence of a material violation of securities law or breach of fiduciary duty or similar violations by the issuer up-the-ladder within the company. If the CLC's or CEO's response to the evidence is not appropriate, then the attorney should report the evidence to the audit committee, to another committee of independent directors, or to the full board.

As directed by Section 404 of Sarbanes-Oxley, in Release 33-8238 in 2003 the SEC issued a final rule on management's report on internal control over financial reporting and certification of disclosure in exchange act periodic reports. The final rule has the following requirements for management's report:[47]

- It must include a statement of management's responsibility for establishing and maintaining adequate internal control over financial reporting;

---

[47] See Chapter 8 for further discussion of these filing requirements.

- Management must assess the effectiveness of internal control over financial reporting as of the end of the most recent fiscal year;
- Management must identify the framework used in the evaluation of internal control over financial reporting;
- The registered public accounting firm that audited the financial statement must state that it has issued an attestation report on management's assessment of internal control over financial reporting (later revised to focus on whether internal control over financial reporting is effective rather than on management's process of evaluation);
- Every fiscal quarter, management must evaluate any change in internal control over financial reporting that might have a material effect.

## Corporate Responsibility and Governance Developments

The American Bar Association Task Force on Corporate Responsibility recommended adoption of these governance policies as ABA policy:

1. The board of directors of a public corporation must engage in active, independent and informed oversight of the corporation's business and affairs, including its senior management.

2. In order to improve the effectiveness of such oversight, the board of directors of a public corporation should adopt governance principles (more fully specified in Part VI of this Report) that (a) establish and preserve the independence and objectivity of directors by eliminating disabling conflicts of interest and undue influence or control by the senior management of the corporation and (b) provide the directors with timely and sufficient information and analysis necessary to the discharge of their oversight responsibilities.

3. The directors should recognize and fulfill an obligation to disclose to the board of directors information and analysis known to them that is relevant to the board's decision making and oversight responsibilities. Senior executive officers should recognize and fulfill an obligation to disclose, to a supervising officer, the general counsel, or the board of directors or committees of the board, information and analysis relevant to such persons' decision making and oversight responsibilities.

4. Providing information and analysis necessary for the directors to discharge their oversight responsibilities, particularly as they relate to legal compliance matters, requires the active involvement of general counsel for the public corporation. (If a public corporation has no internal general counsel, it should identify and designate a lawyer or law firm to act as general counsel. The responsibility for implementing these recommended policies may necessarily be delegated to some extent by the general counsel to subordinate lawyers.)

5. A lawyer representing public corporation shall serve the interests of the entity, independent of the personal interests of any particular director, officer, employee or shareholder.

6. The general counsel of a public corporation should have primary responsibility for assuring the implementation of an effective legal compliance system under the oversight of the board of directors.

 7. Public corporations should adopt practices in which:
   a. The selection, retention, and compensation of the corporation's general counsel are approved by the board of directors.
   b. General counsel meets regularly and in executive session with a committee of independent directors to communicate concerns regarding legal compliance matters, including potential or ongoing material violations of law by, and breaches of fiduciary duty to, the corporation.
   c. All reporting relationships of internal and outside lawyers for a public corporation establish at the outset a direct line of communication with general counsel through which these lawyers are to inform the general counsel of material potential or ongoing violations of law by, and breaches of fiduciary duty to, the corporation.

 8. The model Business Corporation Act and the general corporation laws of the states, and the courts interpreting and applying the duties of directors, should more clearly delineate the oversight responsibility of directors generally, and the unique role that independent directors play in discharging that responsibility in public company settings. (Among the specific oversight matters that should be considered in relation to the Model Business Corporation Act or its commentary and the state corporate laws as well as in relation to important guidance such as the *Corporate Director's Guidebook* are at least the following: selecting, evaluating, and compensating the chief executive officer and other members of senior management; reviewing, approving, and monitoring fundamental financial and business strategies and the performance of the company relative to those strategies; assessing major risks facing the company; and ensuring that reasonable processes are in place to maintain the integrity of the company and the corresponding accountability of senior management, including processes relating to integrity of financial reporting, compliance with law and corporate codes of legal and ethical conduct, and processes designed to prevent improper related party transactions. Federal law (particularly the securities law, including the rules and regulations adopted by the SEC) also plays a significant role in affecting and promoting corporate responsibility.

 9. Engagements of counsel by the board of directors, or by a committee of the board, for special investigations or independent advice should be structured to assure independence and direct reporting to the board of directors or the committee.

 10. The SEC and the state attorney disciplinary authorities should cooperate in sharing information in order to promote effective and appropriate enforcement of rules of conduct applicable to counsel to public corporations.

 11. The courts, law schools and lawyer professional organizations such as the ABA should promote awareness of, and adherence to, the professional responsibilities of lawyers in their representation of public corporations.

 12. Law firms and law departments should adopt procedures to facilitate and promote compliance with rules of professional conduct governing the representation of public corporations. (In its Preliminary Report [at 43], the task force stated its intention to consider issues involving potential conflicts of interest arising out of lawyers' business and investment relationships with clients. The testimony submitted to the Task Force, however, did not

significantly focus on such issues, and the Task Force therefore recommends that further review of the issues be taken by interested professional organizations, including the appropriate ABA entities.)[48]

With respect to audit committees, the ABA Task Force recommended these corporate governance practices:

The board of directors should establish an audit committee, composed exclusively of independent directors.

  a. The audit committee should meet regularly outside the presence of any senior executive officer.

  b. The audit committee should be:
     i. authorized to engage and remove the corporation's outside auditor (or if legally permissible, to recommend such engagement or removal to the Board), and to determine the terms of the engagement of the outside auditor;
    ii. authorized and afforded resources sufficient to engage independent accounting and legal advisers when determined by the committee to be necessary or appropriate; and
    iii. responsible for recommending or establishing policies relating to non-audit services provided by the corporation's outside auditor to the Corporation and other aspects of the Corporation's relationship with the outside auditor that may adversely affect that firm's independence.

  c. The resolution of the board of directors creating the committee should specify whether the foregoing decisions are to be made exclusively by the audit committee, or (where legally permissible) by the full board of directors (or by the independent directors) upon the recommendation of the committee.

## GUIDELINES FOR MINIMIZING LEGAL LIABILITY

Obviously, audit committee directors wish to avoid legal liability. To achieve this objective, the directors should conduct their activities in a manner that is above reproach. As evidenced in federal and state statutes, federal regulations, and court cases, audit committees serve a critically important role in the corporate environment. Not only should they exercise the required standards of care and loyalty in their positions, but they also should foster professionalism as they conduct their directorship.

To assist the members of the audit committee in minimizing their possible legal liability, the following list of guidelines is provided. It is not an all-inclusive list and is open to insertion of additional matters. Note, too, that the guidelines are presented in view of the oversight and advisory capacity of the committee.

---

[48] American Bar Association, *Report of the American Bar Association Task Force on Corporate Responsibility* (Chicago, ABA, 2003), 31–33.

## Minimizing the Audit Committee's Legal Liability: A Checklist[49]

I. The Independent Auditors
  A. Have we inquired about the qualifications of the personnel whom we engaged in the audit?
    1. Review the backgrounds of the executive partner and auditing personnel.
    2. Inquire about the auditing firm's registration with the SEC practice division of the AICPA.
    3. Inquire about the CPA firm's participation in the voluntary peer review professional practice programs.
  B. Have we reviewed their engagement letter?
    The auditor's engagement letter sets forth the nature and scope of the audit engagement in order to avoid any misunderstanding between the auditing firm and the client. This letter constitutes a contract regarding the professional services of the CPA firm.
  C. Is there evidence that the audit examination was properly planned, supervised, and reviewed?
    1. Inquire about the overall audit plan concerning the scope, conduct, and timing of the audit examination.
    2. Discuss the level of knowledge that is required for the corporation and the industry.
    3. Discuss the ratio of staff assistants to supervisors in connection with the level of responsibilities for the audit.
    4. Review or request an outline of the supervisory review procedures of the staff assistant's work and note any disagreements among the audit personnel.
  D. Does the corporate annual report contain a fair and meaningful presentation of the information concerning the financial statements, footnotes, and supplementary information?
    Significant changes in the external reporting practices of the corporation should be discussed (e.g., departures from generally accepted accounting principles, exceptions to the consistent application of accounting principles, and the alternative applications of generally accepted accounting principles).
  E. Have we reviewed the recommendations made in their management letter to assure the auditors' objectivity?
    1. The management letter contains the auditors' recommendations as a result of their evaluation of the system of internal control. Any matters regarding the material weaknesses in the system of internal control should be discussed as well as full compliance with the provisions of the Foreign Corrupt Practices Act.

---

[49] It is advisable that the audit committee document its activities and have in-house counsel or outside legal counsel review documentation for content and use prior to adoption. Such procedures will help protect the audit committee in cases of possible litigation.

    2. Discuss the implementation of the recommendations in the current and prior years' management letters as well as causes of management disagreement with the auditors.

F. Have we reviewed the lawyer's letter concerning litigations, claims, and assessments?

    1. The lawyer's letter contains the opinion of legal counsel with respect to potential litigation, such as a pending lawsuit. Such information is provided to the CPA firms for possible disclosure in the financial statements.

    2. Discuss the accounting treatment concerning the contingency losses and effect on the financial statements.

G. Have we reviewed the letter of management's representation?

The chief financial officer and chief executive officer will furnish a letter to the auditing firm with respect to the corporation's representations concerning the financial position and the results of operations. This letter should be examined in view of the facts in the letter and in the financial statements. This letter is particularly important since it confirms management's responsibilities for the financial statements.

H. Have we reviewed:

    1. Any amendments to the bylaws or corporate charter?

    2. The minutes of the meetings of the board of directors, directors' committees, and stockholders (e.g., compensation committee or finance committees)?

I. Have we reviewed the corporation's compliance with the auditors and legal counsel concerning the:

    1. Securities statutes?

    2. Antitrust laws?

    3. Income tax laws?

    4. Labor laws?

    5. Regulatory laws applicable to the industry?

J. Have we made an evaluation of any material non–arm's-length transactions, such as loans to officers?

K. Have we reviewed:

    1. Results of peer review and PCOAB inspection?

    2. Litigation against the CPA firm?

    3. Adequacy of professional liability insurance?

    4. Independence issues as required by ISB Standard No. 1?

    5. Required disclosures to the audit committee as required by SAS #61 or #114?

    6. Extent of management services provided by CPA firm and impact on independence?

II. The Internal Auditors

A. Have we reviewed the qualifications of the internal audit staff?

    1. Review the backgrounds of the director of internal auditing and the internal auditing group.

    2. Inquire about the internal audit staff's participation in the programs of the Institute of Internal Auditors and other professional societies.

  3. Discuss their qualifications with the independent auditing firm.
B. Have we reviewed their charter or audit plan?
C. Have we considered the reporting responsibility of the internal audit staff?
D. Is there evidence that the work of the internal audit staff was properly planned, supervised, and reviewed?
  See item number C under "The Independent Auditors."
E. Have we reviewed:
  1. Reports on compliance audits?
  2. Reports on operational audits?
  3. Reports on financial audits?
  4. Reports on the system of internal accounting and administrative controls?
     • Have we reviewed the recommendations made in their reports with respect to objectivity?
     • Have we considered the possibility of a long-form report from the Director of Internal Auditing?
F. Have the internal auditors' recommendations in connection with the prior years' internal audit been implemented?
G. Have we scrutinized cases of management disagreements with the internal auditors?
H. Have we reexamined the relationship of the internal audit function to the other departments?
I. How are activities of the internal audit staff and the independent auditors interrelated?
J. If the corporation has an electronic data processing installation, have we considered the use of independent EDP consultants to audit the installation?
III. The Representatives of Management (Chief Executive Officer, Chief Financial Officer, Treasurer, and Controller)
A. Are the qualifications of the representatives of management consistent with the corporate bylaws?
B. Have we reviewed their administrative functions in relationship to the present financial and accounting policies? (See company's organization chart.)
C. Have these individuals exercised their authority in accordance with the corporate bylaws?
D. Have we reviewed the minutes of the meeting of the board of directors concerning their compensation?
E. Have we reviewed their written reports concerning their responses to the deficiencies noted in the internal audit reports?
F. Are all employees who handle cash, securities, and other valuables bonded?
G. Are the financial and accounting policies and procedures set forth in manuals?
H. Are interim financial reports prepared for submission to management on a timely basis?

    I. Is the quality and quantity of information in the interim reports adequate?

    J. Have we discussed cases of management disagreements with the auditors?

    K. Have we discussed:
       1. The engagement letter?
       2. The management letter from the independent auditors?
       3. The letter of management's representations?
       4. The lawyer's letter?

    L. Have we discussed the periodic filings with the various regulatory agencies?

In view of the preceding discussions on the legal position of the audit committee, it is important that audit committee directors fully understand the nature and scope of their legal responsibilities concerning the corporation's outside constituencies and the securities markets. They should, however, keep their legal obligations in proper perspective. Such obligations should be integrated and balanced with the committee's functions so that the committee's purpose is not defeated. In short, directors should discharge their responsibilities in a professional manner and not become totally preoccupied with the legal rules and regulations.

## SOURCES AND SUGGESTED READINGS

American Bar Association. *Corporate Director's Guidebook* (Chicago: ABA, 1978).

American Bar Association. *Corporate Director's Guidebook* (Chicago: ABA, 1994).

American Bar Association. *Report of the American Bar Association Task Force on Corporate Responsibility* (Chicago: American Bar Association, 2003), 1–89.

*Bomark, Inc. v. Hemodynamics, Inc.*, 848 F. Supp. 1335 (W.D.M.I. 1993).

Braiotta, Louis. "Auditing for Honesty." *American Bar Association Journal*, 78, no. 5 (May 1992): 76–79.

Commerce Clearing House. *Federal Securities Law Reporter* (Chicago: Commerce Clearing House, 1972–73, 1974–75, 1977–78 Transfer binder).

Commerce Clearing House. *Federal Securities Law Reporter* (Chicago: Commerce Clearing House, 1984–1985 Transfer binder).

Committee on Corporate Laws, Section of Corporation, Banking and Business Law of the American Bar Association. *Revised Model Business Corporation Act—Chapter 8: Directors and Officers* (Chicago, Ill.: American Bar Association, 1984).

Committee on Corporate Laws of the Section of Business Law. *Model Business Corporation Act—Chapter 8: Directors and Officers* (Chicago, Ill.: American Bar Association, 1998).

Connecticut General Statutes Annotated, Sections 33-318(b)(1) and (2), West 1960 and Supplement 1985.

"Firing Line," *Time* (February 19, 1979): 51.

*Guttman v. Jen-Hsun Huang et al. Nvidia Corporation*, C.A. No. 19571-N.C. (Del. Ch. 2003).

*Haltman, et al. v. Aura Systems, Inc., et al.* 844 F. Supp. 544 (C.D.C.A. 1993).

*In re Caremark, Derivative Litigation Delaware Court of Chancery*, 1996 698 A. 2d 959.

*In re Livent, Inc. Securities Litigation*, 148 F. Supp. 2d 331 (S.D.N.Y. 2001).

*International, Inc. Derivative Litigation*, 698 A.2d 959 (Del. Ch. 1996).

Internal Revenue Code. Chapter 75A, Crimes (1954).

Lancaster, Hal. "Fuss at Cal Life Shows Audit Committee Role Is Crucial, Experts Say." *Wall Street Journal*, March 17, 1980.

*Manzo v. Rite Aid Corporation*, C.A. No. 18451-N.C. (Del. Ch. 2002).

Marsh, Hugh L., and Thomas E. Powell. "The Audit Committee Charter: Rx for Fraud Prevention." *Journal of Accountancy* 167, no. 2 (February 1989): 55–57.

New York Business Corporation Law, *McKinney's Consolidated Laws of New York Annotated* (Brooklyn: Edward Thompson Company, 1963, Book 6).

Petziner, Thomas, Jr. "Heinz Senior Officials Didn't Participate in Profit-Juggling Practices, Panel Says." *Wall Street Journal*, May 9, 1980.

Powers, William C. Report of Investigation by the Special Investigative Committee of the Board of Directors of Enron Corporation (February 1, 2002). Available at http://news.findlaw.com/hdocs/docs/enron/sicreport/.

Sarbanes-Oxley Act of 2002. Section 307, Rules of Professional Responsibility for Attorneys. H.R. Rep. No. 107-610 (2002).

Securities and Exchange Commission, 1993, 1994, 1995, 1996, 1997 *Annual Reports* (Washington, DC: U.S. Government Printing Office).

Securities and Exchange Commission, Release No. 33-8155, Implementation of Standards of Professional Conduct for Attorneys (January 29, 2003).

Securities and Exchange Commission, *The Work of the Securities and Exchange Commission* (Washington, DC: U.S. Government Printing Office, 1974).

Securities Exchange Act Rule 10(b)-5, Title 17, Code of Federal Regulations, Sec. 240 (1974).

United States Code, Titles 15 and 18 (1970).

Verschoor, Curtis C. "A Case Study of Audit Committee Effectiveness at Sundstrand." *Internal Auditing* 4, no. 4 (Spring 1989): 11–19.

Verschoor, Curtis C. "Miniscribe: A New Example of Audit Committee Ineffectiveness." *Internal Auditing* 5, no. 4 (Spring 1990): 13–19.

*Wall Street Journal.* "Playboy Audit Committee Bares Details of Hefner's High Living on Firm's Tab." *Wall Street Journal*, April 4, 1980.

# Chapter 5

# Rules of the Road

## Financial Reports and Their Audits

A primary responsibility of audit committees concerns the integrity, quality, and rigor of the company's people and processes that produce financial reports. This requires oversight of the relationship between the company and its external auditor. The content and structure of financial reports are generally governed by authoritative accounting pronouncements and disclosure requirements that arise from a variety of sources, depending on a company's geographical location and regulatory status. Oversight of the relationship of the company with its external auditors is also subject to various statutory, regulatory, and professional considerations that, likewise, depend on the company's location and status.

Although states' corporation acts in the United States treat accounting and auditing issues as matters to be negotiated among the parties by contract, companies subject to federal regulation by the Securities and Exchange Commission must follow accounting and disclosure requirements contained in Regulations S-X and S-K (www.sec.gov/divisions/corpfin/ecfrlinks.shtml). Most of the accounting provisions in Regulation S-X and the disclosures about them are products of the Financial Accounting Standards Board (FASB; www.fasb.org). Since 1974, the SEC has recognized the FASB's primary responsibility for standards associated with the recognition and measurement of financial statement elements along with the disclosures about the entity's application of those standards. In 1984, the FASB began a long transition in approach from income recognition and measurement to balance sheet recognition and measurement. As part of the implementation of the balance sheet approach, the FASB increasingly has required financial assets and liabilities to be carried at their "fair value" (i.e., current market prices or estimates of them). Fair value measurement has also expanded the scope of financial-instrument disclosures to include much more information about their risk. The FASB currently is working on a comprehensive disclosure standard whose effect would be to provide more uniform structure and content to financial statement disclosures. The standards promulgated by the FASB through its extensive due process currently are referred to as Generally Accepted Accounting Principles (GAAP or U.S. GAAP). In the past, the term "generally accepted accounting principles" referred broadly to a set of concepts and practices followed by accounting professionals, but now the term is reserved for the standards of the FASB. When the SEC recognized the FASB's financial statement responsibility in 1974, it kept for itself the responsibility for general disclosures, which can be found in Regulation S-K.

Outside the United States, most countries treat accounting in their commercial code, capital markets law, or corporation law. Countries with developed capital markets, or aspirations to participate in global capital markets, increasingly have adopted International Financial Reporting Standards (IFRS) of the International Accounting Standards Board (www.iasb.org). In 1974, a coordinative effort began within the accountancy profession to achieve global convergence of accounting standards for companies whose securities trade on stock exchanges; substantial progress has since been made by national financial reporting standards-setters, regulators, stock exchanges, and professional bodies. The FASB and IASB share many common projects and have a program for convergence of their standards (www.fasb.org/jsp/FASB/Page/SectionPage&cid=1176156245663). Twice since 2003, the U.S. SEC has laid out "road maps" for adoption of IFRS by companies subject to SEC registration.

Within the United States, state and federal agencies may require that state- or federally funded organizations also use specific accounting treatments. Federal or state funding occurs frequently in health care, low-income housing development, research, and education. Financial institutions, insurance companies, utilities, and financial intermediaries may also be subject to accounting and disclosure requirements of federal or state oversight agencies. Often these accounting requirements apply only to materials filed with the agencies and not to public financial reports; public financial reporting requirements would be satisfied by reports prepared according to U.S. GAAP as promulgated by the FASB.

The Government Accounting Standards Board (GASB) is organized separately from the FASB by the Financial Accounting Foundation, which is the private sector board that oversees both the FASB and GASB (see www.gasb.org). GASB's mission is to establish and improve standards of state and local governmental accounting and financial reporting that will result in useful information for users of financial reports and guide and educate the public, including issuers, auditors, and users of those financial reports.

Auditing standards constitute the rules of evidence that professional auditors follow in determining whether managements' financial reports conform to accounting standards. Financial report audits of U.S. public companies consider all of the following factors: internal control over financial reporting, the content of the financial statements, and the disclosures associated with the financial statements. External auditors also consider whether management's disclosure of nonfinancial statement material is consistent with their knowledge of the company. Most of the evidence collected by auditors consists of sampling, tracing, and vouching transactions; confirmations with external parties; observation of activities and processes; reperformance of calculations; and identification and verification of documentation.

Generally Accepted Auditing Standards (GAAS) arise from a number of sources. The Public Company Accounting Oversight Board (PCAOB) (www.pcaob.org) was created by the Sarbanes-Oxley Act of 2002 to regulate U.S. public company auditors. It registers, inspects, and disciplines public accounting firms that audit U.S. public companies. It also is responsible for creating the standards used in audits of the financial statements of public companies. Because the jurisdiction of the federal securities acts usually does not include private companies, nonprofits, and government agencies, PCAOB audit standards do not apply in these areas. Rather, the auditing standards set by the Auditing Standards Board (ASB) of the American Institute of Certified Public Accountants (www.aicpa.org) are considered by states' boards of accountancy as authoritative for CPAs in the practice of public accounting; the ASB standards are usually the reference point for audits of private companies. The Government Accountability Office (GAO) publishes the "yellow book" (www.gao.gov/govaud/ybk01.htm), which codifies audit standards (based primarily on the standards of the ASB) to be followed in audits required because of federal funding. The International Audit and Assurance Standards Board (www.iaasb.org)—independently and under its own authority—sets international auditing standards (ISAs) to facilitate the convergence of international and national audit standards. The ASB in the United States has made a concerted effort in recent years to converge as much as possible with ISAs. Nonetheless, U.S. auditing standards tend to be more prescriptive than ISAs, with more details about specific procedures for satisfying the requirement for sufficient, competent evidence for accepting management's assertions.

## AN OVERVIEW OF U.S. GENERALLY ACCEPTED AUDITING STANDARDS

### Nature of Generally Accepted Auditing Standards

While a company's financial statements and related disclosures are the representations and property of its management, the external auditors render an opinion as to whether those statements and disclosures comport to the requirements of U.S. GAAP. The scope paragraph of the standard audit opinion for public companies holds some clues about the work of the auditor. (There are minor differences in these standards for public and private companies due to the AICPA's issuance of Audit Risk Standards in 2006 having not yet been adopted by the PCAOB.)

> We conducted our audit in accordance with the standards of the Public Company Accounting Oversight Board (United States). Those standards require that we plan and perform the audit to obtain reasonable assurance about whether the financial statements are free of material misstatement. An audit includes examining, on a test basis, evidence supporting the amounts and disclosures in the financial statements. An audit also includes assessing the accounting principles used and significant estimates made by management, as well as evaluating the overall financial statement presentation. We believe that our audit provides a reasonable basis for our opinion.[1]

An audit examination depends heavily on authoritative guidelines or rules as established by an appropriate authority. It also depends heavily on professional judgment in the application of auditing procedures. As approved and adopted by the membership of the AICPA, and accepted on an interim basis by the PCAOB, generally accepted auditing standards are characterized at progressively more

[1] American Institute of Certified Public Accountants, *Professional Standards, U.S. Auditing Standards/Attestation Standards*, vol. 1, AU Sec. 508.08.

detailed levels in terms of general standards, fieldwork standards, and reporting standards.

General Standards

1. The audit is to be performed by a person or persons having adequate technical training and proficiency as an auditor.
2. In all matters relating to the assignment, an independence in mental attitude is to be maintained by the auditor or auditors.
3. Due professional care is to be exercised in the performance of the audit and the preparation of the report.

Standards of Field Work

1. The work is to be adequately planned and assistants, if any, are to be properly supervised.
2. A sufficient understanding of the internal control structure is to be obtained to plan the audit and to determine the nature, timing, and extent of tests to be performed.
3. Sufficient competent evidential matter is to be obtained through inspection, observation, inquiries, and confirmations to afford a reasonable basis for an opinion regarding the financial statements under audit.

Standards of Reporting

1. The report shall state whether the financial statements are presented in accordance with generally accepted accounting principles.
2. The report shall identify those circumstances in which such principles have not been consistently observed in the current period in relation to the preceding period.
3. Informative disclosures in the financial statements are to be regarded as reasonably adequate unless otherwise stated in the report.
4. The report shall either contain an expression of opinion regarding the financial statements taken as a whole or an assertion to the effect that an opinion cannot be expressed. When an overall opinion cannot be expressed, the reasons therefore should be stated. In all cases where an auditor's name is associated with financial statements, the report should contain a clear-cut indication of the character of the auditor's work, if any, and the degree of responsibility the auditor is taking.[2]

These auditing standards provide a useful framework for audit committees to assess the quality of the auditors' professional performance during the audit examination and the significance of the opinion in the audit report. Auditing standards differ from audit procedures in the generality of their application and in their specificity. Standards apply to all audit engagements in order to encourage high quality throughout the practice of auditing. The choice of the specific auditing procedures is subject to the auditor's professional judgment regarding the sufficiency and competence of the evidence that is required to accept a particular financial statement assertion. The auditing authorities periodically issue pronouncements on

---

[2] Ibid., AU Sec. 150.03.

auditing matters that represent their interpretations of generally accepted auditing standards. These pronouncements provide the auditors with guidance and direction regarding various auditing procedures in specific auditing situations. In addition to the organizations already mentioned, the Center for Audit Quality (www.thecaq.org), an audit industry association of firms registered with the PCAOB, also offers public company auditors helpful guidance on emerging audit issues.

## AN ANALYSIS OF THE AUDITING STANDARDS

### General Auditing Standards

With respect to the general standards, an individual demonstrates that she possesses adequate technical training and proficiency as an auditor by qualifying for licensure or certification as a Certified Public Accountant in the state where the audit takes place. States also require the registration of CPA firms that perform audits and enforce requirements for quality control systems. The PCOAB accepts state licensure and certification of individual CPAs, but separately registers and inspects CPA firms for their audits of public companies and for their quality control systems. CPAs are subject to an extensive code of professional conduct (www.aicpa.org) and state professional conduct regulations (e.g., see www.op.nysed.gov/part29.htm) and to the regulation of the SEC and PCAOB when auditing public companies. Although CPA firms may provide a variety of client services, their exclusive professional franchise consists of rendering an opinion on whether management's financial statement representations are presented in conformity with Generally Accepted Accounting Principles.

The PCOAB has issued its own standards, Auditing Standards 1 through 7, and has adopted on an interim basis the standards of the Auditing Standards Board (ASB). Exhibit 5.1 gives an overview of the PCAOB's standards. Exhibit 5.4 summarizes the Statements on Auditing Standards of the ASB.

***Auditing Standards of Fieldwork*** The first standard of fieldwork centers around the auditors' objectives, plans, and procedures concerning the particular audit engagement. The AICPA's Auditing Standards Executive Committee points out:

> Audit planning involves developing an overall strategy for the expected conduct and scope of the examination. The nature, extent, and timing of planning vary with the size and complexity of the entity, experience with the entity, and knowledge of the entity's business.[3]

> Supervision involves directing the efforts of assistants who are involved in accomplishing the objectives of the examination and determining whether those objectives were accomplished.[4]

---

[3] *Statement on Auditing Standards No. 22*, "Planning and Supervision" and its amendment for private companies SAS 108 (2006) (New York: AICPA, 1978), par. 3.

[4] Ibid., par. 9.

**EXHIBIT 5.1**   The Auditing Standards of the PCAOB

| | | |
|---|---|---|
| AS 1 | References in Auditors' Reports to the Standards of the Public Company Accounting Oversight Board | Provides language for use in audit reports. |
| AS 2 | An Audit of Internal Control Over Financial Reporting Performed in Conjunction With an Audit of Financial Statements | Replaced by AS 5. |
| AS 3 | Audit Documentation | Specifies the objectives of audit documentation, documentation requirements generally and for specific matters, and retention of and changes to audit documentation. |
| AS 4 | Reporting on Whether a Previously Reported Material Weakness Continues to Exist | Addresses the timing and content of audit work required when an audit of internal control over financial reporting is updated for changes not in conjunction with an audit of financial statements. |
| AS 5 | An Audit of Internal Control Over Financial Statements That Is Integrated with an Audit of Financial Statements | Establishes standards for planning, testing, evaluating deficiencies, and reporting on internal control over financial reporting. |
| AS 6 | Evaluating Consistency of Financial Statements | Considers standards for changes in accounting principles and corrections of material misstatements in previously issued financial statements. |
| AS 7 | Engagement Quality Review and Conforming Amendment to the Board's Interim Quality Control Standards | Enhances the requirement for auditors to perform an objective evaluation of the significant judgments made by the engagement team and the conclusions reached. |

See www.pcaob.org.

The first standard of fieldwork requires that the auditors plan their necessary auditing procedures subsequent to their review of such matters as the corporation's accounting policies and procedures and the industry practices of the particular entity. Also, they are required to develop and administer the necessary levels of proper supervision regarding the audit examination.[5] The first standard of field work details the required communications with the audit committee, board, and management of the company concerning issues that may arise during the course of an audit.

---

[5] For a complete description of the organizational and operational aspects of a public accounting firm, see any standard auditing textbook.

Statement of Audit Standards 99 (SAS 99), "Consideration of Fraud in a Financial Statement Audit," also requires the auditor to plan the audit in such a way as to provide high assurance that the financial statements are free of material misstatements due to fraud. SAS 99 lays out a number of specific procedures as well as general standards for auditors to follow, including communications with management, the audit committee, and the board about matters that come to their attention. Audit committee members should be aware of the content of SAS 99, which is available at the Web sites of both the PCAOB (www.pcaob.org under standards) and the AICPA (www.aicpa.org under professional standards). The PCOAB Web site contains U.S. auditing standards in codified form, while the AICPA site lists U.S. auditing standards chronologically by their SAS numbers and provides links to the codification. Nothing causes more problems for an audit committee than fraudulent financial statements, thus every care should be taken to guard against fraud. An auditor's effective application of SAS 99, coupled with effective internal control over financial reporting, is an important safeguard in reducing the risk of fraudulent financial statements.

The second standard of fieldwork requires that the auditors obtain a sufficient understanding of internal control over financial reporting (see Chapters 6 and 8). Their evaluation of internal control over financial reporting is necessary in order to determine how much to rely on the entity's financial accounting system and to comply with the requirements of the Sarbanes-Oxley Act that public companies have effective internal control over financial reporting. Since the financial statements are the product of the financial reporting system, the auditors must examine internal controls over financial reporting, the related recordings of business transactions, and the effectiveness of the controls. Furthermore, the auditors evaluate the system of internal control to determine the extent of their tests of the accounting records as well as their auditing procedures. The PCAOB has adopted an approach in Auditing Standard 5 that requires an integrated audit of internal control over financial reporting and the financial statements. The external auditor provides opinions about the financial statements' compliance with GAAP and about the effectiveness of management's internal control over financial reporting.

In the third standard of fieldwork, "sufficient appropriate evidential matter" means that the auditors must obtain and examine internal and external documentation that supports the financial accounting representations in the financial statements. For example, the auditors will examine not only sales invoices and other documentations but also correspondence from various parties outside the entity, such as banks and customers. The amount of evidential matter to be examined depends on the auditors' professional judgment. Obviously, the auditors' major objective is to examine sufficient evidence to enable them to express their opinion on the fairness of the presentations in the financial statements. Audits are designed to provide reasonable assurance rather than absolute assurance over the content of financial reports. "Reasonable" in this context has come to mean a "high" level of assurance, usually determined by the persuasiveness of the evidence in the circumstances and the extent and relevance of the procedures used to collect evidence. Because audits rely on evidence gathered by testing samples of items, financial statement audits do not provide exhaustive evidence.

The standards of fieldwork are directly related to the scope of the auditors' examination. The scope of the audit is critically important because the auditors may not express an unqualified opinion on the financial statements if their scope is limited. As the AICPA's Auditing Standards Executive Committee states:

> Restrictions on the scope of his examination, whether imposed by the client or by circumstances such as the timing of his work, the inability to obtain sufficient competent evidential matter, or an inadequacy in the accounting records, may require him to qualify his opinion or to disclaim an opinion.[6]

Thus, the audit committee should be aware of and examine those situations that may lead to a qualified opinion or disclaimer as a result of a limitation on the auditors' scope. Concern about scope restrictions is critically important for audit committees of U.S. public companies because the SEC requires unqualified opinions on registrants' financial statements. If, for example, a limitation on the auditors' observation of physical inventories or the confirmation of accounts receivable would lead to a scope restriction and a qualified opinion or disclaimer of opinion, there would be negative consequences for public offerings and even trading of a listed company's securities.[7]

The Auditing Standards Board realigned and clarified the authority of audit literature and guidance in SAS 95 with a hierarchy of generally accepted auditing standards. The PCAOB has adopted SAS 95 and its amendment, SAS 105, as an interim standard. Exhibit 5.2 identifies the three levels in the hierarchy of generally accepted auditing standards as auditing standards, interpretative publications, and other auditing publications. Because of the extent of the literature in this hierarchy, it is reasonable to expect that audit committees create a systematic process to ensure that they are informed about current authoritative auditing literature.

The auditing standards related to financial reporting are closely associated with generally accepted accounting principles. In the past, important financial reporting issues such as accounting for subsequent events, going concerns considerations, and a hierarchy of GAAP were treated in auditing standards rather than in accounting principles. Recently, the FASB has issued standards, or is in the process of issuing standards, that bring such considerations into GAAP so they apply to management's representations as well as to auditors. Any consideration of auditors' reporting standards must include accounting standards.

## INTEGRATION OF AUDITING AND RELATED ACCOUNTING STANDARDS

The auditors state in the third paragraph of their report that they are expressing an opinion on whether the financial statements are presented fairly in conformity with generally accepted accounting principles. In the United States, the phrase

---

[6] AICPA, *Professional Standards, U.S. Auditing Standards/Attestation Standards*, vol. 1, AU Sec. 508.22. See Chapter 13 for a discussion on the various types of auditing reports.
[7] Ibid., AU Sec. 508.24.

**EXHIBIT 5.2**   GAAS Hierarchy Summary

**Level of Authority**

*Level 1: Auditing Standards*[a] (included the 10 generally accepted auditing standards and the Statements on Auditing Standards).

*Level 2: Interpretive Publications*[b] (includes Interpretations of the SASs, auditing guidance in AICPA Audit and Accounting Guides, and AICPA auditing Statements of Position).

*Level 3: Other Auditing Publications*[c] (includes other AICPA publications not mentioned above; auditing articles in professional journals, including the AICPA's CPA Letter; continuing professional education programs and other instructional materials, textbooks, guide books, audit programs, and checklists; and other auditing publications from state CPA societies, other organizations, and individuals).

*Source: Statement on Auditing Standards No. 95,* "Generally Accepted Auditing Standards" (New York: AICPA, 2002), pars. 1–7.
[a] The auditor should be prepared to justify departures from the SASs.

---

[a] The auditor should be prepared to justify departures from the SASs.
[b] The auditor should be aware of and consider interpretive publications applicable to his audit, and if not applied, the auditor should be prepared to explain how he complied with the SAS provisions.
[c] The third-level publications have no authoritative status; however, they may help the auditor understand and apply the SASs.

"presented fairly in conformity with generally accepted accounting principles" has come to mean that financial statements prepared in conformity with generally accepted accounting principles are also stated fairly. Although an auditor in the United States ethically is permitted to not follow generally accepted accounting principles if their application would create misleading financial statements, such an occurrence would be extremely rare and would require persuasive evidence. In other national jurisdictions, notably in the U.K. but in other jurisdictions as well, auditors separately opine whether the financial statements conform to accounting principles and are "fair and true."

If there are no exceptions noted by the auditors with respect to the consistent application of generally accepted accounting principles and to adequate informative disclosure in the notes to financial statements, then the users normally can rely on such financial statements as fairly presented. The following discussion provides an analysis of the four auditing standards of reporting and the opinion paragraph of the auditors' report.

## Nature of Generally Accepted Accounting Principles

The first auditing standard of reporting requires the auditors to make a statement in their report on whether the financial statements are presented in accordance with generally accepted accounting principles. In the United States, "generally accepted accounting principles" usually refer to the standards of the FASB. The Sarbanes-Oxley Act of 2002 authorized the long-standing practice of the SEC to recognize private sector accounting standards-setters. The SEC has recognized the FASB as such a standards-setter. The AICPA recognizes the standards of the FASB and the IASB as authoritative. Because it is virtually impossible for standards-setters to anticipate all nuances of current and future transactions, various organizations provide nonauthoritative analyses of financial accounting standards that reflect their perspectives on emerging practices. Such organizations can range from auditor-centered groups such as the Center for Audit Quality (www.thecaq.org), financial analyst-centered groups such as the Chartered Financial Analysts Institute (www.cfainstitute.org ), financial statement preparer groups such as Financial Executives International (www.financialexecutives.org), corporate director–centered groups such as the National Association of Corporate Directors (www.nacdonline.org), and professional associations with a mix of constituents such as the AICPA (www.aicpa.org) or state CPA societies. Regulators such as the SEC also offer practice suggestions from time to time through Staff Accounting Bulletins and other communications (www.sec.gov).

The Financial Accounting Standards Board has issued six Statements of Financial Accounting Concepts for business organizations and one statement for financial reporting by nonbusiness organizations. In Chapter 3, these statements of concepts were identified and their implementation was discussed.

Management's selection of accounting principles, methods, or procedures should be based on those principles of accounting that are consistent with GAAP. Adoption of such principles is especially important because it affects the auditors' opinion on the financial statements. If management adopts accounting principles that deviate significantly from GAAP, then the auditors cannot express an unqualified opinion on the statements.[8] Moreover, Rule 203 of the AICPA Rules of Conduct of the Code of Professional Ethics states:

> A member shall not (1) express an opinion or state affirmatively that the financial statements or other financial data of any entity are presented in conformity with generally accepted accounting principles or (2) state that he or she is not aware of any material modifications that should be made to such statements or data in order for them to be in conformity with generally accepted accounting principles, if such statements or data contain any departure from an accounting principle promulgated by bodies designated by Council[9] to establish such principles that have a material effect on the statements or data taken as a whole. If, however, the statements or data contain such a departure and the member can demonstrate that due to unusual circumstances the financial statements or data would otherwise have been misleading, the member can comply with the rule by describing the departure, its approximate effects, if practicable, and the reasons why compliance with the principle would result in a misleading statement.[10]

---

[8] Ibid., AU Sec. 508.35.

[9] See the bodies designated by Council to promulgate technical standards in the Code of Professional Conduct. Available at www.aicpa.org.

[10] AICPA, Rules of Conduct of the Code of Professional Conduct. Available at www.aicpa.org.

Thus, the auditors may express an unqualified opinion when a company uses accounting principles that are inconsistent with GAAP when application of GAAP would be misleading; however, their audit report must be modified to describe the circumstances. As a practical matter, unqualified audit reports that reference GAAP departures are rare.

## GAAP Hierarchy and FASB Accounting Standards Codification

In May 2008, the FASB issued Statement of Financial Accounting Standard No. 162 that adopted the hierarchy for authoritative literature that previously had been part of auditing principles (SAS 95). Exhibit 5.3 summarizes the GAAP hierarchy in effect after May 2008 for nongovernmental entities and state and local governments. The FASB Accounting Standards Codification, adopted in June 2009 in SFAS No. 168, subsequently has set a new standard for identifying authoritative GAAP. The Accounting Standards Codification is now the sole source of authoritative GAAP, although some recourse to the previous hierarchy remains necessary for grandfathered applications. Information about the Accounting Standards Codification is available online at asc.fasb.org.[11]

FASB ASC organizes accounting guidance into areas, topics, subtopics, sections, and subsections without regard to the source of the guidance.

- Areas are the broadest category, grouping topics.
- Topics are the broadest category, containing related content. They correlate with International Accounting Standards (IAS) published by the predecessor of the IASB, the International Accounting Standards Committee, and International Financial Reporting Standards, published by the IASB.
- Subtopics are type or scope subsets of topics.
- Sections identify whether content concerns recognition, measurement, or disclosure, and whether their structure correlates with IAS and IFRS.
- Subsections are further segregation of content.

FASB ASC does not include governmental accounting standards. While its purpose is not to change U.S. GAAP, it does represent a considerable effort to reduce the complexity of searching for authoritative accounting guidance and to facilitate international convergence of accounting standards.

***Consistency***   With respect to the third standard of reporting, auditors are not required to state in their report whether the accounting principles have been applied consistently in the current and preceding periods. As previously mentioned, consistency in the application of accounting principles and adequate informative disclosure in the financial statements can be assumed by users unless the auditors take exception in their audit report. As the FASB affirms in SFAC No. 2:

---

[11] A cross-reference tool that links the original standards to the new ASC codification is available at http://asc.fasb.org/crossref. Note that it does require the user to sign up for a log-on ID and a password. The basic functionality sign-up is free.

**EXHIBIT 5.3** GAAP Hierarchy Summary

| Nongovernmental Entities | State and Local Governments |
|---|---|

**Established Accounting Principles**

**10a.** FASB Statements and Interpretations, APB Opinions, and AICPA Accounting Research Bulletins

**10b.** FASB Technical Bulletins, AICPA Industry Audit and Accounting Guides, and AICPA Statements of Position

**10c.** Consensus positions of the FASB Emerging Issues Task Force and AICPA Practice Bulletins

**10d.** AICPA accounting interpretations, "Qs and As" published by the FASB staff, as well as industry practices widely recognized and prevalent

**12a.** GASB Statements and Interpretations, plus AICPA and FASB pronouncements if made applicable to state and local governments by a GASB Statement or Interpretation

**12b.** GASB Technical Bulletins, and the following pronouncements if specifically made applicable to state and local governments by the AICPA: AICPA Industry Audit and Accounting Guides and AICPA Statements of Position

**12c.** Consensus positions of the GASB Emerging Issues Task Force and AICPA Practice Bulletins if specifically made applicable to state and local governments by the AICPA

**12d.** Q&As published by the GASB staff, as well as industry practices widely recognized and prevalent

**Other Accounting Literature**

**11.** Other accounting literature, including FASB Concepts Statements; APB Statements; AICPA Issues Papers; International Accounting Standards Committee Statements; GASB Statements, Interpretations, and Technical Bulletins; pronouncements of other professional associations or regulatory agencies; AICPA Technical Practice Aids; and accounting textbooks, handbooks, and articles

**13.** Other accounting literature, including GASB Concepts Statements; pronouncements in categories (a) through (d) of the hierarchy for nongovernmental entities when not specifically made applicable to state and local governments; APB Statements; FASB Concepts Statements; AICPA Issues Papers; International Accounting Standards Committee Statements; pronouncements of other professional associations or regulatory agencies: AICPA Technical Practice Aids; and accounting textbooks, handbooks, and articles

Information about a particular enterprise gains greatly in usefulness if it can be compared with similar information about other enterprises and with similar information about the same enterprise for some other period or some other point in time. Comparability between enterprises and consistency in the application of methods over time increases the informational value of comparisons of relative economic opportunities or performance. The significance of information, especially quantitative information, depends to a great extent on the user's ability to relate it to some benchmark.[12]

Such a requirement is necessary because management has some flexibility in selecting accounting methods or procedures from among several alternative accounting methods that may be available for financial reporting. For example, the annual depreciation charges on the entity's plant and equipment may be computed on the basis of several acceptable depreciation methods. Likewise, there are various ways to implement fair value accounting for financial instruments when such instruments do not trade in active markets. As a result, the auditors must satisfy themselves that management has applied the alternative accounting methods on a consistent basis from period to period in order to enhance the comparability of the financial statements. Comparability is a highly sought goal of financial reporting.

Management can convert to an acceptable alternative accounting method in response to changes in economic conditions. For example, economic conditions may lead management to reclassify a security held for trading purposes to one held to maturity, which changes the appropriate accounting valuation method. It is incumbent upon management to justify the change in the accounting methods whereby a particular change enhances fair presentation in the financial statements. Such a change should be disclosed in the notes to financial statements along with the effects of the change on the statements.[13] Moreover, auditors are required to point out the change in application of accounting methods by modifying their report with an additional paragraph following the opinion paragraph.[14] (See "Accounting Changes" in Chapter 10.) Audit committees should pay very close attention to changes in accounting methods, making certain that management's actions are reasonable and supportable in the circumstances.

***Disclosure***   The third reporting standard regarding informative disclosures implies that the information in the financial statements should be relevant to the users of accounting information. The information in the body of the statements, notes, and supplementary materials should be pertinent to the informational needs of the users. The accounting principle related to this particular auditing standard is known as the "full disclosure principle." Under this principle, management has a reporting responsibility to its constituencies to disclose financial information needed for a proper understanding of the financial statements. Such disclosure of information is based on management's judgment. Furthermore, the auditors have a professional obligation to ensure reasonably adequate informative disclosures in the statements.

---

[12] Financial Accounting Standards Board, *Statement of Financial Accounting Concepts No. 2*, "Qualitative Characteristics of Accounting Information" (Stamford, CT: FASB, May 1980), 2. See paras. 120–122 for additional emphasis.

[13] Opinions of the Accounting Principles Board No. 20, *Accounting Changes* (New York: AICPA, 1971), par. 17. See SFAS No. 154 "Accounting Changes and Error Corrections—a replacement of APB Opinion No. 20 and FASB Statement No. 3," as well as PCAOB AS6, "Evaluating Consistency of Financial Statements" (2008).

[14] AICPA, Professional Standards, *U.S. Auditing Standards/Attestation Standards*, vol. 1, AU Sec. 508.16.

The fundamental recognition criteria that determine whether the results of a transaction become part of the financial statements are set forth by the FASB:

An item and information about it should meet four fundamental recognition criteria to be recognized and should be recognized when the criteria are met, subject to a cost-benefit constraint and a materiality threshold. Those criteria are:

*Definitions*—The item meets the definition of an element of financial statements.

*Measurability*—It has a relevant attribute measurable with sufficient reliability.

*Relevance*—The information about it is capable of making a difference in user decisions.

*Reliability*—The information is representationally faithful, verifiable, and neutral.

All four criteria are subject to a pervasive cost-benefit constraint: the expected benefits from recognizing a particular item should justify perceived costs of providing and using the information. Recognition is also subject to a materiality threshold: an item and information about it need not be recognized in a set of financial statements if the item is not large enough to be material and the aggregate of individually immaterial items is not large enough to be material to those financial statements.[15]

The FASB and IASB currently are working on fundamental changes to their conceptual frameworks and related projects on financial statement presentation and revenue recognition that likely will lead to changes in the criteria for recognition of events for accounting purposes. Increasingly, the two boards have adopted an asset and liability recognition approach with measurement at "fair value," and they have projects in progress that would substantially refine their approach to the recognition of such key financial statement elements as assets, liabilities, revenue, and expense.

**Materiality**   With respect to materiality, the FASB indicates:

Individual judgments are required to assess materiality in the absence of authoritative criteria or to decide that minimum quantitative criteria are not appropriate in particular situations. The essence of the materiality concept is clear. The omission or misstatement of an item in a financial report is material if, in the light of surrounding circumstances, the magnitude of the item is such that it is probable that the judgment of a reasonable person relying upon the report would have been changed or influenced by the inclusion or correction of the item.[16]

The Auditing Standards Board has reaffirmed the FASB position on materiality as mentioned in SAS No. 47, and its amendment SAS No. 107 (April 2006), "Audit Risk and Materiality in Conducting an Audit."

---

[15] Financial Accounting Standards Board, *Statement of Financial Accounting Concepts No. 5*, "Recognition and Measurement in Financial Statements of Business Enterprises" (Stamford, CT: FASB, 1984), par. 63.

[16] Financial Accounting Standards Board, *Statement of Financial Accounting Concepts No. 2*, par. 132.

Materiality has a pervasive influence on financial statements. Although the materiality of a particular financial item is a matter of professional judgment, consideration should be given to the significance of the information in relationship to the users' information needs. Such consideration may include the effect of the financial item on the entity's net income or financial condition. For example, an inventory loss of $10,000 would be a material item in the financial statements of a small trading or manufacturing concern because such a loss may represent 5 to 10 percent of the company's assets. However, in a large conglomerate enterprise with billions of dollars in assets, inventory loss of $10,000 would be an immaterial item in the financial statements. Thus, the nature and size of the financial item and its relative importance to the financial statements determine the materiality of the item. No definitive rules or criteria are used to judge materiality since the circumstances regarding each audit examination vary.

In 1999, Arthur Levitt, former SEC chairman, reported, "Staff Accounting Bulletin 99 reemphasizes that the exclusive reliance on any percentage or numerical threshold in assessing materiality for financial reporting has no basis in the accounting literature or in the law." [17] As a result, independent auditors are required to assess both quantitative and qualitative factors in their determination of whether an item is material. Likewise, independent auditors are required to obtain an acknowledgment from management of uncorrected misstatements and discuss these misstatements with the audit committee.

To enhance the usefulness of the financial statements, the predecessor of the FASB, the Accounting Principles Board (APB), adopted a standard with respect to the disclosure of accounting policies. In particular, "the Board believes that the disclosure is particularly useful if given in a separate 'Summary of Significant Accounting Policies' preceding the notes to the financial statements or as the initial note." [18] For example, the disclosures would include, among others, the basis of consolidation, depreciation methods, inventory pricing methods, accounting for research and development costs, and translation of foreign currencies. [19]

The disclosure principle is particularly important because if the auditors do not concur with the adequacy of management's disclosures, then they cannot express an unqualified opinion. Such inadequate disclosures should be stated in their audit report. For further information or additional disclosure matters, see Chapter 10.

The SEC organized an Advisory Committee on Improvements to Financial Reporting (CIFiR), which considered materiality at length during its deliberations

---

[17] Securities and Exchange Commission, *1999 Annual Report* (Washington, DC: U.S. Government Printing Office), 84. For examples of qualitative factors, see *SEC Staff Accounting Bulletin No. 99*, "Materiality" (August 12, 1999) and Staff Accounting Bulletin No. 108, "Considering the Effects of Prior Year Misstatements When Quantifying Misstatements in Current Year Financial Statements" (www.see.gov/interps/account/sab108.pdf). Also see *Statement on Auditing Standards No. 89*, "Audit Adjustments," and *Statement on Auditing Standards No. 90*, "Audit Committee Communications" (New York: AICPA, 1999), and Statement on Auditing Standards No. 114, "The Auditor's Communication with Those Charged with Governance.".

[18] Opinions of the Accounting Principles Board No. 22, *Disclosure of Accounting Policies* (New York: AICPA, 1972), par. 15.

[19] Ibid., par. 13.

in 2006 and 2007. CIFiR's final report, available at www.sec.gov/about/offices/oca/acifr.shtml, embraces a concept of materiality that connects it with what would make a difference in the decision making of a reasonably informed investor in the context of the overall mix of information available. Such an approach to materiality causes managements, boards, and auditors to consider those aspects of financial reporting that would make a difference to such an investor. Previous approaches to materiality were focused on items internal to the financial statements, such as a prescribed percentage of net income, revenue, or net assets. The CIFiR report directs attention to those items that might change investment analysts' assessment of the relative position of the company and of important trends without regard to the absolute or relative size of the item. Although large items remain material, small items could also be material if they were to affect an important metric followed by investment analysts. Being aware of the analysts' models and the bases for their assessments of a company's value is increasingly important for audit committees, managements, and auditors.

*Fairness*   The fourth auditing standard of reporting requires that the independent auditors express their opinion on the fairness of the financial presentation in the financial statements. If for some reason the auditors are unable to express an opinion, then they are required to acknowledge this fact and provide their reasons. Moreover, the auditors are required to disclose the nature of their association and responsibility with the financial statements when their names are associated with the statements. Their professional opinion is based on their informed judgment as a result of the audit. Their opinion should not be construed as an absolute guarantee regarding the accuracy of the financial statements. Furthermore, the Auditing Standards Board points out the following with respect to the term *fairness*:

> The independent auditor's judgment concerning the "fairness" of the overall presentation of financial statements should be applied within the framework of generally accepted accounting principles. Without that framework the auditor would have no uniform standard for judging the presentation of financial position, results of operations, and cash flows in financial statements.[20]

In summary, the auditors should base their judgment on matters such as:

- Whether the accounting principles selected and applied have general acceptance
- Whether the accounting principles are appropriate in the circumstances
- Whether the financial statements, including the related notes, are informative of matters that may affect their use, understanding, and interpretation
- Whether the information presented in the financial statements is classified and summarized in a reasonable manner

---

[20] *Statement on Auditing Standards No. 69, par. 3.*

- Whether the financial statements reflect the underlying events and transactions in a manner that presents the statements within limits that are reasonable and practicable to attain in financial statements[21]

The preceding overview of auditing standards and their integration with related accounting principles underscores the importance of judgment and discretion of management and the independent auditors. Management's application of acceptable accounting principles attested to by an independent auditor enhances the credibility of the financial statements. The audit committee should understand the basis for the auditors' opinions on its company's financial statements. An auditor's inability to express an unqualified opinion on the financial statements usually indicates a serious problem. Auditors resign from engagements when they lose confidence in a company's commitment to appropriate financial reporting or in management's integrity in financial reporting, or when they have an irreconcilable difference with the company on a matter of accounting principle. When an auditor resigns from a public company, or when a public company fires its auditor, both the company and the auditor inform the SEC. When an auditor resigns from a company for one or more of several "reportable conditions," there may be serious underlying management or structural issues at that company that could cause it to underperform for many years. The audit committee needs to be aware of serious disagreements between management and the company's auditors and become involved in their resolution.

Whereas the preceding discussion focuses on the basic framework of auditing standards and the relationship to accounting standards, Exhibit 5.4 is a summary of the more significant auditing standards and related topical areas of interest to audit committees.

## ATTESTATION ENGAGEMENTS

In addition to the generally accepted auditing standards associated with the annual audit of financial statements, the Auditing Standards Board and the Accounting and Review Services Committee of the AICPA have issued a codification of four statements on Standards for Attestation Engagements (SSAEs) and two SSAEs in response to the banking reform legislation (FDICIA). The basic framework for these standards is shown in Exhibit 5.5. The auditor's responsibility for attestation engagements with respect to special reports, reviews, and agreed-upon procedures is discussed in Chapter 13.

---

[21] Ibid., par. 4. With respect to current Securities and Exchange initiatives dealing with such matters as materiality, revenue recognition, in-process research and development, reserves, and audit adjustments, the reader should visit Arthur Levitt's speech, www.sec.gov/news/speeches/spch220.txt. For additional information regarding the guidance on the criteria necessary to recognize restructuring liabilities and asset impairments and the criteria to recognizing revenue, see Staff Accounting Bulletin No. 100, "Restructuring Charges and Asset Impairment" (November 24, 1999) and Staff Accounting Bulletin No. 101 "Revenue Recognition" (December 3, 1999) (Washington, DC: SEC, 1999). See also SFAS No. 146, "Accounting for Costs Associated with Exit or Disposal Activities" (Norwalk, CT: FASB, 2002) and the SEC Staff Accounting Bulletin No. 104, "Revenue Recognition" (Washington, DC: SEC, 2003).

**EXHIBIT 5.4** Summary of Significant Auditing Standards

| Statements on Auditing Standards | Topical Area |
|---|---|
| No. 12, "Inquiry of a Client's Lawyer Concerning Litigation, Claims, and Assessments" | Accounting for contingencies (see SFAS No. 5 and Interpretation No. 14). |
| No. 22, "Planning and Supervision" | Audit plans and execution (superseded for nonpublic companies by SAS No. 108). |
| No. 31, "Evidential Matter" | Management's assertions (superseded for nonpublic companies by SAS No. 106). |
| No. 45, "Omnibus Statement on Auditing Standards—1983" | Related party disclosures (see SFAS No. 57)—(superseded in part by SAS No. 110). |
| No. 47, "Audit Risk and Materiality in Conducting an Audit" | Inherent and control risks (see SFAC No. 2)—(superseded for nonpublic companies by SAS No. 107). |
| No. 50, "Reports on the Application of Accounting Principles" | Other auditors' opinions. |
| No. 54, "Illegal Acts by Clients" | Violations of laws and regulations that have a material direct effect on financial statements. |
| No. 55, "Consideration of the Internal Control Structure in a Financial Statement Audit" | Quality of the control environment and level of control risk (superseded for nonpublic companies by SAS Nos. 109 and 110). |
| No. 56, "Analytical Procedures" | Analysis and evaluation of financial statement information. |
| No. 57, "Auditing Accounting Estimates" | Reasonableness of estimates. |
| No. 58, "Reports on Audited Financial Statements" | Types of auditor's reports. |
| No. 59, "The Auditor's Consideration of an Entity's Ability to Continue as a Going Concern" | Violation of the going-concern assumption. |
| No. 60, "Communication of Control–Structure Related Matters Noted in an Audit" | Reportable conditions (deficiencies in the internal control structure) as noted in the management letter (superseded for nonpublic companies by SAS Nos.112 and 115). |
| No. 61, "Communication with Audit Committees" | Selection of significant accounting policies and discussion of the auditor's disagreement with management (superseded for nonpublic companies by SAS No. 114). |
| No. 62, "Special Reports" | Attestation of other historical financial information. |

*(continued)*

**EXHIBIT 5.4**   *(Continued)*

| Statements on Auditing Standards | Topical Area |
|---|---|
| No. 65, "The Auditor's Consideration of the Internal Audit Function in an Audit of Financial Statements" | Internal control and the quality of the internal audit function. |
| No. 72, "Letters for Underwriters and Certain Other Requesting Parties" (See also SAS No. 76 and No. 86 for amendments.) | Comfort letters to investment banking firms. |
| No. 73, "Using the Work of a Specialist" | Expert opinions (e.g., environmental liabilities). |
| No. 78, "Consideration of Internal Control in a Financial Statement Audit: An Amendment to SAS No. 55" | Revises the definition and description of internal control. |
| No. 79, "Amendment to SAS No. 58, Reports on Audited Financial Statements" | Eliminated the requirement that auditors modify their reports for a significant uncertainty. |
| No. 83, "Establishing an Understanding with the Client" | Communicates the objectives of the engagement, responsibilities of management and the auditors, and any limitations of the engagement. |
| No. 84, "Communications Between Predecessor and Successor Auditors" | Auditor changes (SEC 8-K Report). |
| No. 85, "Management Representations" | Audit evidence acknowledging management's responsibility for the financial statements. |
| No. 87, "Restricting the Use of an Auditor's Report" | Auditor's reports intended only for use by certain parties. |
| No. 89, "Audit Adjustments" | Acknowledges to the auditors that the effects of any uncorrected misstatements brought to management by the auditors are not material, both individually and in the aggregate. Communicates the aforementioned misstatements to the audit committee. |
| No. 90, "Audit Committee Communications" | Discussions about the quality, not just the acceptability, of accounting principles for financial reporting as well as communications of matters related to interim financial information. |
| No. 92, "Auditing Derivative Instruments, Hedging Activities, and Investments in Securities" | Auditing financial statement assertions about derivative instruments, hedging activities, and investment securities (see SFAS No. 133). |
| No. 93, "Omnibus Statement on Auditing Standards—2000" | Withdraws SAS No. 75; amends SAS No. 58; amends SAS No. 84. |

| | |
|---|---|
| No. 94, "The Effect of Information Technology on the Auditor's Consideration of Internal Control in a Financial Statement Audit" | The effect of IT on internal control and assessment of control risk. |
| No. 95, "Generally Accepted Auditing Standards" | Establishes an authoritative hierarchy for GAAS (Amended by SAS No. 105). |
| No. 96, "Audit Documentation" | Revises SAS No. 41, "Working Papers," and requires greater audit documentation. |
| No. 97, "Amendment to SAS No. 50, Reports on the Application of Accounting Principles" | Prohibits an accountant from providing a written report on the application of accounting principles not involving facts and circumstances of a specific entity. |
| No. 98, "Omnibus SAS—2000" | Provides clarifying guidance to SAS Nos. 95, 25, 47, 70, 58, 8, 52, 29, 1. |
| No. 99, "Consideration of Fraud in a Financial Statement Audit" | Revises SAS No. 82, "Consideration of Fraud in a Financial Statement Audit" assessing the risk of material misstatement of the financial statements. |
| No. 100, "Interim Financial Information" | Revises SAS No. 71, "Interim Financial Information Quarterly Reports—SEC 10Q Reports" (see APB No. 28). |
| No. 101, "Auditing Fair Value Measurements and Disclosures" | Accounting basis for measurement or disclosure of a financial statement item is fair value. |
| No. 102, "Defining Professional Requirements in Statements on Auditing Standards" | Identifies unconditional requirements connected to wording in auditing standards such as "must" or "is required" and presumptively mandatory requirements connected to wording such as "should consider." |
| No. 103, "Audit Documentation" | Describes in detail the purpose, content, supervision, control, alteration, and retention standards for audit documentation. |
| No. 104, "Amendment to Statement on Auditing Standard No. 1, *Codification of Auditing Standards and Procedures* ("Due Professional Care in the Performance of Work")" | Addresses the levels of knowledge and skill required to perform an audit, appropriate professional skepticism, and reasonable assurance. |
| No. 105, "Amendment to Statement on Auditing Standards No. 95, *Generally Accepted Auditing Standards*" | Clarifies the hierarchy of auditing standards and requires documentation for departures from presumptively mandatory requirements. |
| No. 106, "Audit Evidence" | Defines audit evidence and identifies thresholds for sufficient competence audit evidence. Identifies types of management's |

(*continued*)

**EXHIBIT 5.4**   *(Continued)*

| Statements on Auditing Standards | Topical Area |
| --- | --- |
| | financial statement assertions and audit evidence appropriate for each type. |
| No. 107, "Audit Risk and Materiality in Conducting an Audit" | Discusses types of audit risks, the user environment in which materiality issues should be framed, and approaches for determining materiality at different levels of specificity in the financial statements. |
| No. 108, "Planning and Supervision" | Examines auditors' responsibilities before audit field work begins, including reaching an understanding with the client about the audit work, choosing the appropriate auditors and specialists, establishing an audit plan, and communicating with the client. |
| No. 109, "Understanding the Entity and Its Environment and Assessing the Risks of Material Misstatement" | In-depth discussion of assessing risks associated with internal control over financial reporting. |
| No. 110, "Performing Audit Procedures in Response to Assessed Risks and Evaluating the Audit Evidence Obtained" | Discusses appropriate audit responses related to different types of financial statement misstatement risk and the collection of related audit evidence. |
| No. 111, "Amendment to Statement on Auditing Standards No. 39, *Audit Sampling*" | Updates audit sampling approaches for new requirements related to planning, evidence gathering, and documentation. Auditors may continue to use judgmental or statistical sampling approaches, although the standard encourages more use of statistical sampling. |
| No. 112, " Communicating Internal Control Related Matters Identified in an Audit" | Defines "significant deficiency" and "material weakness" in audits of internal control over financial reporting and requires the communication to those in governance of significant deficiencies and material weaknesses. |
| No. 113, "Omnibus – 2006" | Codification of changes related to hierarchy of generally accepted auditing standards, consideration of fraud in financial statements, auditing fair value measurements and disclosures, management representations, going concern considerations, auditing accounting estimates, and subsequent events. |

| | |
|---|---|
| No. 114, "The Auditor's Communication With Those Charged With Governance" | Creates standards for the auditor's communication with audit committees, or other subcommittee of the board charged with governance, and with management. |
| No. 115, "Communicating Internal Control Related Matters Identified in an Audit" | Revises the definitions of "material weakness" and "significant deficiency" and the list of significant deficiencies that may indicate a material weakness. |
| No. 116, "Interim Financial Information" | Identifies the circumstances when auditing standards can be applied to interim financial statements of companies that are nonissuers so are not subject to SEC Regulation S-X. |

*Note:* The Auditing Standards Board has rescinded SAS No. 21, "Segment Information." The Board's Audit Issues Task Force has issued an interpretation, "Applying Audit Procedures to Segment Disclosures in Financial Statements" of SAS No. 31, "Evidential Matter." Also see SAS No. 86, "Amendment to SAS No. 72, Letters for Underwriters and Certain Other Requesting Parties."

---

**EXHIBIT 5.5**   Standards for Attestation Engagements

**General Standards**
1. The engagement shall be performed by a practitioner having adequate technical training and proficiency in the attest function.
2. The engagement shall be performed by a practitioner having adequate knowledge in the subject matter.
3. The practitioner shall perform the engagement only if he or she has reason to believe that the subject matter is capable of evaluation or measurement against criteria standards or benchmarks that are available to users.
4. In all matters relating to the engagement, an independence in mental attitude shall be maintained by the practitioner.
5. Due professional care shall be exercised in the performance of the engagement.

**Standards of Fieldwork**
1. The work shall be adequately planned and assistants, if any, shall be properly supervised.
2. Sufficient evidence shall be obtained to provide a reasonable basis for the conclusion that is expressed in the report.

**Standards of Reporting**
1. The report shall identify the subject matter or the assertion being reported on and state the character of the engagement.
2. The report shall state the practitioner's conclusion about the subject matter or the assertion based on the criteria against which the subject matter was measured.
3. The report shall state all of the practitioner's significant reservations about the engagement.

(*continued*)

**EXHIBIT 5.5**  (*Continued*)

4. The report on an engagement to evaluate subject matter that has been prepared based on agreed-upon criteria or an assertion related thereto or on an engagement to apply agreed-upon procedures should contain a statement restricting its use to the parties who have agreed upon such criteria or procedures.

*Source: Statement on Standards for Attestation Engagements No. 9*, "Amendments to Statement on Standards for Attestation Engagements Nos. 1, 2, and 3" (New York: AICPA, 1999), p. 2. Reprinted with permission. Copyright 1999 by the American Institute of Certified Public Accountants, Inc.

Exhibit 5.6 lists the attestation standards and related topical areas of concern to audit committees. The reader may wish to consult other AICPA statements, such as Statements on Standards for Accounting and Review Services, Statements on Standards for Management Consulting Services, Statements on Quality Control Standards, Standards for Performing and Reporting on Quality Reviews, Statements on Responsibilities in Tax Practices, and Statements on Standards for Accountants' Services on Prospective Financial Information. They are available at www.aicpa.org under the professional standards tab.

**EXHIBIT 5.6**  Summary of Significant Standards for Attestation Engagements

| | | |
|---|---|---|
| SSAE 10 (as amended by SSAE 14) | Attest Engagements | Lays down the foundations for attest engagements, including identification of subject matter, assertions, and responsible parties. Establishes professional qualifications, criteria for evidence, content of representation letters. Formulates the essential professional standards for attest engagements. |
| SSAE 10 (as amended by SSAE 11) | Agreed-Upon Procedures Engagements | Identifies the conditions when such engagements are appropriate and their general, field work, and reporting standards |
| SSAE 10 (as amended by SSAE 11) | Financial Forecasts and Projections | Establishes standards for the preparation of financial forecasts and projections. |
| SSAE 10 | Reporting on Pro Forma Financial Information | Codifies the standards for presenting and reporting on pro-forma financial information. |
| SSAE 10 | Reporting on an Entity's Internal Control Over Financial Reporting | Establishes standards similar to audit standards for reporting on |

| | | |
|---|---|---|
| | | internal control over financial reporting when not performed as part of an integrated audit of financial reporting. |
| SSAE 10 | Compliance Attestation | Addresses the standards governing attestation reports on entities' compliance with regulatory or other third-party requirements. |
| SSAE 10 | Management's Discussion and Analysis | Provides guidance on attestations related to management's discussion and analysis required for public companies in Regulation S-K. |
| SSAE 11 | Attest Documentation | Identifies documentation content, extent, and retention requirements for attest engagements. |
| SSAE 12 | Amendment to Statement on Standards for Attestation Engagement No. 10, *Attestation Standards: Revision and Recodification* | Update and recodification of general standards for attest engagements. |
| SSAE 13 | Defining Professional Requirements in Statements on Standards for Attestation Engagements | Explains that "must" and "is required" mean unconditional requirements to perform and that "should" means presumptively mandatory requirements. |
| SSAE 14 | SSAE Hierarchy | Establishes a three-tier hierarchy of standards, authoritative interpretations from the AICPA, and other sources. |
| SSAE 15 | An Examination of an Entity's Internal Control Over Financial Reporting That Is Integrated with an Audit of Its Financial Statements | Converges the standards used by auditors of non-issuers to the PCAOB Standard No. 5 for issuers. |

## INTERNATIONAL AUDITING STANDARDS

Recognizing the movement toward the globalization of the world's securities markets, the International Organization of Securities Commission (IOSCO)[22] has been working with the International Accounting Standards Board (IASB) and the

---

[22] International Federation of Accountants, 1992 Annual Report, p. 3.

International Auditing and Assurance Standards Board (IAASB),[23] which is associated with the International Federation of Accountants (IFAC), to work toward the convergence of national and international accounting and auditing standards. The objective of these initiatives is to enable a company that has complied with global standards to raise capital in a global capital marketplace.

In response to the demand for international auditing standards, IFAC established an International Auditing and Assurance Standards Board. This board has issued a number of pronouncements and related statements, as shown in Exhibit 5.7. Although such standards are adopted on a voluntary basis, the goal of these international organizations and boards is to foster harmonized standards on an international basis. Neither IASB nor IAASB has statutory authority in any country to create financial reporting standards or auditing principles in the same way that the FASB and PCAOB do in the United States. Rather, IASB and IAASB promulgate their standards and principles with the anticipation that sovereign nations will adopt them in order to achieve uniformity in financial reporting and auditing. Many countries have adopted IFRS and International Standards on Auditing (ISA) in whole or in part. Given the audit committee's oversight responsibility for financial reporting, these standards may have an impact on companies at home and abroad. More recently, the IAASB issued an ISA entitled "Communications to Those Charged with Governance." In short, the IAPC, IAASB's predecessor, indicated that such an ISA is needed for these reasons:

---

**EXHIBIT 5.7**   International Auditing Pronouncements

ISA 200—*Overall Objectives of the Independent Auditor and the Conduct of an Audit in Accordance with International Standards on Auditing*

ISA 210—*Agreeing the Terms of Audit Engagements*

ISA 220—*Quality Control for an Audit of Financial Statements*

ISA 230—*Audit Documentation*

ISA 240—*The Auditor's Responsibilities Relating to Fraud in an Audit of Financial Statements*

ISA 250—*Consideration of Laws and Regulations in an Audit of Financial Statements*

ISA 260—*Communication with Those Charged with Governance*

ISA 265—*Communicating Deficiencies in Internal Control to Those Charged with Governance and Management*

ISA 300—*Planning an Audit of Financial Statements*

ISA 315—*Identifying and Assessing the Risks of Material Misstatement through Understanding the Entity and Its Environment*

---

[23] See American Institute of Certified Public Accountants, *Professional Standards*, vol. 2, Sec. AC 9000 for the International Accounting Standards, New York, June 1, 2003.

ISA 320—*Materiality in Planning and Performing an Audit*

ISA 330—*The Auditor's Responses to Assessed Risks*

ISA 402—*Audit Considerations Relating to an Entity Using a Service Organization*

ISA 450—*Evaluation of Misstatements Identified during the Audit*

ISA 500—*Audit Evidence*

ISA 501—*Audit Evidence-Specific Considerations for Selected Items*

ISA 505—*External Confirmations*

ISA 520—*Analytical Procedures*

ISA 530—*Audit Sampling*

ISA 540—*Auditing Accounting Estimates, Including Fair Value Accounting Estimates, and Related Disclosures*

ISA 550—*Related Parties*

ISA 560—*Subsequent Events*

ISA 570—*Going Concern*

ISA 580—*Written Representations*

ISA 600—*Special Considerations—Audits of Group Financial Statements (Including the Work of Component Auditors)*

ISA 610—*Using the Work of Internal Auditors*

ISA 620—*Using the Work of an Auditor's Expert*

ISA 700—*Forming an Opinion and Reporting on Financial Statements*

ISA 705—*Modifications to the Opinion in the Independent Auditor's Report*

ISA 706—*Emphasis of Matter Paragraphs and Other Matter Paragraphs in the Independent Auditor's Report*

ISA 710—*Comparative Information—Corresponding Figures and Comparative Financial Statements*

ISA 720—*The Auditor's Responsibilities Relating to Other Information in Documents Containing Audited Financial Statements*

ISA 800—*Special Considerations—Audits of Financial Statements Prepared in Accordance with Special Purpose Frameworks*

ISA 805—*Special Considerations—Audits of Single Financial Statements and Specific Elements, Accounts or Items of a Financial Statement*

ISA 810—*Engagements to Report on Summary Financial Statements*

International Standard on Quality Control (ISQC) 1—*Quality Controls for Firms That Perform Audits and Reviews of Financial Statements, and Other Assurance and Related Services Engagements*

---

*Note:* ISA and ISQC pronouncements are available at www.ifac.org/iaasb.

It recognizes the need to provide standards and guidance on the auditor's responsibility to communicate matters of governance interest, arising from the audit of financial statements, to those charged with governance of an entity. Although the structures of governance vary from country to country reflecting cultural and legal background, in many jurisdictions the auditor is required to communicate matters of governance interest, arising from the audit of financial statements, to those charged with governance of an entity. Furthermore, the communication of these matters is part of a mechanism by which the external auditors can add value to the role of those responsible for the governance of the entity.[24]

Thus, the IAASB has recognized the benefits of a corporate governance approach to the audit process as a requisite for harmonizing the international accounting and auditing standards. The Public Oversight Board has argued that the auditing profession should shift its focus from a compliance and rule-oriented audit to a corporate governance approach.

## SOURCES AND SUGGESTED READINGS

American Institute of Certified Public Accountants. *Professional Standards, U.S. Auditing Standards/Attestation Standards*, vol. 1. New York: AICPA, 2003.

American Institute of Certified Public Accountants. *Professional Standards, International Auditing*, vol. 2. New York: AICPA, 2003.

American Institute of Certified Public Accountants. *Rules of Conduct of the Code of Professional Ethics*. New York: AICPA, 1997.

Financial Accounting Standards Board. *Statement of Financial Accounting Concepts No. 2*. "Qualitative Characteristics of Accounting Information." Stamford, CT: FASB, 1980.

Financial Accounting Standards Board. *Statement of Financial Accounting Concepts No. 5*. "Recognition and Measurement in Financial Statements of Business Enterprises." Stamford, CT: FASB, 1984.

International Auditing Practices Committee. "Communications to Those Charged with Governance." Exposure Draft. New York: IFA, 1998.

International Federation of Accountants. *1992 Annual Report*. New York: IFA, 1992.

Opinions of the Accounting Principles Board, No. 20. "Accounting Changes." New York: AICPA, 1971.

Opinions of the Accounting Principles Board, No. 22. "Disclosure of Accounting Policies." New York: AICPA, 1972.

Securities and Exchange Commission. *1999 Annual Report*. Washington, DC: U.S. Government Printing Office.

Securities and Exchange Commission. "Materiality." *Staff Accounting Bulletin No. 99*. Washington, DC: SEC, August 12, 1999.

Securities and Exchange Commission. "Restructuring Charges and Asset Impairment." *Staff Accounting Bulletin No. 100*. Washington, DC: SEC, November 24, 1999.

---

[24] *International Auditing Practices Committee*, "Communications to Those Charged with Governance," Exposure Draft (New York: IFA, August 1998), 2–3.

Securities and Exchange Commission. "Revenue Recognition." *Staff Accounting Bulletin No. 101*. Washington, DC: SEC, December 3, 1999.

*Statement of the Accounting Principles Board, No. 4*. "Basic Concepts and Accounting Principles Underlying Financial Statements of Business Enterprises." New York: AICPA, 1970.

*Statement on Auditing Standards No. 22*. "Planning and Supervision." New York: AICPA, 1978.

*Statement on Auditing Standards No. 69*. "The Meaning of Present Fairly in Conformity with Generally Accepted Accounting Principles in the Independent Auditor's Report." New York: AICPA, 1992.

*Statement on Auditing Standards No. 89*. "Audit Adjustments." New York: AICPA, 1999.

*Statement on Auditing Standards No. 99*. "Audit Committee Communications." New York: AICPA, 1999.

*Statement on Standards of Attestation Engagements No. 9*. "Amendments to Statement on Standards for Attestation Engagements Nos. 1, 2, and 3." New York: AICPA, 1999.

# Part Two
# The Planning Function of the Audit Committee

# Chapter 6

# Planning the External Audit

The audit committee's primary responsibilities relate to the oversight of (1) the financial reporting process and (2) the external auditor. In the United States, Section 2(a)(3)(A) of the Sarbanes-Oxley Act states that the audit committee is established "for the purpose of overseeing the accounting and financial reporting processes of the issuer and audits of the financial statements of the issuer." The Sarbanes-Oxley Act goes further to amend Section 10A of the Securities Exchange Act of 1934 to state, "The audit committee of each issuer, in its capacity as a committee of the board of directors, shall be directly responsible for the appointment, compensation, and oversight of the work of any registered public accounting firm employed by that issuer (including resolution of disagreements between management and the auditor regarding financial reporting) for the purpose of preparing or issuing an audit report or related work, and each such registered public accounting firm shall report directly to the audit committee."

Although other countries may not spell out such detailed oversight requirements, certainly most industrialized nations have established expectations that the audit committee should oversee the integrity of the financial reporting process and the appointment of the external auditor.[1] Meeting these expectations begins with an evaluation of the external auditor's plan. It is helpful to begin such an evaluation with an understanding of the external auditor's planning requirements.

As discussed in Chapter 5, the International Auditing and Assurance Standards Board (IAASB) issued, in 2003, revised International Standards on Auditing (ISAs) directed primarily at the planning stage of the audit. Those standards, which collectively are called the "Audit Risk Standards," include:[2]

- ISA 500 (Revised), Audit Evidence
- ISA 315, Understanding the Entity and its Environment and Assessing the Risks of Material Misstatement
- ISA 330, The Auditor's Procedures in Response to Assessed Risks
- An addition to ISA 200, Objective and General Principles Governing an Audit of Financial Statements

---

[1] For example, the "Smith Guidance" for audit committees contained in the UK's Combined Code (2003) states in paragraph 4.13, "The audit committee should assess annually the qualification, expertise and resources, and independence . . . of the external auditors and the effectiveness of the audit process." Paragraph 4.19 goes further to state, "The scope of the external audit should be reviewed by the audit committee with the auditor. If the audit committee is not satisfied as to its adequacy it should arrange for additional work to be undertaken."

[2] See www.ifac.org/IAASB/. Note also that all IAASB pronouncements can be downloaded free of charge from a link on that Web site.

In 2006 the AICPA completed a project to incorporate these revised ISAs into U.S. auditing standards. In connection with that project the AICPA issued its own revised Statements on Auditing Standards (SASs) Nos. 104 to 111. At the time of the writing of this book the PCAOB was in the midst of a project to issue its own audit risk standards, modeled closely after the IAASB standards.

As discussed in the preceding chapter, adequate audit planning is one of the tenets of the generally accepted auditing standards of fieldwork. SAS No. 108 states:

> Audit planning involves developing an overall audit strategy for the expected conduct, organization, and staffing of the audit. The nature, timing, and extent of planning vary with the size and complexity of the entity, and with the auditor's experience with the entity and understanding of the entity and its environment, including its internal control.[3]

This definition is directionally consistent with a similar definition contained in ISA No. 300, par. 2.

Audit planning is an iterative process that involves:

1. Obtaining an understanding of the entity, its environment and its internal control system;
2. Assessing the risk of material misstatement in the financial statements; and
3. Designing audit procedures commensurate with the assessed level of risk.

This process naturally becomes more efficient as the auditor gains experience with the client. However, all three steps must be undertaken for each audit cycle, and sometimes must be adjusted during the audit. An example of the general flow of the full audit process is shown in Exhibit 6.1.

In the final analysis the auditor's primary job is to (1) identify the things that have a reasonable possibility of causing the financial statements to be materially misstated, and (2) design and execute tests to determine whether such misstatements have occurred. In certain public company audits, such as those subject to Section 404 of the Sarbanes-Oxley Act, the auditor's testing also must address the effectiveness of the internal control system as a whole.

The audit committee's proper oversight of the external auditor requires its members to be familiar with (1) how auditors consider the assertions contained in the financial statements, and (2) the planning process that auditors go through (and the terminology that they use to describe it). The remainder of this chapter summarizes the audit planning process and provides some attributes that audit committee members may look for in an effective audit plan.

---

[3] Statement on Auditing Standards No. 108, "Planning and Supervision" (New York: AICPA, 2006), par. 2.

---

**EXHIBIT 6.1** Audit Process Flow

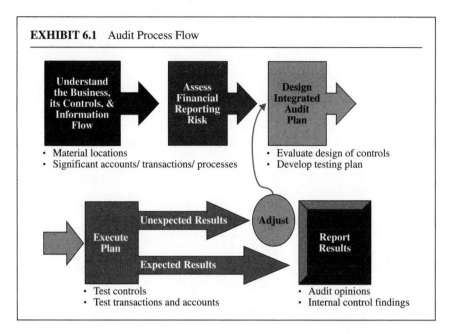

- Material locations
- Significant accounts/ transactions/ processes

- Evaluate design of controls
- Develop testing plan

- Test controls
- Test transactions and accounts

- Audit opinions
- Internal control findings

---

## FINANCIAL STATEMENT ASSERTIONS

Audit committee members may hear the external auditors talking about "relevant financial statement assertions." When management issues financial statements, it implicitly or explicitly makes assertions regarding the recognition, measurement, presentation, and disclosure of information in the financial statements and related disclosures. Financial statement assertions identify the most important elements of a given financial reporting line item or disclosure. During the planning phase of the audit, they allow the auditor to focus attention on what is most important to financial statement users. For example, "existence" is a relevant assertion regarding reported cash (i.e., the assertion that reported cash is real). Conversely the "valuation" of cash generally is not a relevant assertion because cash is cash—its value is equal to its reported value (as long as it really exists). Accordingly, one would expect an auditor to focus an appropriate amount of attention on the existence of cash, but not on its valuation.

As another example, one might ask the following question from the investors' perspective, "Am I more concerned with whether reported revenue is overstated (the existence assertion) or understated (the completeness assertion)?" Investors typically are more concerned with the *existence* of reported revenue than with its *completeness*, unless there is a risk that the company is trying to push revenue inappropriately into a future period. Alternatively, investors typically are more concerned with the *completeness* of reported liabilities (i.e., the risk of their understatement) than they are about their *existence* (i.e., the risk of their overstatement). This type of analysis helps the auditor design the tests that will be employed during the audit.

Contained in both ISA 215[4] and SAS No. 106, the following assertions typically are considered by external auditors. Auditors may describe these assertions in slightly different terms or combine some of them; so while a given audit firm's terminology may be different, these general concepts should be covered:

A. Assertions about classes of transactions and events for the period under audit:
  i. *Occurrence.* Transactions and events that have been recorded have occurred and pertain to the entity.
  ii. *Completeness.* All transactions and events that should have been recorded have been recorded.
  iii. *Accuracy.* Amounts and other data relating to recorded transactions and events have been recorded appropriately.
  iv. *Cutoff.* Transactions and events have been recorded in the correct accounting period.
  v. *Classification.* Transactions and events have been recorded in the proper accounts.
B. Assertions about account balances at the period-end:
  i. *Existence.* Assets, liabilities, and equity interests exist.
  ii. *Rights and obligations.* The entity holds or controls the rights to assets, and liabilities are the obligations of the entity.
  iii. *Completeness.* All assets, liabilities, and equity interests that should have been recorded have been recorded.
  iv. *Valuation and allocation.* Assets, liabilities, and equity interests are included in the financial statements at appropriate amounts, and any resulting valuation or allocation adjustments are recorded appropriately.
C. Assertions about presentation and disclosure:
  i. *Occurrence and rights and obligations.* Disclosed events and transactions have occurred and pertain to the entity.
  ii. *Completeness.* All disclosures that should have been included in the financial statements have been included.
  iii. *Classification and understandability.* Financial information is presented and described appropriately, and disclosures are expressed clearly.
  iv. *Accuracy and valuation.* Financial and other information are disclosed fairly and at appropriate amounts.

## THE RELATIONSHIP BETWEEN RISK AND THE EXTERNAL AUDIT

It is not possible to design a practical audit of financial statements that eliminates all risk of misstatement. Auditors, therefore, must design their audits to (1) focus

---

[4] Reprinted with permission from ISA 215, "Identifying and Assessing the Risks of Material Misstatement through Understanding the Entity and Its Environment," par. A111 (New York: IFAC, 2009). See also SAS No. 106, par. 15. Copyright © April 2009 by the International Federation of Accountants (IFAC). All rights reserved. Used with permission of IFAC. Contact permissions@ifac.org for permission to reproduce, store, or transmit this document.

on audit areas that have the highest likelihood of containing a *material* misstatement, and (2) employ audit methodologies that provide reasonable, but not absolute, assurance that such misstatements do not exist.[5] In doing so, auditors consider two key factors during the planning and conduct of the audit: materiality and audit risk.

## Materiality

Accounting and auditing standards define materiality as "the magnitude of an omission or misstatement of accounting information that, in the light of surrounding circumstances, makes it probable that the judgment of a reasonable person relying on the information would have been changed or influenced by the omission or misstatement."[6] Thus, materiality is influenced by the needs of financial statement users. The standards further recognize that materiality judgments are made in light of surrounding circumstances and necessarily involve both quantitative and qualitative considerations.

At the planning stage materiality affects the nature, timing, and extent of designed audit procedures, including:

1. Financial accounts and disclosures on which to focus
2. Locations, subsidiaries, or divisions to include or exclude from scope

After the planning stage (i.e., during the audit and at its conclusion) materiality is used as a tool to evaluate audit findings and determine whether any uncorrected errors—individually or in the aggregate—render the financial statements materially inaccurate.

Quantitative materiality often is calculated as a percentage of a meaningful financial statement number (e.g., pretax net income, total revenue, or total assets). That calculated number then becomes the starting point for scoping the audit. However, the auditor does not design the audit to detect *only* misstatements that meet or exceed materiality.

Assume an auditor determines that a $100,000 overstatement of pretax net income would result in a material misstatement of the financial statements. If the auditor designs the audit to focus on errors greater than or equal to $100,000, a $90,000 error might go undetected and not result in a material misstatement. Now, however, a mere $10,000 error (aggregated with the $90,000 error) would yield a material misstatement of the financial statements. That $10,000 error is small enough to slip easily through an audit scope based on a $100,000 threshold. For

---

[5] Statement on Auditing Standard No. 1, par. 2 states, "The auditor has a responsibility to plan and perform the audit to obtain reasonable assurance about whether the financial statements are free of material misstatement, whether caused by error or fraud."

[6] This definition was originally included in FASB's Statement of Financial Accounting Concepts No. 2, *Qualitative Characteristics of Accounting Information.* It has also been adopted in Statement on Auditing Standards No. 107, *Audit Risk and Materiality in Conducting an Audit,* par. 4 (New York: AICPA, 2006). It is also consistent with the definition of materiality in ISA 200, par. 6.

that reason auditors typically scope their audits using a concept called "tolerable error."

Tolerable error is the maximum *undetected* error that the auditor is willing to accept within a population, and typically is some fraction (e.g., 75 to 80 percent) of the materiality number. International auditing standards refer to this concept as "performance materiality." This number becomes a benchmark that auditors use to determine if a particular location or class of transactions will be included in the audit scope. It also is used in statistical formulas to determine sample sizes for various audit tests.

Although materiality often is expressed in quantitative terms, it also includes judgmental, qualitative considerations. Some common qualitative considerations are included in Appendix 6A.

Both an organization's management team and the external auditor assess materiality, although the level of formality in those assessments can vary widely. The audit committee should be confident that management's materiality threshold is sensible and is at least as conservative as the external auditor's reasonable assessment of materiality. This may seem counterintuitive. One might argue that the auditor is the last line of defense, and therefore her materiality threshold should be the most conservative, but such is not the case. Organizations should design their internal control systems to provide reasonable assurance that material misstatements do not reach the financial statements.[7] If management's methodology is less conservative than the external auditor's, management in effect is saying that it is willing for some level of material error to fall through the internal control system to the auditors. An indicator of an ineffective system is a control philosophy that says, "The external auditors have this area covered."

## Audit Risk

Audit risk is the risk that the auditor may unknowingly fail to appropriately modify his opinion on financial statements that are materially misstated.[8] It is a function of (1) the risk that the financial statements prepared by management are materially misstated (i.e., risk of material misstatement) and (2) the risk that the auditor will not detect such material misstatement (i.e., detection risk).[9] In other words, the risk that an auditor may fail to identify a material misstatement varies with respect to the level of risk in the area being audited, and with the ability of the auditor's procedures to catch a related misstatement (see Exhibit 6.2).

It follows, then, that the risk of material misstatement and detection risk bear an inverse relationship. The greater the risk of material misstatement, the less the detection risk the auditor can accept. Conversely, the lower the risk of material misstatement, the greater the detection risk that can be accepted by the auditor.[10]

---

[7] See COSO, *Internal Control—Integrated Framework* 1992), Ch. 1, 1.
[8] SAS No. 107, par. 2. (New York: AICPA, 2006); and ISA 200, par. 13(c). (New York: IFAC 2009).
[9] Ibid., SAS No. 107, par. 12; and ISA 200, par. 13(c).
[10] Ibid., SAS No. 107, par. 25; and ISA 200, par. A42.

**EXHIBIT 6.2**   Relationship between Materiality and Risk

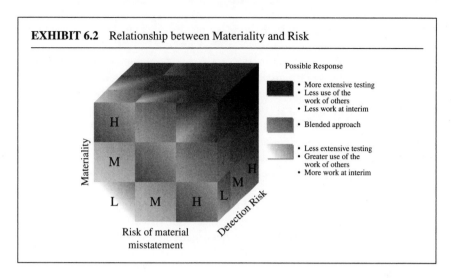

This relationship allows the auditor to design an efficient audit methodology that provides the "reasonable, but not absolute, assurance" discussed earlier.

Evaluating the risk of material misstatement is the most challenging part of audit planning. It requires the auditor to evaluate:[11]

1. *Inherent risk.* The misstatement risk that exists naturally in a given area irrespective of the perceived ability of internal control to mitigate that risk
2. *Control risk.* The risk that an organization's internal control system will not prevent or detect a material misstatement

The segregation of audit risk into its inherent and control risk components helps the auditor design an efficient audit that does not overlook key areas. By excluding the expected effectiveness of internal control from consideration, the inherent risk analysis prevents the auditor from passing over a key risk area simply because she believes (without performing appropriate audit tests) that the internal control system would prevent a related material misstatement.[12] The control risk analysis, on the other hand, provides support for the auditor's increased or decreased level of reliance on the internal control system. This, in turn, helps the auditor modify his plan in proportion to the level of risk.[13]

Some examples of inherent risk considerations include the following:[14]

---

[11] Ibid., SAS No. 107, par. 21; and ISA 200, par. 13(n).

[12] A similar risk assessment philosophy should be employed by organizations in determining how best to monitor their internal control systems. See COSO, *Guidance on Monitoring Internal Control Systems,* vol. 2, (COSO, 2009), par. 56.

[13] The auditor has always been required to consider control risk as part of the broader audit risk assessment. It is not, as some have assumed, a new requirement established by the Sarbanes-Oxley Act of 2002.

[14] See the *AICPA Audit Guide: Assessing and Responding Audit Risk in a Financial Statement Audit,* par. 2.10.

- *Volume.* A high volume of transactions or processes can make small, repetitive errors material in the aggregate.
- *Complexity.* The more complex the processing or accounting that exists in a given area, the greater its susceptibility to material misstatement.
- *Susceptibility of an asset to theft.* The risk of theft not only increases the risk of misstatement, but often is accompanied by creative means to hide the theft.
- *Estimates.* Accounting areas that require significant judgment pose greater financial reporting risks than do areas consisting of routine, factual data.
- *Industry circumstances.* Technological, regulatory, economic or other changes that affect a specific industry can increase financial reporting risk.

Some of the factors that influence inherent risk (e.g., complexity, the level of judgment required, and susceptibility to fraud) can also affect the ability of the internal control system to prevent or detect material errors. Other examples of control risk considerations include:[15]

- *Nature of operations.* The way an organization is structured and the characteristics of its operations can influence control risk. Such characteristics may include degree of centralization, information system complexity, and existence of foreign operations.
- *Changes in operations.* Mergers, joint ventures, acquisitions, system changes, personnel, and other changes are all indicators of increased control risk.
- *Environmental factors.* External dynamics including competition, changes in the market (e.g., supply chain, customer base, or economy), or changes in regulation can influence the internal control system's effectiveness.

The risk of material misstatement (both inherent risk and control risk) rests with the company. Detection risk, on the other hand, rests with the auditor. At its heart detection risk relates to the potential for the auditor to fail in (1) designing the audit properly or (2) executing it effectively.

## Fraud Considerations

In the context of an external audit, fraud is categorized as either misappropriation of assets or intentionally falsifying financial statements. Both forms of fraud can and do have devastating effects on financial statements, investors, management, the board, and employees.

Recognizing that it is not possible to design an audit to catch all fraud, auditing standards nonetheless expect the auditor to plan and perform the audit to obtain reasonable assurance about whether the financial statements are free of material misstatement, whether caused by error *or fraud.*[16] Accordingly, the audit committee should understand how the external auditor has considered the risk of fraud

---

[15] See COSO, *Guidance on Monitoring Internal Control Systems*, vol. 2, par. 58.
[16] See ISA 200, par. 5, and SAS No. 1, par. 2.

in designing his or her audit. This topic is discussed further in "A Perspective on Fraud and the Auditor," found later in this Handbook.

## THE ENGAGEMENT TEAM

The first standard of audit field work states, "The auditor must adequately plan the work and must properly supervise any assistants."[17] Accordingly the audit committee might inquire of the auditor regarding:[18]

- The experience, training, and amount of resources assigned to specific audit areas (e.g., areas with a heightened risk of material misstatement)
- The involvement of experts on complex matters
- When such resources are to be assigned (e.g., at an interim audit period or at key cutoff dates) and how much time they are expected to incur
- How all audit resources are to be managed, directed, and supervised, such as:
  - When and how often team briefing and debriefing meetings are expected to be held
  - How the engagement partner and manager reviews are expected to take place (for example, on-site or off-site)
  - Whether the auditor will utilize a concurring reviewer or other form of engagement quality review

Section 103 of the Sarbanes-Oxley Act required the PCAOB to establish rules for registered audit firms that "provide a concurring or second partner review . . . by a qualified person . . . other than the person in charge of the audit." In July 2009 the PCAOB fulfilled that requirement through the issuance of Auditing Standard No. 7, *Engagement Quality Review* (AS 7), which states:

> An engagement quality review and concurring approval of issuance are required for each audit engagement and for each engagement to review interim financial information conducted pursuant to the standards of the Public Company Accounting Oversight Board ("PCAOB").[19]

Accordingly, every audit of a company listed on a U.S. exchange must include a concurring partner (or equivalent) quality review. Some audit firms also require concurring reviews on audits of private and not-for-profit organizations if the level of audit risk warrants such an approach.

## TYPES OF AUDIT TESTS

Auditors perform two different types of audit tests: tests of controls and substantive procedures. Tests of controls are designed to evaluate the effectiveness of

---

[17] *Statement on Auditing Standard No. 108*, par. 1. New York: AICPA, 2006.

[18] Ibid., par. 15. See also ISA 220, par. 14–15.

[19] Public Company Accounting Oversight Board, *Auditing Standard No. 7*, par. 1.

the internal control system in preventing or in detecting and correcting errors before they result in a material misstatement of the financial statements. Substantive procedures test the output from the financial reporting process and are designed to detect material misstatements at the assertion level. If an auditor's substantive procedure discovers a material error, it is because the internal control system did not.

## Tests of Controls

The external auditor's initial analysis of control risk[20] informs her preliminary risk assessment, but it does not provide enough evidence to support a conclusion as to whether internal control is effective in a given area. Auditors may need and want to obtain such support if:[21]

1. They reasonably believe the internal control system is effective and wants to rely, at least in part, on that system to plan and conduct the audit.
2. Substantive procedures alone cannot provide sufficient audit evidence to support a conclusion that the financial statements are not materially misstated.[22]

In some cases the auditor may be required to test controls, such as in public company audits that must comply with Section 404 of the Sarbanes-Oxley Act, or when required by certain debt or acquisition agreements. However, even in those situations the first condition should still be true. The auditor will obtain little value from testing internal controls that he has reason to believe are ineffective at the outset.

Audit committees should be interested for several reasons in the external auditor's level of internal control testing. First, the audit committee should know whether internal control areas exist that the auditor does not believe are effective enough to warrant any level of audit reliance. Such areas—even if they do not produce material errors in the external financial statements—may nevertheless lead to errors in internal reports used for decision-making purposes. They often are fraught with inefficiencies as well. Second, the auditor's ability to test and rely on the internal control system improves the efficiency of both the financial reporting and the audit processes. Almost without exception, early detection and prevention of financial reporting errors is less costly than fixing them after they become material problems. In addition, a healthy reliance on effective internal control systems helps the auditor spread audit work throughout the year, thus reducing the strain on the organization's resources at the end of the fiscal year and during the auditor's final fieldwork.

---

[20] See the earlier "Audit Risk" section for a description of control risk.

[21] See ISA 330, par. 8, and SAS No. 110, par. 23.

[22] For example, high-volume, highly automated processes that require little manual intervention typically require some level of auditor internal control consideration because substantive procedures alone are either impractical or not sufficient to support a conclusion that the related output is materially correct.

Tests of controls typically begin with a walkthrough in which the auditor obtains an understanding of the design and operation of the control by tracing one or more transactions through the system from beginning to end. Tests of controls can also involve selecting samples of controls at a point in time, or over a period of time, and observing their performance, reperforming them, or obtaining some other evidence that they operated effectively.

Some auditors separate the documentation of their tests of controls into "tests of design" (i.e., determining if the control as designed should be effective) and "tests of effectiveness" (i.e., testing to ensure that the control is operating as designed).

When designing tests of controls, the external auditor does not need to test every control that mitigates a given risk. Rather, controls should be selected for testing that, when evaluated, provide reasonable assurance that the internal control system is operating effectively. Such controls often called are "key controls."[23]

In the United States, both the SEC and the PCAOB encourage a top-down approach to internal control evaluation by focusing first on controls they refer to as "entity-level controls." These controls typically fall into one of three categories:[24]

1. Pervasive controls such as certain control environment controls that have an important, but indirect, effect on the likelihood that a misstatement will be detected or prevented on a timely basis.
2. Controls that monitor the effectiveness of other controls.
3. Entity-level controls that operate at a level of precision to prevent or detect earlier control failures before they can result in a material misstatement.

By focusing first on these entity-level controls, the external auditor may determine that the risk of material misstatement has been addressed adequately at the entity level, thus reducing the need to test controls at the activity level.

### Substantive Procedures

Substantive procedures consist of "tests of details" and "substantive analytical procedures." These are the audit procedures many people associate with "green-eyeshade" auditors.

Professional standards require that auditors perform substantive procedures for each material class of transactions, account balance, and disclosure—regardless of the assessed risk of material misstatement.[25] This requirement reflects the fact that the auditor's risk assessment process has limitations and may not identify

---

[23] See COSO, *Guidance on Monitoring Internal Control Systems* (2009), vol. 2, par. 49–51 and 59–62.
[24] See the PCAOB's Auditing Standard No. 5, *An Audit of Internal Control over Financial Reporting That Is Integrated With an Audit of Financial Statements* (May 2007), par. 24–27; and the SEC's *Securities Exchange Act Release No. 54976* , 12, footnote 29 (December 2006).
[25] See ISA 330, par. 18, and SAS No. 110 par. 9 and 51.

all risks of material misstatement. It also recognizes that even good internal control systems have limitations, and errors may get through.

Tests of details often involve selecting a sample of transactions or accounts and performing one or more of the following:[26]

- *Inspection.* Examining records or documents or performing a physical examination of an asset.
- *Observation.* Watching others perform their duties.
- *External confirmation.* Asking a third party, such as a customer, vendor, or attorney, to confirm independently certain balances, transactions, or facts. The responses to external confirmations often are in paper or electronic form.
- *Recalculation.* Checking the mathematical accuracy of documents or records.
- *Reperformance.* The auditor's independent execution of procedures or controls that originally were performed as part of the organization's internal control system.
- *Inquiry.* Seeking information, both financial and nonfinancial, from knowledgeable persons within or outside the entity. Inquiry alone is not sufficient to draw audit conclusions. It does require some other level of testing support.[27]

Substantive analytical procedures[28] involve examining data and its relationship to other data or to expectations. Such procedures may range from simple comparisons to performing complex analyses using advanced statistical techniques. They can be applied to consolidated financial statement line items, components of those line items, or more granular elements like transaction or journal entry details. Examples may include but are not limited to:

- Analyzing financial trends over time or in comparison to budgets, industry norms, or other expectations
- Comparing financial ratios, such as gross margin percentages, to expectations established in light of current economic or environmental conditions
- Comparing financial information and relevant nonfinancial information, such as payroll costs and number of employees

## Using the Work of Others

External auditors can often enhance the efficiency and effectiveness of their audits by using the work performed by others. Most of the auditing standards that govern the auditor's use of such work relate to the auditor's use of work performed by

---

[26] See ISA 500, par. A14-A22, and SAS No. 110, par 11.

[27] See ISA 315, par. A67, and SAS No. 110, par. 29.

[28] Audit committee members may hear auditors talk about "planning analytics." While planning analytics employ the same tools as substantive analytical procedures, auditors perform them for a different purpose. Auditors use planning analytics early in the audit cycle to help identify inherent and control risks. They employ substantive analytical procedures (which usually are more comprehensive than planning analytics) throughout the audit cycle to determine whether material mis-statements have occurred.

internal audit functions.[29] In the United States, the PCAOB has expanded the auditor's potential use of the work of others, stating:

> the auditor may use the work performed by, or receive direct assistance from, internal auditors, company personnel (in addition to internal auditors), and third parties working under the direction of management or the audit committee that provides evidence about the effectiveness of internal control over financial reporting. In an integrated audit of internal control over financial reporting and the financial statements, the auditor also may use this work to obtain evidence supporting the auditor's assessment of control risk for purposes of the audit of the financial statements.[30]

All of these standards contain the following general criteria for the auditor to consider when deciding whether to use the work of others:

- The nature and scope of specific work performed by others and whether it is likely to be adequate for purposes of the audit
- The assessed risks of material misstatement (a higher level of risk may increase the auditor's need to perform testing directly)
- The degree of subjectivity involved in the evaluation of the audit evidence gathered by the others in support of the relevant assertions
- The objectivity and technical competence of the others performing the work
- Whether their work is likely to be carried out with due professional care
- Whether effective communication is likely to occur between the others and the external auditor
- The planned effect of the work of others on the nature, timing, or extent of the external auditor's procedures

In any event, the auditor—by using the work performed by others—does not relinquish responsibility for the adequacy of his audit support. Accordingly, external auditors should be careful in determining whether to use the work of others and how they will review it.

Audit committees should understand the extent to which auditors plan to use the work of others.[31] They should be confident that the auditor is taking advantage of such work where it makes sense to do so. On the other hand, the audit committee should allow for the auditor's healthy skepticism in situations where she determines reasonably not to use the work of others.

## EVALUATING THE EXTERNAL AUDIT PLAN

With an understanding of (1) the interplay between materiality, the risk of material misstatement and audit risk (see Exhibit 6.3) and (2) the types of tests external

---

[29] See ISA 610 and SAS No. 65.

[30] See PCAOB Auditing Standard No. 5, par. 17.

[31] See ISA 240, par. A14.

**EXHIBIT 6.3**   Materiality, Risk of Material Misstatement, and Audit Risk

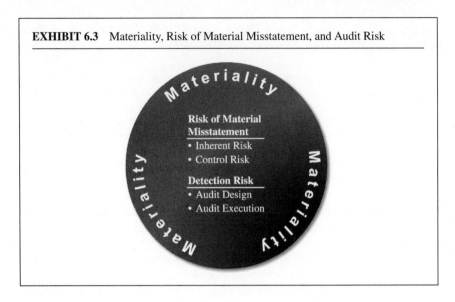

auditors can employ (i.e., tests of controls and substantive tests), the audit committee is prepared to evaluate and oversee the audit plan.

Audit committee members want to be confident of at least four things regarding the external audit plan:

1. It covers all risks that have a reasonable possibility of materially affecting the financial statements, but does not dwell on areas having little chance of a material effect.
2. It focuses appropriately on the internal control system's ability to mitigate those risks without spending substantial time on controls whose failure likely would be:
   a. Immaterial to the financial statements
   b. Detected and corrected in a timely manner by other controls
3. It takes appropriate advantage of the work performed by others (especially internal audit), but does not place reliance on such work where it is not warranted.
4. It focuses appropriately on areas where the risk of fraud is meaningful.

The audit committee also should work with the auditor early in the audit cycle to establish expectations regarding communications and a related timeline. Early identification of audit problems—whether related to errors in the books and records or failure of the organization to provide the necessary audit information, or failure of the auditor to complete the audit plan as designed—can minimize surprises and prevent the unnecessary escalation of costs. Appendix 6B contains a sample external audit plan template that external auditors and audit committees can use first to plan the audit and then to track progress.

Exhibit 6.4 contains an excerpt from the AICPA's Audit Guide, "Assessing and Responding to Audit Risk in a Financial Statement Audit." Audit committee members may find it to be helpful during the planning phase of the external audit.

**EXHIBIT 6.4**   Developing an Audit Strategy

| The overall audit strategy involves the determination of . . . | Examples of which include . . . |
|---|---|
| The characteristics of the audit that define its scope | • The basis of reporting<br>• Industry-specific reporting requirements<br>• The locations of the client |
| The reporting objectives of the engagement related to the timing of the audit and the required communications | • Deadlines for interim and final reporting<br>• Key dates for expected communications with management and those charged with governance |
| Important factors that determine the focus of the audit team's efforts. | • Appropriate materiality and tolerable misstatement levels<br>• Preliminary identification of areas where there may be higher risks of material misstatement<br>• Preliminary identification of material locations and account balances<br>• Plans, if any, to obtain evidence about the operating effectiveness of internal control at the assertion level<br>• How the entity uses IT to capture, store, and process information and whether the use of an IT specialist is necessary for the engagement<br>• Recent, significant, and entity-specific developments related to the client's industry, financial reporting requirements, or other relevant matters |

*Source*: Reprinted with permission from the AICPA's Audit Guide, *Assessing and Responding to Audit Risk in a Financial Statement Audit*. Table 3-1, "Developing an Audit Strategy" (New York: AICPA, 2006).

## SOURCES AND SUGGESTED READINGS

AICPA's Audit Guide. *Assessing and Responding to Audit Risk in a Financial Statement Audit*. New York: AICPA, 2006.

American Institute of Certified Public Accountants. *Audit Guide, Consideration of Internal Control in a Financial Statement Audit*. New York: AICPA, 1996.

American Institute of Certified Public Accountants. *Professional Standards, U.S. Auditing Standards/Attestation Standards*, vol. 1. New York: AICPA, 2003.

COSO. "Internal Control—Integrated Framework." 1992. Available at www.coso.org.

COSO. "Guidance on Monitoring Internal Control Systems." 2009. Available at www.coso.org.

Financial Reporting Council (UK), "The Combined Code on Corporate Governance." www.frc.org.uk (2006).

Hardy, John W., and Larry A. Deppe. "Client Acceptance: What to Look For and Why." CPA Journal 62, No. 5 (May 1992), pp. 20–27.

IAASB pronouncements at www.ifac.org/IAASB/.

Pickett, K. H. Spencer. *Audit Planning: A Risk-Based Approach.* Hoboken, NJ: John Wiley & Sons, 2006.

Securities and Exchange Commission. *Accounting and Auditing Enforcement Release No. 215,* SEC v. Donald D. Sheelen, et al. (February 8, 1989), 42 SEC Docket 1562.

Public Company Accounting Oversight Board, Auditing Standards No. 1-7. Available at www.pcaobus.org.

*Statement on Auditing Standards No. 22.* "Planning and Supervision." New York: AICPA, 1978.

*Statement on Auditing Standards No. 56.* "Analytical Procedures." New York: AICPA, 1988.

*Statement on Auditing Standards No. 61.* "Communication with Audit Committees." New York: AICPA, 1988.

*Statement on Auditing Standards No. 99.* "Consideration of Fraud in a Financial Statement Audit." New York: AICPA, 2002.

*Statement on Auditing Standards No. 108.* "Planning and Supervision." New York: AICPA, 2006.

Sumners, Glenn E., and Barbara Apostolou. "Preparation Can Cut Audit Fees." *Financial Manager* 3, no. 1 (January/February 1990): 46–49.

U.S. General Accounting Office. *Government Auditing Standards, Standards for Audit of Government Organizations, Programs, Activities and Functions.* Washington, DC: U.S. Government Printing Office, 2003.

Walker, Robert. "Know Your Client's Business." *CA Magazine* 124, no. 6 (June 1991), pp. 49–52.

## Video

American Institute of Certified Public Accountants, *Fraud and the Financial Statement Audits: Auditor Responsibilities Under SAS No. 99.* New York: American Institute of Certified Public Accountants, 2003. Length of video: 135 minutes.

# Qualitative Factors That May Influence the Determination of Materiality

Qualitative factors that you may consider when making judgments about materiality include the following:

- The potential effect of the misstatement on trends, especially trends in profitability.
- A misstatement that changes a loss into income or vice versa.
- The potential effect of the misstatement on the entity's compliance with loan covenants, other contractual agreements, and regulatory provisions.
- The existence of statutory or regulatory reporting requirements that affect materiality thresholds.
- A change masked in earnings or other trends, especially in the context of general economic and industry conditions.
- A misstatement that has the effect of increasing management's compensation, for example, by satisfying the requirements for the award of bonuses or other forms of incentive compensation.
- The sensitivity of the circumstances surrounding the misstatement, for example, the implications of misstatements involving fraud and possible illegal acts, violations of contractual provisions such as debt covenants, and conflicts of interest.
- The significance of the financial statement element affected by the misstatement, for example, a misstatement affecting recurring earnings as contrasted to one involving a nonrecurring charge or credit, such as an extraordinary item.
- The effects of misclassifications, for example, misclassification between operating and nonoperating income or recurring and nonrecurring income items, or a misclassification between fund-raising costs and program activity costs in a not-for-profit organization.
- The significance of the misstatement relative to reasonable user needs, for example:
  - Earnings to investors and the equity amounts to creditors.
  - The magnifying effects of a misstatement on the calculation of purchase price in a transfer of interests (buy-sell agreement).
  - The effect of misstatements of earnings when contrasted with expectations.

Obtaining the views and expectations of those charged with governance and management may be helpful in gaining or corroborating an understanding of user needs, such as those illustrated above.

- The definitive character of the misstatement, for example, the precision of an error that is objectively determinable as contrasted with a misstatement that unavoidably involves a degree of subjectivity through estimation, allocation, or uncertainty.
- The motivation of management with respect to the misstatement, for example, (1) an indication of a possible pattern of bias by management when developing and accumulating accounting estimates, (2) a misstatement precipitated by management's continued unwillingness to correct weaknesses in the financial reporting process, or (3) an intentional decision not to follow generally accepted accounting principles.
- The existence of offsetting effects of individually significant but different misstatements.
- The likelihood that a misstatement that is currently immaterial may have a material effect in future periods because of a cumulative effect, for example, that builds over several periods.
- The cost of making the correction. It may not be cost-beneficial for the client to develop a system to calculate a basis to record the effect of an immaterial misstatement. On the other hand, if management appears to have developed a system to calculate an amount that represents an immaterial misstatement, it may reflect a motivation of management.
- The risk that possible additional undetected misstatements would affect the auditor's evaluation.

# Example Audit Planning Schedule

| Month → | Q2 | | | Q3 | | | Q4 | | | Q1-Next Yr | | | Budgeted Hours | Hours to Date | ETC |
|---|---|---|---|---|---|---|---|---|---|---|---|---|---|---|---|
| | 4 | 5 | 6 | 7 | 8 | 9 | 10 | 11 | 12 | 1 | 2 | 3 | | | |
| *Phase I —Planning, risk assessment, and control design* | | ▓ | ▓ | | | | | | | | | | | | |
| Integrated audit planning | | | | | | | | | | | | | | | |
| Review and comment on client's entity-level risk assessment and project plan (i.e., determine locations for testing) | | | | | | | | | | | | | | | |
| Identify significant accounts/cycles and critical assertions | | | | | | | | | | | | | | | |
| Update entity-level control documentation | | | | | | | | | | | | | | | |
| Update activity-level control documentation | | | | | | | | | | | | | | | |
| Evaluate control design effectiveness and note key controls | | | | | | | | | | | | | | | |
| Execute walk-throughs of identified (and potentially key) controls | | | | | | | | | | | | | | | |
| Follow up on previous recommendations for improvement | | | | | | | | | | | | | | | |
| | | | | | | | | | | | | | | | |
| *Phase II —Tests of controls and preliminary financial statement testing* | | | | ▓ | ▓ | ▓ | ▓ | ▓ | ▓ | ▓ | ▓ | | | | |
| Identify key controls | | | | | | | | | | | | | | | |
| Review management's testing methodology | | | | | | | | | | | | | | | |
| Finalize testing strategy for key controls | | | | | | | | | | | | | | | |
| Evaluate competence and objectivity of client's control testers | | | | | | | | | | | | | | | |
| Determine possible use of others' work | | | | | | | | | | | | | | | |

| Task | | | | | | | | | | | | | | | |
|------|--|--|--|--|--|--|--|--|--|--|--|--|--|--|--|
| Determine controls to test and testing procedures | | | | | | | | | | | | | | | |
| Execute and document tests of controls (including review of work of others) | | | | | | | | | | | | | | | |
| Quarterly financial statement reviews | | | | | | | | | | | | | | | |
| *Phase III —Final testing, evaluate results, and wrap up* | | | | | | | | | | | | | | | |
| Evaluate and document deficiencies | | | | | | | | | | | | | | | |
| Make recommendations for improvements | | | | | | | | | | | | | | | |
| Annual audit procedures | | | | | | | | | | | | | | | |
| Communicate and report results | | | | | | | | | | | | | | | |
| Draft opinion | | | | | | | | | | | | | | | |
| Complete review and documentation | | | | | | | | | | | | | | | |
| Issue opinion | | | | | | | | | | | | | | | |
| *Total* | | | | | | | | | | | | | | | |

Legend:

Integrated audit planning & ICFR audit steps

Specific financial statement audit steps

# Chapter 7

# Planning the Internal Audit

The Institute of Internal Auditors (The IIA) defines internal audit as:

> an independent, objective assurance and consulting activity designed to add value and improve an organization's operations. It helps an organization accomplish its objectives by bringing a systematic, disciplined approach to evaluate and improve the effectiveness of risk management, control, and governance processes.[1]

Key to this definition is the concept that internal audit is a consulting activity. It does not provide independent assurance in the same sense that the external auditors do. However, internal auditors[2] are required to maintain their objectivity.[3] As such they serve in that valuable middle ground between management, the audit committee, and the external auditor.

In order to maintain their objectivity, internal auditors typically report directly to the board or the board's audit committee. However, internal auditing standards do recognize that a dual reporting relationship between management and the board can provide the internal auditor with valuable access to both groups.[4]

## COMPONENTS OF THE INTERNAL AUDIT PLAN

### An Overview

Internal audit plans typically cover the following: (1) financial reporting, (2) operational efficiency, and (3) compliance with laws, regulations, and corporate policies. Some internal audit departments, especially in private organizations or small public companies, focus primarily (or exclusively) on operational and compliance audits. However, as organizations grow in size, or as financial reporting risks and complexities increase, management and the board often find it necessary to add financial reporting audits to the scope of the internal audit function.

---

[1] Source: The IIA's *International Professional Practices Framework* (IPPF).

[2] Throughout this Handbook, the term "internal auditor" refers to professionals who follow The IIA's IPPF.

[3] See The IIA's Code of Ethics, Rule of Conduct #2, and The IIA Standard 1100.

[4] The IIA's interpretation of its Standard 1100 states, "To achieve the degree of independence necessary to effectively carry out the responsibilities of the internal audit activity, the chief audit executive has direct and unrestricted access to senior management and the board. This can be achieved through a dual-reporting relationship."

*Financial Reporting Audits*   Chapter 6 covered the external audit plan and addressed the external auditor's use of the work of others, including the work of internal auditors. External auditors are often able to take advantage of financial reporting work performed by internal auditors because it covers some of the same risks, controls, accounts, and disclosures that the external auditor's plan covers.

The most frequent form of internal audit work in this area relates to testing internal control over financial reporting (ICFR). Internal auditors develop a testing plan for ICFR in much the same way that external auditors do, by:[5]

1. Assessing and prioritizing risks to financial reporting objectives
2. Understanding how the internal control systems address those risks and identifying key controls
3. Determining what information is necessary to conclude on the effectiveness of those controls
4. Designing and executing appropriate tests

Management or the audit committee also may request interim financial audits, such as an internal audit of the financial statements at the end of a month or quarter. In such cases internal auditors conduct their examination and express their opinion on the statements. These statements are used within the entity and are not distributed to external users who require independent, audited financial statements. These interim internal audits can improve the reliability of information used for decision making. They also can identify financial reporting problems before they materially affect the external financial statements, thus improving financial reporting quality and external audit efficiency.

As reporting using Extensible Business Reporting Language (XBRL) becomes ubiquitous, many internal audit functions may be asked to verify the related digital tagging of financial statement items. Internal audit also may review management's controls over the safeguarding of assets. Finally, as a result of their financial audit, the audit committee or management may request that the internal auditor function conduct special assignments, such as improving internal control in a given area or implementing a fraud prevention program.

Worth noting is that the continuing increase in public availability of electronic information is leading to a growing army of "auditors" in the outside world. These individuals, many of whom are not trained accountants or auditors, have the time, ability, and electronic tools to analyze available information and identify potential problems. For example, the backdating of stock options scandal in 2005 was uncovered by Erik Lie, an associate professor of finance at the University of Iowa. Lie analyzed proxy statements and insider transaction documents filed with the SEC from more than 2,000 large companies and discovered a pattern in which stocks fell slightly just before options were granted and rose shortly after the grant date.[6] Professor Lie's analysis would not have been practical if not for the

---

[5] See COSO, *Guidance on Monitoring Internal Control Systems* (2009), par. 42–53.
[6] See Professor Lie's study, "On the Timing of CEO Stock Option Awards." Available at http://www.biz.uiowa.edu/faculty/elie/Grants-MS.pdf.

availability of electronic data on so many public companies. Such availability will only increase in the future. Audit committees should be aware of this trend and seek to ensure that their organization's internal audit departments are equipped with the necessary analytical tools.

***Operational Audits***   Operational audits usually are performed by the internal auditing staff. The primary purpose of these audits is to evaluate and improve the efficiency and effectiveness of certain functions. For example, the internal auditors may review the operating efficiency and the effectiveness of the processes within a department. Such a review essentially is a service to management since the auditors generally make recommendations for operational improvements.

In connection with operational audits, internal auditors are often asked to evaluate the performance of individual managers. They also may be tasked with developing process improvements or implementing fraud prevention measures across the organization. Consequently, the internal audit function is an important resource since such a group can serve management, the audit committee, and the full board on an organization-wide basis.

The planning process for an operational audit is similar to that for a financial reporting audit. It involves assessing risks to operational objectives, understanding how the organization's controls manage or mitigate those risks, and assessing the effectiveness of those controls. Many operational audits begin with a theory or an indication that something may be wrong. A good internal control system, with access to reliable analytical information, can help identify operational risk areas and focus internal audit on a potential problem. The substantive analytical procedures discussed in Chapter 6 can be good tools in this regard.

***Compliance Audits***   In contrast to operational audits, compliance audits are oriented toward internal adherence to managerial policies and the entity's compliance with regulatory requirements, if applicable. Periodic compliance audits help protect the organization from the severe consequences of intentional and unintentional violations of policy or law.

The compliance audit plan may be structured on the same basis as the financial reporting and operational audit plans. However, compliance audits often involve legal matters. Accordingly, the scope of the compliance audit may need to be discussed with legal counsel. In some cases, the work may need to be directed by legal counsel and documented according to its requirements in order to preserve legal privilege.

Regardless of the type of audit (financial reporting, operational or compliance), as business accelerates and becomes more complex, internal auditors must increase their capabilities to identify and address potential problems in a timely manner. Good analytical tools, risk assessment methodologies, training, and planning will be increasingly important to the internal audit function. Audit committees should also recognize the tremendous value that an effective internal audit function can bring to the organization and to their committee's oversight responsibilities.

## ENTERPRISE RISK MANAGEMENT

One might combine the above internal audit types under one umbrella, called enterprise risk management (ERM). In fact, COSO has done just that in its 2004 Enterprise Risk Management—Integrated Framework (ERM Framework), although COSO rightly adds organizational strategy as a fourth objective within ERM. Thus, a holistic view of risk management may include the following objectives:[7]

- *Strategic.* Relating to high-level goals, aligned with and supporting the organization's mission
- *Operations.* Relating to effective and efficient use of the organization's resources
- *Reporting.* Relating to the reliability of the organization's reporting
- *Compliance.* Relating to the organization's compliance with applicable laws and regulations

When considered correctly, ERM helps management and the board to see the universe of risks that could affect organizational objectives and to take a rational, measured response to each one. Such responses could include avoiding, accepting, reducing, or sharing the risk. When considered incorrectly, ERM either fails to respond properly to the risk in concert with the organization's objectives or becomes an overengineered mechanical exercise with minimal practical benefit.

Complex organizations often require complex ERM plans, while simple organizations rarely require such plans. In the final analysis, however, all ERM follows the general path outlined in the internal audit testing described above:

1. Assess and prioritize the risk to organizational objectives
2. Determine how best to respond to those risks given the organization's related objectives
3. Determine what information is necessary to conclude on the effectiveness of those responses
4. Design and execute appropriate monitoring procedures

The board delegates to the organization's management team the responsibility for managing and mitigating enterprise risks. However, responsibility for oversight of that process can be confusing. The New York Stock Exchange's rules state the following:

> While it is the job of the CEO and senior management to assess and manage the company's exposure to risk, the audit committee must discuss guidelines and policies to govern the process by which this is handled. The audit committee should discuss the company's major financial risk exposures and the steps management has taken to monitor and control such exposures. The audit committee is not

---

[7] See COSO, *Enterprise Risk Management—Integrated Framework* (2004) 21.

required to be the sole body responsible for risk assessment and management, but, as stated above, the committee must discuss guidelines and policies to govern the process by which risk assessment and management is undertaken. Many companies, particularly financial companies, manage and assess their risk through mechanisms other than the audit committee. The processes these companies have in place should be reviewed in a general manner by the audit committee, but they need not be replaced by the audit committee.[8]

Those same rules state the following regarding the internal audit function:

Listed companies must maintain an internal audit function to provide management and the audit committee with ongoing assessments of the company's risk manage- ment processes and system of internal control. A company may choose to outsource this function to a third party service provider other than its independent auditor.[9]

Other U.S. or global exchanges have not established similar requirements for the audit committee or the internal audit function; but oversight of many organizations' ERM capabilities often falls to those two groups, nonetheless. Accordingly, it may be helpful for audit committee members to have a working knowledge of ERM. Members may find the executive summary to COSO's Enterprise Risk Management—Integrated Framework helpful.[10] Further, in 2009 COSO released a four-page paper titled "Effective Enterprise Risk Oversight— The Role of the Board of Directors." This paper emphasizes the role boards of directors play in overseeing ERM, and points to four specific areas, discussed in COSO's 2004 ERM Framework, that contribute to board risk oversight, including:[11]

1. Understanding the entity's risk philosophy and concurring with the entity's risk appetite
2. Knowing the extent to which management has established effective enterprise risk management of the organization
3. Reviewing the entity's portfolio of risk and considering it in light of the entity's risk appetite
4. Being apprised of the most significant risks and whether management is responding appropriately

## OVERSIGHT AND REPORTING

Internal audit typically reports to the audit committee of the board of directors. In some instances, especially in private organizations, internal audit reports to management. In any event it is important for the audit committee to have

---

[8] See NYSE Rule 303A.07(c)(iii)(D).

[9] Ibid., Rule 303A.07(d). See the discussion on outsourcing internal audit in Chapter 9.

[10] Available at www.coso.org/ERM-IntegratedFramework.htm.

[11] Available at www.coso.org/documents/COSOBoardsERM4pager-FINALRELEASEVERSION82 409.pdf.

open lines of communication with both management and the board. It is also customary for Chief Audit Executives (CAEs) to meet privately with the audit committee or the board at least annually.[12]

The IIA maintains strict standards of conduct and provides robust guidance to its members, many of which have obtained the Certified Internal Auditor (CIA) designation. However, there are no legal restrictions that prevent untrained and uncertified people from calling themselves "internal auditors." Accordingly, audit committee members may want to inquire about the professional qualifications of internal audit personnel. The IIA has set forth a series of broad audit committee oversight responsibilities that committee members may find helpful. The list includes the following:[13]

1. Reviewing and approving the internal audit activity's charter
2. Ensuring communication and reporting lines between the head of internal auditing and the audit committee
3. Reviewing internal audit staffing and ensuring that the function has the necessary resources
4. Reviewing and assessing the annual internal audit plan
5. Overseeing the coordination of the internal auditor with the external auditor
6. Reviewing periodic reports on the results of the internal auditors' work
7. Reviewing management's responsiveness to internal audit's findings and recommendations
8. Monitoring and assessing internal audit effectiveness

The IIA also suggests that CAEs regularly attend and participate in meetings that relate to the board's oversight responsibilities for auditing, financial reporting, organizational governance, and control. This provides the CAE with an opportunity to be apprised of strategic business and operational developments that may influence the audit plan. It also gives the CAE the opportunity to raise at an early stage high-level risk, systems, procedures, or control issues. Meeting attendance also provides an opportunity to exchange information concerning the internal audit function's plans.[14]

## SOURCES AND SUGGESTED READINGS

American Institute of Certified Public Accountants. *The AICPA's "Audit Committee Toolkit."* New York: AICPA, 2004.

American Institute of Certified Public Accountants. "Audit Committee Effectiveness Center." www.aicpa.org/audcommctr/homepage.htm.

American Institute of Certified Public Accountants. *Audit Guide, Consideration of Internal Control in a Financial Statement Audit.* New York: AICPA, 1997.

---

[12] See The IIA's Practice Advisory 1111-1, *Board Interactions.*
[13] See The IIA's publication, *Audit Committee Briefing . . . Internal Audit Standards: Why They Matter*, 4. Available at www.theiia.org/download.cfm?file=83632.
[14] See The IIA's Practice Advisory 1111-1, *Board Interactions.*

Beasley, Mark S., Bruce C. Branson, Bonnie V. Hancock. "ERM: Opportunities for Improvement." *Journal of Accountancy*, 208(3) (September 2009). www.journalofaccountancy.com/Issues/2009/Sep/20091792.

Canadian Institute of Chartered Accountants. "Resources for Audit Committees." Available at www.cica.ca/auditcommittees/item29408.aspx.

COSO. *Guidance on Monitoring Internal Control Systems* (2009). Available at www.coso.org/IC.htm.

COSO. "Effective Enterprise Risk Oversight—The Role of the Board of Directors" (2009). www.coso.org/documents/COSOBoardsERM4pager-FINALRELEASEVERSION82409.pdf.

Fraser, John, and Hugh Lindsay. "20 Questions Directors Should Ask about Internal Audit." Canadian Institute of Chartered Accountants, Toronto, ON, 2004. Available at www.theiia.org/iia/download.cfm?file=2927.

The IIA. "Audit Committee Briefing . . . Internal Audit Standards: Why They Matter" (2005). Available at www.theiia.org/download.cfm?file=83632.

The IIA. "*Audit Committee Effectiveness: What Works Best*, 3rd ed. The IIA Research Foundation (2005). To order, visit www.theiia.org/bookstore/product/audit-committee-effectiveness-what-works-best-3rd-edition-1157.cfm.

The IIA. International Professional Practices Framework.

The IIA's Position Paper. "The Role of Internal Auditing in Enterprise-wide Risk Management" (2009). Available at www.theiia.org/download.cfm?file=62465.

The IIA's Practice Advisory 1111-1. "Board Interactions."

Lie, Erik. "On the Timing of CEO Stock Option Awards." Available at www.biz.uiowa.edu/faculty/elie/Grants-MS.pdf.

# Part Three

# The Monitoring and Reviewing Functions of the Audit Committee

# Chapter 8

# Monitoring the System of Internal Control

Much has been debated and written in recent years about the high cost of evaluating internal control over financial reporting in accordance with Section 404 of the U.S. Sarbanes-Oxley Act of 2002. To a large extent the resulting criticism is warranted as the cost of compliance far outstripped anything the U.S. Congress or the SEC contemplated. The reasons for the high cost are twofold:

1. The marketplace (companies, consultants, and auditors) suffered from a lack of understanding regarding the best way to evaluate internal control.
2. Many companies lacked effective internal control where such control should have been in place.

Several things occurred between 2006 and 2009 to lower the cost of compliance. First, the PCAOB issued a revised auditing standard designed to "increase the likelihood that material weaknesses in internal control will be found before they result in material misstatement of a company's financial statements, and, at the same time, eliminate procedures that are unnecessary."[1] Second, the SEC issued guidance for management regarding its year-end assessment of internal control over financial reporting.[2] Third, COSO issued its 2006 "ICFR—Guidance for Smaller Public Companies" and its 2009 "Guidance on Monitoring Internal Control Systems."[3] The 2006 guidance helped frame the ICFR evaluation process. COSO's 2009 monitoring guidance was designed to help management better utilize its organization's existing internal control monitoring procedures (which should be in place for every organization) to support its assertions, rather than building a separate and often inefficient Section 404 compliance process.

The concept is not new that organizations should have effective internal control systems, and should monitor those systems to ensure that they remain effective. The U.S. Foreign Corrupt Practices Act,[4] passed in 1977, states the following (emphasis added):

---

[1] PCAOB news release dated May 24, 2007, announcing the adoption of Auditing Standard No. 5.

[2] Release 33-8810, "Commission Guidance Regarding Management's Report on Internal Control Over Financial Reporting Under Section 13(a) or 15(d) of the Securities Exchange Act of 1934" (2007).

[3] Available at www.coso.org/IC.htm.

[4] See further discussion of the Foreign Corrupt Practices Act in Chapter 12.

"Every issuer . . . shall-

(A) make and keep books, records, and accounts, which, in reasonable detail, accurately and fairly reflect the transactions and dispositions of the assets of the issuer; and

(B) *devise and maintain a system of internal accounting controls* sufficient to provide reasonable assurances that-
    (i) transactions are executed in accordance with management's general or specific authorization;
    (ii) transactions are recorded as necessary (I) to permit preparation of financial statements in conformity with generally accepted accounting principles or any other criteria applicable to such statements, and (II) to maintain accountability for assets;
    (iii) access to assets is permitted only in accordance with management's general or specific authorization; and
    (iv) the recorded accountability for assets is compared with the existing assets at reasonable intervals and appropriate action is taken with respect to any differences."[5]

The UK's Combined Code states, "The board should maintain a sound system of internal control to safeguard shareholders' investment and the company's assets."[6] The UK's related Guidance on Internal Control goes further stating, "It is the role of management to implement board policies on risk and control. In fulfilling its responsibilities, management should identify and evaluate the risks faced by the company for consideration by the board and design, operate and monitor a suitable system of internal control which implements the policies adopted by the board."[7]

Similar guidance exists in other countries.[8] Regardless of the country of origin, all of this guidance is based on generally accepted good business practices. Audit committee members should take note that laws passed in recent years requiring management and others to report on the effectiveness of internal control over financial reporting are rooted in the expectation that these good business practices are in place. They do not specifically require the establishment of new, large compliance departments. Accordingly, an organization that had good internal control—including good monitoring procedures—before the passage of these laws should be able to comply with the existing reporting requirements without a dramatic, long-term increase in cost or effort. A brief review of the most noteworthy of these laws may be helpful. Note the reasonableness of the requirement in contrast to the amount of compliance effort reported by many organizations.

---

[5] U.S.C. Title 15, Chapter 2B, Section 78m(b)(2).
[6] Combined Code (2006), par. C.2.
[7] The UK's "Guidance on Internal Control" (also known as the "Turnbull Guidance") (www.frc.org.uk/corporate/internalcontrol.cfm) provides direction in applying the internal control provisions of the Combined Code. This quote is from paragraph 18 of that guidance.
[8] For example, see Canada's "Criteria of Control (CoCo)," (www.cica.ca) and South Africa's, "King Code of Governance for South Africa" (www.iodsa.co.za/downloads/documents/King_Code_2009.pdf).

Section 404 of the U.S. Sarbanes-Oxley Act of 2002 required the SEC to establish rules mandating:

(a) . . . each [public company] annual report . . . to contain an internal control report, which shall—
   (1) state the responsibility of management for establishing and maintaining an adequate internal control structure and procedures for financial reporting; and
   (2) contain an assessment, as of the end of the most recent fiscal year of the issuer, of the effectiveness of the internal control structure and procedures of the issuer for financial reporting.

(b) . . . With respect to the internal control assessment required by subsection (a), each registered public accounting firm that prepares or issues the audit report for the issuer shall attest to, and report on, the assessment made by the management of the issuer.

Other countries now have similar requirements. For example, Canada, Japan, and Germany now have laws requiring management to sign certifications regarding internal control and/or risk management practices.[9] Some non-U.S. laws do not require the auditor to issue a separate audit opinion on management's assertion, but they all require some form of written management assertion.

## DEFINITION AND BASIC CONCEPTS

The various forms of international guidance on internal control (e.g., COSO, CoCo, and the Turnbull Guidance) are indistinguishable in most respects. Of all the guidance, COSO's has been vetted most extensively[10] and is the framework used by most U.S.-listed public companies. Accordingly, the following discussion about internal control and monitoring will draw heavily from the COSO Framework and from COSO's 2009 monitoring guidance in particular.

Chapter 1 of the COSO Framework says, "Internal control is a process, effected by an entity's board of directors, management and other personnel, designed to provide reasonable assurance regarding the achievement of objectives in the following categories:

- Effectiveness and efficiency of operations,
- Reliability of financial reporting,
- Compliance with applicable laws and regulations."

---

[9] See the Canadian Securities Administrators' (CSA) Multilateral Instrument 52-109, "CEO and CFO Certification"; Japan's Financial Instruments and Exchange Law, Article 24-4-4 and Article 193-2; and Germany's Stock Corporation Act, Section 91(2).

[10] COSO's Internal Control—Integrated Framework was the first major framework published in 1992. Its Guidance on Monitoring Internal Control Systems (published in 2009) was developed over a two-year period that included two public comment periods.

**EXHIBIT 8.1**   The COSO Framework Cube

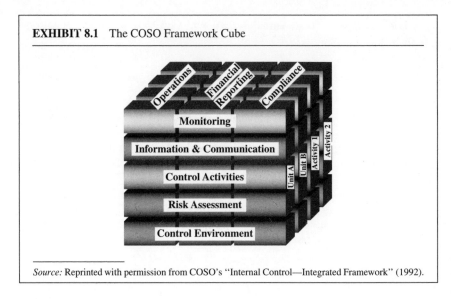

*Source:* Reprinted with permission from COSO's "Internal Control—Integrated Framework" (1992).

Organizations meet these objectives through a process that includes five primary components:[11]

- *Control environment.* Comprises the individual attributes (e.g., integrity, ethical values, and competence) of an organization's people and the propriety of the environment in which they operate. The control environment is the foundation of effective internal control.
- *Risk assessment.* The process whereby an organization identifies and prioritizes risks to its objectives.
- *Control activities.* The related policies and procedures developed to address the risks identified above.
- *Information and communication.* The processes and systems implemented to capture and exchange the information needed in an internal control system.
- *Monitoring.* The processes and procedures designed to help ensure that internal control continues to operate effectively.

The interrelationship between the three objectives and the five components, operating across organizational boundary lines, often is depicted in the graphic shown in Exhibit 8.1.

COSO's 2009 monitoring guidance shows how these components fit together as an overall process, and how the monitoring component covers all five components (Exhibit 8.2).

The COSO Framework states that "monitoring ensures that internal control continues to operate effectively."[12] It also recognizes that risks change over time and that management needs to "determine whether the internal control system

---

[11] See COSO Framework, Ch. 1.
[12] COSO Framework, 69.

**EXHIBIT 8.2**   Monitoring Applied to the Internal Control Process

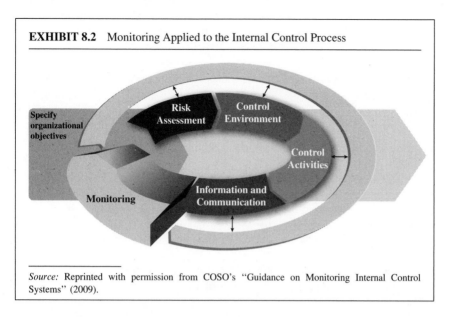

*Source:* Reprinted with permission from COSO's "Guidance on Monitoring Internal Control Systems" (2009).

continues to be *relevant* and able to *address new risks*."[13] Thus, monitoring should evaluate (1) whether management reconsiders the design of controls when risks change and (2) whether controls that have been designed to reduce risks to an acceptable level continue to operate effectively.

When monitoring is effective, it provides the necessary support for management, and others who are charged with governance, to be confident that internal control is operating effectively at any given point in time—including at the end of the year when formal assertions by management may be required. Some additional work may be necessary at year-end to formalize documentation and complete testing in high-risk areas. However, audit committee members should note that large, fourth-quarter efforts, designed solely to comply with Section 404 of Sarbanes-Oxley or similar reporting requirements, likely are indicative of:

1. Inadequate monitoring procedures earlier in the year
2. A weak internal control system that needs correction
3. A duplication of effort already addressed by the organization's effective monitoring procedures

Organizations perform their most effective monitoring when they focus on gathering and evaluating *persuasive information* about the operation of *key controls* that address *meaningful risks* to their objectives.[14] This process includes the following:[15]

---

[13] Ibid., 69 (emphasis added).
[14] See COSO's Guidance on Monitoring Internal Control Systems, vol. I, par. 26.
[15] Ibid., par. 27-47.

1. Understanding and prioritizing risks to organizational objectives
2. Identifying key controls across the internal control system that address those prioritized risks
3. Identifying information that will persuasively indicate whether those controls are operating effectively
4. Developing and implementing cost-effective, ongoing or periodic evaluations that evaluate that persuasive information

By definition, effective monitoring expends little, if any, time or effort on risks that are not meaningful or on controls whose evaluation is not necessary to support a conclusion about internal control effectiveness. To that end, audit committee members may find it helpful to understand the definition of "key control" as contained in COSO's monitoring guidance.

Key controls have one or both of the following characteristics:

- Their failure could materially affect the objectives for which the evaluator is responsible, but might not be detected in a timely manner by other controls.
- Their operation may prevent other control failures or detect such failures before they have an opportunity to become material to the organization's objectives.[16]

The intent of identifying key controls is not to suggest that some controls are more important to the internal control system than others, but to help organizations devote monitoring resources where they can provide the most value. If the failure of a given control likely would be immaterial to the financial statements, then organizations should consider that fact before investing time in testing that control. Similarly, if a given control's failure is likely to be detected and corrected in a timely manner by other controls, then perhaps monitoring should focus on those other controls. Understanding this dynamic can help the audit committee ensure that management, the internal auditor, and the external auditor have an appropriate internal control evaluation scope.

## RESPONSIBILITY FOR THE SYSTEM OF INTERNAL CONTROL

### General Considerations

Everyone in an organization shares some responsibility for internal control. Their roles and responsibilities can be characterized as follows:

- *Management.* The chief executive officer ultimately is responsible for and should assume "ownership" of the system. More than any other individual, the chief executive sets the tone at the top that affects integrity, ethics, and other attributes of a positive control environment. In a large company, the chief executive fulfills this duty by providing leadership and direction to senior

---

[16] Ibid., Vol. I, par. 30-33.

managers, and reviewing the way they are controlling their units' business. Senior managers, in turn, assign appropriate unit personnel the responsibility for establishing more function-specific internal control policies and procedures. In a smaller organization, the influence of the chief executive (often an owner-manager) is usually more direct. Large company or small, where responsibility cascades, a manager effectively is the chief executive of his or her jurisdiction. Of particular note are financial officers and their staff, whose control activities permeate the operating and other units of an enterprise.

- *Board of directors.* Management is accountable to the board of directors, which provides governance, guidance, and oversight. Effective board members are objective, capable, and inquisitive. They also have knowledge of the entity's activities and environment, and commit the time necessary to fulfill their board responsibilities. Management may be dishonest—overriding controls, ignoring or stifling communications from subordinates, and intentionally misrepresenting results to cover its tracks—but a strong, active board will identify and correct such a situation. The board can be particularly effective when sound upward communications channels and capable financial, legal, and internal audit functions are in place.

- *Audit committee.* Audit committee member responsibilities are separate and apart from those of conventional board members. As noted in Chapter 6, the audit committee generally is responsible for overseeing the accounting and financial reporting processes of an organization, and for the appointment, compensation, and oversight of the external auditor.[17] In addition, as discussed in Chapter 7, audit committees of companies listed on the New York Stock Exchange are obligated to review their organization's risk management practices.[18] Whether related to financial reporting, auditor oversight, or enterprise risk management, the audit committee's role is one of oversight, not execution. Accordingly, its procedures should be focused on (1) understanding the risks and (2) verifying that management, the auditors, and others are focused appropriately on those risks. To that end, an effective internal audit function is a valuable tool to the audit committee.

- *Internal auditors.* Internal auditors play an important role in evaluating the effectiveness of control systems and contribute to ongoing effectiveness. Because of its organizational position and authority in an entity, an internal audit function often plays a significant monitoring role.

- *Other personnel.* Virtually all employees are responsible either for producing information used in the internal control system or for taking other actions needed to effect control. A responsibility shared by all personnel is that of upward communication of operations problems, code of conduct non-compliance, and other policy violations or illegal actions.[18]

---

[17] This is especially true under the Sarbanes-Oxley requirements for audit committees of U.S.-listed public companies.
[18] See NYSE Rule 303A.07(c)(iii)(D).

External parties often contribute to achievement of an entity's objectives. External auditors, in bringing an independent and objective view, contribute directly and indirectly—directly through the financial statement audit and indirectly via information that is useful to management and the board in executing their responsibilities. Legislators and regulators, customers and others transacting business with the enterprise, financial analysts, bond raters, and the news media all provide information that is useful to the entity's effecting internal control. External parties, however, are not responsible for, nor are they a part of, the internal control system.

Moreover, auditing standards require external auditors to communicate to the audit committee any identified significant deficiencies or material weaknesses in internal control over financial reporting.[19] The New York Stock Exchange went further by specifying additional audit committee oversight expectations through a modification to Section 303A of its Corporate Governance Standards, which states in part:

(H) report regularly to the board of directors

Commentary: The audit committee should review with the full board any issues that arise with respect to the quality or integrity of the company's financial statements, the company's compliance with legal or regulatory requirements, the performance and independence of the company's independent auditors, or the performance of the internal audit function.

General Commentary to Section 303A.07(c): While the fundamental responsibility for the company's financial statements and disclosures rests with management and the independent auditor, the audit committee must review: (A) major issues regarding accounting principles and financial statement presentations, including any significant changes in the company's selection or application of accounting principles, and major issues as to the adequacy of the company's internal controls and any special audit steps adopted in light of material control deficiencies; (B) analyses prepared by management and/or the independent auditor setting forth significant financial reporting issues and judgments made in connection with the preparation of the financial statements, including analyses of the effects of alternative GAAP methods on the financial statements; (C) the effect of regulatory and accounting initiatives, as well as off-balance sheet structures, on the financial statements of the company; and (D) the type and presentation of information to be included in earnings press releases (paying particular attention to any use of "pro forma," or "adjusted" non-GAAP, information), as well as review any financial information and earnings guidance provided to analysts and rating agencies.

General Commentary to Section 303A.07: To avoid any confusion, note that the audit committee functions specified in Section 303A.07 are the sole responsibility of the audit committee and may not be allocated to a different committee.[20]

---

[19] See SAS No. 115, par. 1; and ISA 265, par. 9.
[20] Securities and Exchange Commission, Release No. 34-50298 (Washington, DC: SEC, August 31, 2004, (www.sec.gov/rules/sro/nyse/34-50298.pdf), Section 303A(7)(c)(iii)(H), 23–24.

## REPORTING REQUIREMENTS

Due to the volume and complexity of the U.S. reporting requirements regarding controls for public companies, this chapter will conclude with a summary of the most common requirements and some examples. Readers should note, however, that during the present era of regulatory reform, the SEC may change these requirements. For that reason audit committee members should work with internal audit, external audit, and management to stay abreast of any modifications.

### Quarterly Certifications and Annual Assertions

Section 302 of the Sarbanes-Oxley Act requires CEOs and CFOs of U.S.-listed companies to file quarterly certifications as to their responsibility for internal control and the accuracy of the financial statements. The text of the law establishing the requirement is reproduced in Chapter 2. The SEC's rule that spells out the form of the certification for the vast majority of U.S. registrants is included in Exhibit 8.3. Audit committee members should note that the SEC expects the wording of these reports, which should be filed as exhibits to the Form 10-Q, to appear *exactly* as written below.

---

**EXHIBIT 8.3**   SEC's Required Quarterly Certification

---

I, [identify the certifying individual], certify that:

1. I have reviewed this [specify report] of [identify registrant];
2. Based on my knowledge, this report does not contain any untrue statement of a material fact or omit to state a material fact necessary to make the statements made, in light of the circumstances under which such statements were made, not misleading with respect to the period covered by this report;
3. Based on my knowledge, the financial statements, and other financial information included in this report, fairly present in all material respects the financial condition, results of operations and cash flows of the registrant as of, and for, the periods presented in this report;
4. The registrant's other certifying officer(s) and I are responsible for establishing and maintaining disclosure controls and procedures (as defined in Exchange Act Rules 13a–15(e) and 15d–15(e)) and internal control over financial reporting (as defined in Exchange Act Rules 13a–15(f) and 15d–15(f)) for the registrant and have:
   a. Designed such disclosure controls and procedures, or caused such disclosure controls and procedures to be designed under our supervision, to ensure that material information relating to the registrant, including its consolidated subsidiaries, is made known to us by others within those entities, particularly during the period in which this report is being prepared;
   b. Designed such internal control over financial reporting, or caused such internal control over financial reporting to be designed under our supervision, to provide reasonable assurance regarding the reliability of financial reporting and the

---

*(continued)*

---

**Exhibit 8.3**  *(Continued)*

---

preparation of financial statements for external purposes in accordance with generally accepted accounting principles;

c. Evaluated the effectiveness of the registrant's disclosure controls and procedures and presented in this report our conclusions about the effectiveness of the disclosure controls and procedures, as of the end of the period covered by this report based on such evaluation; and

d. Disclosed in this report any change in the registrant's internal control over financial reporting that occurred during the registrant's most recent fiscal quarter (the registrant's fourth fiscal quarter in the case of an annual report) that has materially affected, or is reasonably likely to materially affect, the registrant's internal control over financial reporting; and

5. The registrant's other certifying officer(s) and I have disclosed, based on our most recent evaluation of internal control over financial reporting, to the registrant's auditors and the audit committee of the registrant's board of directors (or persons performing the equivalent functions):

a. All significant deficiencies and material weaknesses in the design or operation of internal control over financial reporting which are reasonably likely to adversely affect the registrant's ability to record, process, summarize and report financial information; and

b. Any fraud, whether or not material, that involves management or other employees who have a significant role in the registrant's internal control over financial reporting.

Date:

_____

_____

[Signature]

_____

[Title]

---

*Note:* Reproduced from 17 C.F.R. 229.601(b)(31)(i). Note that asset-backed issuers (as defined in 17 CFR 229.1101) have different certification language. See 17 C.F.R. 229.601(b)(31)(ii) for the required text.

---

In addition to the quarterly certification requirements, management also must file on an annual basis an assertion about the effectiveness of ICFR. That report must contain the following:[21]

1. A statement of management's responsibility for establishing and maintaining adequate ICFR
2. A statement identifying the framework used by management to evaluate the effectiveness ICFR (typically the COSO Framework)

---

[21] See 17 C.F.R. 229.308.

3. Management's assessment of the effectiveness of ICFR as of the end of the most recent fiscal year, including disclosure of any material weakness in ICFR identified by management[22]
4. A statement that the external auditor's opinion includes a report on ICFR

The annual report also must include the external auditor's opinion on ICFR[23] and disclose any material changes in ICFR that occurred during the registrant's last fiscal quarter. Exhibit 8.4 contains an example of a typical annual management assertion regarding ICFR.

---

**EXHIBIT 8.4**   Sample Management Assertion under Sarbanes-Oxley Section 404

**Management's Report on Internal Control Over Financial Reporting**
Management of XYZ Corp. is responsible for establishing and maintaining adequate internal control over financial reporting as defined in Rule 13a-15(f) of the Securities Exchange Act of 1934 as amended (the Exchange Act). The Corporation's internal control over financial reporting is a process designed to provide reasonable assurance regarding the reliability of financial reporting and the preparation of financial statements for external purposes in accordance with accounting principles generally accepted in the United States of America. XYZ Corp.'s internal control over financial reporting includes those policies and procedures that (1) pertain to the maintenance of records, that in reasonable detail, accurately and fairly reflect the transactions and disposition of the Corporation's assets; (2) provide reasonable assurance that transactions are recorded as necessary to permit the preparation of the financial statements in accordance with generally accepted accounting principles and that receipts and expenditures of the Corporation are being made only in accordance with the authorizations of XYZ Corp.'s management and directors; and (3) provide reasonable assurance regarding prevention or timely detection of unauthorized acquisition, use or disposition of the Corporation's assets that could have a material impact on the financial statements.

Because of its inherent limitations, internal control over financial reporting may not prevent or detect misstatements. Also, projections of any evaluation of effectiveness to future periods are subject to the risk that controls may become inadequate due to changes in conditions, or that the degree of compliance with the policies and procedures may deteriorate.

Under the supervision and with the participation of management, including the Chief Executive Officer and the Chief Financial Officer, the Corporation conducted an evaluation of the effectiveness of the internal control over financial reporting based on the framework in "Internal Control—Integrated Framework" promulgated by the Committee of Sponsoring Organizations of the Treadway Commission, commonly referred to as the

*(continued)*

---

[22] Management is not permitted to conclude that ICFR is effective if one or more material weaknesses are present.
[23] As of the date of this writing, nonaccelerated filers would have to meet this requirement only for fiscal years ending on or after December 15, 2009. However, there has been discussion about extending the deadline. Audit committee members should verify whether the SEC retained or extended the 2009 deadline.

**Exhibit 8.4**    (*Continued*)

"COSO" criteria. Based on this evaluation under the "COSO" criteria, management concluded that the internal control over financial reporting was effective as of December 31, 20XY.

There was no change in the Corporation's internal control over financial reporting that occurred during the fourth quarter of 20XY that has materially affected or is likely to materially affect, the Corporation's internal control over financial reporting.

The effectiveness of the internal control structure over financial reporting, as of December 31, 20XY, has been audited by ABC Auditors LLP, an independent registered public accounting firm, as stated in their report included on page 70, which expresses an unqualified opinion on the effectiveness of the Corporation's internal control over financial reporting as of December 31, 20XY.

## Disclosure Controls and Procedures versus ICFR

Audit committee members may hear the terms "disclosure controls and procedures" and "internal control over financial reporting." It is important to understand the differences and similarities.

Disclosure controls and procedures include the processes and controls used to prepare *all* of an organization's filings under the Securities Exchange Act of 1934.[24] They cover all of the information required to be included in a filing, including management's discussion and analysis (MD&A), risk disclosures, *the financial statements*, and so on. The inclusion of controls and procedures that affect the financial statements means that internal control over financial reporting is subsumed in the scope of disclosure controls and procedures.

Internal control over financial reporting (ICFR) is a subset of disclosure controls and procedures that is more narrowly focused on (1) the financial statements, (2) the financial reporting processes, and (3) controls over the safeguarding of assets.

When management issues its quarterly certification under Section 302 of the Sarbanes-Oxley Act, its certification covers the disclosure controls and procedures. Management certifies that controls and other procedures are designed to ensure that information required to be disclosed in the quarterly report is recorded, processed, summarized, and reported within the time periods specified in the SEC's rules and forms. Management also is certifying that controls and procedures are in place to ensure that necessary information is accumulated and communicated to management as appropriate to allow timely decisions regarding required disclosure.[25]

---

[24] The term "disclosure controls and procedures" was first used in connection with U.S. filings under the Securities Exchange Act of 1934. It is now incorporated into other countries' securities laws. For example, beginning in 2005, Canadian securities laws require CEOs and CFOs to file certificates attesting to their disclosure controls and procedures.

[25] See 17 C.F.R. 240.13a-15(e).

When management issues an annual assertion regarding ICFR under Sarbanes-Oxley Section 404, it is asserting to the controls that provide reasonable assurance regarding the reliability of *financial reporting and the preparation of financial statements for external purposes in accordance with generally accepted accounting principles*. As such the ICFR assertion does not cover MD&A and other disclosures not related to the financial statements. The ICFR assertion covers those policies and procedures that:

1. Pertain to the maintenance of records that, in reasonable detail, accurately and fairly reflect the transactions and dispositions of the assets of the issuer.
2. Provide reasonable assurance that transactions are recorded as necessary to permit preparation of financial statements in accordance with generally accepted accounting principles, and that receipts and expenditures of the issuer are being made only in accordance with authorizations of management and directors of the issuer.
3. Provide reasonable assurance regarding prevention or timely detection of unauthorized acquisition, use or disposition of the issuer's assets that could have a material effect on the financial statements.[26]

## AUDIT COMMITTEE EXPECTATIONS

Following is a list of reasonable expectations the audit committee may have of management with respect to the controls and procedures discussed above:

1. *Understanding of objectives.* Management should understand the organization's broad business objectives, as well as the financial reporting objectives of investors and creditors. When organizations venture into new products, industries, or geographies, management should be able to articulate both the business objectives and any implications on financial reporting or other regulatory requirements.
2. *Risk assessment.* Management should be able to explain how it assesses meaningful risks to the organization's objectives. For large and/or complex organizations, this process may be very formal and occur frequently. For small, simpler companies, it may be an informal process that periodically gathers qualified individuals to discuss objectives and related risks. The audit committee's level of experience and study is an important component of its oversight capabilities in this area.
3. *Involvement of appropriate personnel.* The audit committee should be confident that, in all areas of meaningful risk, management has people in place with the right skills, abilities, authority, and objectivity to manage identified risks appropriately.
4. *Proper focus on control.* It is not possible to eliminate all risks, but it is possible to manage them to an acceptable level. Management should be able to

---

[26] See 17 C.F.R. 240.13a-15(f).

articulate how the internal control system is designed to prevent, or detect and correct, errors resulting from meaningful risks before those risks can lead to material errors.

5. *Effective monitoring procedures.* Management's belief that internal control is effective can start with a general belief that people are doing their jobs well, but it should not end there—at least not in relation to meaningful risks. Management must have feedback mechanisms in place—either built into routine operations or operating periodically (such as internal audit's annual review of an area)—that provide persuasive support for a conclusion about the effective design and operation of internal control.

## SOURCES AND SUGGESTED READINGS

Canada. "Criteria of Control (CoCo)" (www.cica.ca).

Canadian Securities Administrators (CSA). Multilateral Instrument 52-109, "Certification of Disclosure in Issuers' Annual And Interim Filings." Available at www.gov.ns.ca/nssc/docs/mi52-109.pdf.

COSO. "Guidance on Monitoring Internal Control Systems" (2009). Available at www.coso.org/IC.htm.

Germany. Stock Corporation Act, Section 91(2).

Japan. Financial Instruments and Exchange Law, Article 24-4-4 and Article 193-2.

New York Stock Exchange. Rule 303A.07(c)(iii)(D).

SAS No. 115, par. 1; and ISA 265, par. 9.

Securities and Exchange Commission. Release 33-8810, "Commission Guidance Regarding Management's Report on Internal Control Over Financial Reporting Under Section 13(a) or 15(d) of the Securities Exchange Act of 1934" (2007).

Securities and Exchange Commission. Release No. 34-50298, Section 303A(7)(c)(iii)(H). Washington, DC: SEC, August 31, 2004, 23–24. Available at www.sec.gov/rules/sro/nyse/34-50298.pdf.

South Africa. "King Code of Governance for South Africa" (2009). Available at http://african.ipapercms.dk/IOD/KINGIII/kingiiireport/.

UK. "Combined Code" (2006). Available at www.frc.org.uk/corporate/combinedcode.cfm.

UK. "Guidance on Internal Control" (also known as the "Turnbull Guidance") (2005). Available at www.frc.org.uk/corporate/internalcontrol.cfm.

U.S. Code of Federal Regulations. Available at www.gpoaccess.gov/cfr/index.html.

# Chapter 9

# Evaluating the Internal and External Audit Function

It has been said that being on an audit committee is a part-time job with full-time responsibilities. There is some truth to this. As such, audit committees rely heavily on internal and external auditors to be their eyes, ears, arms, and legs. Chapters 6 and 7 covered the important topics of overseeing the planning function of both groups. This chapter provides insight into selecting internal and external auditors and overseeing their work once it is planned and in motion.

## SELECTING AND STAFFING AN INTERNAL AUDIT FUNCTION

### Criteria for Selection

As noted in Chapter 7, there are no legal restrictions that prevent untrained and uncertified people from calling themselves "internal auditors." To fill that gap in support of a high level of professionalism, the Institute of Internal Auditors (The IIA, www.theiia.org) established certification and code of ethics requirements, providing a consistent and proven quality control filter for professionals who perform internal audit work. That level of professionalism is apparent in The IIA's standards regarding internal audit charters, as reflected in Exhibit 9.1. By going through the certification process, Certified Internal Auditors demonstrate a level of commitment to the profession of internal auditing. In addition to certification, The IIA also provides ongoing training, research, and audit tools that greatly boost the certified internal auditor's capabilities.

Staffing internal audit is a joint exercise that includes input from the audit committee and management. Together they should match their underlying expectations with the corresponding level of skill, training, and resources necessary to meet them. Several factors—such as size, complexity, level of risk, and geographic diversity—can influence decisions regarding the level of internal audit certification, if any, that may be desired. Following is a list of some other factors that audit committees and management might consider when staffing an internal audit function:

1. *A strong leader.* Internal audit leaders (often called Chief Audit Executives or Directors of Internal Audit) need to have a personality strong enough to deliver constructive criticism to both management and the audit committee. Internal audit functions exist to make organizations better by identifying existing or

**EXHIBIT 9.1**   Practice Advisory 1000-1: Internal Audit Charter

**Primary Related Standard**

**1000 Purpose, Authority, and Responsibility**

The purpose, authority, and responsibility of the internal audit activity must be formally defined in an internal audit charter, consistent with the Definition of Internal Auditing, the Code of Ethics, and the Standards. The chief audit executive must periodically review the internal audit charter and present it to senior management and the board for approval.

**Interpretation:**

*The internal audit charter is a formal document that defines the internal audit activity's purpose, authority, and responsibility. The internal audit charter establishes the internal audit activity's position within the organization; authorizes access to records, personnel, and physical properties relevant to the performance of engagements; and defines the scope of internal audit activities. Final approval of the internal audit charter resides with the board.*

1. Providing a formal, written internal audit charter is critical in managing the internal audit activity. The internal audit charter provides a recognized statement for review and acceptance by management and for approval, as documented in the minutes, by the board. It also facilitates a periodic assessment of the adequacy of the internal audit activity's purpose, authority, and responsibility, which establishes the role of the internal audit activity. If a question should arise, the internal audit charter provides a formal, written agreement with management and the board about the organization's internal audit activity.

2. The chief audit executive (CAE) is responsible for periodically assessing whether the internal audit activity's purpose, authority, and responsibility, as defined in the internal audit charter, continue to be adequate to enable the activity to accomplish its objectives. The CAE is also responsible for communicating the result of this assessment to senior management and the board.

*Source:* Institute of Internal Auditors, *The Professional Practice Framework* (Altamonte Springs, FL: Institute of Internal Auditors, 2009).

potential problems and proposing solutions. They cannot meet that objective if their leaders are afraid to bring potential problems to light.[1]

2. *Reporting relationships.* Internal audit's reporting directly to the audit committee is considered by many to be a best practice. However, as noted in Chapter 7, internal auditing standards do recognize that a dual reporting relationship between management and the board can provide the internal auditor with valuable access to both groups.[2] Regardless of the stated reporting relationship, internal audit functions should:

---

[1] The need increases to identify a strong internal audit leader if management's style is intimidating to the internal audit function or if the management team demonstrates an unwillingness to listen to internal audit. Audit committee members should be aware of the increased financial reporting risk posed by an *overly* aggressive management team.

[2] See Chapter 7, footnote 4.

1. Have frequent, open and direct lines of communication with the audit committee and/or audit committee chairperson
2. Have the freedom to execute all reasonable audit procedures that are necessary to address meaningful organizational risks
3. *Need for specialists.* Organizations with highly complex process or transaction types may need to hire or engage specialists.[3] Some examples might include:
   1. Difficult accounting (e.g., accounting for derivatives)
   2. Complex information systems
   3. Regulatory requirements
   4. Short-term special needs such as a fraud investigation
4. *Geographic diversity.* Organizations with wide geographic reach may benefit from having internal audit personnel located near significant operations. Mapping internal audit staffing to an organization's geographic footprint can reduce travel costs, increase internal audit's ability to make spot-check visits, and help address global cultural differences.
5. *Form of compensation.* Compensation mechanisms that link substantial internal audit benefits to short-term earnings projections can have a negative effect on internal audit quality. The audit committee should be confident that internal audit's form of compensation drives an appropriate focus on audit quality.
6. *Objectivity.* Objectivity or "independence" is an important trait for internal auditors. They should be familiar with the subject matter they are auditing, but they should not be so closely tied to the area that their neutrality is impaired. Many organizations draw internal audit staff out of their operating units. In fact some organizations have an established rotation of operational personnel through internal audit, providing an exchange that helps maintain internal audit's knowledge base and gives operating personnel an appreciation for internal audit's role. However, the audit committee and management should be aware of conflicts that may arise when internal auditors review the work of close friends or opine on the adequacy of procedures the internal auditors helped establish. See more regarding objectivity in the "Internal Audit Independence" section later in this chapter.

To ensure that the organizational framework for the internal auditing function is comprehensive and balanced, the audit committee should consider:

- Corporate auditing philosophy
- Corporate auditing independence
- Logistical matters, such as the size and geographic location of staff

---

[3] The need for a specialist may sometimes be fulfilled by an outsourcing arrangement rather than by hiring a full-time person.

## Internal Audit Philosophy

Continuing developments in corporate accountability and governance necessitate an ongoing appraisal of the entity's auditing philosophy. As noted in Chapter 7, internal audit can include within its scope objectives related to financial reporting, operations, and compliance with laws and regulations; but not all internal audit functions cover all three. For example, many organizations focus their internal audit functions on operational issues—looking for indicators of fraud, waste, and abuse, or improving operational efficiency. The audit committee should understand that philosophy because it means that risks related to financial reporting or regulatory compliance may not receive internal audit attention.

Understanding the auditing philosophy enables the audit committee to verify that internal audit has necessary resources. For example, if the entity has a complex computer environment, then the committee should be satisfied that internal audit has the necessary information technology expertise. Likewise, if the organization determines to change its philosophy (e.g., by increasing its focus on the financial reporting objective), then the audit committee and management will have a better idea of the types of resources that are required to support the new approach.

## Internal Audit Independence

As noted above, objectivity is an important trait for internal auditors. Appropriate levels of independence enable internal audit to (1) design and execute appropriate audit procedures in all necessary areas and (2) report fully its findings and recommendations to management and the audit committee or the full board. COSO's Guidance on Monitoring Internal Control Systems contains some helpful direction regarding the broad concept of objectivity.

> Objectivity refers to the extent to which evaluators and information sources can be expected to perform an evaluation or provide information with no concern about possible personal consequences and no vested interest in manipulating the results for personal benefit or self-preservation. Personal integrity is a primary consideration in assessing objectivity, but other, more easily observed factors include compensation incentives, reporting responsibilities, personal relationships and the degree to which individuals might be otherwise affected by the results of monitoring.[4]

In 2009 the Institute of Internal Auditors issued updated Practice Advisories (PAs) dealing with internal audit's independence and its communication with boards of directors and audit committees:

PA 1110-1. "Organizational Independence" (Exhibit 9.2)
PA 2060-1. "Reporting to Senior Management and the Board" (Exhibit 9.3)

---

[4] COSO, "Guidance on Monitoring Internal Control Systems," vol. 2 (2009), par. 33.

**EXHIBIT 9.2**   Practice Advisory 1110-1: Organizational Independence

**Primary Related Standard**

**1110–1 Organizational Independence**

The chief audit executive must report to a level within the organization that allows the internal audit activity to fulfill its responsibilities. The chief audit executive must confirm to the board, at least annually, the organizational independence of the internal audit activity.

1. Support from senior management and the board assists the internal audit activity in gaining the cooperation of engagement clients and performing their work free from interference.

2. The chief audit executive (CAE), reporting functionally to the board and administratively to the organization's chief executive officer, facilitates organizational independence. At a minimum the CAE needs to report to an individual in the organization with sufficient authority to promote independence and to ensure broad audit coverage, adequate consideration of engagement communications, and appropriate action on engagement recommendations.

3. Functional reporting to the board typically involves the board:
   • Approving the internal audit activity's overall charter.
   • Approving the internal audit risk assessment and related audit plan.
   • Receiving communications from the CAE on the results of the internal audit activities or other matters that the CAE determines are necessary, including private meetings with the CAE without management present, as well as annual confirmation of the internal audit activity's organizational independence.
   • Approving all decisions regarding the performance evaluation, appointment, or removal of the CAE.
   • Approving the annual compensation and salary adjustment of the CAE.
   • Making appropriate inquiries of management and the CAE to determine whether there is audit scope or budgetary limitations that impede the ability of the internal audit activity to execute its responsibilities.

4. Administrative reporting is the reporting relationship within the organization's management structure that facilitates the day-to-day operations of the internal audit activity. Administrative reporting typically includes:
   • Budgeting and management accounting.
   • Human resource administration, including personnel evaluations and compensation.
   • Internal communications and information flows.
   • Administration of the internal audit activity's policies and procedures.

*Source:* Institute of Internal Auditors, *The Professional Practice Framework* (Altamonte Springs, FL: The IIA, 2009).

---

**EXHIBIT 9.3**   Practice Advisory 2060-1: Reporting to Senior Management and the Board

---

**Primary Related Standard**

**2060 Reporting to Board and Senior Management**

The chief audit executive must report periodically to senior management and the board on the internal audit activity's purpose, authority, responsibility, and performance relative to its plan. Reporting must also include significant risk exposures and control issues, including fraud risks, governance issues, and other matters needed or requested by senior management and the board.

**Interpretation:**

*The frequency and content of reporting are determined in discussion with senior management and the board and depend on the importance of the information to be communicated and the urgency of the related actions to be taken by senior management or the board.*

1.  The chief audit executive (CAE) needs to submit activity reports to senior management and the board periodically. Activity reports highlight significant engagement observations and recommendations and inform senior management and the board of significant deviations from approved engagement work schedules, staffing plans, and financial budgets; the reasons for the deviations; and action taken or needed.

2.  Significant engagement observations are those conditions that, in the judgment of the CAE, could adversely affect the organization. Significant engagement observations may include conditions dealing with fraud, irregularities, illegal acts, errors, inefficiency, waste, ineffectiveness, conflicts of interest, and control weaknesses.

3.  Senior management and the board make decisions on the appropriate action to be taken regarding significant engagement observations and recommendations. Senior management and the board may decide to assume the risk of not correcting the reported condition because of cost or other considerations. The board needs to be informed of senior management's decisions on all significant engagement observations and recommendations.

4.  The CAE considers whether it is appropriate to inform the board regarding previously reported, significant engagement observations and recommendations in those instances when senior management and the board assumed the risk of not correcting the reported condition. This may be necessary when there have been significant changes that affect the risk profile.

---

*Source:* Institute of Internal Auditors, *The Professional Practices Framework* (Altamonte Springs, FL: The IIA, 2009)

---

## Structure and Logistics

Organizations, depending largely on their nature, size, and complexity, have different internal auditing needs. Many organizations audit certain locations or lines of business every year, and others do so on a two- or three-year rotation. The selection of major areas is ordinarily based on the materiality and relative risk for

**EXHIBIT 9.4**   Sample Internal Audit Organization Chart

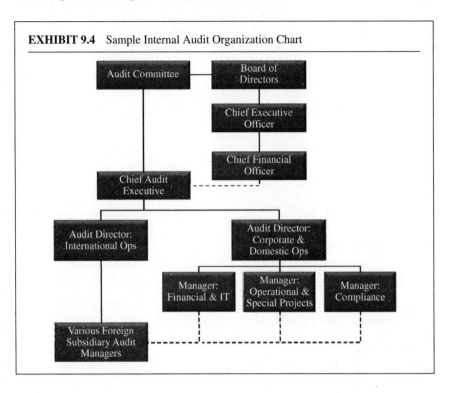

the financial audit (discussed in Chapter 5). In connection with operational or compliance audits, it may be useful to develop some estimate of the relative profit contribution or risk compared to the related audit costs. Consequently, the committee should review the plans and budgets of the internal auditors in relation to the entity's auditing needs and potential auditing benefits.

Equally important, the committee should review the organization chart of the internal auditing function to determine that it is balanced in accordance with the audit plan. An illustrative organization chart in Exhibit 9.4 shows how the internal audit function of a multinational enterprise might be organized on a centralized basis. Note the CAE's dotted-line connection to the CFO. Note also that the audit director for international operations (in this example) oversees local operational and compliance audits in the various foreign locations, but the foreign audit managers also provide assistance to the Corporate and Domestic side for audit projects that require global resources. This structure enables centralized control of audit work related to financial reporting and other significant, enterprise-wide risks.[5]

Anthony J. Ridley, retired general auditor of the Ford Motor Company and past chairman of the Institute of Internal Auditors, recommends that chief audit executives consider an audit committee event matrix for important events that

---

[5] Because the chart is simplified, the organizational arrangements will vary and contain more detail in practice. The objective is to show the reporting and functional relationships of the internal auditing function.

occur outside regularly scheduled meetings. Ridley points out, "The easiest way to resolve this quandary [i.e., the risk of missing a major event] is to ask your audit committee in advance about the things they want to know—and when—and then capture their preferences in an event matrix for ongoing use. The matrix can eliminate much of the guesswork related to providing information to your audit committee." Some of the generic events to be included in the matrix are

- Defalcations and ethics violations
- Litigation
- Regulatory concerns and adverse publicity
- Financial reporting
- Independence and effectiveness of auditors[6]

## Considerations about Outsourcing

Some organizations find it necessary to outsource some or all of their internal audit function. Common reasons include temporary staff shortages, needs for specialized skills, coverage of remote business locations, special project work, and supplemental staff to meet tight deadlines. Small organizations in particular may find it necessary to explore outsourcing due to their inability to hire permanent or full-time internal auditors.

In the late 1990s and early 2000s, many companies outsourced their internal audit functions to the same firm that conducted their external audits. The practice was advantageous in that it improved efficiency, but was disadvantageous in that it impaired the objectivity of both the internal and external auditors.

Most public companies today are prohibited by statute or regulation from outsourcing internal audit services to their external auditors. However, even if it were allowed by law or statute, The IIA does not believe that internal auditing should be outsourced to the same external audit firm that audits the organization's financial statements.[7]

The IIA suggests considering the following factors when evaluating possible outsourcing arrangements:[8]

- Independence of the external service provider
- Allegiance of in-house resources versus that of external service provider
- Professional standards followed by the external service provider
- Qualifications of the service provider
- Staffing—training, turnover, rotation of staff, management
- Flexibility in staffing resources to meet engagement needs or special requests
- Availability of resources
- Retention of institutional knowledge for future assignments
- Access to best practice or insight to alternative approaches

---

[6] Anthony J. Ridley, "An Audit Committee Event Matrix," *Internal Auditor* 57, no. 2 (April 2000): 54.
[7] See The IIA's paper *10 Steps to Effective Co-sourcing* (May 30, 2008).
[8] See The IIA's paper *The Role of Internal Auditing in Resourcing the Internal Audit Activity*, 4.

- Culture of the organization—receptiveness to external service providers
- Insight into the organization by the external service provider
- Coverage of remote locations
- Coordination with in-house internal auditing
- Coordination with external auditor
- Use of internal auditing as a training ground for internal promotions
- Retention, access to, and ownership of work papers
- Acquisition and availability of specialty skills
- Cost considerations
- Good-standing membership in an appropriate professional organization

The IIA provides additional guidance on outsourcing in the Practice Advisory shown in Exhibit 9.5.

---

**EXHIBIT 9.5** Practice Advisory 1210.A1-1: Obtaining External Services to Support or Complement the Internal Audit Activity

**Primary Related Standard**

**1210.A1** The chief audit executive must obtain competent advice and assistance if the internal auditors lack the knowledge, skills, or other competencies needed to perform all or part of the engagement.

1. Each member of the internal audit activity need not be qualified in all disciplines. The internal audit activity may use external service providers or internal resources that are qualified in disciplines such as accounting, auditing, economics, finance, statistics, information technology, engineering, taxation, law, environmental affairs, and other areas as needed to meet the internal audit activity's responsibilities.

2. An external service provider is a person or firm, independent of the organization, who has special knowledge, skill, and experience in a particular discipline. External service providers include actuaries, accountants, appraisers, culture or language experts, environmental specialists, fraud investigators, lawyers, engineers, geologists, security specialists, statisticians, information technology specialists, the organization's external auditors, and other audit organizations. An external service provider may be engaged by the board, senior management, or the chief audit executive (CAE).

3. External service providers may be used by the internal audit activity in connection with, among other things:
   - Achievement of the objectives in the engagement work schedule.
   - Audit activities where a specialized skill and knowledge are needed such as information technology, statistics, taxes, or language translations.
   - Valuations of assets such as land and buildings, works of art, precious gems, investments, and complex financial instruments.
   - Determination of quantities or physical condition of certain assets such as mineral and petroleum reserves.
   - Measuring the work completed and to be completed on contracts in progress.

*(continued)*

---

**Exhibit 9.5**   *(Continued)*

---

- Fraud and security investigations.
- Determination of amounts, by using specialized methods such as actuarial determinations of employee benefit obligations.
- Interpretation of legal, technical, and regulatory requirements.
- Evaluation of the internal audit activity's quality assurance and improvement program in conformance with the *Standards*.
- Mergers and acquisitions.
- Consulting on risk management and other matters.

4. When the CAE intends to use and rely on the work of an external service provider, the CAE needs to consider the competence, independence, and objectivity of the external service provider as it relates to the particular assignment to be performed. The assessment of competency, independence, and objectivity is also needed when the external service provider is selected by senior management or the board, and the CAE intends to use and rely on the external service provider's work. When the selection is made by others and the CAE's assessment determines that he or she should not use and rely on the work of the external service provider, communication of such results is needed to senior management or the board, as appropriate.

5. The CAE determines that the external service provider possesses the necessary knowledge, skills, and other competencies to perform the engagement by considering:
   - Professional certification, license, or other recognition of the external service provider's competence in the relevant discipline.
   - Membership of the external service provider in an appropriate professional organization and adherence to that organization's code of ethics.
   - The reputation of the external service provider. This may include contacting others familiar with the external service provider's work.
   - The external service provider's experience in the type of work being considered.
   - The extent of education and training received by the external service provider in disciplines that pertain to the particular engagement.
   - The external service provider's knowledge and experience in the industry in which the organization operates.

6. The CAE needs to assess the relationship of the external service provider to the organization and to the internal audit activity to ensure that independence and objectivity are maintained throughout the engagement. In performing the assessment, the CAE verifies that there are no financial, organizational, or personal relationships that will prevent the external service provider from rendering impartial and unbiased judgments and opinions when performing or reporting on the engagement.

7. The CAE assesses the independence and objectivity of the external service provider by considering:
   - The financial interest the external service provider may have in the organization.
   - The personal or professional affiliation the external service provider may have to the board, senior management, or others within the organization.
   - The relationship the external service provider may have had with the organization or the activities being reviewed.

- The extent of other ongoing services the external service provider may be performing for the organization.
- Compensation or other incentives that the external service provider may have.

8. If the external service provider is also the organization's external auditor and the nature of the engagement is extended audit services, the CAE needs to ascertain that work performed does not impair the external auditor's independence. Extended audit services refer to those services beyond the requirements of audit standards generally accepted by external auditors. If the organization's external auditors act or appear to act as members of senior management, management, or employees of the organization, then their independence is impaired. Additionally, external auditors may provide the organization with other services such as tax and consulting. Independence needs to be assessed in relation to the full range of services provided to the organization.

9. To ascertain that the scope of work is adequate for the purposes of the internal audit activity, the CAE obtains sufficient information regarding the scope of the external service provider's work. It may be prudent to document these and other matters in an engagement letter or contract. To accomplish this, the CAE reviews the following with the external service provider:
- Objectives and scope of work including deliverables and time frames.
- Specific matters expected to be covered in the engagement communications.
- Access to relevant records, personnel, and physical properties.
- Information regarding assumptions and procedures to be employed.
- Ownership and custody of engagement working papers, if applicable.
- Confidentiality and restrictions on information obtained during the engagement.
- Where applicable, conformance with the Standards and the internal audit activity's standards for working practices.

10. In reviewing the work of an external service provider, the CAE evaluates the adequacy of work performed, which includes sufficiency of information obtained to afford a reasonable basis for the conclusions reached and the resolution of exceptions or other unusual matters.

11. When the CAE issues engagement communications, and an external service provider was used, the CAE may, as appropriate, refer to such services provided. The external service provider needs to be informed and, if appropriate, concurrence should be obtained before making such reference in engagement communications.

*Source:* Institute of Internal Auditors, *The Professional Practice Framework* (Altamonte Springs, FL: The IIA, 2009).

## MONITORING THE INTERNAL AUDIT FUNCTION

The audit committee's routine oversight of internal audit is beneficial for the following reasons. First, it enhances the audit staff's independence and strengthens its image in the corporate structure. Second, the audit committee can help coordinate internal and external audit activity, thus improving the efficiency of both. Third, an effective internal audit function assists the audit committee in discharging its responsibilities in light of its limited time and oversight capacity.

## Appraising the Quality of the Auditing Staff

The IIA's Standards for the Professional Practice of Internal Auditing require that engagements be "performed with proficiency and due professional care."[9] They also require the CAE to "develop and maintain a quality assurance and improvement program."[10] CAEs should be able to articulate to the audit committee how they meet these standards. Criteria for which the audit committee should look include the following:

- Proficiency
- Due professional care
- Continuing professional development
- Internal and external quality assessments
- Reporting on the quality assurance and improvement program

The audit committee also should inquire of the independent auditor regarding the quality of auditing personnel in relation to:

1. The professional qualifications and educational backgrounds of the staff.
2. The use of professional training and development programs for the corporate audit staff. Such programs are available through several professional accounting societies and especially through the Institute of Internal Auditors.[11] Another possible source of training is in-house professional development programs delivered by the independent accounting firm.
3. The performance appraisal and evaluation system. These might include assessments of (1) an auditor's technical knowledge, (2) compliance with audit policies and procedures, (3) administrative skills and work habits, and (4) effectiveness in interpersonal relationships.

In addition audit committee members may find the questions in Exhibit 9.6 helpful.

While each audit committee may develop its own approach to monitoring the activities of the internal audit function, the following summary thoughts should be helpful. In general audit committees should:

1. Assist in the overall internal auditing policy determination and approve such policies to ensure that the staff has authority commensurate with its responsibilities.
2. Review the scope of the internal and external auditing plans in order to maximize the resources allocated to the audit function and minimize the outside auditing fees.
3. Review copies of the internal auditing reports and critically evaluate findings, recommendations, management's response, and courses of action taken. Also,

---

[9] The IIA, *International Professional Practices Framework* (IPPF), Standard 1200 (2009).
[10] Ibid., Standard 1300 (2009).
[11] Such as The IIA's *Certified Internal Auditor* and *Certified Information Systems Auditor* programs.

---

**EXHIBIT 9.6** Vital Checkpoints: Internal Audit Questions for the Audit Committee

---

*Mission Statement.* Each company should develop and disseminate an annual policy statement re the objectives of internal audit.

- ✓ Does a mission statement exist for the internal audit function?
- ✓ Is this mission statement approved by the chief executive officer or senior management?
- ✓ Are the internal audit objectives known and understood by all levels of management?

*Annual Internal Audit Plan.* The senior internal auditor should prepare an annual plan setting forth goals and objectives such as:

- Planned level of audit coverage
- Staffing
- Areas of audit risk
- Degree of coordination with external audit function
- Special projects
- Annual cost
- Compliance with corporate codes of conduct
    - ✓ Is this plan reviewed and approved by appropriate levels of management?
    - ✓ Was this plan reviewed with the external auditors?
    - ✓ Were their comments and/or recommendations incorporated in the plan?
    - ✓ Did they note any deficiencies in the plan that were not incorporated in the final plan?
    - ✓ Has management placed any scope restrictions on the extent of audit coverage?
    - ✓ Does the plan provide coverage of the company's computer control functions?
    - ✓ Do you have the necessary human resources in terms of trained, experienced staff to achieve the annual plan?

*Progress Reports.* The internal auditor should report annually on progress in meeting the previously approved annual plan:

- ✓ Has management adequately addressed the comments and recommendations set forth in your reports?
- ✓ Who receives copies of your reports?
- ✓ Are copies of your recent reports made available to the external auditor?
- ✓ Do they receive appropriate management support?
- ✓ Were there any significant recommendations relating to control weaknesses or company policy that have not been adequately addressed and corrected?
- ✓ Do you monitor that the necessary corrective action has in fact been implemented?
- ✓ Did your audit procedures uncover any instances of employee fraud, questionable or illegal payments, or violations of laws or regulations? (Follow-up questions, as appropriate.)
- ✓ Were any limitations placed on the phase of your audit plan during this period?
- ✓ Did you receive appropriate management support and cooperation?

*(continued)*

**Exhibit 9.6** *(Continued)*

✓ In connection with the audit functions completed during this period, did you review all the related computer control functions? Were they deemed adequate?

✓ Is the computer security system reviewed in connection with these audit procedures? Are they adequate?

✓ Does each computer system reviewed have an adequate backup system and disaster contingency plan?

*Other Areas.* Additional areas can be covered in private meetings with internal auditors as appropriate:

✓ Are you satisfied with the adequacy and competence of financial management in the areas subject to audit review?

✓ Does the internal audit function receive the appropriate level of support from senior management and operating management?

✓ Are you satisfied with the level of cooperation and support from the external auditors?

✓ Are the internal and external audit functions coordinated to maximize the effectiveness of both groups and to minimize any unnecessary duplication of effort?

✓ Have there been any material changes in the internal audit staff that would adversely impact your ability to complete your objective for the current period?

✓ To what extent, if any, have you been assigned special projects that have adversely impacted your ability to achieve your goals?

✓ Are you satisfied that the "tone at the top" is appropriate?

✓ Has the company taken the appropriate action with respect to management comments submitted by the external auditors?

*Further Questions.* Additional internal auditing questions can be addressed privately to financial personnel, senior management, or the external auditor, as appropriate:

✓ Are you satisfied with respect to the level of performance of the internal audit function?

✓ Do the internal auditors perform their duties and responsibilities objectively and professionally?

✓ Do they perform their audits effectively?

✓ Are they considered constructive and effective by operating management?

✓ Do they receive the appropriate level of management support and cooperation?

✓ Does an appropriate degree of mutual respect exist between the internal and external auditors?

✓ Is there an effective working relationship between the internal and external auditors to maximize effectiveness and minimize cost?

---

*Source:* Richard S. Hickok and Jules Zimmerman, *Vital Checkpoints: Internal Audit Questions for the Audit Committee* (New York: Hickok Associates, Inc., 1990). Copyright © 1990 by Hickok Associates, Inc. Reprinted with permission.

review the disposition of the recommendations in the independent auditor's management letter.

4. Review and appraise the staff's organization regarding its auditing philosophy, independence, and logistical operations.

5. Assess the quality of the auditing personnel and training to ensure that the internal auditing function is adequately staffed. Also, the auditing work should be properly planned, supervised, and reviewed.

6. Assure the CAE that the audit committee supports his function in the corporate structure and the director has access to the committee and the functional areas within the entity. Also, obtain assurance that the staff is receiving the proper cooperation from management.

7. Determine the need for special assignments, such as complex areas of accounting or evaluation of computer security.

## SELECTING AND EVALUATING AN EXTERNAL AUDITOR

While nothing prevents untrained and/or uncertified persons from calling themselves internal auditors, such is not true for external auditors. Most countries, and certainly all significant industrialized countries, have laws prohibiting people from calling themselves "independent public accountants"[12] without appropriate training and certification. These restrictions serve as a protective gate for investors, management, and the audit committee by helping to ensure that only qualified people conduct external audits. Certification, however, is only the first hurdle.

Few decisions that audit committees make are more important than the recommendation or selection of external auditors.[13] Audit committee members should, therefore, be diligent in selecting the right auditor, and in evaluating the auditor's performance throughout the engagement. Exhibit 9.7 presents some selection criteria for audit committee consideration. These same criteria also can be used to evaluate the auditor's performance during or at the end of an audit.

### Nonaudit Services

The Sarbanes-Oxley Act prohibits external auditors of U.S. public companies from conducting certain nonaudit services and has established a requirement for boards (usually through their audit committees) to approve any other nonaudit services that are not specifically prohibited. The prohibited services are based on

---

[12] Other terms subject to the same limitations may include "certified public accountant" or "chartered accountant."

[13] In some situations (such as the appointment of the external auditor for a company listed on a U.S. exchange) the audit committee must select and engage the external auditor. In other countries, and with most private organizations, the audit committee might merely *recommend* an audit firm to management, who then makes the decision regarding engaging that firm.

**EXHIBIT 9.7**    External Auditor Selection/Evaluation Criteria

| | |
|---|---|
| 1. Industry experience | Most auditors have experience performing audits of routine, domestic manufacturing companies. Most have also audited benefit plans; but when organizations become large and complex, or when they venture into complicated industries (like the software industry or finance), audit committees need to make sure the external auditors have an appropriate level of experience. This qualification may be necessary for the whole team or for part of the team, depending on the circumstances. |
| 2. Support network available within the firm | No auditor can answer every technical accounting question. The audit committee should be confident that the external auditor has access to specialized technical skills where appropriate. Those resources sometimes are located in a national office, but it is helpful if the firm has specialized resources spread around its geographic footprint. Audit committee members might ask the prospective auditor to describe the process she would go through to answer a technical question that could not be handled by the engagement team alone. |
| 3. Independence | External auditors are subject to strict independence requirements. In most countries, they are also required to communicate their independence to the audit committee. The audit committee should be confident that the external auditor has appropriately evaluated and reported the firm's independence, including considerations of family relationships, investment holdings, or other business relationships. These considerations begin with the immediate engagement team, but they extend to personnel in the firm's local office and—in most public company situations—to the firm as a whole. |
| 4. Reasonableness of audit plan | The audit committee should be confident that the prospective auditor has a reasonable vision for the scope of the audit. That vision should include audit work at or on locations that, on their own, are material to the financial statements. It might also include some smaller locations on a rotating basis or on a limited-scope basis (e.g., testing only balances and controls relevant to inventory or revenue recognition). The audit committee should be confident that the auditor will develop a scope that is adequate but not excessive. |
| | The committee should resist gravitating automatically to the lowest bid in a competitive bid situation. Unusually low bids can indicate the auditor's lack of understanding regarding the necessary scope. Others represent loss-leaders with a plan to make up the difference through special billing. A good way to evaluate bids is to require the proposing firms to quote both hours and fees by major audit area. Committee members then can see where the firms |

|  | differ on hourly rates (which may reflect on the level of personnel they plan to do the work) or on the number of hours (which may reflect on the adequacy of the audit plan). |
|---|---|
| 5. Ability to toe the line | As with Chief Audit Executives, audit committees should be confident that the audit partner in particular has the fortitude to deliver constructive criticism. Audit committees learn of this attribute over time by asking, in executive session, open-ended questions about management's and/or internal audit's performance. The auditor may lack strength if he demonstrates discomfort with the questions, or never or rarely identifies opportunities for improvement. |
|  | This quality is more difficult to evaluate in a new prospective auditor, thus the audit committee may ask (on a no-name basis) about the nature of issues the auditor has communicated to other audit committees. The committee may also ask references to comment on the auditor's ability to communicate difficult information. |
| 6. Form and frequency of communications<br>　a. With management<br>　b. With internal audit<br>　c. With the audit committee | With respect to management and internal audit, the audit committee should expect communication to be frequent and open. It may also reasonably expect the auditor to spend meaningful time in operations talking to managers and employees outside of the executive suite. |
|  | Auditing standards require the auditor to have certain types of communications with the audit committee. The section below, titled **REPORTING BY THE EXTERNAL AUDITOR**, describes those types of communications. At a high level, apart from a demonstrated ability to "toe the line" as discussed above, the audit committee should expect: |
|  | 1. An audit planning discussion early in the year that describes what the auditor plans to do, where he plans to do it, and how much effort he expects it to take.<br>2. Interim (usually quarterly) audit updates that measure progress against the plan established in the planning meeting.<br>3. Immediate communication of major issues such as a suspected fraud, major internal control problem or indication of a prior-period material error.<br>4. A wrap-up presentation that covers all of the required communications discussed below, brings the interim status up to date, and delivers any meaningful recommendations for improvement. |
| 5. Lack of surprises | Audit surprises, in this context, come in two forms: those related to last-minute audit adjustments and those related to last-minute cost overruns. Both can be caused either by the company's failure to get necessary information to the auditor in a timely manner or by the auditor's failure to perform necessary procedures early enough to detect the problem. Such surprises normally are avoidable with |

*(continued)*

**Exhibit 9.7** (*Continued*)

|  |  |
|---|---|
|  | proper interim communication as described above. At every opportunity the audit committee should ask, and the auditor should offer, a status update on information requested from the organization. |
|  | At the beginning of the audit, most auditors provide a list of schedules and information they expect the organization to provide. These often are called "prepared by client" lists or "PBCs," and typically have an agreed-upon date of delivery. Auditors schedule their staffing according to these dates. However, if those dates arrive and the information is not ready, the auditor begins incurring downtime, which later leads to overruns and rushed audit procedures when the information becomes available. Unfortunately, many auditors fail to communicate with the audit committee when these issues arise. Audit committees may find it helpful, therefore, to inquire routinely about the status of requested PBCs. |
| 6. Partner and manager involvement | A typical audit includes between 20 and 30 percent partner/manager time. Some audits, such as simple benefit plan audits, may require less, while highly complex audits may require more. In addition, the mix of partner and manager time varies depending on the number of audit managers and their level of experience. |
|  | In truth, the *quality* of the hours spent, especially by the partner, is more important than the *number* of hours. Early partner involvement in the planning process is critical to designing an effective and efficient audit. When the plan is complete, the partner should perform frequent interim reviews of the audit work. The audit committee also should be confident that the partner is spending enough review time in the field rather than in the firm's offices. |
| 7. Quality control procedures | Auditors of public companies are required to have concurring or second partner reviews,[a] often called "engagement quality reviews." The audit committee should inquire about the skills and involvement of the concurring partner, who should have appropriate industry experience and be available to the engagement team on an as-needed basis. |
| 8. Use of the work of others | The audit committee should be confident that the external auditor is making appropriate but not excessive use of the internal control testing performed by others, including internal audit.[b] |
| 9. Usefulness of recommendations | External auditors are in a unique position to add value beyond the assurance they provide through their audit opinion. Compared to most external parties, the auditors have unprecedented access to business operations and the related books and records. Further, they gain valuable knowledge from best practices they see in many other companies. |

| | A good external auditor is always looking for ways to help organizations be more effective and efficient, especially relative to financial reporting processes. Audit committees should be confident that the auditors they select have a continual-improvement mindset. |
| --- | --- |
| 10. Team chemistry | External auditors have to balance their client relationships with their duty to the users of financial statements. Audit committees should expect the entire audit team to be courteous, respectful, and reliable and, at the same time, to maintain an objective attitude. Auditing standards refer to this as a "healthy skepticism."[c] Committee members should make periodic inquiries of management regarding the relationship with the auditor, looking equally for signs of excessive tension and excessive collegiality.[d] The committee should ask the auditor about the nature of management's interactions. |

---

[a] See Preliminary note to Rule 2-01 of Regulation S-X, 17 CFR 210.2-01.

[b] See the Sarbanes-Oxley Act of 2002, Section 201.

[c] The 2009 SEC Handbook, Section 603.07 states, "SEC registrants may, of course, change auditors at their discretion. It is imperative, however, that when a new auditor is engaged that auditor possess the integrity, objectivity and independence required by professional and Commission standards. The auditor must, at all times, maintain a 'healthy skepticism' to ensure that a review of a client's accounting treatment is fair and impartial."

[d] The AICPA's Audit Committee Toolkit (2004) states: "In considering information gathered through the process of evaluating the independent auditor, it is important that the audit committee give consideration to the source of the information. For example, if the CFO/controller comments that they believe the auditor went too far in certain areas, that would probably carry less weight in your deliberations than if the CFO/controller comments that certain areas were not tested adequately. As with all deliberative processes, the audit committee should consider the different perspectives and motivations of those having input into the deliberations."

three primary criteria: (1) an auditor cannot function in the role of management, (2) an auditor cannot audit her own work, and (3) an auditor cannot serve in an external advocacy role for her client.[14] The prohibited services include:[15]

1. Bookkeeping or other services related to the accounting records or financial statements of the audit client.
2. Financial information systems design and implementation.
3. Appraisal or valuation services, fairness opinions, or contribution-in-kind reports.
4. Actuarial services.
5. Internal audit outsourcing services.
6. Management functions or human resources.

---

[14] See Preliminary note to Rule 2-01 of Regulation S-X, 17 CFR 210.2-01.

[15] See the Sarbanes-Oxley Act of 2002, Section 201.

7. Broker or dealer, investment adviser, or investment banking services.
8. Legal services and expert services unrelated to the audit.
9. Any other service that the PCAOB determines, by regulation, is impermissible.

The above prohibited nonaudit services are U.S. requirements, but they also reflect the types of services that audit committees of non-U.S. companies may consider as potential impairments to an external auditor's objectivity. Further, some international organizations currently are exploring equivalent, or even more stringent, prohibitions on nonaudit services.[16]

Thousands of examples of good audit committee preapproval policies are available on the Internet through the investor relations section of most public company Web sites. To provide readers with the current models, and to preserve space, links to two such examples are presented below.

- McDonalds Corporation: www.aboutmcdonalds.com/mcd/investors/corporate_governance/audit_committee_policy.html
- PepsiCo Inc.: www.pepsico.com/Investors/Corporate-Governance/Policy-for-Audit-Audit_Related-and-Non_Audit-Services.html

## REPORTING BY THE EXTERNAL AUDITOR

Auditing standards require the external auditor to communicate certain things to "those charged with governance," which usually includes management and the board (through the audit committee).[17] Chapter 10 covers in detail the required communications between auditors and audit committees. In general the audit committee should expect the auditor to communicate:

1. The auditor's responsibilities in relation to the financial statement audit
2. Planned scope and timing of the audit
3. Significant findings from the audit
4. Auditor independence

Exhibit 9.8 lists the types of communications the audit committee should expect from the auditor and a general time frame within which those communications might be made.

In addition to the communications above, the audit committee might inquire of the external auditor regarding the results of any recent regulatory inspections (such as an inspection by the PCAOB). The audit committee might also ask the auditor to provide summaries of new or pending standards, regulations, or requirements related to accounting, tax, or corporate governance.

---

[16] The UK Financial Reporting Council's (FRC's) "Guidance on Audit Committees" (October 2008) establishes broad expectations of audit committee oversight of nonaudit services. In addition—as of the date of this writing—the FRC's Auditing Practices Board is set to begin a consultation on nonaudit fees that could result in greater prohibitions than those outlined in the United States.
[17] See ISA 260 and SAS No. 114.

**EXHIBIT 9.8**   Required External Auditor Communications to the Audit Committee

| Communications | When Delivered[*] |
|---|---|
| Independence and retention matters | Prior to acceptance and annually |
| Auditor's responsibilities under the relevant auditing standards | Prior to commencing services |
| Audit committee preapproval of services | Prior to commencing services |
| Fraud and illegal acts | When event becomes known |
| Inquiries and investigations by authorities | When event becomes known |
| Significant accounting policies, judgments, and estimates | End of audit |
| Auditor's judgments about the quality of accounting principles | End of audit |
| Audit adjustments, including uncorrected misstatements | End of audit |
| Disagreements with management | End of audit |
| Difficulties encountered when performing the audit | End of audit |
| Management's consultations with other accountants | End of audit |
| Material weaknesses and significant deficiencies in internal control | Prior to issuing report |
| Auditor's internal quality control procedures | Prior to issuing report |
| Material issues raised during most recent quality control or peer review | Prior to issuing report |
| Material written communications with management | Prior to filing |

[*] If necessary, all of these matters should be discussed promptly on an interim basis with the audit committee.

## SOURCES AND SUGGESTED READINGS

American Institute of Certified Public Accountants, "Audit Committee Toolkit." New York: AICPA, 2004.

"An Ounce of Prevention," *Journal of Accountancy* (October 2007). Available at www.journalofaccountancy.com/Issues/2007/Oct/AnOunceOfPrevention.

Brannen, Laurie. "Upfront: Top 10 Questions In Establishing An Internal Audit Function." *Business Finance Magazine*. March 1, 2004.

CCH Incorporated. *2009 SEC Handbook: Rules and Forms for Financial Statements and Related Disclosure, 19th Edition.* Section 603.07. December 2008.

COSO. "Guidance on Monitoring Internal Control Systems" (2009). Available at www.coso.org/IC.htm.

Cummings, John. "10 Best Practices for Co-Sourcing Internal Audit." *Business Finance Magazine.* June 16, 2008.

Institute of Internal Auditors. Position Paper, "The Role of Internal Auditing in Resourcing the Internal Audit Activity" (January 2009).

Institute of Internal Auditors. "10 Steps to Effective Co-sourcing." (May 30, 2008). Available at www.theiia.org/theiia/newsroom/news-releases/index.cfm?i=6183.

Institute of Internal Auditors. *The Professional Practices Framework.* Altamonte Springs, FL: Institute of Internal Auditors, 2009.

International Federation of Accountants. ISA 260. "Communication with Those Charged with Governance" (2009).

International Federation of Accountants. ISA 265. "Communicating Deficiencies in Internal Control to Those Charged with Governance and Management" (2009).

Morrow, John F., and Joan Pastor. "Eight Habits of Highly Effective Audit Committees." *Journal of Accountancy*, September 2007. Available at www.journalofaccountancy.com/Issues/2007/Sep/EightHabitsOfHighlyEffectiveAuditCommittees.htm.

Ridley, Anthony J. "An Audit Committee Event Matrix." *Internal Auditor 57, no. 2 (April 2000): 53–56.*

Sarbanes-Oxley Act of 2002, Section 201.

Statements on Auditing Standards No. 114, "The Auditor's Communication with Those Charged with Governance" (2006), and its international counterpart, ISA 260.

UK Financial Reporting Council (FRC). "Guidance on Audit Committees" (October 2008). Available at www.frc.org.uk/documents/pagemanager/frc/Smith_Guidance/Guidance%20on%20Audit%20Committees%20October%202008.pdf.

# Chapter 10

# Communications between Auditors and Audit Committees

One of the more important responsibilities of the audit committee involves a number of communications with the independent auditor about the review of management's accounting policies that are used in accounting for the transactions of the company, and the cooperation between management and the auditor. Through such communications and review of the significant accounting policies and critical accounting policies and estimates, the audit committee can obtain assurance on behalf of the board of directors that management is fulfilling its financial accounting reporting responsibilities. The review is conducted with the independent public accountants in order to determine the integrity and objectivity of the financial statements, based on management's formulation and implementation of the corporate accounting policies.

In its issuing release (Release No. 33-8183) dealing with audit committee interactions with auditors concerning accounting policy issues, the SEC famously quoted Warren Buffett on the role and responsibilities of audit committees:

> Their function . . . is to hold the auditor's feet to the fire. And, I suggest . . . the audit committee ask [questions] of the auditors [including]: if the auditor were solely responsible for preparation of the company's financial statements, would they have been prepared in any way differently than the manner selected by management? They should inquire as to both material and non-material differences. If the auditor would have done anything differently than management, then explanations should be made of management's argument and the auditor's response.

## AUDIT COMMITTEE'S REVIEW OBJECTIVE

The audit committee represents an independent check on corporate management with respect to its responsibilities for reporting its stewardship accountability to outside constituencies. In particular, the audit committee is responsible for assuring that management has prepared the financial statements in conformity with generally accepted accounting principles (GAAP). It must assess not only management's judgment regarding the application of accounting principles but also the adequacy of the disclosures in the financial statements.[1] The American Institute of Certified Public Accountants summarizes the committee's review objective in this way:

> The audit committee should meet with management and the external auditor to review the financial statements and the audit results. This is an especially important function of the audit committee.

> Some audit committees confine their review of the financial statements to major or critical items, while others examine the statements in considerable detail. The scope of the review is something each audit committee must set forth for itself, bearing in mind that at the conclusion of the meeting the members should have a comprehensive understanding of any major financial reporting problems encountered, how they were resolved, and whether the resolution is satisfactory. Factors affecting the extent of the review include the committee's confidence in management, the system of internal accounting control, and the external auditor; the existence of any unresolved differences between the auditor and management; the extent of adjustments or additional disclosures, if any, proposed by the auditor; and any unusual occurrences during the year. The committee's major concern throughout the review should be whether the financial statements fairly present the company's financial results in conformity with generally accepted accounting principles.[2]

## SEC Rules

In January 2003, the Securities and Exchange Commission issued final rules in Release No. 33-8183 addressing independent auditors' responsibilities to report on a timely basis certain information to the audit committee. These rules are pursuant to Section 204, Auditor Reports to Audit Committees, of the Sarbanes-Oxley Act of 2002. The final rules state,

> In particular, the Sarbanes-Oxley Act requires that the auditor report to the audit committee on a timely basis (a) all critical accounting policies used by the registrant, (b) alternative accounting treatments that have been discussed with management along with the potential ramifications of using those alternatives, and (c) other written communications provided by the auditor to management, including a schedule of unadjusted audit differences. These rules strengthen the relationship between the audit committee and the auditor.[3]

The auditing standards of the PCAOB (for public companies) and of the AICPA (for nonpublic entities) also address the importance of the auditor's communications with the audit committee concerning accounting policies and

---

[1] For a more detailed discussion of accounting principles, see Chapter 5.

[2] American Institute of Certified Public Accountants, *Audit Committees, Answers to Typical Questions about Their Organization and Operations* (New York: AICPA, 1978): 16–17.

[3] Securities and Exchange Commission, Release No. 33-8183, "Strengthening the Commission's Requirements Regarding Auditor Independence," January 28, 2003, www.sec.gov/rules/final/33-8183.htm, p. 3.

other accounting treatments in AU 380. Both AU 380 and SEC Release 33-8183, whose changes were reflected in Regulation S-X, identify the following items as ones that the auditor should discuss with the audit committee:

- *Significant accounting policies.* The audit committee should expect auditors to keep them informed of management's initial choices in accounting policies and their implementation, as well as any changes in the policies or their applications. Audit committees should be especially alert to discussing with the auditors accounting policy choices and applications for difficult, new, or unusual transactions and in areas of changing practices. Areas of concern include revenue recognition, off-balance sheet financing, derivative accounting, and fair value accounting applications.
- *Management judgments and accounting estimates.* The audit committee should focus on areas where judgments and estimates have a significant impact on the financial statements. Not only should the audit committee understand the impact of judgments and estimates on the reported numbers, but it also should be comfortable with their reasonableness and the auditor's process and procedures for gathering evidence of their reasonableness.
- *Audit adjustments.* An audit adjustment is a proposed financial statement change that arose from the audit procedures, regardless of whether it is actually "booked." The audit committee should be aware of, and understand the reasoning behind, audit adjustments that the auditor considers significant to the financial reporting process.
- *Auditor's judgments about the quality of the entity's accounting principles.* Relative to SEC audit engagements, auditors and management must discuss with the audit committee their perceptions of the quality of the accounting policies, not simply their acceptability. Because audit committees have oversight responsibility for the quality of the financial reporting process, they should encourage a frank and open discussion about differences in assessments of the quality of accounting policies. Such a discussion is also a best practice for non-SEC audit engagements.
- *Other information in documents containing audited financial statements.* Audited financial statements usually appear in connection with other information presented by the company about its activities, such as in Management's Discussion and Analysis. The audit committee should discuss with the auditor the level of responsibility the auditor accepts for this other information. In addition, the audit committee should assure itself that the auditor agrees that the other information does not contain statements that are inconsistent with the audited financial statements.
- *Disagreements with management.* The auditors should discuss any disagreements with management over the choice and application of accounting principles, the bases for estimates and judgments, the scope of the audit, the wording of the audit opinion, and other matters that have a significant effect on the financial reporting process.
- *Consultation with other accountants.* If the auditor is aware that management has consulted with one or more other accounting firms or consultants about

an accounting policy and its application, or about an accounting estimate, the auditor should inform the audit committee of his assessment of the consultation.

- *Major issues discussed with management prior to retention.* The auditor should discuss the major issues related to accounting principles and auditing standards that were discussed with management during the proposal and hiring stages.
- *Difficulties encountered in performing the audit.* The audit committee and auditor should discuss issues and difficulties that occurred while the audit was in progress, such as time schedule and cooperative work issues.

## ACCOUNTING POLICY DISCLOSURES

### Accounting Policies

Management is required to present a summary of the significant accounting policies as part of the financial statements in the annual report. Such disclosure of significant accounting policies sets forth the accounting principles and methods used to prepare the financial statements. A summary of significant accounting policies frequently includes:

- Basis of consolidation and use of estimates and assumptions
- Depreciation methods
- Financial instruments
- Inventory pricing methods
- Accounting for research and development costs
- Basis for foreign currency translation
- Accounting treatment for:
  - Pension plans
  - Intangible assets, such as goodwill
  - Income taxes and investment credits
  - Revenue recognition on long-term construction contracts
- Accounting changes
- Fair value applications
- Industry practices

Obviously, the disclosure of the key accounting policies will vary from company to company. The audit committee's job consists of satisfying itself of the appropriateness of management's judgments. The audit committee's oversight role is aided by the independent auditors' assessment of the adequacy of management's disclosures of key accounting policies. If management's disclosures are inadequate, the independent auditors cannot express an unqualified opinion on the financial statements.

Therefore, as part of its financial review responsibilities, the committee should discuss "any significant disagreement between management and the independent accountants and whether such disagreement has been resolved to the satisfaction of both."[4]

## Critical Accounting Policies

The SEC amended Regulation S-X in 2003 as follows:

[E]ach public accounting firm registered with the Board that audits an issuer's financial statements must report to the issuer's audit committee (1) all critical accounting policies and practices used by the issuer, (2) all material alternative accounting treatments within GAAP that have been discussed with management, including the ramifications of the use of the alternative treatments and the treatment preferred by the accounting firm, (3) other material written communications between the accounting firm and management of the issuer such as any management letter or schedule of "unadjusted differences," and (4) in the case of registered investment companies, all non-audit services provided to entities in the investment company complex that were not pre-approved by the investment company's audit committee. The required reports need not be in writing, but must be provided to the audit committee before the auditor's report on the financial statements is filed with the Commission.[5]

## Accounting Changes

According to the Accounting Principles Board:

A change in accounting by a reporting entity may significantly affect the presentation of both financial position and results of operations for an accounting period and the trends shown in comparative financial statements and historical summaries. The change should therefore be reported in a manner which will facilitate analysis and understanding of the financial statements.[6]

There are basically three types of accounting changes, which follow.

*Change in Accounting Principle*   A change in accounting principle results from the adoption of a generally accepted accounting principle different from the one used previously for reporting purposes. For example, a change in the method of inventory pricing is a common change in accounting principles. Although there is a presumption that an accounting principle, once adopted, should not be changed, management may overcome this presumption if it justifies the use of an alternative acceptable accounting principle on the basis that such a change in accounting method enhances the fairness in the presentation of the financial

---

[4] Schornack, "The Audit Committee," 76.

[5] Securities and Exchange Commission, Release No. 33-8183, "Strengthening the Commission's Requirements Regarding Auditor Independence," January 28, 2003, www.sec.gov/rules/final/33-8183.htm, p. 45.

[6] Opinions of the Accounting Principles Board No. 20, "Accounting Changes" (New York: AICPA, 1971), par. 1.

statements. Accounting principles also change because standards-setters issue new standards to replace old ones. When the FASB issues a new standard supplanting an older one, companies must change to the new approach in order to maintain compliance with GAAP.

With respect to the disclosure of a change in accounting principle, the Board stated:

> The nature of and justification for a change in accounting principle and its effect on income should be disclosed in the financial statements of the period in which the change is made. The justification for the change should explain clearly why the newly adopted accounting principle is preferable.[7]

**Change in Accounting Estimate**   Certain accounting actions are based on management's judgment regarding the use of estimates. Accounting estimates affect almost every item in the financial statements. Some of the more common estimates involve those of:

- Useful lives of assets
- Uncollectible accounts receivable
- The in process inventories
- Warranty usage
- Completion of projects

Thus, as management acquires additional information and more experience concerning such matters as the economic life of plant and equipment assets and probable uncollectible receivables, a change in accounting estimate may occur. Changes in accounting estimates usually are reflected prospectively.

**Change in the Reporting Entity**   A change in reporting entity occurs as a result of a change in the entity's composition, such as a merger. As the Board points out:

> One special type of change in accounting principle results in financial statements which, in effect, are those of a different reporting entity. This type is limited mainly to (a) presenting consolidated or combined statements in place of statements of individual companies, (b) changing specific subsidiaries comprising the group of companies for which consolidated financial statements are presented, and (c) changing the companies included in combined financial statements. A different group of companies comprise the reporting entity after each change.[8]

Management has "choices among accounting principles or procedures," and such choices affect "the major areas in the financial statements requiring

---

[7] Ibid., par. 17. Additional reporting matters should be discussed with the chief financial officer and/or the external auditor. See also APB No. 20 amendment SFAS No. 154, "Accounting Changes and Error Corrections—a replacement of APB Opinion No. 20 and FASB Statement No. 3" (Norwalk, CT: FASB, 2005).

[8] Opinions of the Accounting Principles Board No. 20, par. 12.

subjective determinations."[9] Hence, a major objective of the committee is to review with the external auditor management's choices of accounting principles and methods in order to obtain assurance that its choices not only are in compliance with the current accounting standards, but also are properly disclosed.

## GUIDELINES FOR REVIEWING ACCOUNTING POLICY DISCLOSURES

### General Approach

In reviewing the accounting policy disclosures, the audit committee should adopt a systematic review approach. Such an approach should include:

1. *Preliminary review.* Before meeting with management and the external auditors, the committee should be familiar with such matters as:
   a. The nature of the accounting practices of the business and its industry. It should request a summary of the entity's financial reporting requirements. If necessary, the committee may wish to review the accounting policies and procedures manual and other documented information regarding the relationship between the accounting system and internal accounting controls. Are such accounting practices in line with industry practices?
   b. A summary of the minutes of the meetings of the stockholders, board of directors, and other standing committees of the board, particularly the finance committee. The accounting policies should reflect the board's authorization regarding the financial accounting affairs of the entity.
   c. The prior year's financial statements and audit reports and a summary of the effect of accounting pronouncements of the FASB, AICPA, and SEC on the statements. Are there any trends that have a disproportionate effect on the financial status of the entity?
   d. The impact of accounting changes and the rationale for such changes in the previous accounting periods.
   e. The prior years' government reports, such as the SEC and IRS report filings. The committee may wish to engage the services of tax counsel or legal counsel concerning such matters.
   In addition to the preceding matters, the committee should request a written summary of an annual review of the accounting policy disclosures from the chief financial officer, executive audit partner, and executive internal auditor. Such a summary review will enable the committee to identify major financial reporting problems that affect the accounting policies. Obviously, the committee can expedite its review through the use of such summaries and thus make best use of its review time. Much of the preliminary review activities can occur during the initial and preaudit segments of the auditing cycle, as discussed in Chapters 6 and 7.

---

[9] Schornack, "The Audit Committee," 75–76.

2. *Postaudit review.* During the committee's review of the drafts of the financial statements, it should give consideration to the following matters with the aforementioned parties:

a. Proposed management changes in accounting policies, such as a change in the inventory pricing methods and the external auditor's concurrence. Also, proposed changes in such policies concerning the new reporting requirements of the FASB, SEC, and other regulatory agencies.[10]

b. Changes in the entity's operations, such as a merger with or acquisition of another entity, and the related effects on existing accounting policies. Certain accounting standards govern the accounting treatment for the basis of valuing such investments (e.g., equity versus cost method of accounting). In view of the recommendations of the other standing committees and the approval of the board, the accounting policies should reflect such resolutions.

c. The committee should judge the existing accounting policies in light of the objectives of financial reporting that were discussed in Chapter 3. Such financial reporting objectives serve as a criterion for judging management's selection of accounting methods.[11]

d. Since many independent accounting firms engaged in auditing publicly held corporations implement quality control review programs, the committee should ask the external auditor to review the disclosure checklist items that are applicable to the significant accounting policies. As a basis for discussion, the committee can use the auditor's summary review memo, previously requested, in order to reconcile significant disclosure matters. Moreover, the committee may wish to request a copy of the accounting firm's disclosure checklist concerning the financial statements. Such disclosure checklists are usually cross-referenced to the disclosure requirements in the accounting pronouncements. An illustrative accounting policy disclosure checklist in Exhibit 10.1 shows how the audit committee might document its review.[12]

While all members of the committee may not possess the requisite accounting knowledge, each should approach his review task with imagination, perceptiveness, and resourcefulness in order to assure themselves that the policies are reasonable and consistent with the financial reporting requirements of the FASB, AICPA, SEC, and other regulatory agencies. Furthermore, the committee should exercise judgment regarding the need for the use of specialists in areas of complex accounting, tax, and legal matters. For example, several independent consultants, who are retired partners of CPA firms, sit on corporate audit committees to assist

---

[10] SEC matters regarding proxy materials should be discussed at this point, particularly compliance with the rules of the AICPA's SEC Practice Section. See Chapter 7.

[11] The reader should review in Chapter 5 such concepts as consistency, full disclosure, materiality, and fairness in financial statement presentation as well as certain enhanced financial disclosures sections of the Sarbanes-Oxley Act that are in Chapter 2.

[12] This checklist is not all-inclusive, and additional matters may be inserted based on the committee's judgment.

**EXHIBIT 10.1**   Accounting Policy Disclosures: A Checklist

| | Yes | No | Remarks |
|---|---|---|---|
| 1. Summary of the significant accounting policies reviewed by the external auditor, chief financial officer, and internal auditor. Summaries obtained. | _____ | _____ | |
| 2. Accounting policies are consistent in relationship to the industry practices (conservative or liberal). | _____ | _____ | |
| 3. Current reporting requirements are reflected in the accounting policies. | _____ | _____ | |
| 4. Accounting changes reviewed and the external auditor's concurrence obtained. | _____ | _____ | |
| 5. Disclosure of significant accounting policies is adequate to support the auditor's unqualified opinion. | _____ | _____ | |
| 6. Major financial reporting problems resolved satisfactorily. | _____ | _____ | |
| 7. Unresolved differences between the auditor and management reviewed. | _____ | _____ | |
| 8. Additional disclosures reviewed. | _____ | _____ | |
| 9. Unusual occurrences during the year, such as a disposal of a segment of the business properly disclosed in the financial statements. | _____ | _____ | |
| 10. Accounting policies are consistent with a fair presentation of the financial statement in conformity with generally accepted accounting principles. | _____ | _____ | |
| 11. Accounting policies reflect the board's authorization regarding financial and accounting matters. | _____ | _____ | |

Signed by: _____   Date _____

(Should be signed by the chairman of the audit committee)*

_____

* See Chapter 4 with respect to procedures to document audit committee activities.

with complex accounting issues.[13] In short, the primary objective of the committee's review should be to scrutinize management's judgment in selecting the accounting principles and methods used in the preparation of the financial statements and to recommend the statements for the approval of the board of directors.

_____

[13] Obviously, a retired partner would not sit on the audit committee of a corporation that is a client of her former firm. Two commentators point out that "analysts, stakeholders, the press, juries and jurists, and the public would not be persuaded that a retired partner of an audit firm could perform effectively as a member of the audit committee of a client of the partner's firm." Dan M. Guy and Stephen A. Zeff, "Independence and Objectivity: Retired Partners on Audit Committees," *CPA Journal* 72, no. 7 (July 2002): 34.

## Benchmarking

Audit committees should consider adopting a benchmarking program for comparing their company's accounting policy disclosures to those of peer and aspirant companies (the independent auditors and management can assist with choosing such companies). Benchmarking is an area in which audit committees may choose to engage independent advisors to help them understand whether their company is performing at an acceptable level.

## SOURCES AND SUGGESTED READINGS

American Institute of Certified Public Accountants. *Audit Committees, Answers to Typical Questions about Their Organization and Operations.* New York: AICPA, 1978.

American Institute of Certified Public Accountants. *Meeting the Financial Reporting Needs of the Future: A Public Commitment from the Public Accounting Profession.* New York: AICPA, 1993.

American Institute of Certified Public Accountants. Practice Alert 2000-2, "Quality of Accounting Principles-Guidance for Discussions with Audit Committees." www.aicpa. org/audcommctr/practice_alert_2000-2.

Bristol-Myers Squibb Company. 2002 Annual Report.

Exxon Corporation. 1992 Annual Report.

Ford Motor Company. 1990 Annual Report.

Gerson, James S., J. Robert Mooney, Donald F. Moran, and Robert K. Waters. "Oversight of the Financial Reporting Process—Part I." *CPA Journal* 59, no. 7 (July 1989): 22–28.

Gerson, James S., J. Robert Mooney, Donald F. Moran, and Robert K. Waters. "Oversight of the Financial Reporting Process—Part II." *CPA Journal* 59, no. 8 (August 1989): 40, 42–47.

Guy, Dan M., and Stephen A. Zeff. "Independence and Objectivity: Retired Partners on Audit Committees." *CPA Journal* 72, no. 7 (July 2002): 30–34.

McKesson Corporation. 1998 Annual Report.

Opinions of the Accounting Principles Board, No. 20. "Accounting Changes." New York: American Institute of Certified Public Accountants, 1971.

Opinions of the Accounting Principles Board, No. 22. "Disclosure of Accounting Policies." New York: American Institute of Certified Public Accountants, 1972.

Palmer, Russell E. "Audit Committees—Are They Effective? An Auditor's View." *Journal of Accountancy* 144, no. 3 (September 1977): 76–79.

Public Oversight Board. A Special Report by the Public Oversight Board of the SEC Practice Section, AICPA. Stamford, CT: Public Oversight Board, 1993.

Schornack, John J. "The Audit Committee—A Public Accountant's View." *Journal of Accountancy* 147, no. 4 (April 1979): 73–77.

Securities and Exchange Commission. Release No. 33-8183, "Strengthening the Commission's Requirements Regarding Auditor Independence," January 28, 2003. www.sec. gov/rules/final/33-8183.htm.

Statements on Auditing Standards No. 114. "The Auditor's Communication with Those Charged with Governance" (2006), and its international counterpart, ISA 260.

# Chapter 11

# A Perspective on Fraud and the Auditor

In the aftermath of Enron, WorldCom, and the passage of the Sarbanes-Oxley Act of 2002, at least for public companies, audit committees have been vested with significantly greater authority with respect to oversight of financial reporting matters. The "client" of the independent auditor is no longer "senior management"; it is now unequivocally the audit committee of the board of directors. In the context of internal controls over financial reporting, the audit committee's oversight responsibilities extend over senior management, but significant interactions are expected to occur with the independent auditor as well as the internal auditors. All of these developments collectively have led to a situation where, whenever material fraud is alleged or uncovered, the real question has become "Where was the audit committee?" Certainly, in this new era of corporate governance and accountability, audit committees find themselves having to address not only heightened risk of fraud, but also other sensitivities such as actual, perceived, or potential conflicts of interest, as well as attending to anonymous tips and complaints, including whistle-blower concerns brought to their attention, and interacting closely with general counsel on matters of compliance such as the Foreign Corrupt Practices Act (FCPA).

In view of the general misconception concerning the auditor's responsibility for the detection of fraud, the purpose of this chapter is to examine the implications of management fraud relative to the external and internal auditors and the audit committee. Moreover, audit committee members will not only examine the meaning and rationale for management fraud, but will also explore ways to safeguard the entity against such fraud. A significant reason for this shift in focus can be traced to specific provisions of the Sarbanes-Oxley Act of 2002. The audit committee's monitoring of certain general business practices, such as conflicts of interest, will be discussed in Chapter 12.

## MEANING OF FRAUD IN A FINANCIAL STATEMENT AUDIT

In the Auditing Standards Board of the AICPA, fraud and its characteristics are described in this way:

> Fraud is a broad legal concept and auditors do not make legal determinations of whether fraud has occurred. Rather, the auditor's interest specifically relates to acts that result in a material misstatement of the financial statements. The primary factor

that distinguishes fraud from error is whether the underlying action that results in the misstatement of the financial statements is intentional or unintentional. For purposes of the Statement, *fraud* is an intentional act that results in a material misstatement in financial statements that are the subject of an audit.[1]

The Board describes the types of misstatements as follows:

- *Misstatements arising from fraudulent financial reporting* are intentional misstatements or omissions of amounts or disclosures in financial statements designed to deceive financial statement users where the effect causes the financial statements not to be presented, in all material respects, in conformity with generally accepted accounting principles (GAAP). Fraudulent financial reporting may be accomplished by the following:
  - Manipulation, falsification, or alteration of accounting records or supporting documents from which financial statements are prepared
  - Misrepresentation in or intentional omission from the financial statements of events, transactions, or other significant information
  - Intentional misapplication of accounting principles relating to amounts, classification, manner of presentation, or disclosure

Fraudulent financial reporting need not be the result of a grand plan or conspiracy. It may be that management representatives rationalize the appropriateness of a material misstatement, for example, as an aggressive rather than indefensible interpretation of complex accounting rules, or as a temporary misstatement of financial statements, including interim statements, expected to be corrected later when operational results improve.

- *Misstatements arising from misappropriation of assets* (sometimes referred to as theft or defalcation) involve the theft of an entity's assets where the effect of the theft causes the financial statements not to be presented, in all material respects, in conformity with GAAP. Misappropriation of assets can be accomplished in various ways, including embezzling receipts, stealing assets, or causing an entity to pay for goods or services that have not been received. Misappropriation of assets may be accompanied by false or misleading records or documents, possibly created by circumventing controls. The scope of this Statement includes only those misappropriations of assets for which the effect of the misappropriation causes the financial statements not to be fairly presented, in all material respects, in conformity with GAAP.[2]

In addition, the Institute of Internal Auditors defines fraud as:

Any illegal acts characterized by deceit, concealment or violation of trust. These acts are not dependent upon the application of threat of violence or of physical force. Frauds are perpetrated by individuals and organizations to obtain money, property or services; to avoid payment or loss of services; or to secure personal or business advantages.[3]

---

[1] Statement on Auditing Standards no. 99, "Consideration of Fraud in a Financial Statement Audit" (New York: AICPA, 2002), par. 5.
[2] Ibid., par. 6.
[3] Institute of Internal Auditors, *The Professional Practices Framework* (Altamonte Springs, FL: The IIA, 2009).

With respect to the identification of fraud, the Institute's *Standards for the Professional Practice of Internal Auditing* indicates:

> The internal auditor should have sufficient knowledge to identify the indicators of fraud but is not expected to have the expertise of a person whose primary responsibility is detecting and investigating fraud.[4]

With respect to fraudulent financial reporting, the National Commission on Fraudulent Financial Reporting defined such reporting as:

> intentional or reckless conduct, whether act or omission, that results in materially misleading financial statements. Fraudulent financial reporting can involve many factors and take many forms. It may entail gross and deliberate distortion of corporate records, such as inventory count tags, or falsified transactions, such as fictitious sales or orders. It may entail the misapplication of accounting principles. Company employees at any level may be involved, from top to middle management to lower-level personnel. If the conduct is intentional, or so reckless that it is the legal equivalent of intentional conduct, and results in fraudulent financial statements, it comes within the Commission's operating definition of the term *fraudulent financial reporting*.

> Fraudulent financial reporting differs from other causes of materially misleading financial statements, such as unintentional errors. The Commission also distinguished fraudulent financial reporting from other corporate improprieties, such as employee embezzlements, violations of environmental or product safety regulations, and tax fraud, which do not necessarily cause the financial statements to be materially inaccurate.[5]

Although there is a distinction between fraudulent financial reporting and misappropriation of assets, this chapter addresses both types of fraud. Suffice it to say that one major distinction is their incidence-to-impact ratio. They seem to follow the 80-20 rule; thus, 80 percent-plus of all frauds are probably of the asset misappropriation variety but seem to exert only some 20 percent of the impact, while management fraud, with an incidence ratio of less than 20 percent, appears to have 80 percent plus impact, including in global financial markets. (Consider the case of Satyam Computer Systems, a global technology outsourcing provider that was listed in the New York, Amsterdam, and Bombay Stock Exchanges.)

Although both the private sector and public sector have initiated action, particularly the Foreign Corrupt Practices Act of 1977 and Sections 301 and 302 of the Sarbanes-Oxley Act of 2002 (discussed in Chapter 1), to protect the business community against management fraud, it is apparent that such legislative mandates will not completely eliminate this corporate problem. Since the passage of Sarbanes-Oxley in the United States, management fraud cases continue to

---

[4] Ibid., section 1210. A2., 9 For further information regarding the identification of fraud and the internal auditor's responsibility for detection, see Practice Advisory 1210. A2-1 and 1210.A2-2.
[5] National Commission on Fraudulent Financial Reporting, *Report of the National Commission on Fraudulent Financial Reporting* (Washington, DC: NCFFR, 1987), 2.

be discussed in the news media: consider the 2008 Wall Street financial meltdown, at least part of which appears to be based on mortgage fraud (cf. SEC action against Countrywide Financial and its key leaders). The cost of management fraud to the business community is indeterminable, primarily because many cases are undisclosed or undiscovered. Furthermore, the cost of compliance to safeguard the entity from management fraud is increasing. Consequently, the cost in money and time to businesses and consumers to reform corporate behavior, as well as the cost of liability insurance, is constantly increasing. For example, see the summarized findings from the 2008 *Report to the Nation* by the Association of Certified Fraud Examiners in Exhibit 11.1.

---

**EXHIBIT 11.1**   Association of Certified Fraud Examiners, 2008 *Report to the Nation*, Occupational Fraud and Abuse

---

The Association of Certified Fraud Examiners (ACFE) conducts a bi-annual survey of its members and prepares a *Report to the Nation on Occupational Fraud & Abuse* (*Report to the Nation*). The 2008 *Report to the Nation* is based on data compiled from 959 cases of occupational fraud from a wide range of industries that were investigated between January 2006 and February 2008. Information from these cases was reported by the Certified Fraud Examiners (CFEs) who investigated the cases. The 2008 report summarized the following findings:

- Participants in the survey estimated that U.S. organizations lose 7% of their annual revenues to fraud, an increase from the 5% estimated in the 2006 *Report to the Nation*. Applied to the projected 2008 United States Gross Domestic Product (GDP), this 7% figure translates to approximately $994 billion in fraud losses.
- Occupational fraud schemes tend to be extremely costly. The median loss caused by the occupational frauds in this study was $175,000. More than one-quarter of the frauds involved losses of at least $1 million.
- Occupational fraud schemes frequently continue for years before they are detected. The typical fraud in the study lasted two years from the time it began until the time it was caught by the victimized organization.
- The most common fraud schemes were corruption, which occurred in 27% of all cases, and fraudulent billing schemes, which occurred in 24% of all cases (different types of fraud are discussed later in this chapter). Financial statement fraud was the most costly category, with a median loss of $2 million.
- Occupational frauds are much more likely to be detected by a tip than by audits, controls, or other means. Forty-six percent of the cases were detected by tips from employees, customers, vendors, and other sources.
- The implementation of anti-fraud controls appears to have a measurable impact on an organization's exposure to fraud. For example, organizations that conducted surprise audits suffered a median loss of $70,000, while those that did not conduct them had a median loss of $270,000. Similar reductions were found in fraud losses for organizations that had anonymous fraud hotlines, offered employee support programs, provided fraud training for managers, and had internal audit or fraud examination departments.
- While fraud can occur in any type of organization, the industries most commonly victimized were banking and financial services, government, and health care. The industries with the largest median losses were manufacturing, banking, and insurance.

- Small businesses continue to be especially vulnerable to occupational fraud, with a median loss of $200,000. Check tampering and fraudulent billing were the most common small business fraud schemes.
- Lack of adequate controls was most commonly cited (35%) as the factor that allowed fraud to occur. Next most common were lack of management review (17%) and override of existing controls (17%).
- Seventy-eight percent of victimized organizations modified their anti-fraud controls after discovering that they had been defrauded. This typically involved enhancing controls, conducting surprise audits, and providing fraud training to managers and employees.
- Occupational frauds were most often committed by the accounting department or upper management. Not surprisingly, frauds committed by executives were particularly costly, resulting in a median loss of $853,000.
- Occupational fraudsters are generally first-time offenders. Only 7% had prior convictions, and only 12% had been terminated previously for fraud-related conduct.
- Fraud perpetrators often display behavioral traits that serve as indicators of possible illegal behavior. The most commonly cited red flags were perpetrators living beyond their apparent means (39%) or experiencing financial difficulties (34%). In financial statement fraud cases, which tend to be the most costly, excessive organizational pressure to perform was a particularly strong warning sign.

*Source:* Association of Certified Fraud Examiners, *2008 Report to the Nation, Occupational Fraud and Abuse* (Austin, TX: ACFE, 2008).

In 2008, The Institute of Internal Auditors (The IIA), The American Institute of Certified Public Accountants (AICPA), and the Association of Certified Fraud Examiners (ACFE) collaborated on a landmark guidance paper titled *Managing the Business Risk of Fraud: A Practical Guide.* This guidance outlines five key principles of a management process for fraud risk and recommends ways in which boards, senior management, and internal auditors can fight corporate fraud. A dedicated task force of more than 20 experts in the field of fraud risk identification, mitigation, and investigation spent two years developing the guidance. It contains the following definition:

Fraud is any intentional act or omission designed to deceive others, resulting in the victim suffering a loss and/or the perpetrator achieving a gain.

The principles enunciated in the 2008 IIA/AICPA/ACFE guidance paper are summarized in Exhibit 11.2.[6]

---

[6] In an article entitled "Six Common Myths about Fraud," Joseph T. Wells, chairman of the Association of Certified Fraud Examiners, identifies such myths as (1) most people will not commit fraud; (2) fraud is not material; (3) most fraud goes undetected; (4) fraud is usually well concealed; (5) the auditor can't do a better job in detecting fraud; and (6) prosecuting fraud perpetrators deters others. For further discussion, see *Journal of Accountancy* 169, no. 2 (February 1990): 82–88. Also see Joseph T. Wells, "Occupational Fraud: The Audit as Deterrent," *Journal of Accountancy* 193, no. 4 (April 2002): 24–28.

---

**EXHIBIT 11.2**   2008 IIA/AICPA/ACFE Core Principles in "Managing the Business Risk of Fraud"

---

The *2008 IIA/AICPA/ACFE Guidance Paper, "Managing the Business Risk of Fraud"* indicated the importance for organizations to establish a diligent and ongoing effort to protect themselves from acts of fraud. To support these efforts, the *Guidance* set out five key principles that organizations can follow for proactively establishing an environment that will help effectively manage fraud risk.

These principles are:

**Principle 1.** As part of an organization's governance structure, a fraud risk management program should be in place, including a written policy (or policies) to convey the expectations of the board of directors and senior management regarding managing fraud risk.

**Principle 2.** Fraud risk exposure should be assessed periodically by the organization to identify specific potential schemes and events that the organization needs to mitigate.

**Principle 3.** Prevention techniques to avoid potential key fraud risk events should be established, where feasible, to mitigate possible impacts on the organization.

**Principle 4.** Detection techniques should be established to uncover fraud events when preventive measures fail or unmitigated risks are realized.

**Principle 5.** A reporting process should be in place to solicit input on potential fraud, and a coordinated approach to investigation and corrective action should be used to help ensure potential fraud is addressed appropriately and timely.

---

In October 1997, Ernst & Young's Fraud Investigative Group in the United Kingdom surveyed senior executives in 11,000 major organizations in 32 countries. Based on 1,205 responses, Ernst & Young reported these findings:

- The experience of organisations participating in our surveys shows that the curse of fraud continues. More than half had been defrauded in the last 12 months. 30 percent had suffered more than five frauds in the last five years.

- 84 percent of the worst frauds were committed by employees, nearly half of whom had been with the organization for over five years.

- Most of the worst frauds were committed by management.

- 87 percent of respondents thought the incidence of fraud would increase, or at best remain static, over the next 5 years. Yet less than half of these organisations had done as much as they cost effectively could to protect their business against fraud.

- Only 13 percent of fraud losses had been recovered—including insurance recoveries.

- Respondents' replies indicated that the better the directors' understanding of the business as a whole, the lower the incidence of fraud they suffered.

- However, less than half the respondents believed that their directors had a good understanding of areas outside their core business, including remote and overseas operations.

- Less than a quarter of the respondents believed their directors had a good understanding of electronic communication or information technology.
- With the millennium approaching fast, three in four organisations had failed to include within their Year 2000 projects an assessment of the vulnerability of their computer systems to fraud.
- The proportion of organisations with fraud reporting policies was higher than in our last survey, but communication of these to the workforce was still poor.[7]

As David Sherwin, head of Ernst & Young's Fraud Investigation Group, asserts:

Companies need to act positively to prevent fraud from happening in the first place. They should ensure all the simple steps are conscientiously applied.

Areas of neglect include:

- *Lack of knowledge of the workings of remote sites and overseas operations.* Senior management reveals that it still doesn't make regular visits to remote locations in order to ensure that adequate controls are in place—placing too much reliance, instead, on local management.
- *Poor understanding by directors of electronic communications and IT.* Although computer systems are being widely reviewed to eliminate "millennium bomb" problems, the vulnerability of these systems to fraud was checked by only one in four companies surveyed.
- *Inadequate fraud-reporting policies for staff.* While most companies are developing such policies, communication remains poor. Over half the companies said they were opposed to hotlines to enable staff to report fraud. Such opposition was lowest in the U.S. and greatest in continental Europe.[8]

## Intentional Distortions of Financial Statements

Concerning management's deliberate misrepresentations in the entity's financial position and results of operations, L. B. Sawyer, A. A. Murphy, and M. Crossley report:

Management fraud has been found in overstatements of inventory to show healthy assets which are, in truth, sickly . . . the acceptance of inferior goods to conceal a tottering cash position . . . delayed key expenditures to increase current profits to the detriment of the long-range survival of the company . . . overstatements of receivables to puff both assets and sales . . . fictitious sales which construct a facade of vigorous business volume . . . and understatements of liabilities to gloss over the financial picture.[9]

---

[7] Ernst & Young, *Fraud: The Unmanaged Risk, An International Survey of the Effect of Fraud on Business* (London: Ernst & Young, 1998), 1.

[8] Ernst & Young, *Ernst's & Young's Business Upshot* (Cleveland, OH) (July/August 1998), 3.

[9] Lawrence B. Sawyer, Albert A. Murphy, and Michael Crossley, "Management Fraud: The Insidious Specter," *Internal Auditor* 36, no. 2 (April 1979): 12–13.

With respect to legal cases concerning management fraud and the audit committee, the reader should review the cases in Chapter 4. Such a review indicates that the SEC and the courts have ruled on the establishment of the audit committee by the registrant in order to comply with the provisions of the federal securities laws. As a result, the legal obligations of audit committee members have intensified because their standard duty of care and loyalty to the entity has increased in light of the management fraud activities. Consequently, the audit committee will look to the internal and external auditing executives as well as legal counsel for assistance in preventing management fraud. In short, since management fraud is perpetrated by the top executives of the entity, it is ordinarily conducted on a sophisticated basis and requires the professional expertise of auditors, legal counsel, or special investigators.

The rationale for management fraud is essentially attributable to "different pressures" that force management into deliberate misrepresentations of accounting information as well as the misappropriations of assets.[10] Sawyer, Murphy, and Crossley summarize the reasons:

- "Executives sometimes take rash steps from which they cannot retreat," such as setting unattainable objectives regarding the earnings per share figure. Such rash actions may involve actually lying to the external auditors in order to inflate the bottom line of the entity.
- "Profit centers may distort facts to hold off divestments," whereby management of a subsidiary will deliberately manipulate transactions and alter documents and records to falsify its profitability performance.
- "Incompetent managers may deceive in order to survive," based on their actual performance versus their reported results.
- "Performance may be distorted to warrant larger bonuses," through the manipulation of the reported figures regarding the company's incentive plans.
- "The need to succeed can turn managers to deception," whereby such individuals place personal gain and self-interest before their stewardship accountability to their constituencies (discussed in Chapter 2).
- "Unscrupulous managers may serve interests which conflict," as discussed in Chapter 4 in relation to the state and federal statutory laws covering the directors and officers. Such laws provide a standard duty of care and loyalty to the entity.
- "Profits may be inflated to obtain advantages in the marketplace," whereby the perpetrators are confident that "their own abilities transcend any fear of detection."
- "People who control both the assets and their records are in a perfect position to falsify the latter." Thus a sound system of internal control, discussed in Chapter 8, is essential.[11]

---

[10] Ibid., p. 17.
[11] Ibid., 17–19.

Expanding on the aforementioned rationale and motivation for fraudulent financial reporting, the National Commission on Fraudulent Financial Reporting characterized various situations and opportunities:

Fraudulent financial reporting usually occurs as the result of certain environmental, institutional, or individual forces and opportunities. These forces and opportunities add pressures and incentives that encourage individuals and companies to engage in fraudulent financial reporting and are present to some degree in all companies. If the right combustible mixture of forces and opportunities is present, fraudulent financial reporting may occur.

A frequent incentive for fraudulent financial reporting that improves the company's financial appearance is the desire to obtain a higher price from a stock or debt offering or to meet the expectations of investors. Another incentive may be the desire to postpone dealing with financial difficulties and thus avoid, for example, violating a restrictive debt covenant. Other times the incentive is personal gain: additional compensation, promotion, or escape from penalty for poor performance.

Situational pressures on the company or an individual manager also may lead to fraudulent financial reporting. Examples of these situational pressures include:

1. *Sudden decreases in revenue or market share.* A single company or an entire industry can experience these decreases.

2. *Unrealistic budget pressures, particularly for short-term results.* These pressures may occur when headquarters arbitrarily determines profit objectives and budgets without taking actual conditions into account.

3. *Financial pressure resulting from bonus plans that depend on short-term economic performance.* This pressure is particularly acute when the bonus is a significant component of the individual's total compensation.

Opportunities for fraudulent financial reporting are present when the fraud is easier to commit and when detection is less likely. Frequently these opportunities arise from:

1. *The absence of a board of directors or audit committee that vigilantly oversees the financial reporting process.*

2. *Weak or nonexistent internal accounting controls.* This situation can occur, for example, when a company's revenue system is overloaded from a rapid expansion of sales, an acquisition of a new division, or the entry into a new, unfamiliar line of business.

3. *Unusual or complex transactions.* Examples include the consolidation of two companies, the divestiture or closing of a specific operation, and agreements to buy or sell government securities under a repurchase agreement.

4. *Accounting estimates requiring significant subjective judgment by company management.* Examples include reserves for loan losses and the yearly provision for warranty expense.

5. *Ineffective internal audit staffs.* This situation may result from inadequate staff size and severely limited audit scope.

A weak corporate ethical climate exacerbates these situations. Opportunities for fraudulent financial reporting also increase dramatically when the accounting principles for transactions are nonexistent, evolving, or subject to varying interpretations.[12]

The rationale for management fraud is based on the various pressures from the internal and external environment of the corporation. Moreover, such frauds are augmented by the economic motives of the perpetrator as well as the organizational structure of the entity.

## Computer Fraud

In addition to management fraud, computer fraud has been a major, constant problem of the business community. As far back as 1987, the National Commission on Fraudulent Financial Reporting concluded:

> The increasing power and sophistication of computers and computer-based information systems may contribute even more to the changing nature of fraudulent financial reporting. The last decade has seen the decentralization and the proliferation of computers and information systems into almost every part of the company. This development has enabled management to make decisions more quickly and on the basis of more timely and accurate information. Yet by doing what they do best—placing vast quantities of data within easy reach—computers multiply the potential for misusing or manipulating information, increasing the risk of fraudulent financial reporting.[13]

As defined by Brandt Allen:

> Computer fraud is . . . any defalcation or embezzlement accomplished by tampering with computer programs, data files, operations, equipment or media and resulting in losses sustained by the organization whose computer system was manipulated.[14]

---

[12] National Commission on Fraudulent Financial Reporting, Report of the National Commission on Fraudulent Financial Reporting: 23–24. For a good discussion, see James D. Stice, W. Steve Albrecht, and Leslie M. Brown, "Lessons to be Learned—ZZZZ Best, Regina, and Lincoln Savings," CPA *Journal* 61, no. 4 (April 1991): 52–53. A recent study of 75 fraud and 75 no-fraud firms noted that no-fraud firms with outside members on the board of directors significantly reduce the likelihood of financial statement fraud. See Mark S. Beasley, "An Empirical Analysis of the Relation between the Board of Director Composition and Financial Statement Fraud," *Accounting Review* 71, no. 4 (October 1996): 443–465. For additional reading, see Best Practices Council of the National Association of Corporate Directors, *Coping with Fraud and Other Illegal Activity* (Washington, DC: National Association of Corporate Directors, 1998); Mark S. Beasley, Joseph V. Carcello, and Dana R. Hermanson, *Fraudulent Financial Reporting: 1987–1997 An Analysis of U.S. Public Companies* (New York: COSO of the Treadway Commission, 1999).

[13] National Commission on Fraudulent Financial Reporting, Report of the National Commission on Fraudulent Financial Reporting, 28. The reader may wish to review the *Equity Funding Corporation of America* case, which illustrates the use of computers to create fictitious insurance policies and, in turn, overstate assets by more than $120 million and overstate the corporation's earnings. See *United States v. Weiner*, 578 F. 2d 757 (9th Cir.), *cert. denied*, 439 U.S. 981 (1978).

[14] Brandt Allen, "The Biggest Computer Frauds: Lessons for CPA's," *Journal of Accountancy* 143, no. 5 (May 1977), 52.

For an expanded discussion of computer fraud, see *The Computer and Internet Fraud Manual* published by the Association of Certified Fraud Examiners (ACFE). More recently, ACFE Founder and Chairman Joseph Wells has edited a compendium of cases of computer fraud—see *Computer Fraud Casebook: The Bytes That Bite* (2009).

## THE EXTERNAL AUDITOR'S RESPONSIBILITY

### An Overview[15]

The AICPA's fraud-related audit standard (SAS No. 99, "Consideration of Fraud in a Financial Statement Audit") contains significant implications for audit committees. This fraud standard provides external auditors with revised and expanded guidelines on consideration of fraud risk during a financial statement audit (i.e., material misstatements of financial statements resulting from intentional acts such as asset misappropriation or fraudulent financial reporting). Nevertheless, under SAS No. 99, the auditor's responsibility to plan and perform the audit to obtain reasonable assurance about whether the financial statements are free of material misstatements, whether caused by error or fraud, has not changed. However, external auditors are required to give consideration of fraud throughout the audit, and they place increased emphasis on the need for heightened professional skepticism.

SAS No. 99 covers two types of material fraud: (1) fraudulent financial reporting, involving intentional material misstatements or omissions of material amounts or disclosures in the financial statements, and (2) misappropriation of assets, involving the theft of an entity's assets.

The standard requires the external auditors to identify and document fraud risks rather than fraud risk factors (e.g., risk of misappropriation of inventory). Additionally, the standard renames the categories of fraud risk factors: (1) incentive/pressure, (2) opportunity, and (3) attitudes/rationalization. (For additional information, see appendix to SAS No. 99 as well as Chapter 6.) SAS No. 99 establishes the following process to address the potential for intentional material misstatements in the financial statements. The standard requires the auditors to:

- Gather information necessary to identify the risks of material misstatements
- Identify risks of material misstatements
- Assess identified risks
- Respond to the results of the assessment
- Evaluate audit evidence
- Communicate fraud to interested parties
- Document the auditors' consideration of fraud[16]

---

[15] In addition to the external auditor's role and responsibility for detecting fraud and illegal acts, the reader may wish to consult other auditing standards with respect to the internal auditor, fraud examiner, and government auditors. See the Bibliography for the applicable reference.

[16] *Statement on Auditing Standards no. 99*, "Consideration of Fraud in a Financial Statement Audit," par. 2. For further reference, see Douglas R. Carmichael, "The Auditor's New Guide to Errors, Irregularities and Illegal Acts," *Journal of Accountancy* 166, no. 3 (September 1988): 40–48.

With respect to the effect of fraud on the auditor's report, the SAS 99 states:

The auditor should evaluate whether identified risks of material misstatement due to fraud can be related to specific financial-statement account balances or classes of transactions and related assertions, or whether they relate more pervasively to the financial statements as a whole. Relating the risks of material misstatement due to fraud to the individual accounts, classes of transactions, and assertions will assist the auditor in subsequently designing appropriate auditing procedures.

Certain accounts, classes of transactions, and assertions that have high inherent risk because they involve a high degree of management judgment and subjectivity also may present risks of material misstatement due to fraud because they are susceptible to manipulation by management. For example, liabilities resulting from a restructuring may be deemed to have high inherent risk because of the high degree of subjectivity and management judgment involved in their estimation. Similarly, revenues for software developers may be deemed to have high inherent risk because of the complex accounting principles applicable to the recognition and measurement of software revenue transactions. Assets resulting from investing activities may be deemed to have high inherent risk because of the subjectivity and management judgment involved in estimating fair values of those investments.

In summary, the identification of a risk of material misstatement due to fraud involves the application of professional judgment and includes the consideration of the attributes of the risk, including:

- The *type* of risk that may exist, that is, whether it involves fraudulent financial reporting or misappropriation of assets
- The *significance* of the risk, that is, whether it is of a magnitude that could lead to result in a possible material misstatement of the financial statements
- The *likelihood* of the risk, that is, the likelihood that it will result in a material misstatement in the financial statements[a]
- The *pervasiveness* of the risk, that is, whether the potential risk is pervasive to the financial statements as a whole or specifically related to a particular assertion, account, or class of transactions.[17]

Finally, the external auditor has a responsibility to communicate fraud to the audit committee or board of directors. More specifically:

(i) AU 316.22, *Consideration of Fraud in a Financial Statement Audit*, requires the independent auditor to inquire directly of the audit committee (or at least its chair) regarding the audit committee's views about the risks of fraud and whether the audit committee has knowledge of any fraud or suspected fraud affecting the entity.

---

[a] The occurrence of material misstatements of financial statements due to fraud is relatively infrequent in relation to the total population of published financial statements. However, the auditor should not use this as a basis to conclude that one or more risks of a material misstatement due to fraud are not present in a particular entity.

---

[17] Ibid., pars. 38, 39, 40.

(ii) AU 316.79, *Consideration of Fraud in a Financial Statement Audit*, requires the independent auditor to communicate with those charged with governance fraud involving senior management and fraud (whether caused by senior management or other employees) that causes a material misstatement of the financial statements. In addition, the auditor should reach an understanding with those charged with governance regarding the nature and extent of communications with those charged with governance about misappropriations perpetrated by lower-level employees.

(iii) The disclosure of possible fraud to parties other than the client's senior management and its audit committee ordinarily is not part of the auditor's responsibility and ordinarily would be precluded by the auditor's ethical or legal obligations of confidentiality unless the matter is reflected in the auditor's report. The auditor should recognize, however, that in the following circumstances a duty to disclose to parties outside the entity may exist:

   a. To comply with certain legal and regulatory requirements[a]
   b. To a successor auditor when the successor makes inquiries in accordance with SAS No. 84, *Communications Between Predecessor and Successor Auditors*[b] (*AICPA, Professional Standards*, vol. 1, AU sec. 315)
   c. In response to a subpoena
   d. To a funding agency or other specified agency in accordance with requirements for the auditors of entities that receive governmental financial assistance[c]

Because potential conflicts between the auditor's ethical and legal obligations for confidentiality of client matters may be complex, the auditor may wish to consult with legal counsel before discussing matters covered by paragraphs 79 through 81 with parties outside the client.[18]

---

[a] These requirements include reports in connection with the termination of the engagement, such as when the entity reports an auditor change on Form 8-K and the fraud or related risk factors constitute a *reportable event* or is the source of a *disagreement*, as these terms are defined in Item 304 of Regulation S-K. These requirements also include reports that may be required, under certain circumstances, pursuant to Section 10A(b)1 of the Securities Exchange Act of 1934 relating to an illegal act that has a material effect on the financial statements.
[b] SAS No. 84 requires the specific permission of the client.
[c] For example, *Government Auditing Standards* (the Yellow Book) require auditors to report fraud or illegal acts directly to parties outside the audited entity in certain circumstances.

In addition to fraud in a financial statement audit, the external auditor has a responsibility for detecting illegal acts by client companies. As defined by the Auditing Standards Board:

The term *illegal acts*, for purposes of this Statement, refers to violations of laws or governmental regulations. Illegal acts by clients are acts attributable to the entity whose financial statements are under audit or acts by management or employees acting on behalf of the entity. Illegal acts by clients do not include personal misconduct by the entity's personnel unrelated to their business activities.[19]

---

[18] Ibid., pars. 79, 80, 81, 82.
[19] *Statement on Auditing Standards, no. 54*, "Illegal Acts by Clients" (New York: AICPA, 1988), par. 2. For further discussion, see Donald L. Neebes, Dan M. Guy, and O. Ray Whittington, "Illegal Acts: What Are the Auditor's Responsibilities?" *Journal of Accountancy* 171, no. 1 (January 1991): 82–84, 86, 88, 90–93.

Although the external auditor may recognize that the client has committed an illegal act, the determination of whether the act is illegal is dependent on legal judgment. Therefore, the auditor would consult with legal counsel or await a court ruling, depending on the circumstances.

In view of the fact that illegal acts vary in their relation to the financial statements, the Auditing Standards Board makes this distinction between direct and indirect effects:

> The auditor considers laws and regulations that are generally recognized by auditors to have a direct and material effect on the determination of financial statement amounts. For example, tax laws affect accruals and the amount recognized as expense in the accounting period; applicable laws and regulations may affect the amount of revenue accrued under government contracts. However, the auditor considers such laws or regulations from the perspective of their known relation to audit objectives derived from financial statement assertions rather than from the perspective of legality *per se*. The auditor's responsibility to detect and report misstatements resulting from illegal acts having a direct and material effect on the determination of financial statement amounts is the same as that for fraud as described in SAS No. 99, "Consideration of Fraud in a Financial Statement Audit."
>
> Entities may be affected by many other laws or regulations, including those related to securities trading, occupational safety and health, food and drug administration, environmental protection, equal employment, and price-fixing or other antitrust violations. Generally, these laws and regulations relate more to an entity's operating aspects than to its financial and accounting aspects, and their financial statement effect is indirect. An auditor ordinarily does not have sufficient basis for recognizing possible violations of such laws and regulations. Their indirect effect is normally the result of the need to disclose a contingent liability because of the allegation or determination of illegality. For example, securities may be purchased or sold based on inside information. While the direct effects of the purchase or sale may be recorded appropriately, their indirect effect, the possible contingent liability for violating securities laws, may not be appropriately disclosed. Even when violations of such laws and regulations can have consequences material to the financial statements, the auditor may not become aware of the existence of the illegal act unless he is informed by the client, or there is evidence of a governmental agency investigation or enforcement proceeding in the records, documents, or other information normally inspected in an audit of financial statements.[20]

Warning signals for possible illegal acts are presented in Exhibit 11.3.

Finally, the auditor is required to communicate with the audit committee in this way:

> The auditor should assure himself that the audit committee, or others with equivalent authority and responsibility, is adequately informed with respect to illegal acts that come to the auditor's attention. The auditor need not communicate matters that are clearly inconsequential and may reach agreement in advance with the audit committee on the nature of such matters to be communicated. The communication

---

[20] Ibid., pars. 5, 6.

---

**EXHIBIT 11.3**   Warning Signals of Possible Illegal Acts

---

- Unauthorized transactions, improperly recorded transactions, or transactions not recorded in a complete or timely manner in order to maintain accountability for assets
- Investigation by a governmental agency, an enforcement proceeding, or payment of unusual fines or penalties
- Violations of laws or regulations cited in reports of examinations by regulatory agencies that have been made available to the auditor
- Large payments for unspecified services to consultants, affiliates, or employees
- Sales commissions or agents' fees that appear excessive in relation to those normally paid by the client or to the services actually received
- Unusually large payments in cash, purchases of bank cashiers' checks in large amounts payable to bearer, transfers to numbered bank accounts, or similar transactions
- Unexplained payments made to government officials or employees
- Failure to file tax returns or pay government duties or similar fees that are common to the entity's industry or the nature of its business

---

*Source: Statement on Auditing Standards No. 54, "Illegal Acts by Clients," par. 9.*

---

should describe the act, the circumstances of its occurrence, and the effect on the financial statements. Senior management may wish to have its remedial actions communicated to the audit committee simultaneously. Possible remedial actions include disciplinary action against involved personnel, seeking restitution, adoption of preventive or corrective company policies, and modifications of specific control procedures. If senior management is involved in an illegal act, the auditor should communicate directly with the audit committee. The communication may be oral or written. If the communication is oral, the auditor should document it.[21]

With respect to detection of management fraud and reporting illegal acts, the Public Oversight Board set forth these recommendations.

Recommendation V-1

1. Accounting firms should assure that auditors more consistently implement, and be more sensitive to the need to exercise the professional skepticism required by, the auditing standard that provides guidance on the auditor's responsibility to detect and report errors and irregularities.

Recommendation V-2

2. The Auditing Standards Board, the Executive Committee of the SEC Practice Section or some other appropriate body should develop guidelines to assist auditors in assessing the likelihood that management fraud which may affect financial information may be occurring and to specify additional auditing procedures when there is a heightened likelihood of management fraud.[22]

---

[21] Statement on Auditing Standards, no. 54, "Illegal Acts by Clients," par. 17.

[22] Public Oversight Board, A Special Report by the Public Oversight Board of the SEC Practice Section, AICPA (Stamford, CT: POB, 1993), p. 43.

Recommendation V-14

3. The accounting profession should support carefully drafted legislation requiring auditors to report to the appropriate authorities, including the SEC, suspected illegalities discovered by the auditor in the course of an audit if the client's management or board of directors fails to take necessary action with respect to such suspected illegalities and the auditor believes that they are or may be significant to the entity. The profession should seek adequate guidance as to the types of illegalities that would be encompassed by this requirement.[23]

It is reemphasized that the auditor's purpose is to express an objective opinion on the fairness of the presentation in the financial statements. A review of the scope paragraph of the external auditor's standard report explicitly indicates that he should plan and perform the audit to obtain reasonable assurance about whether the financial statements are free of material misstatement. Such a statement is also acknowledged to the client company in the engagement letter, whereby the auditor explicitly states that the audit may not detect all material irregularities.

It should be recognized that the auditor's examination in full compliance with the promulgated auditing standards is not a guarantee that fraud is totally nonexistent. As noted in the preceding discussion on computer fraud, a sophisticated scheme along with collusion may go undetected by the independent auditor. As a result, it is incumbent on the audit committee to obtain reasonable assurance from the external auditors that management has taken the necessary actions to protect the assets of the entity. Such assurance is obtained through the committee's review of the auditor's management letter regarding management's responsibility for the financial accounting system and the related internal controls as well as appropriate fidelity bond insurance coverage.

In view of the nature and complex problems of management fraud, the AICPA's standing committee on methods, perpetration, and detection of fraud has provided a time-tested list of warning signals of the possible existence of fraud. (See Exhibit 11.4.)

This checklist of warning signals is particularly important as a guide to the audit committee in its inquiries of the audit partner to identify the auditor's alertness to the possibility of fraud. For example, the committee may wish to correlate the checklist of warning signals with the auditor's management letter in order to identify potential problem areas. The major objective is to determine whether the auditor is taking a fresh look at the current year's audit examination versus merely rolling over examinations from previous years. Furthermore, the committee's review of the checklist will enable it to create an environment "that fosters morality and high business ethics."[24] "The systems should provide checks and balances and reports that cause flares to streak across the corporate sky if improprieties are practiced."[25]

---

[23] Ibid., p. 55.
[24] Sawyer, Murphy, and Crossley, "Management Fraud," 24.
[25] Ibid.

**EXHIBIT 11.4** Warning Signals of the Possible Existence of Fraud

1. Highly domineering senior management and one or more of the following, or similar, conditions are present:
   - An ineffective board of directors and/or audit committee.
   - Indications of management override of significant internal accounting controls.
   - Compensation or significant stock options tied to reported performance or to a specific transaction over which senior management has actual or implied control.
   - Indications of personal financial difficulties of senior management.
   - Proxy contests involving control of the company or senior management's continuance, compensation, or status.
2. Deterioration of quality of earnings evidenced by:
   - Decline in the volume or quality of sales (e.g., increased credit risk or sales at or below cost).
   - Significant changes in business practices.
   - Excessive interest by senior management in the earnings per share effect of accounting alternatives.
3. Business conditions that may create unusual pressures:
   - Inadequate working capital.
   - Little flexibility in debt restrictions such as working capital ratios and limitations on additional borrowings.
   - Rapid expansion of a product or business line markedly in excess of industry averages.
   - A major investment of the company's resources in an industry noted for rapid change, such as a high technology industry.
4. A complex corporate structure where the complexity does not appear to be warranted by the company's operations or size.
5. Widely dispersed business locations accompanied by highly decentralized management with inadequate responsibility reporting system.
6. Understaffing which appears to require certain employees to work unusual hours, to forego vacations, and/or to put in substantial overtime.
7. High turnover rate in key financial positions such as treasurer or controller.
8. Frequent change of auditors or legal counsel.
9. Known material weaknesses in internal control which could practically be corrected but remain uncorrected, such as:
   - Access to computer equipment or electronic data entry devices is not adequately controlled.
   - Incompatible duties remain combined.
10. Material transactions with related parties exist or there are transactions that may involve conflicts of interest.
11. Premature announcements of operating results or future (positive) expectations.
12. Analytical review procedures disclosing significant fluctuations which cannot be reasonably explained, for example:
    - Material account balances.
    - Financial or operational interrelationships.
    - Physical inventory variances.
    - Inventory turnover rates.
13. Large or unusual transactions, particularly at year-end, with material effect on earnings.
14. Unusually large payments in relation to services provided in the ordinary course of business by lawyers, consultants, agents, and others (including employees).

(*continued*)

---

**Exhibit 11.4**   (*Continued*)

---

15. Difficulty in obtaining audit evidence with respect to:
    - Unusual or unexplained entries.
    - Incomplete or missing documentation and/or authorization.
    - Alterations in documentation or accounts.
16. In the performance of an examination of financial statements unforeseen problems are encountered, for instance:
    - Client pressures to complete audit in an unusually short time or under difficult conditions.
    - Sudden delay situations.
    - Evasive or unreasonable responses of management to audit inquiries.

---

*Source:* American Institute of Certified Public Accountants, *CPA Letter* 59, No. 5 (March 12, 1979), 4.

## THE INTERNAL AUDITOR'S RESPONSIBILITY

As previously noted, the annual audit examination does not guarantee the non-existence of fraud. However, through a sound system of internal control, adequate fidelity bond insurance, and effective internal and external audits, the entity can be reasonably protected against fraud. Nevertheless, on the discovery of fraud, it is essential that the board of directors call for a careful and competent investigation of the situation. Although such an investigation is a burden on the entity, "corporate heads, including the boards of directors, should regard the occurrence as a business problem, not a legal problem."[26] Hence the board, through its audit committee, should demonstrate that it has taken the necessary course of action to properly uncover the fraud in order to maximize on its recovery from the fidelity bond insurance company.

Fraud risk governance must start with the governing board. The board helps to set the tone for fraud risk management and can encourage management to establish specific policies that encourage ethical behavior and promote the prevention and detection of fraud. The board is also responsible for monitoring the effectiveness of the organization's fraud risk management program. It can do this by assigning to a member of management the responsibility for the fraud risk management program and reporting to the board on its effectiveness.

Working closely with the audit committee, the internal audit function plays an important role in contributing to the overall governance of a fraud risk management program. This is primarily evident from the objective assurance the internal audit function provides to the board and management that the controls in place to manage fraud risks are designed adequately and operate effectively. Specifically, internal auditors may conduct proactive auditing to search for corruption, misappropriation of assets, and financial statement fraud. They can thus be regarded as both a fraud detection and deterrence measure—they can assist in the deterrence of fraud by examining and evaluating the adequacy and effectiveness of the

---

[26] Sawyer, Murphy, and Crossley, "Management Fraud," 20.

system of internal control, commensurate with the extent of the exposure or risk in the various segments of the organization's operations. Some such activities described in AU 316.86 are determining whether:

- Appropriate authorization policies for transactions are established and maintained.
- Policies, practices, procedures, reports, and other mechanisms are developed to monitor activities and safeguard assets, particularly in high-risk areas.
- Recommendations need to be made for the establishment or enhancement of cost-effective controls to help deter fraud.

## INVESTIGATING KNOWN FRAUD[27]

Although the approach to an investigation may vary, Sawyer, Murphy, and Crossley point out that "an executive should be assigned to coordinate . . . the investigation."[28] Ordinarily, the executive is the director of internal auditing. However, the audit committee may wish to engage special investigators and/or external auditors so that both groups may coordinate their efforts with the internal auditors. Moreover, the surety company usually makes its own investigation because it must attest to the validity of the entity's claim. However, it is important to recognize that such an investigation should not be made solely by the surety company because its objective is to minimize the claim for the loss. Thus the audit committee should ensure that the investigation is properly coordinated with the auditors or the special investigators and the surety company. In particular, the committee should be assured that (1) the suspect has not been notified of the present investigation; (2) the investigation has been properly planned in advance and will be conducted expeditiously to prevent covering up the evidence; (3) all corporate transactions involving the suspect and the methods used to perpetrate the fraud have been properly investigated and documented; (4) the existence of possible collusion has been carefully considered; (5) the dollar amount of the defalcation has been properly ascertained and the amount of the funds recovered; and (6) any legal action, if appropriate, has been taken against the perpetrator(s). Such assurance is obtained through the committee's review of the reports from the auditors, legal counsel, and the surety company as well as its consultation with the external audit partner regarding disclosure matters in the financial statements.

From the preceding discussion, it is evident that the audit committee should recognize not only the primary purpose of the annual audit examination but also the implications of the auditor's responsibility for the detection of fraud. The committee will look primarily to the internal and external auditors for assistance concerning the necessary measures for the prevention of fraud. For example, it

---

[27] For further reference, see Denzil Y. Causey, "The CPA Guide to Whistle Blowing," *CPA Journal* 58, no. 8 (August 1988): 26–37; Timothy L. Williams and W. Steve Albrecht, "Understanding Reactions to Fraud," *Internal Auditor* 47, no. 4 (August 1990): 45–51. As discussed in Chapter 2, the reader should review Section 806 dealing with whistle-blowing protection for employees.

[28] Ibid.

may request a periodic survey of the fraud prevention measures within the entity. Such a survey may be done by the internal audit group to determine the soundness of the system of internal control. Consequently, during its review of the audit plans, the committee should address the need for a survey of the fraud prevention measures. When such a survey is conducted, the committee should review the internal auditor's report with the outside audit partner to obtain the partner's assessment of the entity's fraud prevention activities. The committee should be satisfied that there is adequate follow-up regarding the internal auditor's recommendations so that if and when fraud should occur, it can be confident that the cause of the fraud was not related to recommendations that were overlooked. Such an oversight on the part of the committee may be a cause for an unrecovered insurance claim. It is obvious that the audit committee must be alert not only to the possibility of fraud but also to the steps necessary to safeguard the entity from such fraud.

Hugh L. Marsh and Thomas E. Powell conclude:

> It would be a misconception to believe the possibility of fraud is the only reason for establishing a chartered audit committee. While the primary role has been to oversee management's financial and reporting responsibilities, it is only one task. Nevertheless, the Treadway Commission's investigations indicated that audit committees could serve very effectively to reduce the incidence of fraud. When fraudulent financial reporting did occur despite the existence of an audit committee, the following important points in the audit committee's charter often had been omitted:
>
> *Authorization for resources.* As noted by the Treadway Commission, only in unusual circumstances would an audit committee need a separate staff, but the means for accomplishing this should be addressed.
>
> *Issues related to CPAs' independence.* The press has made much ado about the practice of some CPAs using audit services as a "loss leader" for management advisory services. Strong opinions have been expressed on both sides of this issue, but it would seem prudent for the audit committee to oversee management's judgments about the independence of its CPAs.
>
> *Seeking a second opinion.* Some observers speak of it disparagingly as "opinion shopping"; others refer to it as seeking a technically correct opinion. But any time a second opinion is sought, the audit committee should know what the issues were and how they were resolved.
>
> *Preservation of internal auditor independence.* Internal auditors occupy the unique position of "independent" staff members. This independence is strengthened and ensured through audit committee action. Direct and unrestricted access to records is essential and the audit committee should concur with the appointment and discharge of the director of internal audit.[29]

A good reference for audit committees concerned about fraud risk is the work edited by former AICPA General Counsel Michael R. Young, "Accounting

---

[29] Hugh L. Marsh and Thomas E. Powell, "The Audit Committee Charter: Rx for Fraud Prevention," *Journal of Accountancy* 167, no. 2 (February 1989): 55–57.

Irregularities and Financial Fraud."[30] Two recent publications, one from Deloitte[31] and one Ernst & Young,[32] are also worth consulting.

## THE AUDIT COMMITTEE'S OVERSIGHT APPROACH TO FRAUD RISK ASSESSMENT

As part of their oversight of the audit process and the SAS No. 99 requirements, audit committees need to assure the full board of directors of any indications of possible fraud and illegal acts, including management's remedial actions. More specifically, audit committees can expect to have discussions with their external auditors regarding fraud risk areas during the information-gathering phase. Likewise, audit committees will be notified about fraud findings and reportable conditions during the communication phase.

To achieve effective oversight responsibility for fraud risk areas, audit committees should consider this two-step approach:

1. Complete a profile worksheet with the details of the entity's potential fraud risk area.
2. Address a set of representative questions for the preaudit and postaudit meetings.

### Audit Committee's Profile Worksheet—Fraud Risk Areas

Given the thrust of the new fraud standard, it is reasonable to expect that audit committees will include a statement regarding their fraud risk discussions in their written charter, which is disclosed in the entity's annual proxy statement. Exhibit 11.5 shows a suggested format for a profile worksheet.

To adequately plan a review of the fraud risk areas, audit committees need knowledge about the entity's:

- Business model and industry
- Business risks and internal control environment
- Policies and procedures for detecting fraud and illegal acts
- Accounting industry practices
- Complex business transactions and significant contracts
- Financial reporting process

Likewise, audit committees need to review:

- The operational characteristics of the entity and the vulnerability of the industry to changing economic conditions and competitive pressures. Such a review

---

[30] Michael R. Young (ed.), *Accounting Irregularities and Financial Fraud: A Corporate Governance Guide*, 2nd edition (New York: Aspen Publishers, 2002).

[31] Bishop, T.J.F., and Hydoski, F.E., *Corporate Resiliency: Managing the Growing Risk of Fraud and Corruption* (Hoboken, NJ: John Wiley & Sons, 2009)

[32] Sharma, R., & Sherrod, M. (eds.), *The Guide to Investigating Business Fraud* (New York: AICA, 2009).

**EXHIBIT 11.5** Audit Committee's Profile Worksheet of the Entity's Fraud Risk Areas

| Audit Committee Practice Area Knowledge Areas | Management | Internal Auditors | External Auditors | Legal Counsel | Board of Directors | Compliance with SEC, SROs, ASB, or Sarbanes-Oxley Act | Comments |
|---|---|---|---|---|---|---|---|
| ***Industry Matters*** | | | | | | | |
| Competition | ✓ | ✓ | ✓ | | | | |
| Economic conditions | ✓ | ✓ | ✓ | | | | |
| Technology | ✓ | ✓ | ✓ | | | | |
| Government regulations | ✓ | ✓ | ✓ | ✓ | | | |
| Industry accounting practices | ✓ | ✓ | ✓ | | | | |
| ***Entity's Business Matters*** | | | | | | | |
| Organizational structure (management integrity) | | | ✓ | | ✓ | | |
| Business and product segments (Business model profile) | ✓ | ✓ | ✓ | | | | |
| Policies and procedures for detecting fraud, illegal acts, and whistle-blower protection (e.g., conflicts-of-interests (related party transactions) monitoring, compliance with the corporate code of conduct, monitoring compliance with laws and regulations, and management override of control(s)) | ✓ | ✓ | ✓ | ✓ | ✓ | ✓ | |
| Management's risk assessment process (business risk profile and internal control concepts) | ✓ | ✓ | ✓ | | | | |
| Accounting policies and practices | ✓ | ✓ | ✓ | | | | |
| Complex business transactions and contracts | ✓ | ✓ | ✓ | ✓ | | | |
| Frequent change of legal counsel | | | | | ✓ | | |

| | | | | | |
|---|---|---|---|---|---|
| Financial reporting process (quarterly and annual financial statements) | ✓ | ✓ | ✓ | | ✓ | ✓ |
| Internal communication process | ✓ | ✓ | ✓ | ✓ | ✓ | ✓ |
| External communication process | ✓ | | ✓ | | ✓ | ✓ |
| ***External Audit Process*** | | | | | | |
| Selection or retention of auditors (terms of service, qualifications, composition, and independence of the audit engagement team) | ✓ | ✓ | ✓ | | ✓ | ✓ |
| Frequent change of auditors (disagreement on GAAP, which indicates opinion shopping) | ✓ | ✓ | ✓ | | ✓ | ✓ |
| Quantity of lawsuits against the CPA firm | ✓ | ✓ | ✓ | ✓ | ✓ | |
| Nonacceptance of recommendations in the management letter (breakdowns in internal controls) | ✓ | ✓ | ✓ | | | ✓ |
| ***Internal Audit Process*** | | | | | | |
| Approve hiring or termination of the internal auditing executive (term of service, qualifications and composition of the internal audit groups) | | ✓ | ✓ | | ✓ | |
| Departmental organization and size | | ✓ | ✓ | | | |
| Reporting responsibility | | ✓ | | | | |
| Scope restrictions and access to requested information | | ✓ | | | | |
| Quantity of special projects and investigations dealing with material noncompliance | | ✓ | ✓ | ✓ | | ✓ |

usually would include recent annual and interim financial statements, SEC filings (1O-Qs and 10-Ks), annual proxy statement, the entity's Web site, and analytical review procedures (e.g., absolute data comparison, financial ratio data). In addition, an evaluation of management integrity would include biographical information on senior executives and financial management.

- Management's risk assessment process and related internal controls (i.e., the components of COSO's Internal Control—Integrated Framework)
- Management's policies and procedures with respect to:
  - Conflicts-of-interest statements
  - Corporate code of conduct
  - Laws and regulations
  - Management override of controls
- Industry accounting practices, with particular emphasis on the appropriateness of accounting principles
- Complex business transactions (e.g., restructuring charges)
- Financial reporting process at the individual financial account and transaction class level
- Internal and external communication processes
- Internal and external auditing processes

## Audit Committee's Meetings and Agendas—Fraud Risk Areas

Based on the profile worksheet, audit committees need to know what questions to ask with respect to the auditors' assessment of fraud risk and their response to the overall audit approach.

During the preaudit meeting, audit committees can elicit information that is helpful in setting objectives and implementation measures related to fraud prevention and detection. For example, audit committees may ask the auditors to expand the scope of their examination with respect to areas of revenue recognition or misappropriation of inventory. This information is also useful in setting objectives in areas such as internal audit and special investigations. Exhibits 11.6 and 11.7 provide questions that enable audit committees to establish specific objectives related to fraud risk areas.

During the postaudit meeting, audit committees need answers to questions dealing with fraud detection, illegal acts, and breakdowns in internal control that arose in the audit engagement. Exhibit 11.7 indicates some representative questions.

In reviewing the financial statements, audit committees should request a fraud risk assessment at the financial account and transaction class level. They should be alert to areas that involve judgment in recognition, valuation, measurement, and disclosure, as well as management's assertions regarding asset realization and liability measurement.

In addition, audit committees should be alert to situations that involve breakdowns in the system of internal control. As previously noted, audit committees should review and study the areas of COSO's Internal Control—Integrated Framework in the context of the auditors' fraud risk assessment.

**EXHIBIT 11.6**　Representative Questions for Preaudit Meetings—Fraud Risk Planning

- To what extent can the planned audit scope be relied on to detect fraud? (See audit engagement letter for the auditors' responsibilities.)
- What steps were taken by the audit engagement team in assessing the likelihood that fraud, which may affect financial information, may be occurring?
  - Inquiries of management and employees other than management
  - Observations with regard to preliminary analytical procedures, including procedures related to revenue recognition (i.e., unusual and unexpected results)
  - Consideration of fraud risk factors relative to fraudulent financial reporting and misappropriation of assets (incentives/pressures, opportunities, and attitudes/rationalizations)
  - Consideration of other information (e.g., integrity of management)
  - Identification of fraud risks, including type of risk, significance, likelihood, and pervasiveness
  - Assessment of identified fraud risks and consideration of the entity's programs and controls to prevent, detect, and mitigate fraud
  - Response to fraud risk assessment in the overall audit approach, including the nature, timing, and extent of audit procedures as well as additional procedures related to management override of controls
- What areas will be emphasized due to the heightened likelihood of fraud?
- What areas require special attention by the audit committee? (e.g., Sarbanes-Oxley's Corporate and Criminal Fraud Accountability provision, including record retention and destruction procedures as well as whistleblower protection)
- Were there any allegations of unethical behavior in the financial reporting process?

**EXHIBIT 11.7**　Representative Questions for Postaudit Meeting—Fraud Risk Areas

- To what extent did the actual scope of the fraud risk audit findings differ from the preaudit plan? What were the causes for the difference?
- Did management restrict the scope of the audit or access to requested information?
- Were there disagreements with management on accounting policies and practices, including estimates and assumptions?
- What recommendations were made to management to improve the system of internal control?
- What assessment was given to the entity's policies and procedures for detecting conflicts of interests (e.g., related party transactions) and management override of controls, including directives of the board of directors?
- Were there any incidents of noncompliance with laws and regulations, including the provisions of Sarbanes-Oxley?
- Were there any incidents of noncompliance with the corporate code of conduct?
- What were the accounting treatments with respect to complex transactions, unusual transactions, and material contracts?
- Were there any proposed accounting adjustments, including immaterial uncorrected adjustments?

Finally, audit committees should be concerned with material audit adjustments and immaterial uncorrected misstatements, including aggressive versus conservative accounting policies and any changes in accounting principles.

In sum, the new fraud standard will affect the audit committee's preaudit and postaudit meetings and related agendas, and it will presumably help engender a high degree of integrity in both the audit processes and the financial reporting process.

Thus audit committees need to review and discuss with the internal and external auditors and financial management:

1. Premature revenue recognition situations, such as those related to unshipped products and bill and hold sales not at the customer request
2. Unrealistic assumptions related to accounting estimates cookie jar reserves
3. Big Bath restructuring charges in which certain expenses belong to future periods
4. The key provisions of the Sarbanes-Oxley Act of 2002 that relate to such matters as personal loans to executives (Section 402) and disclosure of off-balance sheet transactions and other relationships (Section 401).

### SOURCES AND SUGGESTED READINGS

American Institute of Certified Public Accountants. *CPA Letter* 59, no. 5 (March 12, 1979): 1–6.

American Institute of Certified Public Accountants. *Management Antifraud Programs and Controls*. For more information on fraud prevention and deterrence, visit the AICPA's Antifraud Resource Center, www.aicpa.org/antifraud.

Association of Certified Fraud Examiners. Annual Fraud Conference, www.CFEnet.com.

Association of Certified Fraud Examiners. *Fraud Statistics Fact Sheet*. Austin, TX: ACEF, 1993.

Association of Certified Fraud Examiners. *Report to the Nation on Occupational Fraud Abuse*. Austin, TX: ACEF, 1996, 2002.

Beasley, Mark S. "An Empirical Analysis of the Relation Between the Board of Director Composition and Financial Statement Fraud." *Accounting Review* 71, no. 4 (October 1996): 443–465.

Brandt, Allen. "The Biggest Computer Frauds: Lesson for CPAs." *Journal of Accountancy* 143, no. 5 (May 1977): 52–62.

Carmichael, Douglas R. "The Auditor's New Guide to Errors, Irregularities and Illegal Acts." *Journal of Accountancy* 166, no. 3 (September 1988): 40–48.

Causey, Denzil Y. "The CPA Guide to Whistle Blowing." *CPA Journal* 58, no. 8 (August 1988): 26–37.

Ernst & Young. *Fraud: The Unmanaged Risk, An International Survey of the Effect of Fraud on Business*. London: Ernst & Young, 1998.

Institute of Internal Auditors bookstore. Visit their Web site at www.theiia.org for information on fraud, ethics, law.

Marsh, Hugh L., and Thomas E. Powell. "The Audit Committee Charter: Rx for Fraud Prevention." *Journal of Accountancy* 167, no. 2 (February 1989): 55–57.

Menkus, Belden. "Eight Factors Contributing to Computer Fraud." *Internal Auditor* 47, no. 5 (October 1990): 71–73.

National Commission on Fraudulent Financial Reporting. *Report of the National Commission on Fraudulent Financial Reporting.* Washington, DC: NCFFR, 1987.

Neebes, Donald L., Dan M. Guy, and O. Ray Whittington. "Illegal Acts: What Are the Auditor's Responsibilities?" *Journal of Accountancy* 171, no. 1 (January 1991): 82–84, 86, 88, 90–93.

Public Oversight Board. *A Special Report by the Public Oversight Board of the SEC Practice Section, AICPA.* Stamford, CT: POB, 1993.

Sawyer, Lawrence B., Albert A. Murphy, and Michael Crossley. "Management Fraud: The Insidious Specter." *Internal Auditor*, 36, no. 2 (April 1979): 11–25.

*Statement on Auditing Standards No. 54.* "Illegal Acts by Clients." New York: AICPA, 1988.

*Statement on Auditing Standards No. 55.* "Consideration of the Internal Control Structure in a Financial Statement Audit." New York: AICPA, 1988.

*Statement on Auditing Standards No. 99.* "Consideration of Fraud in a Financial Statement Audit." New York: AICPA, 2002.

Stice, James D., W. Steve Albrecht, and Leslie M. Brown. "Lessons to be Learned—ZZZZ Best, Regina, and Lincoln Savings." *CPA Journal* 61, no. 4 (April 1991): 52–53.

*United States v. Weiner*, 578 F. 2d 757 (9th Cir), *cert. denied*, 439 U.S. 981 (1978).

Wells, Joseph T., "Six Common Myths About Fraud." *Journal of Accountancy* 169, no. 2 (February 1990): 82–88.

Williams, Timothy L., and W. Steve Albrecht. "Understanding Reactions to Fraud." *Internal Auditor*, no. 4 (August 1990): 45–51.

Young, Michael R. (ed.). *Accounting Irregularities and Financial Fraud.* New York: Aspen Law & Business, A Wolters Kluwer Company, 2002.

The reader also may wish to visit the Web sites of other organizations as noted in the Appendix.

## Additional Suggested Readings

Albrecht, W. S., M. B. Romney, D. J. Cherrington, I. R. Payne, and A. J. Roe. *How to Detect and Prevent Business Fraud.* Englewood Cliffs, NJ: Prentice-Hall, 1982.

Association of Certified Fraud Examiners. *Professional Standards and Practices for Certified Fraud Examiners.* Austin, TX: ACFE, 2002.

Association of Certified Fraud Examiners. *The White Paper.* Austin, TX: ACFE, published bimonthly.

Bloom Becker, Buck. *Spectacular Computer Crimes.* New York: Dow Jones Irwin, 1990.

Bologna, G. Jack, and Robert J. Lindquist. *Fraud Auditing and Forensic Accounting.* New York: John Wiley & Sons, 1987.

Bologna, G. Jack, Robert J. Lindquist, and Joseph Wells. *The Accountant's Handbook of Fraud & Commercial Crime.* New York: John Wiley & Sons, 1992.

Coderre, David G. "Fraud Detection: A Revealing Look at Fraud." Ekaros Analytical, 2004.

Davia, Howard R., Patrick C. Coggins, John C. Wildeman, and Joseph T. Kastantin. *Management Accountants' Guide to Fraud Discovery and Control*. New York: John Wiley & Sons, 1992.

Domanick, Joe. *Faking It in America*. Chicago: Contemporary Books, 1989.

Elliott, Robert K., and John J. Willingham. *Management Fraud: Detection and Deterrence*. New York: Petrocelli Books, 1980.

Glover, Hubert D., and James C. Flagg. *Effective Fraud Detection and Prevention Techniques*. Altamonte Springs, FL: The IIA, 1993.

Institute of Internal Auditors. "Fraud Findings." *Internal Auditor* (published monthly).

Institute of Internal Auditors. *The Professional Practice Framework*. Altamonte Springs, FL: The IIA, 2009.

Jackson, Ira A., and Jane Nelson. "Profits with Principles." Doubleday, 2004.

Jacobson, Alan. *How to Detect Fraud Through Auditing*. Altamonte Springs, FL: The IIA, 1990.

Kellogg, Irving. *Fraud, Window Dressing, and Negligence in Financial Statements*. New York: McGraw-Hill, 1991.

O'Gara, John D. *Corporate Fraud: Case Studies in Detection and Prevention*. Hoboken, NJ: John Wiley & Sons, 2004.

Wells, J.T. (ed.). *Computer Fraud Casebook: The Bytes that Bite*. Hoboken, NJ: John Wiley & Sons, 2009.

# Chapter 12

# The Audit Committee, Corporate Culture, and Tone at the Top

The audit committee contributes to fulfilling the board of directors' responsibility for internal control over financial reporting and the maintenance of appropriate books and records, for encouraging an appropriate company culture, and for ensuring a positive tone at the top. Some specific areas in which the audit committee has a role concern various types of sensitive payments. Such payments could encompass bribes or other questionable payments, executive perquisites and compensation, political contributions, and charitable contributions. Applicable to all of these areas is the joint problem of ensuring that sensitive payments are legal and, if they are legal, that they are properly authorized and reported. Audit committees should make certain that systems and personnel are in place to assure that an appropriate example is set at the top of the organization and that it is well imbedded in the culture of the company.

## QUESTIONABLE FOREIGN PAYMENTS

### Nature of Questionable Foreign Payments

The Foreign Corrupt Practices Act of 1977 prohibited all U.S. companies (both private and public), foreign companies registered with the SEC, and their directors, officers, stockholders, employees, and agents from bribing foreign government officials. The act prohibits the use of mails or any means or instrumentalities of interstate commerce to make corrupt payments or authorize payments regarding "anything of value" to:

1. Any foreign official
2. Any foreign political party or official thereof
3. Any person, while knowing or having reason to know that all or a portion of the payment will be offered to any of the preceding groups or any candidate for foreign political office[1]

---

[1] The act is contained in Title I of Public Law No. 95-213.

Certain payments, referred to as "facilitating" or "grease" payments, are not covered under the act because they are treated by the act as ministerial or clerical. Nonetheless, with respect to disclosure of such ministerial or clerical payments, the SEC indicates:

> These so-called facilitating payments have been deemed to be material where the payments to particular persons are large in amount or the aggregate amounts are large, or where corporate management has taken steps to conceal them through false entries in corporate books and records.[2]

Management is responsible for identifying and determining how payments for customs documents, minor permits, and other such transactions that essentially are facilitating payments should be authorized, accounted for, reported, and disclosed. The audit committee oversees management's activities in these areas.

---

**EXHIBIT 12.1**    Selected Cases and Alleged Violations—Foreign Corrupt Practices Act

| Date Filed | Release No. | Nature of Alleged Violations |
|---|---|---|
| 12/21/00 | LR-16839 | On December 21, 2000, the Commission instituted settled administrative proceedings against a registrant for books and records violations resulting from payments of $22 million to foreign officials by one of the company's wholly owned subsidiaries in Argentina. These improper payments were made in violation of the Foreign Corrupt Practices Act of 1997 (FCPA). The company also consented to the entry of a judgment in U.S. District Court ordering it to pay a $300,000 penalty. |
| 1/15/02 | LR-17310 | The Commission filed a civil action against two former officers of registrant, alleging that they authorized over $500,000 in bribery payments to Haitian customs officials to reduce the company's import taxes by approximately $1.5 million. |
| 8/1/02 | LR-17651 | The Commission instituted settled cease-and-desist proceedings against the registrant and obtained an order directing it to pay a $150,000 penalty based on its expansion into Venezuela and Nicaragua. |

*Source:* Securities and Exchange Commission, *2001 Annual Report* (page 4) and *2002 Annual Report* (page 9) (Washington, DC: U.S. Government Printing Office, 2001, 2002).

---

[2] Securities and Exchange Commission, "Report of the Securities and Exchange Commission on Questionable and Illegal Corporate Payments and Practices," submitted to the Senate Banking, Housing and Urban Affairs Committee, May 12, 1976, at 27.

The Organization of Economic Cooperation and Development (OECD) reached an accord with its member countries to address the problem of bribery in international business. As Donald J. Johnston, secretary-general of the OECD, points out:

> The Convention on Combating Bribery of Foreign Public Officials in International Business Transactions is an instrument which will permit OECD and other countries to move in a coordinated manner to adopt national legislation to make it a crime to bribe foreign public officials. The Convention sets a high standard for national laws. It includes a broad, clear definition of bribery; it requires dissuasive penalties; it sets a strong standard for enforcement; and it provides for mutual legal assistance. The entry into force provisions are designed to encourage signatories to act quickly and in concert.[3]

The Convention contains 17 articles. Article 8 includes an accounting provision that states:

1. In order to combat bribery of foreign public officials effectively, each Party shall take such measures as may be necessary, within the framework of its laws and regulations regarding the maintenance of books and records, financial statement disclosures, and accounting and auditing standards, to prohibit the establishment of off-the-books accounts, the making of off-the-books or inadequately identified transactions, the recording of non-existent expenditures, the entry of liabilities with incorrect identification of their object, as well as the use of false documents, by companies subject to those laws and regulations, for the purpose of bribing foreign public officials or of hiding such bribery.
2. Each Party shall provide effective, proportionate and dissuasive civil, administrative or criminal penalties for such omissions and falsifications in respect of the books, records, accounts and financial statements of such companies.[4]

Obviously, the negotiated convention by the OECD with its member nations is a major step toward solving the problem of bribery in international business. Presumably, the OECD's convention will be adopted by the individual governments of the member countries.

## Summary Guidelines: Historical Perspective

To monitor questionable foreign payments effectively, the audit committee should review corporate policy and other documentation that supports management's compliance with such policy. Concerning corporate policy, the American Assembly's recommendations regarding the standards of corporate conduct are useful in formulating policy guidelines:

---

[3] Organization of Economic Cooperation and Development, Convention on Combating Bribery of Foreign Public Officials in International Business Transactions (Paris: OECD, 1997), at 3.
[4] Ibid., 8.

Although American corporations operating overseas should give due regard to the ethical judgments of other societies, each U.S. corporation can maintain only one set of universal principles that must not be compromised in foreign subsidiaries. Some U.S. practices of a less important nature may be adjusted to custom, practice, and law; such cases should be evaluated before the fact and stated publicly.

American corporations should proscribe bribery and kickbacks everywhere . . . American corporations operating in foreign lands should not be prohibited by American law from contributing to political parties when such contributions are legal under that country's laws, expected as part of good corporate responsibility, and are disclosed.[5]

The desirability of such a corporate policy became evident in a Conference Board study where the Board surveyed 35 firms on their approaches to the problem of improper payments. Survey results revealed that "a handful" of companies were free of problems because they had effective corporate policies and practices.[6] Such companies "simply enjoin company employees from any illegal activity or conflicts of interest."[7] But "many companies reported sharp divisions in their management ranks regarding the types of payments that should be enjoined."[8] Thus, to avoid any misunderstanding among the employees, it is necessary to define clearly the proper and improper payments within the context of the Foreign Corrupt Practices Act.

## The External Auditor's Responsibility

As noted in Chapter 11, the external auditor's examination cannot guarantee that irregularities or illegal acts are nonexistent. According to the Auditing Standards Board:

Certain illegal acts have a direct and material effect on the determination of financial statement amounts. Other illegal acts, such as those described,[9] may, in particular circumstances, be regarded as having material but indirect effects on financial statements. The auditor's responsibility with respect to detecting, considering the financial statements effects of, and reporting these other illegal acts is described in this Statement. These other illegal acts are hereinafter referred to simply as *illegal acts*. The auditor should be aware of the possibility that such illegal acts may have occurred. If specific information comes to the auditor's attention that provides evidence concerning the existence of possible illegal acts that could have a material indirect effect on the financial statements, the auditor should apply audit procedures, specifically directed to ascertaining whether an illegal act has occurred. However, because of the characteristics of illegal acts as explained above, an audit made in

---

[5] American Assembly, *The Ethics of Corporate Conduct*, Pamphlet 52 (New York: Columbia University, April 1977): 6–7.

[6] James Greene, "Assuming Ethical Conduct Abroad," *Conference Board Information Bulletin*, No. 12 (November 1976): 1.

[7] Ibid., 3.

[8] Ibid.

[9] See Chapter 11 for additional emphasis.

accordance with generally accepted auditing standards provides no assurance that illegal acts will be detected or that any contingent liabilities that may result will be disclosed.[10]

While the external auditors can assist the audit committee in the sensitive payments area, it is important to recognize that:

[w]ith respect to high level executive conflicts of interest, the Board of Directors has the obligation, in selecting such executives, to make exhaustive background checks of prospective candidates such as are now being followed in filling high U.S. Government posts.[11]

Such investigations of the candidates will not only help curtail the problem of improper payments and conflicts of interest but also will strengthen the board's image in the business community. As a result, the major objective is to review the corporate policy and internal monitoring procedures, as discussed in this chapter and the preceding chapter, with the external auditors.

In short, as Grover R. Heyler, partner of Latham and Watkins, concludes, ". . . directors need to go beyond what the auditors might be able to do."[12] In addition to the annual questionnaires regarding sensitive areas, Heyler suggests that:

- A conflict-of-interest committee can be established.
- The board can require reports on trading in the company's stock.
- Controls on the disclosure of inside information and press releases can be initiated.
- Provisions can be made for some independent review of relationships between the company and firms affiliated with insiders.[13]

## CORPORATE PERQUISITES AND EXECUTIVE COMPENSATION

### Corporate Perquisites

During the latter part of the 1970s, the SEC scrutinized the area of perquisites, or "perks," as evidenced by several SEC releases. For example, SEC Release No. 33-5758, issued in November 1976, stated:

. . . it has been suggested that disclosure should be required of the numerous emerging forms of indirect compensation or "perquisites" now given to management personnel.

---

[10] Statement on Auditing Standards, No. 54, "Illegal Acts by Clients" (New York: AICPA, 1988), par. 7.

[11] Herbert Robinson and J. Karl Fishbach, "Commercial Bribery—The Corporation as Victim," *Financial Executive* 47, no. 4 (April 1979): 16.

[12] Boltz, Heyler, James, and Wheat, "Corporate Directors' Responsibilities," 20.

[13] Ibid.

Furthermore, in April 1977 the SEC asked, in Securities Exchange Act Release No. 13482, "Should the Commission amend its proxy rules . . . to provide for more detailed or comprehensive disclosure of management remuneration?" Finally, in August 1977, the SEC issued Interpretative Release No. 33-5856, "Disclosure of Management Remuneration," whereby it pointed out that the securities acts require not only the disclosure of direct remuneration paid to directors and officers but also personal benefits " . . . sometimes referred to as 'perquisites.'" The Commission determined that certain personal benefits received by management from the corporation should be reported as remuneration:

> Among the benefits received by management which the Commission believes should be reported as remuneration are payments made by registrants for the following purposes: (1) home repairs and improvements; (2) housing and other living expenses (including domestic service) provided at principal and/or vacation residences of management personnel; (3) the personal use of company property such as automobiles, planes, yachts, apartments, hunting lodges, or company vacation houses; (4) personal travel expenses; (5) personal entertainment and related expenses; and (6) legal, accounting, and other professional fees for matters unrelated to the business of the registrant. Other personal benefits which may be forms of remuneration are the following: the ability of management to obtain benefits from third parties, because the corporation compensates, directly or indirectly, the bank or supplier for providing the loan or services to management; and the use of the corporate staff for personal purposes.

> Certain incidental personal benefits which are directly related to job performance may be omitted from aggregate reported remuneration provided they are authorized and properly accounted for by the company. Parking places, meals at company facilities, and office space and furnishings at company-maintained offices are a few examples of personal benefits directly related to job performance.

> In addition, certain incidental benefits received by management which are ordinary and necessary to the conduct of company business may not be forms of remuneration. These job-related benefits are benefits which are available to management employees generally, which do not relieve the individual of expenditures normally considered to be of a personal nature and which are extended to management solely for the purposes of attracting and maintaining qualified personnel, facilitating their conduct of company business, or improving their efficiency in job performance. While itemized expense accounts may be considered job-related benefits whose value would be excluded from the aggregate remuneration reported, some may be forms of remuneration if they are excessive in amount or conferred too frequently. In any case, management is usually in the best position to determine whether a certain benefit should be viewed as a form of remuneration based on the facts and circumstances involved in each situation.

> The value of all forms of remuneration should be included within the appropriate item(s) of disclosure. Nonmonetary forms of remuneration must be valued as accurately as possible. The appropriate valuation may be based upon appraisals, the value of the benefit to the recipient, the valuation assigned for tax purposes, or some other appropriate standard.

Although the SEC release attempted to resolve the disclosure problem of perquisites, many accounting practitioners and corporate executives raised questions regarding the disclosure of certain items. In an attempt to resolve the issues, the SEC issued a second Interpretive Release, No. 33-5904, which contained questions and interpretative responses of the Commission's Division of Corporation Finance. In particular, the questions related to (a) the use of company property; (b) membership in clubs and professional associations; (c) medical, insurance, and other reimbursement plans; (d) payments for living and related expenses; (e) use of corporate staff; (f) benefits from third parties; (g) company products; and (h) business expenses. Specifically, the Commission asserted:[14]

> Corporations make a great variety of expenditures which relate to management, many of which result in benefits to executives. Whether these constitute remuneration usually depends upon the facts and circumstances involved in each situation. In general, expenditures which simply assist an executive in doing his job effectively or which reimburse him for expenses incurred in the performance of his functions are not remuneration, while expenditures made for his personal benefit or for purposes unrelated to the business of the company would constitute remuneration. In some instances, expenditures may serve both purposes, and if neither is predominant, allocation to the extent reasonably feasible may be called for.

> In determining whether the value of specific benefits should be included in aggregate remuneration, registrants should keep in mind that full disclosure of the remuneration received by officers and directors is important to informed voting and investment decisions. In particular, remuneration information is necessary for an informed assessment of management and is significant in maintaining public confidence in the corporate system. Of course, accurate and sufficiently detailed books and records are prerequisites to the appropriate disclosure of remuneration information.[15]

Of particular importance to the audit committee is SEC Release No. 33-6003, issued in December 197 to amend Regulation S-K. This release affects not only item 4 of the S-K but also proxy materials and other filing forms. For example, this release increases all remuneration paid to or accrued by the corporation's five highest-paid officers or directors whose total remuneration exceeds $50,000 annually.[16]

As mentioned in Chapter 3, in October 1992 the SEC adopted amendments to the executive officer and director compensation disclosure requirements. With respect to perquisites, Release Nos. 33-6962, 34-31327 and 1C-19032 pertaining to Regulation S-K set forth:

---

[14] In addition to the SEC releases cited, the reader should review Release No. 33-5950, "Proposed Amendments to Disclosure Forms Regulations" (July 1978), with the independent auditors.

[15] Although the SEC has stated that perquisites of less than $10,000 per individual may be excluded in the aggregate remuneration, such exclusion should be disclosed in the registrant's transmittal letter.

[16] As of October 21, 1992, this amount was increased to $100,000, as discussed in Chapter 3. For further reference, see Kathleen T. McGahran, "SEC Disclosure Regulation and Management Perquisites," *Accounting Review* 63, no. 1 (January 1988): 23–41; and Coopers and Lybrand, "Executive Perquisites Study Release: An Overview of the Findings," Executive Briefing (May 1992): 1–3.

*Perquisites.* Several commenters suggested that, to reflect inflation, the perquisites and other personal benefits reporting threshold should be raised from the lesser of $25,000 or 10% of reported salary and bonus, and that the requirement to itemize each perquisite or benefit in a footnote be eliminated. Given the effect of inflation since the last revision of Item 402 in 1983, which has been taken into account in the Commission's upward adjustment of the dollar benchmark for designating the named executives, the Commission similarly has increased the perks/personal benefits threshold in the final rule to call for disclosure only when the aggregate value of these items exceeds the lesser of either $50,000 or 10% of total salary and bonus disclosed in the Summary Compensation Table.

As proposed, the registrant would have been required to identify each perquisite included in the amount reported in a footnote to the Other Annual Compensation column. The Item has been revised to require footnote or textual narrative disclosure of the nature and value of any particular perquisite or benefit only for those perks valued at more than 25% of the sum of all perquisites reported as Other Annual Compensation for that executive.[17]

In view of these new disclosure requirements in the company's annual proxy statement, the audit committee should ensure that the compensation committee and management are complying with the requirement regarding compensation and perquisite disclosure. Such information should be reviewed by general counsel and the independent auditors.

Corporate perquisites again became a major issue—in the context of a number of corporate failures—during the early 2000s. Perhaps the most notorious of these cases was that of Tyco, where chairman and CEO Dennis Kozloswki and several others members of management and the board came under scrutiny for possible excesses. In Section 402, the Sarbanes-Oxley Act addressed some aspects of perceived abuses by restricting the loans that boards could make to executives and directors, and it devoted several sections to new disclosures related to executive and director compensation. The SEC adopted additional regulations on proxy disclosures related to the compensation of executives and the board. Because some perquisites were associated with services rendered to individuals in management who are able to affect the financial reporting process, the PCAOB—by extending the independence rules—restricted the ability for audit firms to provide tax planning and return preparation services to those individuals. The extended disclosures required by the SEC appear in Release No. 33-8765.[18] In addition, the SEC has proposed further revisions to proxy disclosures that relate to compensation and corporate governance disclosures.[19]

Corporate governance activists have also been more aggressive regarding demands for more disclosures about both the compensation and perquisites that accrue to officers and directors of public corporations. Some organizations,

---

[17] Securities and Exchange Commission, "Executive Compensation Disclosure," *Federal Register* 57, no. 204 (October 21, 1992): 48131.

[18] Securities and Exchange Commission, "Executive Compensation Disclosure," *Federal Register* 71, no. 250 (December 29, 2006): 78338.

[19] See Securities and Exchange Commission, "Proxy Disclosure AND Solicitation Enhancements" at www.sec.gov/rules/proposed/2009/33-9052.pdf.

including the National Association of Corporate Directors (NACD) and the International Corporate Governance Network (ICGN) (www.icgn.org), have published guidelines or best practices concerning the effective management of relationships with investors. The ICGN has global guidelines that are representative of the approach of institutional investors:

Three principles underpin these updated guidelines: *transparency*, so investors can clearly understand the program and see total pay; *accountability*, to ensure boards maintain the proper alignment in representing owners in part by obtaining shareowner approval of a remuneration report; and *performance-based*, so the programs are linked to relevant measures of company performance over an appropriate timescale. This should also reflect due regard for the reputational aspects of remuneration.

Because of the congruence of compensation and perquisites with individuals with the potential power to manipulate accounting records and financial reporting, GAAS requires auditors to pay close attention to risk factors associated with those incentives, especially as they relate to financial statement fraud. Executives and directors whose compensation depends heavily upon meeting certain performance targets associated either with numbers reported in the financial statements, or stock prices that may be affected by analysts' expectations of financial statement outcomes, may have incentives to commit financial statement fraud in order to achieve their desired results. SAS 99 has several provisions that concern the work of the external auditor regarding these risks.

## Summary Guidelines

In monitoring corporate perquisites, the audit committee should give consideration to these three matters:

1. All perquisites should be formally approved by the board of directors as recommended by the compensation or audit committee. Such approval should be duly noted in the minutes of the board's meetings and the committee's meetings.
2. The perquisites should be clearly defined in view of the SEC releases regarding the nature of such payments or reimbursements. As discussed in this chapter, such SEC releases provide guidance to the auditors and management in connection with the entity's compliance with the securities laws. Such perks should not be excessive or unusual in light of the rulings.
3. The committee should request a report from the internal auditors concerning the status of the entity's perquisites.[20] In reviewing the audit report, the

---

[20] It may be advisable to retain the outside auditors to review the travel and entertainment expenses for several of the senior executives each year. It is imperative that the company have an appropriate approval system of expense accounts. In its 1987 report, the National Commission on Fraudulent Financial Reporting recommended that "the committee should review in-house policies and procedures for regular review of officers' expenses and perquisites, including any use of corporate assets, inquire as to the results of the review, and, if appropriate, review a summarization of the expenses and perquisites of the period under review" (Washington, DC: National Commission on Fraudulent Financial Reporting, 1987), 180.

committee should obtain assurance in writing that the internal accounting and administrative controls (discussed in Chapter 8) are effective. Also, the committee should inquire about management's method of valuation of personal benefits and related tax consequences. Therefore, it is desirable to discuss the tax implications with the corporate tax specialist or outside tax advisor in order to coordinate the income tax and SEC reporting requirements.

## EXECUTIVE COMPENSATION

Most modern boards have a compensation committee that deals with systems for compensating the CEO and other executives, and at times with the general compensation system of the company. For several reasons, the audit committee also has an interest in the compensation system. The systems for determining executive compensation and the level of executive compensation have significant impacts on the reported financial statements in both current and future periods. Issues may exist related to the recognition of future payments to executives and of stock options, which are interwoven with executive compensation in most public corporations. Executive compensation, especially in the form of various bonuses, has become an area of deep scrutiny by the public, media, regulators, investors, corporate governance organizations, and reform activists. The audit committee's role focuses on internal control over financial reporting. In the case of executive compensation, this means a keen concern for the tone at the top of the organization and for the corporate culture.

Backdating stock options, a relatively recent scandal, has undergone intense scrutiny. Some of the more egregious cases have led to civil and criminal litigation. A comparatively large number of public companies had to restate their financial statements because of options backdating. The systems that monitor and prevent such activities are part of internal control over financial reporting. Other practices related to stock options, such as "spring-boarding," should also be of concern to audit committees. Associating stock option grants advantageously to time periods sensitive to company announcements of good news and bad news is, perhaps, not strictly in violation of any law, but it can be indicative of issues in the tone at the top.

Issues concerning executive compensation also have come under scrutiny because of the large bonuses awarded by financial services institutions just before many of them were bailed out by the federal government. The SEC has instituted special rules for limits on executive compensation for companies participating in various federal bailout programs, and it has revised the disclosures concerning executive compensation. In addition, the SEC is again considering whether to permit shareholders, through the proxy process, a "say on pay" for officers and directors. There is discussion as to whether the "say on pay" should be advisory to the board or authoritative. The U.K. has adopted an advisory vote by shareholders that apparently has eased some of the tension in that environment between boards and shareholders. A number of organizations have adopted policies, guidelines, and best practices concerning boards' management of executive compensation issues.

On November 7, 2006, the SEC amended the disclosure requirements for executive and director compensation, related-person transactions, director independence and other corporate governance matters, and for security ownership of officers and directors. These amendments affect disclosure in proxy and information statements, periodic reports, current reports, and other filings under the Securities Exchange Act of 1934 and to registration statements under the Exchange Act and the Securities Act of 1933. Disclosures about these matters must be provided in plain English. The amendments are intended to make proxy and information statements, reports, and registration statements easier to understand. Their intent also is to provide investors with a clearer and more complete picture of the compensation earned by a company's principal executive officer, principal financial officer, highest-paid executive officers, and members of its board of directors, as well as to provide better information about key financial relationships among companies and their executive officers, directors, significant shareholders and their immediate family members.

SEC Releases No. 33-8732A and 34-54302A require disclosures for executives and directors, and include the following information by different classes of compensation:

- Fees or compensation earned or paid in cash
- Stock awards
- Stock option awards
- Nonequity incentive plan compensation
- Change in pension value and nonqualified deferred compensation earnings
- All other compensation
- Total compensation, which is the sum of the others

## CORPORATE CONTRIBUTIONS

In addition to the usual practice of monitoring certain business practices, such as compliance with the Foreign Corrupt Practices Act in regard to perquisites and travel and entertainment, audit committees may also be requested by the board of directors to review other business practices, such as corporate contributions to charities and political campaigns, to ensure compliance with laws, regulations, and corporate policy.

### Charitable Contributions

According to R. A. Schwartz, corporate contributions or philanthropy may be defined as "a philanthropic transfer of wealth to be a one way flow of resources from a donor to a donee, a flow voluntarily generated by the donor though based on no expectation that a return flow, or economic quid pro quo, will reward the act."[21] Furthermore, as reported by C. Lowell Harriss:

---

[21] R. A. Schwartz, *Corporate Philanthropic Contributions*, pamphlet 72 (New York University, 1968): 480.

The interests and kinds of involvement differ enormously from firm to firm, as do the dollar outlays in corporate giving. Deductions on corporate tax returns of contributions have been rising, from \$252 million in 1950 to \$1,350 million in 1976. But such contributions represent less than 1 percent of profits and less than 5 percent of the community's total philanthropy.[22]

Corporate contributions also consist of nonmonetary giving, which includes:

- Employees' personal time in nonprofit activities
- Company property, such as the firm's auditorium
- Loans at concessionary rates
- Job training for the disadvantaged and disabled.[23]

As Harriss observes in a Conference Board study by James F. Harris and Anne Klepper, "If a price tag were put on all such nonmonetary or indirect aid in 1974, the estimate of corporate contributions would double (to well over \$2 billion)."[24]

*BusinessWeek* observed that "total corporate giving has remained flat at \$6.1 billion since 1990." Typically, "corporation donations are usually 1% to 2% of pretax domestic income." For example, more companies have developed a strategic plan and target charities more directly related to their operations.[25]

Concerning the justification of corporate contributions, Schwartz notes that:

- Gifts that will enhance the public image of a corporation can advantageously shift the demand curve for a corporation's product.
- The compatibility of corporate giving with monetary profit maximization is further suggested by the benefits a firm can derive from "farming out" research programs to educational institutions, while reaping both the gains of subsequent technological advances and the beneficial publicity with the gift.[26]

On the other hand, critics of corporate charity, notably economist Milton Friedman, have argued that, lacking shareholders' approval, the public interest is not served when managers of corporations divert funds from business purposes to charitable purposes. This group views charitable contributions as a distribution of funds that belong to shareholders. If shareholders want to support charitable activities, then they can do so from their own funds.

---

[22] C. Lowell Harriss, *Corporate Giving: Rationale and Issues: Two Essays on Corporate Philanthropy and Economic Education* (Los Angeles: International Institute for Economic Research, October 1978): 2.

[23] Ibid., 3.

[24] See James F. Harris and Anne Klepper, *Corporate Philanthropic Public Service Activities* (New York: The Conference Board, 1976).

[25] Lois Therrien, "Corporate Generosity Is Greatly Depreciated," *BusinessWeek* (November 2, 1992): 118–120.

[26] Schwartz, *Corporate Philanthropic Contributions*, 480. For further reference, see Harry L. Freeman, "Corporate Strategic Philanthropy," *Vital Speeches* 58, no. 8 (February 1, 1992): 246–250; Betty S. Coffee and Jia Wang, "Board Composition and Corporate Philanthropy," *Journal of Business Ethics* 11, no. 10 (October 1992): 771–778.

This charitable contributions issue has become somewhat more complicated because of the many ways in which such contributions can be made. For example, pledging to contribute to specified parties a certain percentage of profits from sales may increase business revenues and profits by creating new customers. In some cases, companies can trace their customer base to the goodwill that accrues from engagement in local communities through charitable activities.

Charitable organizations also have developed a broad array of programs for corporate support, many of which may not satisfy IRS requirements for exempt income to the organization or for a charitable deduction to the corporation. Fairly complex IRS rules determine whether money given to a charitable organization is a donation, sponsorship, dues, advertising, fees for services, or other form of business expense to the donor. Some corporations attempt to manage their charitable contributions by creating a private foundation, which is funded annually by contributions from the corporation. Generally, oversight responsibility falls to the audit committee to ensure appropriate management of internal control and other issues associated with the tone at the top.

Although the Foreign Corrupt Practices Act covers illegal contributions abroad, it is also illegal to make political contribution through the use of corporate funds in U.S. federal elections. As noted by Roderick M. Hills, former chairman of the SEC: "The 'chance' of 'Watergate' gave us the opportunity for better government, and began a series of corporate investigations that already have improved our vision and raised corporate behavioral standards."[27] Thus, it is necessary "to create an internal reporting system that will place these rather difficult payment questions squarely before the independent directors, outside auditors, and outside counsel."[28]

## Political Contributions

Corporate support of political campaigns has long been the subject of hot debate, centering on whether corporations should be granted "individual" First Amendment rights of free speech, or be curtailed in their ability to speak because of their economic power. In 2009, this debate was being considered by the Supreme Court of the United States in connection with a documentary film—funded in part by a corporation—about one of the 2008 presidential hopeful candidates. Political contributions by corporations have been restricted for many years. As a practical matter, almost all corporations' involvement in the political process is accomplished through one or more of three means:

* Establishment of a Political Action Committee, a separate organization that can receive contributions from individual executives and employees, but not directly from the corporation
* Involvement with a lobbying organization that is registered with the appropriate federal or state agency and that complies with their rules and reporting requirements

---

[27] Roderick M. Hills, "Views on How Corporations Should Behave," *Financial Executive* 44, no. 11 (November 1976): 34.
[28] Ibid., 32.

- Participation in a trade association that has a lobbying or government affairs function

If a corporation is involved with lobbying or has a PAC, its audit committee should ensure that the systems and people are in place to comply with the law and regulations, and to satisfy the reporting requirements. Political contributions can be a highly sensitive area where small abuses can escalate into major problems. Prudence and oversight, especially regarding culture and tone at the top, can ensure the avoidance of embarrassments, both to the corporation's executives and to its directors.

## Summary Guidelines

Ferdinand K. Levy and Gloria M. Shatto summarize four evaluative principles regarding corporate charitable contributions programs:

1. If the gift is not legal or if it is questionable, don't make it.
2. The contribution should represent the corporation and should not be a personal gift or whim of one executive.
3. Contributions "in kind" or well specified are generally preferable to unrestricted gifts.
4. Each contribution should stand alone and be capable of being justified on the basis of some type of cost-benefit analysis.[29]

Moreover, "the entire corporate giving program . . . must be open to the public and should be capable of both an internal and external audit."[30] Thus, it is clear that the audit committee should review the corporation's policy concerning its contributions and adhere to the monitoring practices discussed earlier in this chapter.

James A. Joseph notes that foundations need to:

- Clarify what is private and what is public;
- Reaffirm the moral authority of the traditional notion of public trust;
- Examine whether the enthusiasm with which foundations portray nonprofit voluntary activities as a distinctive sector may contribute to the tendency of critics and supporters to overlook the diversity within that sector;
- Demonstrate to the public that responsible governance and efficient management are all part of the public trust; and
- Reflect, retain, and reaffirm principles and practices that are fundamental to effectiveness in philanthropy.[31]

---

[29] Ferdinand K. Levy and Gloria M. Shatto, "A Common Sense Approach to Corporate Corporations," *Financial Executive* 46, No. 8 (September 1978), p. 37.
[30] Ibid., p. 38.
[31] James A. Joseph, "Reaffirming Our Public Accountability," *Foundation News* 33, No. 4 (July/August 1992): 44–45.

The following financial statement disclosure regarding this subject is presented to inform the reader of management's representations to the stockholders.

> *Schering-Plough*—Through corporate giving, the Schering-Plough Foundation and
> employee voluntarism—contributed much in 1992 to the communities where it
> operates; to health care, educational and arts organizations; and to those in need. The
> Foundation made grants totaling $2.8 million in 1992, complementing corporate
> contributions of $1.9 million.[32]

The Council for Institutional Investors has adopted a monitoring and disclosure policy related to the board's responsibilities for corporate charitable and
political contributions (www.cii.org):

> Board Monitoring, Assessment and Approval: The board of directors should monitor,
> assess and approve all charitable and political contributions (including trade association
> contributions) made by the company. The board should ensure that only contributions
> consistent with and aligned to the interests of the company and its shareowners are
> approved. The terms and conditions of such contributions should be clearly defined and
> approved by the board.
>
> Disclosure: The board's guidelines for contribution approval should be publicly disclosed
> as a corporate contributions policy. The board should disclose on an annual basis the
> amounts and recipients of all monetary and nonmonetary contributions made by the
> company during the prior fiscal year. If any expenditures earmarked for political or
> charitable activities were provided to or through a third party, then those expenditures
> should be included in the report.

## CONCLUSION

Recent business and audit failures of major corporations demonstrate that
audit committees need to monitor and enforce a conflicts-of-interest policy
statement to help ensure the integrity of the company as well as to avoid civil
or criminal penalties. To assist the audit committee with the review and discussion, Exhibit 12.2 contains the overall content of a conflicts-of-interest program.
Of course, this program may be modified and is by no means all-inclusive.

Additionally, Exhibit 12.3 contains a discussion of possible warning signals
and red flags related to the Enron debacle.

In summary, audit committees have increasingly assumed additional responsibilities such as those discussed in this chapter. Perhaps the most challenging are
directing and monitoring special investigations related to management fraud and
fraudulent financial reporting, as discussed in Chapters 4 and 11. Based on the
ever-increasing duties and responsibilities of the audit committee, the role of
monitoring business practices will continue to expand into additional areas in
the future.

---

[32] Schering-Plough, 1992 Annual Report, 4.

**EXHIBIT 12.2**    Conflicts-of-Interest Program

| Description | Presentation (Estimated) |
|---|---|
| Review and discuss[a] with the business ethics and compliance officer such matters as: | One day, presentation, and group discussion |

- Company's conflicts-of-interest policies and prevention and detection procedures in view of the Sarbanes-Oxley Act (Sections 206, 303, 304, 305, 306, 307, 402, 403, 406, 501, 802, 806), SEC rules, and SROs listing standards
- Results of special investigations into conflicts-of-interest situations, corrective action taken, SEC disclosure (Form 8-K), and press releases, if appropriate
- Audit findings of directors, officers, and employees compliance with the company's code of conduct, including the code of ethics for senior financial officers and internal auditors
- Recommended improvements in management controls to mitigate non-compliance with the above activities and related party transactions, including the issuance of both internal or external audit reports as well as the board of directors policy statement
- Changes in the conflicts-of-interest policies and practices in view of company acquisitions, divestitures, and joint ventures
- Compliance with loan covenants and funding of pension plans
- Certification of periodic compliance with the conflicts-of-interest policy statements by appropriate employees
- Provisions for continuous surveillance and enforcement

---

[a]In the absence of a business ethnics and compliance officer, the chief audit executive may present and discuss the program with the audit committee.

---

**EXHIBIT 12.3**    Lessons from the Enron Effect

- The audit committee should be informed about the financial and operational aspects of the company and therefore should receive sufficient and timely information. If the audit committee meeting is scheduled to coincide with the regular full board meetings, then the committee must receive written information well in advance of the meetings.
- To be vigilant, the audit committee should ask probing questions about the propriety of the company's financial reporting process and the quality of its internal controls. This task requires the committee to keep abreast of financial reporting developments affecting the company.
- To be an effective independent overseer, the audit committee must be positioned between senior management and the external auditors. This organizational structure allows the audit committee to question management's judgments about financial reporting matters and to suggest improvements in the internal control systems. The

committee's charter defines its mission, duties, and responsibilities; plans its annual agenda; and documents its findings and conclusions.
- Failure on the part of the audit committee to review and evaluate the financial statements and related accounting policies in accordance with generally accepted accounting principles is clearly malfeasance.
- One of the conclusions from the Report of the Special Investigation Committee of the Board of directors of Enron Corporation (Powers Report) was:

> The Board, and in particular the Audit and Compliance Committee, has the duty of ultimate oversight over the Company's financial reporting. While the primary responsibility for financial reporting abuses discussed in the Report lies with management, the participating members of the Committee believe those abuses could and should have been prevented or detected at an earlier time had the Board been more aggressive and vigilant (p. 24).

For example, red flags that fraudulent financial reporting may be occurring (and the appropriate action item) include:

- Overoptimistic news release with respect to earnings. *Action item:* Analyze annual and interim earnings trends to avoid increased opportunities for managing earnings
- Industry accounting practices in contrast to unusual revenue recognition policies to increase earnings. *Action item:* Access significant accounting policies that are industry-specific from a financial reporting data base and review this information with both internal and external auditors.
- Rapid growth of the organization. *Action item:* Investigate reasons for rapid expansion in relationship to both top-line and bottom-line double-digit annual growth rates as well as significant increases in year-to-year changes relative to past performance.
- Significant changes in accounting practices and estimates by management with an excessive interest in earnings. *Action item:* Compare these changes with industry norms and determine the reason for them.
- Conflict-of-interest and significant contracts that affect financial statements. Frequent related-party transactions and failure to enforce the corporate code of conduct. *Action item:* Determine management's intent to disclose such contracts as well as how the firm addresses conflict-of-interest situations and monitors compliance with the code. If necessary, conduct or authorize a special investigation and retain independent counsel and other professionals.
- Unexplained significant fluctuations in account balances. *Action item:* Focus on analytical review procedures and discuss the findings with both internal and external auditors.
- Breakdowns in the system of internal control. *Action item:* Obtain assurance from both the internal and external auditors that management has evaluated the weaknesses and recommendations in the management letter and that corrective action has been taken.
- Scope restrictions placed by management on both the internal and external auditors. *Action item:* Give assurance to the auditors that they have unrestricted and free access to the audit committee.

Audit committee members should be highly attuned to the potential of fraudulent financial reporting. Failure on the part of the audit committee to question management's representations may be the basis for audit committee malfeasance, since the audit committee and the board may be held liable for failure to know what they were responsible for recognizing.

---

*Source:* This discussion is adapted from an article by Louis Braiotta, Jr., "Lessons from the Enron Effect," at www.smartpros.com (March 2002).

## SOURCES AND SUGGESTED READINGS

American Assembly. *The Ethics of Corporate Conduct*. Pamphlet 52. New York: Columbia University, April 1977: 1–11.

Beresford, Dennis R., and James D. Bond. "Foreign Corrupt Practices Act—Its Implications to Financial Management." *Financial Executive* 46, no. 8 (August 1978): 26–32.

Boltz, Gerald E., Grover R. Heyler, David L. James, and Francis M. Wheat. "Corporate Directors' Responsibilities." *Financial Executive* 45, no. 1 (January 1977): 12–21.

Braiotta, Louis, Jr., "Lessons from the Enron Effect." March 2002. www.smartpros.com.

Business Roundtable. *Corporate Governance and American Competitiveness*. New York: The Business Roundtable, 1990.

Charles E. Simon and Company. "An Examination of Questionable Payments and Practices." *Journal of Accountancy* 145, no. 4 (May 1978): 7.

Coffee, Betty S., and Jia Wang. "Board Composition and Corporate Philanthropy." *Journal of Business Ethics* 11, no. 10 (October 1992): 771–778.

Coopers & Lybrand. "Executive Perquisites Study Release: An Overview of the Findings." *Executive Briefing* (May 1992).

Department of Justice. "Foreign Corrupt Practices Act Option Procedure." Code of Federal Regulations, Sec. 28, Part 77, 1978.

Foreign Corrupt Practices Act. Title I of Public Law No. 95-213, December 19, 1977.

Freeman, Harry L. "Corporate Strategic Philanthropy." *Vital Speeches* 58, no. 8 (February 1, 1992): 246–250.

Gerson, James S., J. Robert Mooney, Donald F. Moran, and Robert K. Waters. "Oversight of the Financial Reporting Process—Part I." *CPA Journal* 59, no. 7 (July 1989): 22–28.

Greene, James. "Assuring Ethical Conduct Abroad." *The Conference Board Information Bulletin No. 2* (November 1976): 1–18.

Gustavson, Sandra G., and Jere W. Morehead. "Complying with the Amended Foreign Corrupt Practices Act." *Risk Management* 37, no. 4 (April 1990): 76–82.

Hanson, Walter E. "A Blueprint for Ethical Conduct." Statement in "Quotes." *Journal of Accountancy* 145, no. 6 (June 1978): 80–84.

Harris, James F., and Anne Klepper. *Corporate Philanthropic Public Service Activities*. New York: The Conference Board, 1976.

Harriss, C. Lowell. "Corporate Giving: Rationale and Issues." *Two Essays on Corporate Philanthropy and Economic Education*. Los Angeles: International Institute for Economic Research, October 1978: 1–13.

Hills, Roderick M. "Views on How Corporations Should Behave." *Financial Executive* 44, no. 11 (November 1976): 32–34.

Joseph, James A. "Reaffirming Our Public Accountability." *Foundation News* 33, no. 4 (July/August 1992): 44–45.

Levy, Ferdinand K., and Gloria M. Shatto. "A Common Sense Approach to Corporate Contributions." *Financial Executive* 46, no. 9 (September 1978): 36–40.

Marsh, Hugh L. "The Foreign Corrupt Practices Act: A Corporate Plan for Compliance." *Internal Auditor* 36, no. 2 (April 1979): 72–76.

McGrahan, Kathleen T. "SEC Disclosure Regulation and Management Perquisites." *Accounting Review* 63, no. 1 (January 1988): 23–41.

National Commission on Fraudulent Financial Reporting. *Report of the National Commission on Fraudulent Financial Reporting.* Washington, DC: NCFFR, 1987.

Omnibus Trade and Competitiveness Act, Title V of Public Law No. 100-418. August 23, 1988.

Organization of Economic Cooperation and Development. *Convention on Combating Bribery of Foreign Public Officials in International Business Transactions.* Paris: OECD, 1997.

Piturro, Marlene C. "Just Say . . . Maybe." *World Trade* 5, no. 5 (June 1992): 86–91.

Roberts, Judith L. "Revision of the Foreign Corrupt Practices Act by the 1988 Omnibus Trade Bill: Will It Reduce the Compliance Burdens and Anticompetitive Impact?" *Brigham Young University Law Review*, no. 2 (1989): 491–506.

Robinson, Herbert, and J. Karl Fishbach. "Commercial Bribery—The Corporation as Victim." *Financial Executive* 47 no. 4 (April 1979): 16–19 and 50–51.

Schwartz, R. A. *Corporate Philanthropic Contributions.* Pamphlet 72. New York: New York University, June 1968: 479–497.

Securities and Exchange Commission. "Executive Compensation Disclosure." *Federal Register* 57, no. 204 (October 21, 1992): 48126–48159.

Securities and Exchange Commission. "Executive Compensation Disclosure," *Federal Register* 71, no. 250 (December 29, 2006): 78338.

Securities and Exchange Commission Proposal. "Proxy Disclosure AND Solicitation Enhancements." July 10, 2009. Available at www.sec.gov/rules/proposed/2009/33-9052.pdf.

Securities and Exchange Commission. "Report of the Securities and Exchange Commission on Questionable and Illegal Corporate Payments and Practices." Washington, DC: SEC, May 12, 1976.

*Statement on Auditing Standards, No. 54.* "Illegal Acts by Clients." New York: AICPA, 1988.

Taylor, John C. III. "Preventing Improper Payments Through Internal Controls." *The Conference Board Record* 13, no. 8 (August 1976): 17–19.

Therrien, Lois. "Corporate Generosity Is Greatly Depreciated." *Business Week* (November 2, 1992): 118–120.

"Triton Energy Corp. Justice Department Probing for Possible Law Violations." *Wall Street Journal*, (May 20, 1993).

Zipser, Andy. "Crude Grab? How a Tiny Producer Lost Its Indonesian Stake." *Barron's* 72, no. 21 (May 25, 1992): 12–15.

# Part Four

# The Reporting Function and the Audit Committee

# Chapter 13

# Independent Auditors' Reports

The independent auditors' report is the expression of their professional opinion on the financial statements. As discussed in Chapter 2, although the financial statements are management's responsibility, the independent auditors have a responsibility to attest to the fairness of management's representations in the statements through their audit report.

This chapter will familiarize the audit committee with the different types of audit opinions and other audit reports regarding matters such as interim financial information and special reports.[1] An understanding of the audit opinions and other audit reports provides an important opportunity for each audit committee member to obtain additional insight into the nature and importance of the independent auditors' reporting responsibility.

## THE AUDITORS' REPORTS ON AUDITED FINANCIAL STATEMENTS

As discussed in earlier chapters, the independent auditors or accountants report their objective opinion on the fairness of the representations in the financial statements. Such an expression of their opinion is required in accordance with generally accepted auditing standards as promulgated by the Auditing Standards Board. Increasingly, for U.S. public company audits, the Public Company Accounting Oversight Board (PCAOB) provides the ground rules for how independent auditors should conduct their audits and report the results. Earlier chapters have noted that corporate management has full responsibility for the fairness of the representations in the financial statements. Such a distinction concerning the responsibility for the financial statements is particularly important because if the independent auditors do not concur with the fairness of management's representations, they are required to inform the users of the financial statements of their exceptions. In particular, the fourth auditing standard of reporting is restated for additional emphasis.

---

[1] Attestation engagements with respect to other information, such as reports on internal control and compliance with specified laws and regulations, were discussed in Chapter 5.

## The Standard Auditors' Report (Unqualified Opinion)

The auditor must, in his or her audit report, either express an opinion regarding the financial statements taken as a whole[2] or state that an opinion cannot be expressed. When the auditor cannot express an overall opinion, the auditor should state the reason in the auditor's report. In all cases where an auditor's name is associated with financial statements, the auditor should clearly indicate the character of the auditor's work, if any, and the degree of responsibility the auditor is taking[3] for the auditor's report.

A particular report, the Standard Auditors' Report (Unqualified Opinion), is used by the auditors when they have no exceptions regarding management's representations in the financial statements. In practice, such a report is often described as a "clean opinion." Explicit in the auditors' unqualified report is that their examination has been performed within the general auditing guidelines or standards as set forth by the PCAOB (for U.S. public company audits) or by the AICPA (for U.S. audits of nonpublic organization's).[4] In addition, their unqualified opinion informs the users of the financial statements that such statements have been prepared by management in conformity with generally accepted accounting principles applied on a consistent basis. Such an unqualified opinion is based not only on their examination of the financial statements but also on tests of the accounting records that underlie such statements.

While the auditors' report is not explicit with respect to the system of internal control, it implies that the entity's internal control structure is adequate. However, since the inception in 1977 of the Foreign Corrupt Practices Act, this audit report has been reevaluated in terms of its content because it is argued that the auditors should make their report explicit with respect to management's adherence to the accounting provision in the act. Furthermore, with the passage of the Sarbanes-Oxley Act in 2002—specifically Section 404 that concerns internal controls over financial reporting—for public companies, independent auditors opine separately on whether internal controls over financial reporting are effective (evaluated against a well-established internal control framework, such as COSO).

## Independent Auditors' Reports

As discussed in Chapter 8 of this book, Section 302 of the Sarbanes-Oxley Act of 2002 requires specific representation on the system of internal control. (See Section 302(a)(4) regarding the certifications required from the CEO and CFO.)

---

[2] According to the Auditing Standards Board, the phrase "taken as a whole" with respect to the financial statements applies to the statements of both the current period and one or more prior periods presented on a comparative basis. See Statement on Auditing Standards No. 58 "Reports on Audited Financial Statements" (New York: AICPA, 2008), par. 04.

[3] The reader may wish to review Chapter 5 at this point.

[4] Space constraints prohibit a full analysis of non-U.S. reporting requirements, but International Auditing Standards (in particular ISA 700) establish reporting requirements similar to those in the United States.

Additionally, Section 404 of the Sarbanes-Oxley Act requires management to report annually on its assessment of the effectiveness of internal controls. The act also requires the company to file a report from its independent auditors regarding the expression of an opinion as to whether management's assessment is fairly stated. It is evident that the users of the financial statements rely on the auditors' report to determine whether the statements are fairly presented. As a result, the auditors' report must be clear and concise with respect to the findings and results of the audit examination. To achieve this objective, the Auditing Standards Board has developed audit reports or opinions, which are summarized here:

- *Unqualified opinion.* An unqualified opinion states that the financial statements present fairly, in all material respects, the financial position, results of operations, and cash flows of the entity in conformity with generally accepted accounting principles. This is the opinion expressed in the standard report.
- *Explanatory language added to the auditor's standard report.* Certain circumstances, while not affecting the auditor's unqualified opinion on the financial statements, may require that the auditor add an explanatory paragraph (or other explanatory language) to her report.
- *Qualified opinion.* A qualified opinion states that, except for the effects of the matter(s) to which the qualification relates, the financial statements present fairly, in all material respects, the financial position, results of operations, and cash flows of the entity in conformity with generally accepted accounting principles.
- *Adverse opinion.* An adverse opinion states that the financial statements do not present fairly the financial position, results of operations, or cash flows of the entity in conformity with generally accepted accounting principles.
- *Disclaimer of opinion.* A disclaimer of opinion states that the auditor does not express an opinion on the financial statements.[5]

To cover attest engagements, such as those where an accountant is engaged to issue, or does issue, an examination, a review, or an agreed-upon procedures report on subject matter, or an assertion about the subject matter (other than for financial statement audits typically covered by the Statements on Auditing Standards), the Auditing Standards Board has issued *Statement on Standards for Attestation Engagements*, now recodified in SSAE Nos. 10 through 15. Given the demand from the investing public for management's assertions about the effectiveness of the entity's internal control and the requirements of the Sarbanes-Oxley Act, it is reasonable to expect that the audit committee understands this type of attestation engagement. Thus, it is important for the audit committee to review closely and discuss the recommendations in the annual management letter from the independent auditors.

---

[5] Statement on Auditing Standards No. 58, "Reports on Audited Financial Statements" (New York: AICPA, 1988), par. 10. For additional reference, see Robert S. Roussey, Ernest L. Ten Eyck, and Mimi Blanco-Best, "Three New SASs: Closing the Communication Gap," *Journal of Accountancy* 166, no. 6 (December 1988): 44–52.

## Explanatory Language with the Auditor's Standard Report

The Auditing Standards Board requires independent auditors to modify their standard audit report under certain circumstances. Such a modification may require the addition of an explanatory paragraph or other explanatory language. More specifically, the circumstances include instances when:

a. The auditor's opinion is based in part on the report of another auditor.

b. To prevent the financial statements from being misleading because of unusual circumstances, the financial statements contain a departure from an accounting principle promulgated by a body designated by the AICPA Council to establish such principles.*

c. There is substantial doubt about the entity's ability to continue as a going concern.

d. Accounting principles, or the method of their application, have changed materially between periods.

e. Certain circumstances exist relating to reports on comparative financial statements.

f. Selected quarterly financial data required by SEC Regulation S-K has been omitted or has not been reviewed.

g. Supplementary information required by the Financial Accounting Standards Board (FASB) or the Governmental Accounting Standards Board (GASB) has been omitted, the presentation of such information departs materially from FASB or GASB guidelines, the auditor is unable to complete prescribed procedures with respect to such information, or the auditor is unable to remove substantial doubts about whether the supplementary information conforms to FASB or GASB guidelines.

h. Other information in a document containing audited financial statements is materially inconsistent with information appearing in the financial statements.[6]

---

* For further reference, see "Departures from the New Standard Auditor's Report on Financial Statements of Business Enterprises: A Survey of the Application of Statement on Auditing Standards, No. 58," *Financial Report Survey* (New York: AICPA, 1990).

Certain circumstances may arise, for example, when the auditors may not be independent or must rely on the report of another auditor. With respect to the latter, the auditors' reporting obligations are based on their decisions whether to make reference to the other auditors' report. Therefore, if the auditors decide to make reference to the report of another auditor as a basis, in part, for their opinion, their report should disclose this fact.[7] When auditors decide to make no reference to the report of another auditor because of their acceptance of the auditor's independence and reputation, the standard short-form unqualified report is acceptable.

However, when the auditors are not independent—for example, there is a conflict of interest between the public accounting firm and the client—they should

---

[6] American Institute of Certified Public Accountants, *Professional Standards, U.S. Auditing Standards/Attestation Standards*, Vol. 1 (New York: AICPA, 2008), AU Sec. 508.11.

[7] Ibid., AU Sec. 508.12.

disclaim an opinion with respect to the financial statements and should state specifically that they are not independent.[8]

In addition to their expression of an unqualified opinion, the auditors may wish to emphasize certain matters regarding the financial statements. For example, they may need to indicate that the corporation has had significant transactions with related parties, such as transactions between the entity and the officers or directors.[9] They may also need to disclose an unusually important subsequent event that occurred after the date of the financial statements. Obviously, such matters are disclosed based on the professional judgment of the auditors. However, while the auditors may wish to emphasize certain matters, they can express an unqualified opinion.

To familiarize the audit committee with various examples of the wording in the auditors' modified unqualified report, a model report is presented in Exhibit 13.1.

---

**EXHIBIT 13.1**   Independent Auditor's Report: Example 1

**Opinion Based in Part on Report of Another Auditor**

We have audited the consolidated balance sheets of ABC Company as of December 31, 20X2 and 20X1, and the related consolidated statements of income, retained earnings, and cash flows for the years then ended. These financial statements are the responsibility of the Company's management. Our responsibility is to express an opinion on these financial statements based on our audits. We did not audit the financial statements of B Company, a wholly owned subsidiary, which statements reflect total assets of $_____ and $_____ as of December 31, 20X2 and 20X1, respectively, and total revenues of $_____ and $_____ for the years then ended. Those statements were audited by other auditors whose report has been furnished to us, and our opinion, insofar as it relates to the amounts included for B Company, is based solely on the report of the other auditors.

We conducted our audits in accordance with auditing standards generally accepted in the United States of America. Those standards require that we plan and perform the audit to obtain reasonable assurance about whether the financial statements are free of material misstatement. An audit includes examining, on a test basis, evidence supporting the amounts and disclosures in the financial statements. An audit also includes assessing the accounting principles used and significant estimates made by management, as well as evaluating the overall financial statement presentation. We believe that our audits and the report of other auditors provide a reasonable basis for our opinion.

In our opinion, based on our audits and the report of other auditors, the consolidated financial statements referred to above present fairly, in all material respects, the financial position of ABC Company as of December 31, 20X2 and 20X1, and the results of its operations and its cash flows for the years then ended in conformity with accounting principles generally accepted in the United States of America.[a]

---

[a]*Statement on Auditing Standards No. 58*, par. 13, as amended by ASB interpretation.

*(continued)*

---

[8] Ibid., AU Sec. 504.09.
[9] Ibid., AU Sec. 508.19.

**Exhibit 13.1** *(Continued)*

**Lack of Consistency**

As discussed in Note X to the financial statements, the Company changed its method of computing depreciation in 20X2.[b]

**An Entity's Ability to Continue as a Going Concern**

The accompanying financial statements have been prepared assuming that the Company will continue as a going concern. As discussed in Note X to the financial statements, the Company has suffered recurring losses from operations and has a net capital deficiency that raises substantial doubt about its ability to continue as a going concern. Management's plans in regard to these matters are also described in Note X. The financial statements do not include any adjustments that might result from the outcome of this uncertainty.[c]

---

[b] Professional Standards, *U.S. Auditing Standards/Attestation Standards*, Vol. 1, AU Sec. 508.17.

[c] *Statement on Auditing Standards No. 59*, "The Auditor's Consideration of an Entity's Ability to Continue as a Going Concern" (New York: AICPA, 1988), par. 13. For further discussion, see John E. Ellingsen, Kurt Pany, and Peg Fagan, "SAS No. 59: How to Evaluate Going Concern," *Journal of Accountancy* 168, No. 1 (January 1989), 24–31.

## OTHER AUDITING OPINIONS

### The Qualified Opinion

According to the Auditing Standards Board, the auditors may express a qualified opinion that "'except for' the effects of the matter to which the qualification relates, the financial statements" are presented fairly.[10] Concerning the "exceptions" noted by the auditors, the Board delineated these circumstances:

> There is a lack of sufficient competent evidential matter or there are restrictions on the scope of the audit that have led the auditor to conclude that he cannot express an unqualified opinion and he has concluded not to disclaim an opinion.

> The auditor believes, on the basis of his audit, that the financial statements contain a departure from generally accepted accounting principles, the effect of which is material, and he has concluded not to express an adverse opinion.[11]

With respect to the aforementioned circumstances, an example of the auditors' report is illustrated in Exhibit 13.2.

---

[10] Ibid., AU Sec. 508.20.

[11] Ibid., AU Sec. 20.

---

**EXHIBIT 13.2** Independent Auditor's Report: Example 2

**Scope Limitations**

[Same first paragraph as the standard report]
Except as discussed in the following paragraph, we conducted our audits in accordance with auditing standards generally accepted in the United States of America. Those standards require that we plan and perform the audit to obtain reasonable assurance about whether the financial statements are free of material misstatement. An audit includes examining, on a test basis, evidence supporting the amounts and disclosures in the financial statements. An audit also includes assessing the accounting principles used and significant estimates made by management, as well as evaluating the overall financial statement presentation. We believe that our audits provide a reasonable basis for our opinion.

We were unable to obtain audited financial statements supporting the Company's investment in a foreign affiliate stated at $\_\_\_\_\_$ and $\_\_\_\_\_$ at December 31, 20X2 and 20X1, respectively, or its equity in earnings of that affiliate of $\_\_\_\_\_$ and $\_\_\_\_\_$, which is included in net income for the years then ended as described in Note X to the financial statements; nor were we able to satisfy ourselves as to the carrying value of the investment in the foreign affiliate or the equity in its earnings by other auditing procedures. In our opinion, except for the effects of such adjustments, if any, as might have been determined to be necessary had we been able to examine evidence regarding the foreign affiliate investment and earnings, the financial statements referred to in the first paragraph above present fairly, in all material respects, the financial position of X Company as of December 31, 20X2 and 20X1, and the results of its operations and its cash flows for the years then ended in conformity with accounting principles generally accepted in the United States of America.[a]

**Departure from a Generally Accepted Accounting Principle**

[Same first and second paragraphs as the standard report]
The Company has excluded, from property and debt in the accompanying balance sheets, certain lease obligations that, in our opinion, should be capitalized in order to conform with generally accepted accounting principles. If these lease obligations were capitalized, property would be increased by $\_\_\_\_\_$ and $\_\_\_\_\_$, long-term debt by $\_\_\_\_\_$ and $\_\_\_\_\_$, and retained earnings by $\_\_\_\_\_$ and $\_\_\_\_\_$ as of December 31, 20X2 and 20X1, respectively. Additionally, net income would be increased (decreased) by $\_\_\_\_\_$ and $\_\_\_\_\_$ and earnings per share would be increased (decreased) by $\_\_\_\_\_$ and $\_\_\_\_\_$, respectively, for the years then ended.

In our opinion, except for the effects of not capitalizing certain lease obligations as discussed in the preceding paragraph, the financial statements referred to above present fairly, in all material respects, the financial position of X Company as of December 31, 20X2 and 20X1, and the results of its operations and its cash flows for the years then ended in conformity with accounting principles generally accepted in the United States of America.[b]

---

[a] *Professional Standards, U.S. Auditing Standards/Attestation Standards*, Vol. 1, AU Sec. 26 (New York: AICPA, 2008).
[b] Ibid., AU 508 Sec. 39.

(*continued*)

**Exhibit 13.2**   (*Continued*)

**Inadequate Disclosure**

[Same first and second paragraphs as the standard report]

The Company's financial statements do not disclose [describe the nature of the omitted disclosures]. In our opinion, disclosure of this information is required by generally accepted accounting principles.

In our opinion, except for the omission of the information discussed in the preceding paragraph, . . . [c]

---

[c] Ibid., AU 508 Sec. 42. For further reference, see Jack C. Robertson, "Analysts' Reactions to Auditors' Messages in Qualified Reports," *Accounting Horizons* 2, No. 2 (June 1988), pp. 82–89.

## The Adverse Opinion

The adverse opinion is expressed by the auditors when, in their judgment, "the financial statements taken as a whole are not presented fairly in conformity with generally accepted accounting principles."[12] The adverse opinion is appropriate where the auditors' exceptions are so material that the statements as a whole are not fairly presented. Thus, the distinction between the adverse opinion and qualified opinion is predicated on the concept of materiality discussed in Chapter 5. When the auditors express an adverse opinion, their audit report should disclose "all the substantive reasons" for the opinion as well as "the principal effects of the subject matter" on the financial statements, "if reasonably determinable."[13] "If the effects are not reasonably determinable, the report should so state."[14] If management applies accounting principles that are not in conformity with acceptable principles (discussed in Chapter 5), then the auditors are required to render an adverse opinion. For example, if management refuses to disclose material information in the notes to the statements, such inaction constitutes a violation of the disclosure principle. Therefore, an adverse opinion is appropriate. Such a violation of the disclosure principle would materially distort the financial statements taken as a whole. However, the expression of an adverse opinion is infrequent in practice because management opts for an unqualified opinion and as a result makes the necessary adjustments.

An example of an adverse opinion is shown in Exhibit 13.3.

---

[12] Ibid., AU Sec. 58.
[13] Ibid., AU Sec. 59.
[14] Ibid.

---

**EXHIBIT 13.3**   Independent Auditor's Report: Example 3

---

**Adverse Opinion**

[Same first and second paragraphs as the standard report]

As discussed in Note X to the financial statements, the Company carries its property, plant, and equipment accounts at appraisal values, and provides depreciation on the basis of such values. Further, the Company does not provide for income taxes with respect to differences between financial income and taxable income arising because of the use, for income tax purposes, of the installment method of reporting gross profit from certain types of sales. Generally accepted accounting principles require that property, plant, and equipment be stated at an amount not in excess of cost, reduced by depreciation based on such amount, and that deferred income taxes be provided.

Because of the departures from generally accepted accounting principles identified above, as of December 31, 20X2 and 20X1, inventories have been increased $_____ and $_____ by inclusion in manufacturing overhead of depreciation in excess of that based on cost; property, plant, and equipment, less accumulated depreciation, is carried at $_____ and $_____ in excess of an amount based on the cost to the Company; and deferred income taxes of $_____ and $_____ have not been recorded; resulting in an increase of $_____ and $_____ in retained earnings and in appraisal surplus of $_____ and $_____, respectively. For the years ended December 31, 20X2 and 20X1, cost of goods sold has been increased $_____ and $_____, respectively, because of the effects of the depreciation accounting referred to above and deferred income taxes of $_____ and $_____ have not been provided, resulting in an increase in net income of $_____ and $_____, respectively.

In our opinion, because of the effects of the matters discussed in the preceding paragraphs, the financial statements referred to above do not present fairly, in conformity with accounting principles generally accepted in the United States of America, the financial position of X Company as of December 31, 20X2 and 20X1, or the results of its operations or its cash flows for the years then ended.

---

*Source:* Professional Standards, *U.S. Auditing Standards/Attestation Standards*, vol. 1 (New York: AICPA, 2008), AU 508 Sec. 60.

---

## Disclaimer of Opinion

When the auditors lack sufficient information to form an opinion regarding the financial statements, their report should indicate that they are unable to express an opinion. For example, it is appropriate to express a disclaimer of opinion when the auditors have not conducted "an examination sufficient in scope" to warrant the expression of an opinion on the statements taken as a whole.[15] In contrast to the qualified opinion, the disclaimer of opinion means that the auditors do not have sufficient knowledge about the fairness of management's representations in the financial statements. Furthermore, the auditors should indicate in their report the reason for the disclaimer of opinion. Thus, although the circumstances regarding the issuance of the qualified opinion may be the same for a disclaimer of opinion, the distinction is made between the former and the latter based on the degree of

---

[15] Ibid., AU Sec. 62.

---

**EXHIBIT 13.4**    Independent Auditor's Report: Example 4

---

**Disclaimer of Opinion**

We were engaged to audit the accompanying balance sheets of X Company as of December 31, 20X2 and 20X1, and the related statements of income, retained earnings, and cash flows for the years then ended. These financial statements are the responsibility of the Company's management.

[Second paragraph of standard report should be omitted]

The Company did not make a count of its physical inventory in 20X2 or 20X1, stated in the accompanying financial statements at $_____ as of December 31, 20X2, and at $_____ as of December 31, 20X1. Further, evidence supporting the cost of property and equipment acquired prior to December 31, 20X1, is no longer available. The Company's records do not permit the application of other auditing procedures to inventories or property and equipment.

Since the Company did not take physical inventories and we were not able to apply other auditing procedures to satisfy ourselves as to inventory quantities and the cost of property and equipment, the scope of our work was not sufficient to enable us to express, and we do not express, an opinion on these financial statements.

---

*Source: Professional Standards, U.S. Auditing Standards and Attestation Standards*, vol. 1 (New York: AICPA, 2008), AU 508 Sec. 63. Revised in March 2006 to reflect conforming changes necessitated by the issuance of SAS No. 105 on *Audit Evidence*.

---

materiality with respect to each circumstance. Making such a distinction is contingent on the auditors' professional judgment. Accordingly, the audit committee should inquire about the public accounting firm's criteria for judging materiality as it relates to the financial statements.

Exhibit 13.4 is an example of a disclaimer of opinion resulting from an inability to obtain "sufficient appropriate audit evidence" because of a scope limitation. (The phrase "sufficient appropriate audit evidence" comes from SAS No. 105, one of many "Risk Assessment Standards" issued by the AICPA in 2006.)

## OTHER REPORTS OF THE AUDITORS

### Report on Interim Financial Statements

In addition to the auditors' opinion on the annual financial statements, the Auditing Standards Board states:

> The Securities and Exchange Commission (SEC) requires[a] a registrant to engage an independent accountant to review the registrant's interim financial information, in accordance with this Statement, before the registrant files its quarterly report on Form 10-Q or Form 10-QSB. Although this Statement does not require an accountant to issue a written report on a review of interim financial information, the SEC requires that an accountant's review report be filed with the interim financial information if, in any filing, the entity states that the interim financial information has been reviewed by an independent public accountant.

SAS No. 84, *Communications Between Predecessor and Successor Auditors (AICPA, Professional Standards,* vol. 1, AU sec. 315), requires a successor auditor to contact the entity's predecessor auditor and make inquiries of the predecessor auditor in deciding whether to accept appointment as an entity's independent auditor. Such inquiries should be completed before accepting an engagement to perform an initial review of an entity's interim financial information.[16]

---

[a]The Securities and Exchange Commission (SEC) requirement is set forth in Rule 10-01(d) of Regulation S-X for Form 10-Q and item 310(b) of Regulation S-B for Form 10-QSB.

With respect to the independent auditors' objective of a review of interim financial statements, the Auditing Standards Board points out:

> The objective of a review of interim financial information pursuant to this Statement is to provide the accountant with a basis for communicating whether he or she is aware of any material modifications that should be made to the interim financial information for it to conform with generally accepted accounting principles. The objective of a review of interim financial information differs significantly from that of an audit conducted in accordance with generally accepted auditing standards. A review of interim financial information does not provide a basis for expressing an opinion about whether the financial statements are presented fairly, in all material respects, in conformity with generally accepted accounting principles. A review consists principally of performing analytical procedures and making inquiries of persons responsible for financial and accounting matters, and does not contemplate (a) tests of accounting records through inspection, observation, or confirmation; (b) tests of controls to evaluate their effectiveness; (c) obtaining corroborating evidence in response to inquiries; or (d) performing certain other procedures ordinarily performed in an audit. A review may bring to the accountant's attention significant matters affecting the interim financial information, but it does not provide assurance that the accountant will become aware of all significant matters that would be identified in an audit. Paragraph 22 of this Statement provides guidance to the accountant if he or she becomes aware of information that leads him or her to believe that the interim financial information may not be in conformity with generally accepted accounting principles.[17]

To achieve their review objective, the independent auditors should apply these topical procedures:

- Establishing an understanding with the client regarding the services to be performed in an engagement to review interim financial information (pars. 8–9)

---

[16] *Statement on Auditing Standards No. 100*, "Interim Financial Information" (New York: AICPA, 2002), pars. 3 and 4. SAS No. 100 was issued to improve the guidance on performing reviews of interim financial information of public companies. The SEC requires that the registrant submit timely filings of interim financial information. For further information, see the AICPA's Professional Issues Task Force Practice Alert 2000-4, *Quarterly Review Procedures for Public Companies* (New York: AICPA, 2000). See also SAS No. 116, "Interim Financial Information" that amends SAS No. 100 to accomodate reviews on nonpublic companies (January 2009).

[17] Ibid., par. 7.

- Obtaining knowledge of the entity's business and its internal control (pars. 10–14)
- Requiring analytical procedures, inquiries, and other review procedures (emphasis added—comparing disaggregated revenue data by month and by product line or operating segment during the current interim period with that of comparable prior periods (pars. 15–23)
- Obtaining written representation from management concerning such matters as management's responsibility for the financial statements (par. 24)
- Evaluating the results of interim review procedures (pars. 25–28)
- Communicating to the management, the Audit Committee, and others (pars. 29–36)
- Reporting on a review of interim financial information (pars. 37–46)
- Obtaining the client's representation concerning the review engagement (pars. 47–50)
- Preparing documentation for the review of interim financial information (pars. 51–52)[18]

The audit committee's review of the reports of the independent auditors' limited reviews of the interim financial statements is an important task—one that can enable the committee to alert the board of directors to possible changes in accounting policies and thus minimize unanticipated financial reporting implications at the end of the year.[19]

With respect to communication with audit committees, the Auditing Standards Board requires the following procedures:

> As a result of conducting a review of interim financial information, the accountant may become aware of matters that cause him or her to believe that (a) material modification should be made to the interim financial information for it to conform with generally accepted accounting principles or (b) that the entity filed the Form 10-Q or Form 10-QSB before the completion of the review. In such circumstances, the accountant should communicate the matter(s) to the appropriate level of management as soon as practicable.

> If, in the accountant's judgment, management does not respond appropriately to the accountant's communication within a reasonable period of time, the accountant should inform the audit committee or others with equivalent authority and responsibility (hereafter referred to as the audit committee) of the matters as soon as practicable. This communication may be oral or written. If information is communicated orally, the accountant should document the communication.

---

[18] Ibid. See paragraphs parenthetically noted above.

[19] In its 1987 report, the National Commission on Fraudulent Financial Reporting recommended that "the audit committee's oversight responsibilities undertaken on behalf of the board of directors extend to the quarterly reporting process. The audit committee should review the controls that management has established to protect the integrity of the quarterly reporting process. This review should be ongoing" (p. 48). As noted earlier, *SAS No. 100* provides the agenda items for the audit committee's review of quarterly reporting. Such a review will help minimize opportunities for managing earnings through improper revenue recognition or deferred expense recognition.

If, in the accountant's judgment, the audit committee does not respond appropriately to the accountant's communication within a reasonable period of time, the accountant should evaluate whether to resign from the engagement to review the interim financial information and as the entity's auditor. The accountant may wish to consult with his or her attorney when making these evaluations.

When conducting a review of interim financial information, the accountant may become aware of fraud or possible illegal acts. If the matter involves fraud, it should be brought to the attention of the appropriate level of management. If the fraud involves senior management or results in a material misstatement of the financial statements, the accountant should communicate the matter directly to the audit committee as described in SAS No. 99, *Consideration of Fraud in a Financial Statement Audit* (AICPA, *Professional Standards*, vol. 1, AU sec. 316.79–82). If the matter involves possible illegal acts, the accountant should assure himself or herself that the audit committee is adequately informed, unless the matter is clearly inconsequential.[a] (See SAS No. 54, *Illegal Acts by Clients [AICPA, Professional Standards*, vol. 1, AU sec. 317.17].)

Control deficiencies identified during the audit that, upon evaluation, are considered significant deficiencies or materials weaknesses must be communicated in writing to management and those charged with governance as a part of each audit, including significant deficiencies and material weaknesses that were communicated in previous audits, and have not yet been remediated. [b] Nothing precludes the auditor from also communicating to management and those charged with governance those matters that the auditor believes to be of potential benefit to the entity (e.g., recommendations for operational or administrative efficiency, or for improving internal control), or to fulfill requests for communicating control deficiencies that are not significant deficiencies or material weaknesses.

---

[a] The accountant may have additional communication responsibilities pursuant to SAS No. 54, *Illegal Acts by Clients* (AICPA, *Professional Standards*, vol. 1, AU sec. 317); Section 10A of the Securities Exchange Act of 1934; and SAS No. 99, *Consideration of Fraud in a Financial Statement Audit* (AICPA, *Professional Standards*, vol. 1, AU sec. 316).

[b] SAS No. 112, *Communicating Internal Control Related Matters Identified in an Audit,* and PCAOB Auditing Standard No. 5, par. 78-92.

Exhibit 13.5 details significant findings from the audit, as well as other matters, that need to be communicated to those charged with governance of the entity as noted in AU 380: "The Auditor's Communication with Those Charged with Governance."

A comprehensive summary of the requirements for the independent auditor to "communicate with those charged with governance" (a new phrase introduced by SAS No. 114, superseding SAS No. 60, issued in 2006) appears in Appendix A of AU 380. It is reproduced for ready reference in Exhibit 13.6.

The two technical accounting pronouncements related to interim financial reports are Accounting Principles Board Opinion No. 28 and Financial Accounting Standards Board Statement No. 3. Audit Committee members may wish to review these pronouncements prior to their meetings with the independent auditors. In particular, they should inquire about the methods of recognizing revenues and expenses and how the annual operating costs are allocated to the

---

**EXHIBIT 13.5**  Significant Audit Findings and Other Matters to Be Communicated to Those Charged with Governance

---

**Significant Findings from the Audit**

AU 380.34 The auditor should communicate with those charged with governance the following matters:

a. The auditor's views about qualitative aspects of the entity's significant accounting practices, including accounting policies, accounting estimates, and financial statement disclosures.

b. Significant difficulties, if any, encountered during the audit.

c. Uncorrected misstatements, other than those the auditor believes are trivial, if any.

d. Disagreements with management, if any.

e. Other findings or issues, if any, arising from the audit that are, in the auditor's professional judgment, significant and relevant to those charged with governance regarding their oversight of the financial reporting process.

AU 380.35 Unless all of those charged with governance are involved in managing the entity, the auditor also should communicate:

a. Material, corrected misstatements that were brought to the attention of management as a result of audit procedures. The auditor also may communicate other corrected immaterial misstatements, such as frequently recurring immaterial misstatements that may indicate a particular bias in the preparation of the financial statements.

b. Representations the auditor is requesting from management. The auditor may provide those charged with governance with a copy of management's written representations.

c. Management's consultations with other accountants.

d. Significant issues, if any, arising from the audit that were discussed, or the subject of correspondence, with management.

---

interim periods. The major objective is to identify and comprehend management's methods of reporting interim financial information because the stockholders use the information to predict earnings for the year.

An example of a report on reviewed interim financial information presented in a quarterly report is illustrated next.

## Independent Accountant's Report

We have reviewed the accompanying [*describe the interim financial information or statements reviewed*] of ABC Company and consolidated subsidiaries as of September 30, 20X1, and for the three-month and nine-month periods then ended. This (These) financial information (statements) is (are) the responsibility of the company's management.

We conducted our review in accordance with standards established by the American Institute of Certified Public Accountants. A review of interim financial information consists principally of applying analytical procedures to financial data and making inquiries of persons responsible for financial and accounting matters. It is substantially less in scope than an audit conducted in accordance

---

**EXHIBIT 13.6** Requirements to Communicate with Those Charged with Governance in Other Statements on Auditing Standards

---

A1. Requirements for the auditor to communicate with those charged with governance are included in other Statements on Auditing Standards. This section does not change the requirements in:

a. Paragraph 17 of section 317, *Illegal Acts by Clients*, to communicate with the audit committee or others with equivalent authority and responsibility illegal acts that come to the auditor's attention.

b. Paragraph 22 of section 801, *Compliance Auditing Considerations in Audits of Governmental Entities and Recipients of Governmental Financial Assistance*, to communicate to management and the audit committee or others with equivalent authority and responsibility when the auditor becomes aware during an audit in accordance with generally accepted auditing standards that the entity is subject to an audit requirement that may not be encompassed in the terms of the engagement, and that an audit with generally accepted auditing standards may not satisfy the relevant legal, regulatory, or contractual requirements.

c. Paragraph 22 of section 316, *Consideration of Fraud in a Financial Statement Audit*, to inquire directly of the audit committee (or at least its chair) regarding the audit committee's views about the risks of fraud and whether the audit committee has knowledge of any fraud or suspected fraud affecting the entity.

d. Paragraph 79 of section 316, *Consideration of Fraud in a Financial Statement Audit*, to communicate with those charged with governance fraud involving senior management and fraud (whether caused by senior management or other employees) that causes a material misstatement of the financial statements. In addition, the auditor should reach an understanding with those charged with governance regarding the nature and extent of communications with those charged with governance about misappropriations perpetrated by lower-level employees.

e. Paragraph 20 of section 325, *Communicating Internal Control Related Matters Identified in an Audit*, to communicate in writing to management and those charged with governance control deficiencies identified during an audit that upon evaluation are considered significant deficiencies or material weaknesses.

---

with generally accepted auditing standards, the objective of which is the expression of an opinion regarding the financial statements taken as a whole. Accordingly, we do not express such an opinion.

Based on our review, we are not aware of any material modifications that should be made to the accompanying financial information (statements) for it (them) to be in conformity with accounting principles generally accepted in the United States of America.

*[Signature]*
*[Date]*[20]

---

[20] Ibid., par. 38.

## Special Reports

According to the Auditing Standards Board, special reports apply to:

- Financial statements that are prepared in conformity with a comprehensive basis of accounting other than generally accepted accounting principles (e.g., cash-basis statements)
- Specified elements, accounts, or items of a financial statement (e.g., working capital position)
- Compliance with aspects of contractual agreements or regulatory requirements related to audited financial statements (e.g., restrictions relative to a bond indenture).
- Financial presentations to comply with contractual agreements or regulatory provisions (e.g., restrictions relative to dividend payments, such as maintaining specified financial ratios)
- Financial information presented in prescribed forms or schedules that require a prescribed form of auditor's report (e.g., filings with a regulatory agency)[21]

Of particular importance to the audit committee are the second and fourth items in the preceding list, because the committee may request the auditors to report on royalties, sales for the purpose of computing a rental fee, employee profit participation, or the adequacy of the provision for taxes. Moreover, the auditors may issue a special report in connection with a proposed acquisition, the claims of creditors, or management's compliance with contractual agreements. While such reports may be appropriate under the preceding circumstances, it is suggested that the committee give consideration to the cost/benefit advantages from such reports. As indicated earlier, the committee should give strong consideration to the internal auditing staff regarding its request for special reports.

It is evident that the auditors' professional opinion on the financial statements augments the integrity and objectivity of management's representations in such statements. In addition, the audit committee should be familiar with the auditors' reports because each member has an obligation to provide the impetus to ensure that the proper audit opinion is rendered. Accordingly, the committee should review the audit report during the postaudit review period to determine the audit opinion on the financial statements for the current fiscal period. If an opinion other than an unqualified opinion will be issued, the committee should review and discuss the matters in question with the independent auditors and the senior accounting officers to obtain their concurrence on the auditors' exceptions. Such review meetings may be conducted separately or jointly. The primary objective is to identify the audit opinion exceptions and advise the board of directors of them so that the board may deal with them in a timely manner.

---

[21] *Statement on Auditing Standards No. 62*, "Special Reports" (New York: AICPA, 1989), par. 1. With respect to agreed-upon procedures engagements, see *Section 501 of Statement of Standards for Attestation Engagement No. 10* (New York: AICPA, 2001).

## SOURCES AND SUGGESTED READINGS

AICPA. SAS No. 112, "Communicating Internal Control Related Matters Identified in an Audit." *Professional Standards*, vol. 1, 2008. New York: AICPA. (Note that there were updates and conforming changes made in November 2006 that were not reflected in the 4th edition of *The Audit Committee Handbook*.)

American Institute of Certified Public Accountants. *Professional Standards, U.S. Auditing Standards/Attestation Standards*, vol. 1. New York: AICPA, 2008.

Ellingsen, John E., Kurt Pany, and Peg Fagan. "SAS No. 59: How to Evaluate Going Concern." *Journal of Accountancy* 168, no. 1 (January 1989): 24–31.

National Commission on Fraudulent Financial Reporting. *Report of the National Commission on Fraudulent Financial Reporting*. Washington, DC: NCFFR, 1987.

Robertson, Jack C. "Analysts' Reactions to Auditors' Messages in Qualified Reports." *Accounting Horizons* 2, no. 2 (June 1988): 82–89.

Roussey, Robert S., Ernest L. Ten Eyck, and Mimi Blanco-Best. "Three New SASs: Closing the Communication Gap." *Journal of Accountancy* 166, no. 6, (December 1988): 44–52.

*Statement on Auditing Standards No. 58.* "Reports on Audited Financial Statements." New York: AICPA, 1988.

*Statement on Auditing Standards No. 59.* "The Auditor's Consideration of an Entity's Ability to Continue as a Going Concern." New York: AICPA, 1988.

*Statement on Auditing Standards No. 62.* "Special Reports." New York: AICPA, 1989.

Statement on Auditing Standards No. 100, "Interim Financial Information." New York: AICPA, 2002.

# Chapter 14

# The Audit Committee's Report and Concluding Observations

The audit committee of the board of directors is elected by the board in order to allow committee members to focus their attention on corporate accountability matters in greater depth than would be practical for the full board. As far back as in 1953, a well-argued *Journal of Accountancy* editorial noted:

> Corporate directors do carry heavy responsibilities, for the reasonable discharge of which they may be called to account. The financial statements are the company's most important representation to the stockholders and the public. The independent audit is accepted as an additional assurance of the fairness of the statements. If the board of directors has no knowledge of the circumstances under which the auditors are appointed, or any limitations that may be placed on their work, or of questions they may raise about internal control or accounting, or of major problems that may arise about disclosure of unusual transactions in financial statements—will the board be considered to have discharged its responsibilities reasonably?

Along the lines of the questions raised in the *Journal of Accountancy* that the editorial comments quoted, the board of directors sets forth the duties and responsibilities of the audit committee in the committee's charter. It is therefore incumbent on the committee to report regularly to the board of directors that it is properly performing its defined responsibilities. Examples of audit committee charters were presented in Chapter 2. At this point, the reader may wish to revisit the components and narrative discussion in those charters.

The manner in which audit committees report varies from board to board, but, as noted by the *Conference Board*,[1] substantially all audit committees report to the board at least annually and often more frequently. In addition, as noted in Chapter 2, the Securities and Exchange Commission has required that registrants provide

---

[1] The Conference Board found that "almost every audit committee in the survey (98 percent, or 664 companies) gives a formal accounting of its activities at least once a year," a finding essentially unchanged since the 1978 survey. However, the frequency of reports to the board has risen, from a median of two for all companies in 1978 to three reports in 1987; just 14 percent report only once a year. See Jeremy Bacon, *The Audit Committee: A Broader Mandate*, Report No. 914 (New York: The Conference Board, 1988), 17.

in their proxy statements a report from the audit committee to the shareholders. Likewise, the New York Stock Exchange has set forth a reporting requirement to the board of directors.

The purpose of this chapter is to provide guidance to the chair and members of the audit committee with respect to their reporting responsibilities to the board following each committee meeting or in a written format as outlined herein.

This chapter also presents concluding observations and some perspectives on future developments.

## PURPOSE OF THE AUDIT COMMITTEE'S REPORT

The audit committee's report is the basis for reporting on the board of directors' charge to the committee. It should be addressed to the full board of directors and explain the committee's findings and recommendations primarily concerning the overall effectiveness of both the internal and external auditing functions and other areas within their original jurisdiction as defined by the board. In addition, the report should be based on their participation in the audit planning process as well as their monitoring activities, as discussed in the preceding chapters. Such a report is critically important to the board for these reasons:

- It communicates to the board financial, accounting, and auditing matters of particular interest that were noted in the audit directors' reviews and discussions with the internal and external auditing executives and the senior representatives of management, such as the chief financial officer. To the extent that Section 407 of the Sarbanes-Oxley Act of 2002 requires the presence of at least one "Audit Committee Financial Expert" (ACFE) for particularly complex and significant accounting transactions (e.g., derivative financial instruments), it is critical that the ACFE explain to the rest of the board the implications of entering into such transactions—some of them could represent leveraged bets that could become a catastrophic risk. This actually happened in the case of Barings Bank, the Amaranth Hedge Fund, Societe Generale, etc.—in all these cases, the activities of a "rogue trader" led to devastating losses and even bankruptcy.
- Their report not only contains an independent and objective appraisal of the audit functions but also provides assurance to the board that management is fulfilling its stewardship accountability to its outside constituencies, particularly the stockholders. (A useful source of reference is "20 Questions Directors Should Ask About Internal Audit" by Fraser & Lindsay, 2004, published by the Canadian Institute of Chartered Accountants in cooperation with the Institute of Internal Auditors and the Institute of Directors.)
- The report reflects the audit committee members' responsibility to exercise the legal duty of care in view of the fiduciary principle, discussed in Chapter 4. The reader should reread this chapter prior to the preparation of the report.
- The report calls the board's attention to nonfinancial accounting matters of significance, such as conflicts of interest and other general business practices.

Audit committee members are in a unique position within the framework of corporate accountability because they provide a constructive dimension to the board in helping the directors discharge their fiduciary responsibility to the stockholders. Through a review of their functions (discussed in Chapter 2), it is clearly evident that the scope of their position is broad-based. Such a position enables audit committee members to obtain a broad perspective of the entity's business operations and its industry. As a result of their knowledge and their exposure to the subjects discussed in this text, they are in a position to recognize the auditing needs of the entity and to understand matters of compliance with corporate policies. Although they are not directly involved in the day-to-day accounting and auditing management activities, their seasoned business experience permits them to monitor changes in accounting and auditing standards that affect the financial reporting responsibilities of both the board of directors and the officers of the corporation. The audit committee members are also able to monitor the entity's internal control systems to ensure that they are functioning effectively over time. Furthermore, because of their independent stature and posture in the corporate framework and their broad overview of the entity, they are not restricted to one particular function in the organization. Equally important, they can anticipate potential financial reporting problems and communicate management's course of action to solve such problems.

In short, audit committee members have a critical role in developing their report for the board because of their responsibility to formulate recommendations based on their meetings with the auditors and senior financial officers. Such recommendations are a result of their review of the coordinated efforts of the above executives and their discussions with those executives. Consequently, it is incumbent on the audit directors to develop a report that is responsive to the needs and interests of the board of directors.

The New York Stock Exchange has issued this directive with respect to the audit committee's assistance with board oversight:

(viii) report regularly to the board of directors.

Commentary: The audit committee should review with the full board any issues that arise with respect to the quality or integrity of the company's financial statements, the company's compliance with legal or regulatory requirements, the performance and independence of the company's independent auditors, or the performance of the internal audit function.

General Commentary to Section 303A(7)(d): While the fundamental responsibility for the company's financial statements and disclosures rests with management and the independent auditor, the audit committee must review: (A) major issues regarding accounting principles and financial statement presentations, including any significant changes in the company's selection or application of accounting principles, and major issues as to the adequacy of the company's internal controls and any special audit steps adopted in light of material control deficiencies; (B) analyses prepared by management and/or the independent auditor setting forth significant financial reporting issues and judgments made in connection with the preparation of the financial statements; (C) the effect of regulatory and accounting initiatives, as well as off-balance sheet structures, on the financial statements of the company; and (D) the type and presentation of information to be included in earnings press releases (paying particular attention to any use of "pro forma," or "adjusted" non-GAAP, information), as well as review any financial information and earnings guidance provided to analysts and rating agencies.

General Commentary to Section 303A(7): To avoid any confusion, note that the audit committee functions specified in Section 303A(7) are the sole responsibility of the audit committee and may not be allocated to a different committee.[2]

## GUIDELINES FOR PREPARING THE REPORT

### General Comments

In view of audit directors' oversight, monitoring, and advisory capacity, it is important to recognize that their report should convey this position to the other board members. Moreover, the audit directors should communicate their findings and recommendations and avoid any final decisions, since such decisions are not within the province of the committee. Therefore, it is desirable to reexamine the committee's charge from the board and to develop the report in response. This particular charge has been discussed in Chapter 2, and it is suggested that the reader review the committee's functions at this time.

In developing their report, the audit directors should be particularly alert to present or potential financial reporting and compliance problems. Such a charge is a difficult task for a member of the committee. However, subsequent to their orientation program, along with their continuous committee meetings, each member's ability to recognize such problems will be enhanced. Obviously, such a skill is not acquired from only a few meetings. Nevertheless, through an understanding of the entity's business and other subjects as discussed in this text, each member can assess his or her own strengths and weaknesses and develop the necessary proficiency. Furthermore, the quality of their report will be contingent on not only each member's perceptiveness and inquisitiveness, but also their creativity concerning appropriate recommendations to the board. For example, during the committee's preaudit planning segment of the auditing cycle, the members should inquire of and discuss with auditors and management any particular matters of which they should be aware regarding the audit examination. The committee can then identify areas for possible recommendations to the board. For these reasons, the committee has a key role in evaluating and understanding the accounting policies of the corporation. Clearly, audit committee members should plan their agenda to allow each member sufficient time to study and review the subjects for the report. In summary, each member should keep the board's expectations in proper perspective during the report

---

[2] Securities and Exchange Commission, Release No. 34-47673, "Proposed Rule Change Relating to Corporate Governance," April 11, 2003, www.sec.gov/ruls/SRO/34-47672.htm.

development period and realize that fellow board members will be relying on the report regarding the board's overall final decisions.

## Sources of Information for the Report

Although the sources of information for the report will vary among different audit committees, the following recapitulation of the common sources discussed in the text is applicable:

1. Independent auditors
   a. Engagement letter and independence confirmation letter
   b. Management letter and audit committee reports
   c. Interim financial audit reports
   d. Annual auditors' report in the corporate annual report
   e. Special audit reports, if applicable
2. Corporate management
   a. Lawyer's letter for the outside auditors
   b. Management's letter of representation to the outside auditors
   c. Minutes of meetings of the board and its other standing committees, such as the audit and finance committees[3]
   d. Minutes of the annual stockholders meeting
   e. The annual corporate report and proxy materials
   f. Compliance reports with the regulatory agencies, particularly the SEC and the IRS
   g. Management report in the annual report
   h. Releases to employees and the general report through the public relations office
3. Internal auditors
   Reports on the following:
   a. Compliance audits (especially in areas of vulnerability, such as FCPA compliance)
   b. Operational audits
   c. Financial audits
   d. Internal control system
   e. Risk management, including Enterprise-wide Risk Management (ERM) initiatives
   f. Governance, Risk, and Compliance (commonly referred to as "GRC")
   g. Long-form internal audit report, if available
   h. Special survey reports, such as conflicts of interest and fraud prevention measures

---

[3] The minutes of the audit committee's meetings should be documented. Such a record of the committee's proceedings during the year facilitates the preparation of the report. The chairman of the audit committee should be satisfied that the recorded minutes of each committee meeting are sufficient and adequate in terms of the committee's findings, conclusions, and recommendations.

**4.** Other sources of information
   a. Audit committee's professional development program
   b. Interviews with the chief executive officer, chief financial officer, and legal counsel
   c. Bulletins within the organization and outside the organization, such as the newsletters from the professional accounting firms

## Report Preparation

The audit committee's report is essentially an informational report that contains its overall assessment of the preceding sources of information along with its separate or joint meetings with the auditors and the representatives of management. Ordinarily, such a report will be prepared by the chair of the committee prior to the issuance of the annual corporate report and subsequent to the committee's postaudit conference. However, it may be desirable to issue an interim committee report with respect to special matters, such as interim financial information, so that such matters are communicated to the board in a timely manner. Thus it is highly probable that the audit committee may issue more than one report during the fiscal period.

During the phases of the auditing cycle, the audit committee will have several review meetings concerning the auditing activities and compliance matters. Such review meetings along with the minutes of those meetings assist the committee in the preparation of the report. Although the content of the report may evolve from the transcripts of their meetings, it is important that audit committee members provide sufficient time to develop their report. Moreover, they should be satisfied not only that the facts are properly documented in the minutes but also that their proposal recommendations are practical and reasonable.

In contrast to the independent auditors' report, discussed in Chapter 13, the audit committee's report is not standardized by a professionally recognized accounting organization, such as the AICPA. (Note: The AICPA's Audit Committee Toolkit is a valuable reference.) Nonetheless, the committee's report should describe the activities of their meetings, which consist primarily of their reviews, discussions, findings, and recommendations. In developing the content of the report, the committee's comments should not contradict the audit report opinion of the external auditors or the conclusions of the director of internal auditing. Therefore, subsequent to the preparation of the first draft of the report, the report content should be checked against the sources of information, primarily the audit reports, to avoid potential misunderstandings among the other board members.

Although there are no definitive rules on the subjects, length, and format for the internal report to the board of directors, the committee should give consideration to these points:[4]

---

[4] The author believes it may be desirable to prepare a formal report (as illustrated) in view of not only the potential legal liability of the committee but also the professionalism of the audit committee members.

1. The title of the report should be Audit Committee's Report.
2. The report should be addressed to the board of directors and dated.
3. The charge of the audit committee should be stated in the beginning of the report. Such information should be taken from the corporate bylaws or from a formal resolution passed by the board.
4. The report should contain a statement of the scope of the committee's review. For example, the scope of the report may include the following statement:

> We have made a review of the corporate audit policy statement and related internal and external auditing plans and results for the (period of review) in order to determine whether such functions were being performed in an effective manner. Our review included a discussion of the following: (1) a summary of the entity's financial reporting requirements and the annual report and proxy materials; (2) the system of internal accounting control and the scope of the audit; (3) the coordinated activities between the internal and external auditors regarding the scope of the audit; (4) management's judgment in the selection and application of accounting principles in the preparation of the financial statements; and (5) the entity's compliance with the applicable laws and regulations, particularly the federal securities laws and income tax laws, with the independent auditors and legal counsel.

5. A summary of the committee's review activities and a general discussion of such activities for the current fiscal period. The report should contain a chronological account of the committee's meeting activities. The subjects for the report will consist of the committee's reviews during the phases of the auditing cycle. For example, the committee should describe all significant accounting changes and related accounting policy disclosure matters that were approved during the postaudit review segment of the auditing cycle. For additional guidance on the subjects for the report, the reader should review the check list and other guidelines as discussed in the preceding chapters.
6. A summary of the committee's recommendations regarding such matters as the selection of the public accounting firm and changes in the internal auditing policies. Such recommendations may be incorporated with the preceding step. The reader should review the salient points in Chapter 9 regarding the selection or reappointment of the independent public accounting firm. Also, the committee will approve certain matters, such as financial statement disclosure matters (e.g., changes in accounting policies) as well as the audit and nonaudit fees.
7. The report should be signed by the chair, and names of other committee members should be disclosed in the report.
8. The committee may wish to provide attachments of certain reports, such as the independent auditors' management letter, management's letter of representation to the auditors, and other special reports based on its discretion.

---

**EXHIBIT 14.1**   Illustrative Audit Committee Internal Report

---

(To Board of Directors)                              (Date of Report)

(Charge of the audit committee)

(Scope of committee's reviews)

(Summary of the committee's review activities in chronological order)

(Summary of the committee's recommendations)

Respectfully Submitted,

Signed by: _____

(Name of chairman)

(Names of other committee members)

(Attachments, if appropriate)

---

A suggested format for the report is presented in Exhibit 14.1. Subsequent to their recommendations, audit committee members may wish to use this paragraph:

> Based on our reviews, we are confident that management has fulfilled its reporting stewardship accountability in connection with the financial statements, and we are assured that both the internal and external auditors have properly discharged their appropriate auditing responsibilities.

Finally, publicly held corporations are required by the SEC and self-regulatory organizations to disclose a report of the audit committee's activities in their annual proxy statements. Such action exemplifies the committee's role as representatives of the stockholders. An example of the committee's report of Wal-Mart Stores, Inc., is shown in Exhibit 14.2.[5]

---

[5] In 1987, the National Commission on Fraudulent Financial Reporting recommended that "the Securities and Exchange Commission require all annual reports to stockholders to include a letter from the chairman of the audit committee describing the committee's responsibilities and activities." For further reference, see the Report of the National Commission on Fraudulent Financial Reporting (Washington, DC: NCFFR, 1987). In addition, in 1988, the MacDonald Commission in Canada supported the recommendation of the National Commission on Fraudulent Financial Reporting: "Indeed, we would go further. We advocate a publicly stated mandate from the board to the audit committee. The committee's annual reporting to the shareholders would then describe specifically what it did to discharge its mandate." See the Report of the Commission to Study the Public's Expectations of Audits (Toronto: Canadian Institute of Chartered Accountants, 1988), p. 36. For further reference, see Marilyn R. Kintzel, "The Use of Audit Committee Reports in Financial Reporting," *Internal Auditing* 6, no. 4 (Spring 1991), 16–24; and Frank Urbancic, "The Usefulness of Audit Committee Reports: Assessments and Perceptions," *Journal of Applied Business Research* 7, no. 3 (Summer 1991), 36–41. As noted in Chapter 10, Exhibit 10.1, the Blue Ribbon Committee on Improving the Effectiveness of Corporate Audit Committees recommends that the SEC require all reporting companies to include a letter from the auditee in the company's annual report to shareholders and Form 10-K Annual Report (see Chapter 2 for further details).

**EXHIBIT 14.2**   Audit Committee Report of Wal-Mart Stores, Inc.

Wal-Mart's Audit Committee consists of four directors, each of whom has been determined by the Board to be "independent" as defined by the listing standards of the New York Stock Exchange (NYSE) and the applicable rules of the SEC. The members of the Committee are Aida M. Alvarez; James I. Cash, Jr.; Arne M. Sorenson; and Christopher J. Williams, the chair of the Audit Committee. The Audit Committee is governed by a written charter adopted by the Board. A copy of the current Audit Committee charter is available in the "Corporate Governance" section of the "Investors" page of our corporate Web site at www.walmartstores.com.

Wal-Mart's management is responsible for Wal-Mart's internal controls and financial reporting and the preparation of Wal-Mart's consolidated financial statements. Wal-Mart's independent accountants are responsible for auditing Wal-Mart's annual consolidated financial statements in accordance with the standards of the Public Company Accounting Oversight Board. The independent accountants also are responsible for issuing a report on those financial statements and a report on Wal-Mart's internal control over financial reporting. The Audit Committee monitors and oversees these processes. The Audit Committee is responsible for selecting, engaging, and overseeing Wal-Mart's independent accountants.

As part of the oversight process, the Audit Committee regularly meets with management of the Company, the Company's independent accountants, and the Company's internal auditors. The Audit Committee often meets with each of these groups separately in closed sessions. Throughout the year, the Audit Committee had full access to management, the independent accountants and the Company's internal auditors. To fulfill its responsibilities, the Audit Committee did, among other things, the following:

- reviewed and discussed with Wal-Mart's management and the independent accountants Wal-Mart's audited consolidated financial statements for fiscal 2009;
- reviewed management's representations that those consolidated financial statements were prepared in accordance with generally accepted accounting principles and fairly present the consolidated results of operations and consolidated financial positions of the Company for the fiscal years covered by those consolidated financial statements;
- discussed with the independent accountants the matters required by Statement on Auditing Standards 61, as modified or supplemented, and SEC rules, including matters related to the conduct of the audit of Wal-Mart's consolidated financial statements;
- received written disclosures and the letter from E&Y required by applicable independence standards, rules and regulations relating to E&Y's independence from Wal-Mart, and discussed with E&Y its independence from Wal-Mart;
- based on the discussions with management and the independent accountants, the independent accountants' disclosures and letter to the Audit Committee, the representations of management and the reports of the independent accountants, the Audit Committee recommended to the Board that Wal-Mart's audited annual consolidated financial statements for fiscal 2009 be included in Wal-Mart's Annual Report on Form 10-K for the fiscal 2009 filing filed with the SEC;
- reviewed all audit and non-audit services performed for Wal-Mart by E&Y and considered whether E&Y's provision of non-audit services was compatible with maintaining its independence from Wal-Mart;
- selected and appointed E&Y as Wal-Mart's independent accountants to audit and report on the annual consolidated financial statements of Wal-Mart to be filed with the SEC prior to Wal-Mart's Annual Shareholders' Meeting to be held in calendar year 2010;

*(continued)*

> - monitored the progress and results of the testing of internal controls over financial reporting pursuant to Section 404 of SOX, reviewed a report from management and the internal auditors of the Company regarding the design, operation and effectiveness of internal controls over financial reporting, and reviewed an attestation report from E&Y regarding the effectiveness of internal controls over financial reporting; and
> - received reports from management regarding the Company's policies, processes, and procedures regarding compliance with applicable laws and regulations and the Statement of Ethics, all in accordance with the Audit Committee's charter.
>
> The Audit Committee submits this report:
>
> **Aida M. Alvarez**
> **James I. Cash. Jr.**
> **Arne M. Sorenson**
> **Christopher J. Williams, Chair**
>
> *Source:* Wal-Mart Stores, Inc. *2009 Annual Meeting and Proxy Statement*, 16–17.

## CONCLUDING OBSERVATIONS

Over the past two decades, the audit committee of the board of directors has evolved into a viable mechanism (an independent oversight group) in promoting a high degree of integrity in both the internal and external auditing processes as well as the financial reporting process. Although the evolutionary process that created the audit committee was relatively slow, the major impetus toward the mandatory establishment of the committee came from the New York Stock Exchange in June 1978. Its adoption of mandatory audit committees as a listing requirement on the stock exchange has established standards to improve the accountability of corporate boards of directors and managers to their outside constituencies. Since the adoption of the listing requirement, the stock exchange(s) of an increasing number of countries with developed or emerging equity markets have adopted audit committees to increase transparency in their stock exchanges, which, in turn, helps facilitate foreign investment. Indeed, it is reasonable to expect that this trend will continue. The managements of stock exchanges have accepted the audit committee as a key mechanism within the corporate framework to help the board of directors not only address the needs of information users who rely on dependable financial reporting but also properly discharge its financial and fiduciary responsibilities to shareholders and other constituencies. Thus to the extent that the audit committee can monitor the internal and external audit processes and understand the perceived financial accounting information needs of the entity's constituencies, it can provide a balance in the corporate financial reporting process.

As Harold M. Williams, former chairman of the SEC, once stated in an address before the Securities Regulation Institute:

> Although the American Institute of Certified Public Accountants recently concluded that it should not compel public companies to establish audit committees as a

pre-condition to obtaining an independent auditor's certification, it reiterated its
support for the audit committee concept. In addition, the Foreign Corrupt Practices
Act, and the importance which it places on establishing mechanisms to insure that
the company has a functioning system of internal accounting controls, has given
added impetus to the audit committee movement.

Thus, at this point, the central task is to define the audit committee's responsibilities
and enhance the quality of the committee's work.[6]

In light of Williams' comments, the first edition of this book was written to
respond to the central task of clearly defining the audit committee's responsibilities as well as to enhance the quality of the committee's work. The audit
committee is fundamental to the improvement of the board of directors' stewardship accountability to its constituencies. Agreeing with the spirit behind the
National Association of Corporate Directors (NACD) Blue Ribbon Commission
on Audit Committees statement that "all audit committees can improve, whatever
their current level of excellence," Exhibit 14.3 lays out some areas where audit
committees might focus to enhance their overall quality and effectiveness.

It is clearly evident from the public and private sector initiatives in the 1980s
and 1990s, as well as the Sarbanes-Oxley Act of 2002, that the concept of audit
committees has continued as an integral part of corporate governance and
accountability. The 2008 Wall Street financial crisis clearly indicated that
enterprise risk management systems in the financial services industry may
have brought the risks to the surface, but there was often inadequate understanding from or communications with the board for any serious, timely response
to the risks to be considered and implemented. Specifically, at least some fault
was attributed to the composition of certain audit committees in the financial
services industry. The members of such committees seemed ill-prepared to
understand and appreciate the kinds of risks being assumed by the concerned
investment and commercial banks. The lack of solid and well-understood
reporting relationships among risk officers, the disclosure committee, and the
audit committee, coupled with a lack of understanding of complex financial
instruments, may underpin the subprime mortgage crisis. "The subprime crisis
may do for risk officers what Sarbanes-Oxley did for the internal auditor's
relationship with the audit committee," Holly Gregory, a partner at the New York
City-based Weil, Gotshal and Manges law firm, said at a December 2007 meeting
of the Directorship Institute.[7]

There is no question that both public and private sectors have recognized that
audit committees have made important contributions in promoting the investing
public's confidence in the integrity of the auditing processes and the financial
reporting process. Equally important, audit committees have become a key
element in the entity's system of internal control to help engender a high degree

---

[6] Harold M. Williams, "Corporate Accountability—One Year Later," address presented at the Sixth
Annual Securities Regulation Institute, San Diego, California, January 18, 1979.

[7] KPMG Banking Insider article titled "Subprime Crisis Forges a New Disclosure-Audit Committee
Dynamic," by Gary Larkin, Audit Committee Insights, January 11, 2008.

---

**EXHIBIT 14.3**   NACD Blue Commission Report—How Audit Committees Can Initiate and Maintain Best Practices

---

- Committee Purpose
  - Why do we exist?
  - What is our value?
  - To whom?
  - Why?
  - What are our specific responsibilities?
  - What do Board members and others expect from us?
  - Committee Composition
  - Do we have the right membership?
  - How can we bring it to the level this corporation requires?
- Committee Processes/Best Practices
  - How do we, the members and the chair of the committee, most effectively carry out our roles?
  - How do we use auditors, management, and others?
  - How should we?
- Self-Assessment
  - Does the committee evaluate itself regularly and competently?
- Time Management
  - Does the committee receive information far enough in advance to allow members to prepare fully?
  - Does the committee have enough time?
  - Does it use the time it does have wisely?
- Agenda Planning
  - Does the committee consider the right issues?
- Reporting Accountability
  - What needs to be reported?
  - To whom?
  - When?
  - Is excessive time devoted to show and tell, limiting the time available for more meaningful full discussion of risk areas and other priority matters?
  - Is the reporting responsive to committee expectations?

---

of credibility in financial reporting, which, in turn, helps safeguard the securities market. Their independent oversight responsibility in the internal control environment helps to ensure the independence of both internal and external auditors. As a result, the full board of directors is assured of objective financial reporting by management.

## Future Perspectives Revisited

The first edition of this book was published 39 years ago. Over those 39 years, dynamic changes have occurred in corporate governance, particularly as it has affected audit committees. In the authors' view, the future will bring further changes and added duties and responsibilities for members of audit committees.

The intent here is not to comment fully on each of these possible developments but merely to use a crystal ball, presenting the views of one informed commentator on audit committee activities since the third edition.

## Reporting

- As recommended by the Treadway Report, reports of audit committees will increasingly be included in corporate annual reports.
  *Reality check.* The Securities and Exchange Commission and the self-regulatory organizations now require that audit committees' reports be included in the annual proxy statement to shareholders.
- Corporate management will be required to include in its annual report a statement about the adequacy of the company's internal control, and the company's external auditors will be required to comment on that statement.
  *Reality check.* The Sarbanes-Oxley Act of 2002 and the SEC rules implementing the act now require that the annual report contain a report on management's responsibility for internal controls and assessment of the effectiveness of internal controls for financial reporting, including the independent auditors' attestation report on management's assertion related to the annual audit.
- Future legislation will require the external auditor to report to appropriate authorities, such as the SEC, suspected illegalities discovered by the auditor if the company's management or board of directors (i.e., audit committee) fails to take appropriate action.
  *Reality check.* The Private Securities Litigation Reform Act of 1995 requires external auditors who detect illegal acts to report their findings to the SEC if the client fails to take appropriate action on such acts that have a material effect on the financial statements. The Sarbanes-Oxley Act of 2002 established a whistle-blower communication process under Section 301.
- The form and content of financial statements will be revised over time, as suggested by the Public Oversight Board. In addition, disclosures of business risks and uncertainties will result in further disclosures in financial reports and in modification to the standard auditor's reports. Both of these factors will have future implications for audit committees.
  *Reality check.* The Sarbanes-Oxley Act of 2002 replaced the Public Oversight Board with the Public Company Accounting Oversight Board to oversee the accounting profession.
- The Treadway Report included a recommendation that corporate audit committees have additional responsibilities with respect to an entity's unaudited quarterly earnings report. Although this recommendation has not been adopted by many corporations, it is the author's belief that audit committees' oversight in the future will include quarterly reporting to further ensure the integrity of the interim reporting process.
  *Reality check.* The Sarbanes-Oxley Act of 2002 requires that the CEO and the CFO must certify annual and quarterly reports, including disclosure controls and procedures. The New York Stock Exchange has required audit committee

members to discuss annual and quarterly financial statements with management and the independent auditors.

## Other Areas of Future Change

*Internal Auditing*  As noted in the 1988 Conference Board Research Report ("The Audit Committee: A Broader Mandate"), audit committees are believed to have significantly improved procedures and practices related to the internal auditing function. It is expected that this will continue.

The Treadway Commission recommended that all public companies have an internal audit function. For a variety of reasons (e.g., the current economic environment) many companies, particularly those in the middle and small "cap" range, have not adopted this recommendation.

The authors believe that demands will continue for requiring an internal audit function for all public companies. Furthermore, in those instances in which it may not be economically feasible or practicable to establish a fully staffed internal audit function, this service will be procured from outside firms that specialize in providing such services to the middle and small markets.

*Reality check.* The New York Stock Exchange has set forth a requirement that each listed company must have an internal audit function. Additionally, under the Sarbanes-Oxley Act of 2002, it is unlawful for independent auditors to provide internal audit outsourcing services to SEC audit clients.[8]

*Enhanced Audit Committee Liability*  The Conference Board Report ("The Audit Committee: A Broader Mandate") indicated that CEOs and CFOs could be deemed to have a special responsibility or knowledge that could increase the possibility of their being sued in a class action. However, most believed that corporate indemnification, D&O insurance, and state statutory protection would be sufficient to offset the additional exposure.

Nevertheless, in view of increasing litigation against members of boards serving on corporate audit committees, it is prudent for audit committee directors to follow the guidance of the Treadway Report and good audit committee practices, as set forth in this book. It is increasingly important from a litigation point of view for an audit committee to do its job well and to document that fact.

*Reality check.* As indicated in Chapter 4, the audit committee legal liability exposure is under both state and federal statutory laws. With the enactment of the Sarbanes-Oxley Act, it is reasonable to expect that the committee's enhanced legal liability may be in the area of internal governance. For example, the audit committee should know when to retain the services of independent advisors. However, as evidenced by other cases and in particular the *Caremark International* case, the audit committee must demonstrate active oversight and due diligence in discharging its responsibilities.

---

[8] A useful source of reference is *20 Questions Directors Should Ask about Internal Audit* by Fraser & Lindsay, 2004, published by the Canadian Institute of Chartered Accountants in cooperation with the Institute of Internal Auditors and the Institute of Directors.

## Independent Advisors

The Federal Deposit Insurance Corporation Improvement Act of 1991 (FDICIA) sets forth a number of requirements with respect to audit committees, as noted elsewhere in this book. It further requires larger depository financial institutions to provide independent counsel to audit committees. The Treadway Report also recommended that audit committees have the authority to retain expert consultants or advisors to assist them as needed in meeting their duties and responsibilities, or possibly to evaluate the committee's performance.

In view of the ever-expanding duties and responsibilities of audit committees and, perhaps, increased liability in the future, it is not unreasonable to assume that committees will increasingly seek outside independent advisors to assist them in the effective performance of their charter.

*Reality check.* As previously mentioned, the Sarbanes-Oxley Act of 2002 enables audit committees to engage independent advisors at the company's expense.

While the dynamic changes in corporate governance and the financial reporting needs of investors continue to impact the role and responsibility of audit committees, to limit the potential litigation risk, the board of directors should consider the overall performance of the committee and reexamine periodically the terms of reference in the committee's charter, as set forth in this book.

Recognizing that audit committees have an independent oversight function and operate on a part-time basis, the board and management should avoid diluting the activities of the committee by inappropriately expanding the scope of its charter. For this reason, the board should approve any modifications in the terms of reference of the audit committee.

Clearly, the rapidly changing environment in both the corporate and financial communities necessitates the need for a continuing education program for audit committees. Such a program would enable the committee to cope with recent accounting, auditing, and financial reporting developments and thus enable members better to assist their full boards of directors with discharging their fiduciary responsibilities to the shareholders. The self-regulatory organizations (NYSE and NASDAQ) have set forth recommendations regarding continuing education for boards of directors and their standing committees. Professor Jane F. Mutchler has proposed "a more holistic view of auditing." She combines the dictionary definition of auditing and the definition of assurance services from the AICPA Special Committee on Assurance Services (Elliott Committee):

> an independent, methodological examination and review of a situation or condition and a reporting of the results of the examination to improve the quality of information or its context for decision makers.[9]

Given this definition, Mutchler concludes:

> If we view auditing in this context, a whole new world beyond financial statement auditing opens up. Now we are talking about systems auditing, operational auditing,

---

[9] Jane F. Mutchler, "Report of the Chairperson," Auditing Section/American Accounting Association, *Auditor's Report* 20 (Fall 1996), 1–2.

ethics auditing, risk auditing, management auditing, business process auditing. This not only provides a vision for new services to be offered but also, and perhaps more important for our organization, provides a whole new vision for curriculum and research issues.[10]

In a study dealing with boards of directors and corporate governance over the next 10 years, Oxford Analytica reported with respect to the oversight function:

The key question regarding the oversight function of corporate boards concerns their ability to discipline or even replace management for poor performance before a company is overtaken by a crisis. This is no easy task: challenging the management of a company, even if it is not performing well, requires board members to be well-informed and confident. They are also very likely to need the backing of powerful stakeholders as a counterweight to the power of the CEO.

Oversight is thus likely to be most effective where directors:

- Possess and have a reputation for considerable expertise relevant to evaluating the firm's performance; and

- Respond to the interests of major shareholders, or are individuals who enjoy the backing of major shareholders.

Certain organizational and structural changes may enhance the ability of the board to keep a watchful eye on management's actions. The rise of the audit committee in U.S., Canadian, and UK corporations is one of the most important such developments and merits careful examination.[11]

Recently, both corporate America and the accounting profession have come under increased Congressional scrutiny because of major accounting scandals that have shaken the global capital markets. Since the Enron and WorldCom fallout, a number of public and private sector institutions have issued reforms with respect to audit committees and corporate governance. The 2008 Wall Street financial crisis has further intensified the need for and pace of these reforms in ushering in a new era of corporate governance and accountability in which the audit committee will likely be a key player. Presumably these reforms and the new regulatory and legal framework will provide guidance and assistance to boards of directors and their audit committee in effectively discharging their fiduciary responsibilities to shareholders. Likewise these reforms will enable audit committees to maintain quality in their oversight of the audit processes and financial reporting process to restore investor confidence in the financial reporting system.

This latest edition has examined the chronological events and developments in both the public and private sectors associated with audit committees. Such examination is essential in order to enhance their effectiveness. Given the increasing

---

[10] Ibid., 2.

[11] Oxford Analytica, *Board Directors and Corporate Governance, Trends in the G7 Countries over the Next Ten Years, Executive Report* (Oxford: Oxford Analytica, 1992), 7. For an expanded discussion of forward-looking activities of audit committees, see Arthur L. Ruffing, Jr., "The Future Role of the Audit Committee," *Directors & Boards* 18, no. 3 (Spring 1994), 51–54.

pervasiveness and the number of audit committees, it is reasonable to expect that they will continue to receive a high level of attention from the investing public.

## SOURCES AND SUGGESTED READINGS

Bacon, Jeremy. *The Audit Committee: A Broader Mandate*, Report No. 914. New York: The Conference Board, 1988.

Canadian Institute of Chartered Accountants. *Report of the Commission to Study the Public's Expectations of Audits (MacDonald Commission)*. Toronto: CICA, 1988.

Fraser, J., and H. Lindsay. *20 Questions Directors Should Ask About Internal Audit*. Toronto: Canadian Institute of Chartered Accountants, 2004.

*Journal of Accountancy*. Editorial. "Relations of Auditors with Boards of Directors. *Journal of Accountancy*, 96 (December 1953): 680.

Kintzel, Marilyn R. "The Use of Audit Committee Reports in Financial Reporting." *Internal Auditing* 6, No. 4 (Spring 1991): 16–24.

Mutchler, Jane F. "Report of the Chairperson." *The Auditor's Report* 20 (Fall 1996): 1–2.

National Commission on Fraudulent Financial Reporting. *Report of the National Commission on Fraudulent Financial Reporting*. Washington, DC: NCFFR, 1987.

Oxford Analytica. *Board Directors and Corporate Governance, Trends in the G7 Countries over the Next Ten Years, Executive Report*. Oxford: Oxford Analytica, 1992.

Ruffing, Arthur L., Jr., "The Future Role of Audit Committee." *Directors & Boards* 18, no. 3 (Spring 1994): 51–54.

Securities and Exchange Commission. *Release No. 34-47672, Proposed Rule Change Relating to Corporate Governance*, April 11, 2003. Available at www.sec.gov/ruls/SRO/34-47672.htm.

Urbancic, Frank. "The Usefulness of Audit Committee Reports: Assessments and Perceptions." *Journal of Applied Business Research* 7, no. 3 (Summer 1991): 36–41.

Williams, Harold M. "Corporate Accountability—One Year Later," January 18, 1979. Address presented at the Sixth Annual Securities Regulation Institute, San Diego, California.

# Appendix

# Professional Accounting Associations, Business Organizations, Boards, Commissions, and Directors Publications

Accounting Principles Board
   (see Financial Accounting Standards Board (FASB))
   www.fasb.org

American Accounting Association
   www.aaahq.org

The American Assembly
   www.americanassembly.org

American Bar Association
   www.abanet.org

American Institute of Certified Public Accountants
   www.aicpa.org

American Law Institute
   www.ali-aba.org

Association for Investment Management and Research
   (see CFA Institute)
   www.cfainstitute.org

Association of Certified Fraud Examiners
www.acfe.com

Association of Government Accountants
www.agacgfm.org

Australian Institute of Company Directors
www.companydirectors.com.au

The Business Roundtable
www.businessroundtable.org

The Canadian Institute of Chartered Accountants
www.cica.ca

CFA Institute
www.cfainstitute.org

Committee of Sponsoring Organizations of the Treadway Commission (COSO)
www.COSO.org

The Conference Board
www.conference-board.org

The Corporate Board
www.corporateboard.com

Corporate Board Member
www.boardmember.com

Directors & Boards
www.directorsandboards.com

Directorship LLC
www.directorship.com

Financial Accounting Standards Board
www.fasb.org

Financial Executives International
www.financialexecutives.org

Financial Industry Regulatory Authority (FINRA)
(formerly National Association of Securities Dealers (NASD))
www.finra.org

Governmental Accounting Standards Board
www.gasb.org

Heidrick and Struggles
www.H-S.com

Institute of Corporate Directors
www.icd.ca

The Institute of Internal Auditors
www.theiia.org

Institute of Management Accountants
www.imanet.org

International Accounting Standards Board
www.iasb.org

International Auditing and Assurance Standards Board
www.ifac.org/iaasb

International Federation of Accountants (IFAC)
www.ifac.org

International Organization of Securities Commissions (IOSCO)
www.iosco.org

Investor Responsibility Research Center
www.irrc.org

Korn/Ferry International
www.kornferry.com

National Association of Corporate Directors
www.nacdonline.org

National Association of Securities Dealers
(see Financial Industry Regulatory Authority (FINRA))
www.finra.org

National Investor Relations Institute
www.niri.org

New York State Society of Certified Public Accountants
www.nysscpa.com

New York Stock Exchange (NYSE Euronext)
www.nyse.com

NYSE Euronext (New York Stock Exchange)
www.nyse.com

The Open Compliance and Ethics Group
www.oceg.org

Organisation for Economic Co-operation and Development
www.oecd.org

Oxford Analytica Ltd.
www.oxan.com

Public Company Accounting Oversight Board
www.pcaobus.org

Russell Reynolds Associates
www.russellreynolds.com

Society of Corporate Secretaries and Governance Professionals, Inc.
www.governanceprofessionals.org

U.S. Government Accountability Office
www.gao.gov

U.S. Securities and Exchange Commission
www.sec.gov

# About the Authors

**Louis Braiotta, Jr., CPA** is an Associate Professor of Accounting in the School of Management at the State University of New York at Binghamton from 1981 to present. He is a CPA in the State University of New York and received a BBA from Pace University and an MBA from the Iona Graduate School of Business Administration. Prior to his professorial appointment, he was associated with Ernst & Ernst (now Ernst & Young) and was a corporate auditor with GAF Corporation. He was an adjunct member of the accounting faculty at Pace University Graduate School of Business Administration and is a consulting expert and/or expert witness for various attorneys at law specializing in federal and state securities laws that deal with audit committee effectiveness.

Professor Braiotta is the author of numerous articles, papers, book reviews, and coauthor of *The Essential Guide to Effective Corporate Board Committees*. He is a member of the American Institute of CPAs, the New York State Society of CPAs, the Institute of Internal Auditors, and the American Accounting Association. He is also an honorary faculty member of the Foundation for Accounting Education and Research. He was a member of the editorial board of the Institute of Internal Auditors (The Internal Auditor) and the International Publications Policy Committee.

Professor Braiotta has taught undergraduate accounting courses at the introductory, intermediate, advanced, and graduate level. He is a recipient of the State University of New York Chancellor's Award for Excellence in Teaching, the University Award for Excellence in Teaching, the School of Management's Accounting and Management Organization, Outstanding Professor of the Year for Excellence in Teaching Award, as well as the New York State Society of CPA's Foundation for Accounting Education Distinguished Service Award. Recently, he received the New York State Society of CPA's Dr. Emanuel Saxe Outstanding CPA in Education Award. He is listed in Who's Who in the East and Notable Americans and is the recipient of the Outstanding Young Men of America Award.

**R. Trent Gazzaway, CPA** is the national managing partner of audit services for Grant Thornton LLP and the former managing partner of public policy and corporate governance. In addition to leading Grant Thornton's audit practice, he collaborates with members of Congress, regulators, and key policy groups to shape policy affecting the accounting profession, investors, businesses, and the global capital markets.

Recently, Mr. Gazzaway led the Committee of Sponsoring Organizations of the Treadway Commission (COSO) project team in developing guidance on effective monitoring of internal control (www.coso.org). Completed in December 2008, the project was designed to make dramatic improvements in the efficiency and effectiveness of the internal control evaluation process. Mr. Gazzaway is also one of four steering committee chairmen who led the development of the Open Compliance and Ethics Group's framework for integrating governance, risk management and compliance into business processes (www.oceg.org). Mr. Gazzaway is a member of the advisory board of the Enterprise Risk Management Initiative (www.mgt.ncsu.edu/erm) at NC State University's College of Management. He is also a board member at The Institute for Fraud Prevention.

Mr. Gazzaway was recognized in 2005 and again in 2008 by *Treasury & Risk Management* magazine as one of the "100 most influential people in finance." In 2006, he was recognized by *Business Finance* magazine as one of 60 top "Influencers" in finance and accounting, and in 2008 he was selected "Auditor of the Year" by Institutional Investor's *Compliance Reporter* publication. He is a member of the American Institute of Certified Public Accountants, the Institute of Internal Auditors, the American Accounting Association, and the National Association of Corporate Directors.

**Robert H. Colson, Ph.D.** is a partner in the Public Policy and External Affairs Group of Grant Thornton LLP. Mr. Colson is responsible for the firm's engagement with academic researchers and a wide range of policy leaders associated with capital markets, accounting, auditing, financial regulation, and corporate governance.

Prior to joining Grant Thornton, Mr. Colson was editor-in-chief of *The CPA Journal* and Managing Director for Quality Enhancement at the New York State Society of Certified Public Accountants, where he was responsible for the Society's technical committees and its peer review and ethics programs. He led the Society's policy engagement related to accounting and auditing issues with standards setters, regulators, and legislators in New York, the U.S. federal government, and overseas.

Mr. Colson previously devoted 24 years to faculty and administrative responsibilities at The Ohio State University, the University of Michigan, Case Western Reserve University, and Daemen College in Amherst, New York, where he published extensively on auditing, internal auditing, and accounting topics; developed numerous courses in two accounting masters programs and two MBA programs; developed cases about accounting system design; and was a litigation consulting expert on fraud, internal control, accounting, and auditing. He has contributed to more than 100 publications in academic and professional journals and hundreds of presentations and panels in a variety of venues.

Mr. Colson is a current and former member of numerous committees and task forces of the American Accounting Association, Financial Executives International, the American Institute of Certified Public Accountants, the New York State Society of Certified Public Accountants, and the Academy of Accounting Historians. He is a founding member of the board of advisors of the Millstein

Center for Corporate Governance and Performance at Yale University, a trustee of the Committee for Economic Development, and a trustee of the SEC Historical Society. He is on the editorial board of *Research in Accounting Regulation* and serves as an ad hoc referee for other journals.

**Dr. Sridhar Ramamoorti, ACA, CPA/CITP/CFF, CIA, CFE, CFSA, CRP, CGAP, CGFM, CICA, FCPA, CFFA** currently is a principal with Infogix Advisory Services, Infogix, Inc., a software company and specialized professional services provider in the governance, risk, and compliance (GRC), continuous control monitoring, and forensics space. Infogix Advisory Services focuses on mitigating and managing "information for decision making risk"—a major concern of the C-level suite and boards today—by optimizing IT Governance, deploying Continuous Control Monitoring, and assuring effective "GRC with information integrity"® outcomes.

Dr. Ramamoorti's blended academic-practitioner background spans more than 25 years of auditing, consulting, and academic experience. As a corporate governance partner at Grant Thornton LLP, he contributed to key thought leadership initiatives in corporate governance and accountability, published in research and professional journals, and represented the firm at college and university advisory boards as well as professional organizations. A Grant Thornton authoring team member for the 2009 COSO *Guidance on Monitoring Internal Control Systems,* Dr. Ramamoorti is a co-author on the second edition of a definitive textbook (translated into Spanish and Japanese) published by the Institute of Internal Auditors.

Prior to joining Grant Thornton, Dr. Ramamoorti was the Sarbanes-Oxley Advisor for Ernst & Young LLP's National Advisory Practices in North America. He was an Ernst & Young in-house faculty for fraud awareness training for more than one thousand U.S. audit partners and principals, and has provided technical consultation on Sarbanes-Oxley, professional standards, financial reporting and auditing matters, and antifraud programs and controls. Earlier, he was a principal in Arthur Andersen LLP's Professional Standards Group and served as a key liaison for the multimillion dollar Andersen-MIT research collaboration. Before re-entering professional accountancy practice, Dr. Ramamoorti was an accountancy professor at the University of Illinois at Urbana-Champaign. He earned a bachelor's degree in Commerce from Bombay University, India, and M.Acc. and Ph.D. degrees from the Ohio State University. Dr. Ramamoorti holds numerous professional certifications, serves on editorial boards, and has published widely.

Active in the profession, Dr. Ramamoorti was Chairman of the Academy for Government Accountability, and a Trustee of the IIA Research Foundation. He is a Co-Chairman of the 2010 Global Common Body of Knowledge Study of the IIA, spanning more than 160 countries. Dr. Ramamoorti speaks internationally in the United States, Brazil, Canada, France, India, Japan, the Netherlands, Qatar, South Africa, Spain, Turkey, and the United Arab Emirates.

# Index